Springer Series in Operations Research

Editors:
Peter Glynn   Stephen Robinson

Springer

New York
Berlin
Heidelberg
Barcelona
Budapest
Hong Kong
London
Milan
Paris
Santa Clara
Singapore
Tokyo

Springer Series in Operations Research

Julien Bramel   David Simchi-Levi

The Logic of Logistics

Theory, Algorithms, and
Applications for Logistics Management

With 19 Illustrations

Springer

Julien Bramel
Management Science Division
Graduate School of Business
Columbia University
New York, NY 10027
USA

David Simchi-Levi
Department of Industrial Engineering
and Management Sciences
Northwestern University
Evanston, IL 60208
USA

Series Editors:
Peter Glynn
Department of Operations Research
Stanford University
Stanford, CA 94305
USA

Stephen Robinson
Department of Industrial Engineering
University of Wisconsin
Madison, WI 53786
USA

Library of Congress Cataloging-in-Publication Data
Bramel, Julien.
 The logic of logistics : theory, algorithms, and applications for
logistics management / Julien Bramel, David Simchi-Levi.
  p. cm. — (Springer series in operations research)
 Includes bibliographical references and index.
 ISBN 0-387-94921-6 (hardcover : alk. paper)
 1. Business logistics 2. Operations research. I. Simchi-Levi,
David. II. Title. III. Series
 HD38.5.B73 1997
 658.5—dc21   96-37582

Printed on acid-free paper.

Production managed by Steven Pisano; manufacturing supervised by Joe Quatela.
Photocomposed pages prepared from the authors' LaTeX files.
Printed and bound by Maple-Vail Book Manufacturing Group, York, PA.
Printed in the United States of America.

9 8 7 6 5 4 3 2 1

ISBN 0-387-94921-6 Springer-Verlag New York Berlin Heidelberg   SPIN 10523466

Preface

This book grew out a number of distribution and logistics graduate courses we have taught over the last ten years. In the first few years, the emphasis was on very basic models such as the traveling salesman problem, and on the seminal papers of Haimovich and Rinnooy Kan (1985), which analyzed a simple vehicle routing problem, and Roundy (1985), which introduced power-of-two policies and proved that they are effective for the one warehouse multi-retailer distribution system. At that time, few results existed for more complex, realistic distribution problems, stochastic inventory problems or the integration of these issues.

In the last few years however, there has been renewed interest in the area of logistics among both industry and academia. A number of forces have contributed to this shift. First, industry has realized the magnitude of savings that can be achieved by better planning and management of complex logistics systems. Indeed, a striking example is Wal-Mart's success story which is partly attributed to implementing a new logistics strategy, called cross-docking. Second, advances in information and communication technologies together with sophisticated decision support systems now make it possible to design, implement and control logistics strategies that reduce system-wide costs and improve service level. These decision support systems, with their increasingly user-friendly interfaces, are fundamentally changing the management of logistics systems.

These developments have motivated the academic community to aggressively pursue answers to logistics research questions. Indeed, in the last five years considerable progress has been made in the analysis and solution of logistics problems.

This progress was achieved, in many cases, using an approach whose purpose is to ascertain characteristics of the problem or of an algorithm that are *independent of the specific problem data.* That is, the approach determines characteristics of the solution or the solution method that are intrinsic to the problem and not the data. This approach includes the so-called worst-case and average-case analyses which, as illustrated in the book, help not only to understand characteristics of the problem or solution methodology, but also provide specific guarantees of effectiveness. In many case, the insights obtained from these analyses can then be used to develop practical and effective algorithms for specific complex logistics problems. Our objective in writing this book is to describe these tools and developments.

Of course, the work presented in this book is not necessarily an exhaustive account of the current state of the art in logistics. The field is too vast to be properly covered here. In addition, the practitioner may view some of the models discussed as simplistic and the analysis presented as complex. Indeed, this is the dilemma one is faced with when analyzing very complex, multi-faceted, real-world problems. By focusing on simple yet rich models that contain important aspects of the real-world problem, we hope to glean important aspects of the problem that might be overlooked by a more detail-oriented approach.

The book is written for graduate students, researchers and practitioners interested in the mathematics of logistics management. We assume the reader is familiar with the basics of linear programming and probability theory and, in a number of sections, complexity theory and graph theory, although in many cases these can be skipped without loss of continuity. The book provides:

- A thorough treatment of performance analysis techniques including worst-case analysis, probablistic analysis and linear programming based bounds.

- An in-depth analysis of a variety of vehicle routing models focusing on new insights obtained in recent years.

- A detailed, easy-to-follow analysis of complex inventory models.

- A model that integrates inventory control and transportation policies and explains the observed effectiveness of the cross-docking strategy.

- A description of a decision support system for planning and managing important aspects of the logistics system.

Parts of this book are based on work we have done either together or with others. Indeed, some of the chapters originated from papers we have published in journals such as *Mathematics of Operations Research, Mathematical Programming Operations Research*, and *IIE Transactions*. We rewrote most of these, trying to present the results in a simple yet general and unified way. However, a number of key results, proofs and discussions are reprinted without substantial change. Of course, in each case this was done by providing the appropriate reference and by obtaining permission of the copyright owner. In the case of *Operations Research* and *Mathematics of Operations Research*, it is the Institute for Operations Research and Management Science.

Acknowledgments

It is our pleasure to acknowledge all those who helped us with this manuscript. First and foremost we would like to acknowledge the contribution of our colleague, Dr. Frank Chen of Northwestern University. It is because of his help that Chapter 11 covers so well classical and new results in stochastic inventory systems. Similarly, we are indebted to our colleague, Professor Rafael Hassin of Tel-Aviv University and a number of referees, in particular, Professor James Ward of Purdue University, for carefully reading the manuscript and providing us with detailed comments and suggestions. In addition, we would like to thank Northwestern's Ph.D. students, Philip Kaminsky, Ana Muriel and Jennifer Ryan, who read through and commented on various chapters or parts of earlier drafts. Their comments and feedback were invaluable.

We would like to thank Edith Simchi-Levi who is the main force behind the development of the decision support system described in Chapter 15 and who carefully edited many parts of the book.

It is also a pleasure to acknowledge the support provided by the National Science Foundation, the Office of Naval Research and the Fund for the City of New York. It is their support that made the development of some of the theory presented in the book possible.

Finally, thanks go to Mr. Joel Abel of Waukegan, IL, for the figures and Ms. Aimee Emery-Ortiz of Northwestern University for her administrative and overall support.

Of course, we would like to thank our editor Martin Gilchrist of Springer-Verlag who encouraged us throughout, and helped us complete the project. Also, thanks to Steven Pisano and the editorial staff at Springer-Verlag in New York for their help.

Julien Bramel
David Simchi-Levi

Contents

IV   Hierarchical Models   201

V   Logistics Algorithms in Practice   237

1
Introduction

1.1 What Is Logistics Management?

Fierce competition in today's global markets, the introduction of products with short life cycles and the heightened expectation of customers have forced manufacturing enterprises to invest in and focus attention on their logistics systems. This, together with changes in communications and transportation technologies, for example, mobile communication and overnight delivery, has motivated continuous evolution of the management of logistics systems.

In these systems, items are produced at one or more factories, shipped to warehouses for intermediate storage and then shipped to retailers or customers. Consequently, to reduce cost and improve service levels, logistics strategies must take into account the interactions of these various levels in this *logistics network*. This network consists of suppliers, manufacturing centers, warehouses, distribution centers and retailer outlets, as well as raw materials, work-in-process inventory and finished products that flow between the facilities; see Figure 1.1.

The goal of this book is to present the state-of-the-art in the *science of logistics management*. But what exactly is *logistics management*? According to the Council of Logistics Management, a nonprofit organization of business personnel, it is

> the process of planning, implementing, and controlling the efficient, effective flow and storage of goods, services, and related information from point of origin to point of consumption for the purpose of conforming to customer requirements.

This definition leads to several observations. First, logistics management takes into consideration every facility that has an impact on system effectiveness and

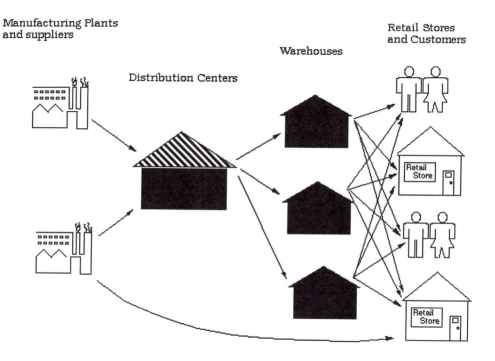

FIGURE 1.1. The logistics network.

plays a role in making the product conform to customer requirements; from supplier and manufacturing facilities through warehouses and distribution centers to retailers and stores. Second, the goal in logistics management is to be *efficient* and cost *effective* across the entire system; the objective is to minimize system-wide costs, from transportation and distribution to inventory of raw material, work in process and finished goods. Thus, the emphasis is not on simply minimizing transportation cost or reducing inventories, but rather on a *systems approach* to logistics management. Finally, because logistics management evolves around *planning, implementing and controlling* the logistics network, it encompasses many of the firm's activities, from the strategic level through the tactical to the operational level.

Indeed, following Hax and Candea's (1984) treatment of production-inventory systems, logistical decisions are typically classified in the following way.

- The **strategic level** deals with decisions that have a long-lasting effect on the firm. This includes decisions regarding the number, location and capacities of warehouses and manufacturing plants, or the flow of material through the logistics network.

- The **tactical level** typically includes decisions that are updated anywhere between once every quarter and once every year. This includes purchasing and production decisions, inventory policies and transportation strategies including the frequency with which customers are visited.

- The **operational level** refers to day-to-day decisions such as scheduling, routing and loading trucks.

1.2 Examples

In this section we introduce some of the logistics management issues that form the basis of the problems studied in the first four parts of the book. These issues span a large spectrum of logistics management decisions, at each of the three levels mentioned above. Our objective here is to briefly introduce the questions and the tradeoffs associated with these decisions.

Distribution Network Configuration

Consider the situation where several plants are producing products serving a set of geographically dispersed retailers. The current set of warehouses is deemed to be inappropriate, and management wants to reorganize or redesign the distribution network. This may be due, for example, to changing demand patterns or the termination of a leasing contract for a number of existing warehouses. In addition, changing demand patterns may entail a change in plant production levels, a selection of new suppliers and, in general, a new flow pattern of goods throughout the distribution network. The goal is to choose a set of warehouse locations and capacities, to determine production levels for each product at each plant, to set transportation flows between facilities (either from plant to warehouse or warehouse to retailer) in such a way that total production, inventory and transportation costs are minimized and various service level requirements are satisfied.

Production Planning

A manufacturing facility must produce to meet demand for a product over a fixed finite horizon. In many real-world cases it is appropriate to assume that demand is known over the horizon. This is possible, for example, if orders have been placed in advance or contracts have been signed specifying deliveries for the next few months. Production costs consist of a fixed amount, corresponding, say to machine set-up costs or times, and a variable amount, corresponding to the time it takes to produce one unit. A holding cost is incurred for each unit in inventory. The planner's objective is to satisfy demand for the product in each period and to minimize the total production and inventory costs over the fixed horizon. Obviously, this problem becomes more difficult as the number of products manufactured increases.

Inventory Control

Consider a retailer that maintains an inventory of a particular product. Since customer demand is random, the retailer only has information regarding the probabilistic distribution of demand. The retailer's objective is to decide at what point to reorder a new batch of products, and how much to order. Typically, ordering costs consist of two parts: a fixed amount, independent of the size of the order, for example, the cost of sending a vehicle from the warehouse to the retailer, and a variable amount dependent on the number of products ordered. A linear inventory holding cost is incurred at a constant rate per unit of product per unit time. The retailer must determine an optimal inventory policy to minimize the expected cost of ordering and holding inventory. As before, this problem becomes even more difficult as the number of products offered increases and the order cost is dependent on the *set* of items ordered.

Cross Docking

Wal-Mart's recent success story highlights the importance of a logistics strategy referred to as *cross docking*. This is a distribution strategy in which the stores are supplied by central warehouses which act as coordinators of the supply process, and as transshipment points for incoming orders from outside vendors, but which do not keep stock themselves. We refer to such warehouses as cross docking points. The questions are obvious: how many cross docking points are necessary? What are the savings achieved using a cross docking strategy? How should a cross docking strategy be implemented in practice?

Integration of Inventory and Transportation

A warehouse serves a set of retailers with a variety of products. To reduce operating costs, management must determine the appropriate balance between inventory and transportation costs. The tradeoff is clear. Frequent trips between warehouse and retailer means each shipment is small, inventory costs are low and transportation costs are high. Infrequent trips entail large shipments, high inventory costs and low transportation costs. Assume, for simplicity, that each retailer experiences constant deterministic demand for the product. The objective is to construct an inventory policy and a transportation strategy, specifying vehicle routes and schedules and the frequency with which the retailers are visited, so as to minimize system-wide inventory and transportation costs.

Vehicle Fleet Management

A warehouse supplies products to a set of retailers using a fleet of vehicles of limited capacity. A dispatcher is in charge of assigning loads to vehicles and determining vehicle routes. First, the dispatcher must decide how to partition the retailers into groups that can be feasibly served by a vehicle, that is, whose loads fit in a vehicle. Second, the dispatcher must decide what sequence to use so as to minimize cost. Typically, one of two cost functions is possible: in the first the objective is to minimize the number of vehicles used, while in the second the focus is on reducing the total distance traveled. The latter is an example of a single-depot Capacitated Vehicle Routing Problem (CVRP), where a set of *customers* has to be served by a fleet of vehicles of limited capacity. The vehicles are initially located at a *depot* (in this case, the warehouse) and the objective is to find a set of vehicle routes of minimal total length.

Truck Routing

Consider a truck that leaves a warehouse to deliver products to a set of retailers. The order in which the retailers are visited will determine how long the delivery will take and at what time the vehicle can return to the warehouse. Therefore, it is important that the vehicle follow an efficient route. The problem of finding the minimal length route, in either time or distance, from a warehouse through a set of retailers is an example of a Traveling Salesman Problem (TSP). Clearly, truck routing is a subproblem of the fleet management example above.

Packing Problems

In many logistics applications, a collection of items must be packed into boxes, bins or vehicles of limited size. The objective is to pack the items such that the number of bins used is as small as possible. This problem is referred to as the Bin-Packing Problem (BPP). For example, it appears as a special case of the CVRP when the objective is to minimize the number of vehicles used to deliver the products. Bin-packing also appears in many other applications, including cutting standard length wire or paper strips into specific customer order sizes. It also often appears as a subproblem in other combinatorial problems.

Delivery with Time-Windows

In many cases, it is necessary to deliver products to retailers or customers during specific *time-windows*. That is, a particular retailer or customer might require delivery between 9am and 11am. When each retailer specifies a time window, the problem of finding vehicle routes that meet capacity constraints and time window constraints becomes even more difficult.

Pickup and Delivery Systems

In some distribution systems, each customer specifies a pickup location and a delivery or destination location. The dispatcher needs to coordinate the pickup and delivery of the products so that each customer pickup/delivery pair is handled by a single truck and the total distance traveled is as small as possible. Thus, a truck route must satisfy the vehicle capacity constraint, the time-window requirement for each pickup and delivery, and must guarantee that a pickup is always performed before its associated delivery.

1.3   Modeling Logistics Problems

The reader observes that most of the problems and issues described in the previous section are fairly well defined mathematically. These are the type of issues, questions and problems addressed in this book. Of course, many issues important to logistics are difficult to quantify and therefore to address mathematically; we will not cover these in this book. This includes topics related to information systems, outsourcing, third party logistics, strategic partnering, etc. For a detailed analysis of these topics we refer the reader to the upcoming book by Simchi-Levi et al. (1997).

The fact that the examples provided in the previous section can be defined mathematically is, obviously, meaningless unless all required data are available. As we discuss in Part V of this book, finding, verifying and tabulating the data are typically very problematic. Indeed, inventory holding costs, production costs, extra vehicle costs and warehouse capacities are often difficult to determine in themselves. Furthermore, identifying the data relevant to a particular logistics problem adds another layer of complexity to the data gathering problem. Even when the data do exist, there are other difficulties related to modeling complex real-world problems. For example, in our analysis we ignore issues such as variations in travel times, variable yield in production, inventory shrinkage, forecasting, crew scheduling, etc. These issues complicate logistics practice considerably.

For most of this book, we assume that all relevant data, for example, production costs, production times, warehouse fixed costs, travel times, holding costs, etc., are given. As a result, each logistics problem analyzed in Parts I–IV is well defined and thus *merely* a mathematical problem.

1.4 Logistics in Practice

How are logistics problems addressed in practice? That is, how are these difficult problems *solved* in the real world. In our experience, companies use several approaches. First and foremost, as in other aspects of life, people tend to repeat what has worked in the past. That is, if last year's safety stock level was enough to avoid backlogging demands, then the same level might be used this year. If last year's delivery routes were successful, that is, all retailers received their deliveries on time, then why change them? Second, there are so-called "rules of thumb" which are widely used and, at least on the surface, may be quite effective. For example, it is our experience that many logistics managers often use the so-called "20/80 rule" which says that about 20% of the products contribute to about 80% of total cost and therefore it is sufficient to concentrate efforts on these critical products. Logistics network design, to give another example, is an area where a variety of rules of thumb are used. One such rule might suggest that if your company serves the continental U.S. and it needs only one warehouse, then this warehouse should probably be located in the Chicago area; if two are required, then one in Los Angeles and one in Atlanta should suffice. Finally, some companies try to apply the experience and intuition of logistics experts and consultants; the idea being that what has worked well for a competitor should work well for itself.

Of course, while all these approaches are appealing and quite often result in logistics strategies that make sense, it is not clear how much is lost by not focusing on the *best* (or close to the best) strategy for the particular case at hand. Indeed, recently, with the advent of cheap computing power, it has become increasingly affordable for many firms, not just large ones, to acquire and use sophisticated *decision support systems* to *optimize* their logistics strategies. In these systems, data are entered, reviewed and validated, various algorithms are executed and a *suggested solution* is presented in a user-friendly way. Provided the data are correct and the system is solving the appropriate problem, these decision support systems *can substantially reduce system-wide cost*. Also, generating a satisfactory solution is typically only arrived at after an iterative process in which the user evaluates various scenarios and assesses their impact on costs and service levels. Although this may not exactly be considered "optimization" in a strict sense, it usually serves as a useful tool for the user of the system.

These systems have as their nucleus models and algorithms in some form or another. In some cases, the system may simply be a computerized version of the rules of thumb above. In more and more instances, however, these systems apply techniques that have been developed in the operations research, management science and computer science research communities.

In this book, we present the current state-of-the-art in mathematical research in the area of logistics. Most of the problems listed above have at their core extremely difficult combinatorial problems in the class called $\mathcal{NP}$-Hard problems. This implies that it is very unlikely that one can construct an algorithm that will always find the optimal solution, or the best possible decision, in computation time that is polynomial in the "size" of the problem. The interested reader can refer to the excellent book by Garey and Johnson (1979) for details on computational complexity. Therefore, in many cases an algorithm that consistently provides the optimal solution is not considered a reachable goal, and hence heuristic, or approximation, methods are employed.

1.5   Evaluation of Solution Techniques

A fundamental research question is how to evaluate heuristic or approximation methods. Such methods can range from simple "rules of thumb" to complex, computationally intensive, mathematical programming techniques. In general, these are methods that will find good solutions to the problem in a reasonable amount of time. Of course, the terms "good" and "reasonable" depend on the heuristic and on the problem instance. Also, what constitutes reasonable time may be highly dependent on the environment in which the heuristic will be used; that is, it depends on whether the algorithm needs to solve the logistics problem in *real-time*.

Assessing and quantifying a heuristic's effectiveness is of prime concern. Traditionally, the following methods have been employed.

- **Empirical Comparisons**: Here, a representative sample of problems is chosen and the performance of a variety of heuristics is compared. The comparison can be based on solution quality or computation time, or a combination of the two. This approach has one obvious drawback: deciding on a good set of test problems. The difficulty, of course, is that a heuristic may perform well on one set of problems but may perform poorly on the next. As pointed out by Fisher (1995), this lack of robustness forces practitioners to "patch up" the heuristic to fix the troublesome cases, leading to an algorithm with growing complexity. After considerable effort, a procedure may be created that works well for the situation at hand. Unfortunately, the resulting algorithm is usually extremely sensitive to changes in the data, and may perform poorly when transported to other environments.

- **Worst-Case Analysis**: In this type of analysis, one tries to determine the maximum deviation from optimality, in terms of relative error, that a heuristic can incur on *any* problem instance. For example, a heuristic for the BPP might guarantee that any solution constructed by the heuristic uses at most 50% more bins than the optimal solution. Or, a heuristic for the TSP might guarantee that the length of the route provided by the heuristic is at most twice the length of the optimal route. Using a heuristic with such a guarantee allays some of the fears of suboptimality, by guaranteeing that we are within a certain percentage of optimality. Of course, one of the main drawbacks of this approach is that a heuristic may perform very well on most instances that are likely to appear in a real-world application, but may perform extremely poorly on some highly contrived instances. Hence, when comparing algorithms it is not clear that a heuristic with a better worst-case performance guarantee is necessarily more effective in practice.

- **Average-Case Analysis**: Here, the purpose is to determine a heuristic's average performance. This is stated as the average relative error between the heuristic solution and the optimal solution under specific assumptions on the distribution of the problem data. This may include probabilistic assumptions on the depot location, demand size, item size, time windows, vehicle capacities, etc. As we shall see, while these probabilistic assumptions may be quite general, this approach also has its drawbacks. The most important includes the fact that an average-case analysis is usually only possible for large size problems. For example, in the BPP, if the item sizes are uniformly distributed (between zero and the bin capacity), then a heuristic that will be "close to optimal" is one that first sorts the items in nonincreasing order and then, starting with the largest item, pairs each item with the largest item with which it fits. In what sense is it close to optimal? The analysis shows that as the problem size increases (the number of items increases), the relative error between the solution created by the heuristic and the optimal solution decreases to zero. Another drawback is that in order for an average-case analysis to be tractable it is sometimes necessary to assume independent customer behavior. Finally, determining what probabilistic assumptions are appropriate in a particular real-world environment is not a trivial problem.

Because of the advantages and potential drawbacks of each of the approaches, we agree with Fisher (1980) that these should be treated as complementary approaches rather than competing ones. Indeed, it is our experience that the logistics algorithms that are most successfully applied in practice are those with good performance in at least two of the above measures.

We should also point out that characterizing the worst-case or average-case performance of a heuristic may be technically very difficult. Therefore, a heuristic may perform very well on average, or in the worst-case, but *proving* this fact may be beyond our current abilities.

1.6   Additional Topics

We emphasize that due to space and time considerations we have been obliged to omit some important and interesting results. These include results regarding yield management, machine scheduling, random yield in production, dynamic and stochastic fleet management models, etc. We refer the reader to Graves et al. (1993) and Ball et al. (1995), for excellent surveys of these and other related topics.

Also, while there exist many elegant and strong results concerning approaches to certain logistics problems, there are still many areas where little, if anything, is known. This is, of course, partly due to the fact that as the models become more complex and integrate more and more issues that arise in practice, their analysis becomes more difficult.

Finally, we remark that it is our firmly held belief that logistics management is one of the areas in which a rigorous mathematical analysis yields not only elegant results but, even more importantly, has had and will continue to have, a significant impact on the practice of logistics.

1.7   Book Overview

This book is meant as a survey of a variety of results covering most of the logistics area. The reader should have a basic understanding of complexity theory, linear programming, probability theory and graph theory. Of course, the book can be read easily without delving into the details of each proof.

The book is organized as follows. In Part I, we concentrate on performance analysis techniques. Specifically, in Chapter 2 we discuss some of the basic tools required to perform worst-case analysis, while in Chapter 3 we cover average-case analysis. Finally, in Chapter 4 we investigate the performance of mathematical programming based approaches.

In Part II, we consider Vehicle Routing Problems, paying particular attention to heuristics with good worst-case or average-case performance. Chapter 5 contains an analysis of the single-depot Capacitated Vehicle Routing Problem when all customers have equal demands, while Chapter 6 analyzes the case of customers with unequal demands. In Chapter 7 we perform an average-case analysis of the Vehicle Routing Problem with Time Window constraints. We also investigate set-partitioning based approaches and column generation techniques in Chapter 8.

Part III concentrates on production and inventory problems. We start with lot sizing in two different deterministic environments, one with constant demand (Chapter 9) and the second with varying demand (Chapter 10). Chapter 11 presents results for stochastic inventory models.

Part IV deals with hierarchical problems in logistics networks and, in particular, with the integration of the different levels of decisions described in Section 1.1. Chapter 12 analyzes distribution network configuration and facility location, also referred to as site selection, problems. Chapter 13 analyzes problems in the coordination of inventory control and distribution policies.

In Part V, we look at case studies concerning the design of decision support tools for large scale logistics applications. In Chapter 14 we report on the development of a decision support tool for school bus routing and scheduling in the City of New York, while in Chapter 15 we look at a network configuration case.

Finally, Figure 1.2 illustrates the precedence relationship between chapters. For example, an arrow between the numbers 2 and 5 indicates that it is recommended that Chapter 2 be read before Chapter 5.

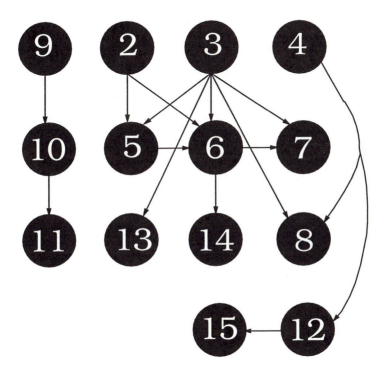

FIGURE 1.2. The precedence relationship between chapters.

Part I

PERFORMANCE

ANALYSIS TECHNIQUES

2

Worst-Case Analysis

2.1 Introduction

Since most complicated logistics problems, for example, the Bin-Packing Problem and Traveling Salesman Problems, are $\mathcal{NP}$-Hard it is unlikely that polynomial time algorithms will be developed for their optimal solutions. Consequently, a great deal of work has been devoted to the development and analyses of heuristics. In this chapter we demonstrate one important tool, referred to as *worst-case performance analysis*, which establishes the maximum deviation from optimality that can occur for a given heuristic algorithm. We will characterize the worst-case performance of a variety of algorithms for the Bin-Packing Problem and the Traveling Salesman Problem. The results obtained here serve as important building blocks in the analysis of algorithms for vehicle routing problems.

Worst-case effectiveness is essentially measured in two different ways. Take a generic problem, and let I be a particular instance. Let $Z^*(I)$ be the total cost of the optimal solution, for instance I. Let $Z^H(I)$ be the total cost of the solution provided by the heuristic H on instance I. Then, the *absolute performance ratio of heuristic H* is defined as:

$$R^H \doteq \inf \left\{ r \geq 1 \mid \frac{Z^H(I)}{Z^*(I)} \leq r, \text{ for all } I \right\}.$$

This measure, of course, is specific to the particular problem. The absolute performance ratio is often achieved for very small problem instances. It is therefore desirable to have a measure that takes into account problems of large size only. This measure is the *asymptotic performance ratio*. For a heuristic H, this ratio is defined as:

$$R_\infty^H \doteq \inf \left\{ r \geq 1 \mid \exists n \text{ such that } \frac{Z^H(I)}{Z^*(I)} \leq r, \text{ for all } I \text{ with } Z^*(I) \geq n \right\}.$$

This measure sometimes gives a more accurate picture of a heuristic's performance. Note that $R_\infty^H \leq R^H$.

In general, it is important to also show that no better worst-case bound (for a given heuristic) is possible. This is usually achieved by providing an example, or family of examples, where the bound is tight, or arbitrarily close to tight.

In this chapter, we will analyze several heuristics for two difficult problems, the Bin-Packing Problem and the Traveling Salesman Problem, along with their worst-case performance bounds.

2.2   The Bin-Packing Problem

The Bin-Packing Problem (BPP) can be stated as follows: given a list of n real numbers $L = (w_1, w_2, \ldots, w_n)$, where we call $w_i \in (0, 1]$ the size of item i, the problem is to assign each item to a bin such that the sum of the item sizes in a bin does not exceed 1, while minimizing the number of bins used. For simplicity, we also use L as a set, but this should cause no confusion. In this case, we write $i \in L$ to mean $w_i \in L$.

Many heuristics have been developed for this problem since the early 1970s. Some of the more popular ones are First-Fit (FF), Best-Fit (BF), First-Fit Decreasing (FFD) and Best-Fit Decreasing (BFD) analyzed by Johnson et al. (1974). First-Fit and Best-Fit assign items to bins according to the order they appear in the list without using any knowledge of subsequent items in the list; these are *online* algorithms. First Fit can be described as follows: place item 1 in bin 1. Suppose we are packing item j; place item j in the lowest indexed bin whose current content does not exceed $1 - w_j$. The BF heuristic is similar to FF except that it places item j in the bin whose current content is the *largest* but does not exceed $1 - w_j$. In contrast to these heuristics, FFD first sorts the items in non increasing order of their size and then performs FF. Similarly, BFD first sorts the items in non-increasing order of their size and then performs BF. These are called *offline* algorithms.

Let $b^H(L)$ be the number of bins produced by a heuristic H on list L. Similarly, let $b^*(L)$ be the minimum number of bins required to pack the items in list L; that is, $b^*(L)$ is the optimal solution to the bin-packing problem defined on list L.

The best asymptotic performance bounds for the FF and BF heuristics are given in Garey et al. (1976) where they show that

$$b^{FF}(L) \leq \left\lceil \frac{17}{10} b^*(L) \right\rceil,$$

and

$$b^{BF}(L) \leq \left\lceil \frac{17}{10} b^*(L) \right\rceil.$$

Here $\lceil x \rceil$ is defined as the smallest integer greater than or equal to x.

The best asymptotic performance bounds for FFD and BFD have been obtained by Baker (1985) who shows that

$$b^{\text{FFD}}(L) \le \frac{11}{9} b^*(L) + 3,$$

and

$$b^{\text{BFD}}(L) \le \frac{11}{9} b^*(L) + 3.$$

Johnson et al. (1974) provide instances with arbitrarily large values of $b^*(L)$ such that the ratios $\frac{b^{\text{FF}}(L)}{b^*(L)}$ and $\frac{b^{\text{BF}}(L)}{b^*(L)}$ approach $\frac{17}{10}$ and instances where $\frac{b^{\text{FFD}}(L)}{b^*(L)}$ and $\frac{b^{\text{BFD}}(L)}{b^*(L)}$ approach $\frac{11}{9}$. Thus, the maximum deviation from optimality for all lists that are sufficiently "large" is no more than 70% times the minimal number of bins in the case of FF and BF, and 22.2% in the case of FFD and BFD.

We now show that by using simple arguments one can characterize the absolute performance ratio for each of the four heuristics. We start however by demonstrating that in general we cannot expect to find a polynomial time heuristic with absolute performance ratio less than $\frac{3}{2}$.

Lemma 2.2.1 *Suppose there exists a polynomial time heuristic H for the BPP with $R^H < 3/2$; then $\mathcal{P} = \mathcal{NP}$.*

Proof. We show that if such a heuristic exists, then we can solve the $\mathcal{NP}$-Complete 2-Partition Problem in polynomial time. This problem is defined as follows: given a set $A = \{a_1, a_2, \ldots, a_n\}$, does there exist an $A_1 \subset A$ such that $\sum_{a_i \in A_1} a_i = \sum_{a_i \in A \setminus A_1} a_i$?

For a given instance A of 2-Partition we construct an instance L of the bin-packing problem with items sizes a_i and bins of capacity $\frac{1}{2} \sum_A a_i$. Observe that if there exists an A_1 such that $\sum_{A_1} a_i = \sum_{A \setminus A_1} a_i = \frac{1}{2} \sum_A a_i$, then the heuristic H must find a solution such that $b^H(L) = 2$. On the other hand, if there is no such A_1 in the 2-Partition Problem, then the corresponding Bin-Packing Problem has no solution with less than 3 bins and hence $b^H(L) \ge 3$.

Consequently, to solve the 2-Partition Problem, apply the heuristic H to the corresponding bin-packing problem. If $b^H(L) \ge 3$, there is no subset A_1 with the desired property. Otherwise there is one. Since 2-Partition is $\mathcal{NP}$-Complete, this implies $\mathcal{P} = \mathcal{NP}$. ∎

Let XF be either FF or BF and let XFD be either FFD or BFD. In this section we prove the following result due to Simchi-Levi (1994).

Theorem 2.2.2 *For all lists L,*

$$\frac{b^{\text{XF}}(L)}{b^*(L)} \le \frac{7}{4},$$

and

$$\frac{b^{\text{XFD}}(L)}{b^*(L)} \le \frac{3}{2}.$$

In view of Lemma 2.2.1 it is clear that FFD and BFD have the best possible absolute performance ratios for the Bin-Packing Problem, among all polynomial time heuristics. As Garey and Johnson (1979, p. 128) point out, it is easy to construct examples in which an optimal solution uses 2 bins while FFD or BFD uses 3 bins. Similarly, Johnson et al. give examples in which an optimal solution uses 10 bins while FF and BF use 17 bins. Thus, the absolute performance ratio for FFD and BFD is exactly $\frac{3}{2}$ while it is at least 1.7 and no more than $\frac{7}{4}$ for FF and BF.

We now define the following terms which will be used throughout this section. An item is called *large* if its size is (strictly) greater than 0.5; otherwise it is called *small*. Define a bin to be of type I if it has only small items, and of type II if it is not a type I bin; that is, it has at least one large item in it. A bin is called *feasible* if the sum of the item sizes in the bin does not exceed 1. An item is said to *fit* in a bin if the bin resulting from the insertion of this item is a feasible bin. In addition, a bin is said to be *opened* when an item is placed in a bin that was previously empty.

2.2.1   First-Fit and Best-Fit

The proof of the worst-case bounds for FF and BF, the first part of Theorem 2.2.2, is based on the following observation. Recall XF=FF or BF.

Lemma 2.2.3 *Consider the jth bin opened by XF ($j \geq 2$). Any item that was assigned to it before it was more than half full does not fit in any bin opened by XF prior to bin j.*

Proof. The property is clearly true for FF, and in fact holds for any item assigned to the jth bin, $j \geq 2$, not necessarily to items assigned to it before it was more than half full. To prove the property for BF, suppose by contradiction, item i was assigned to the jth bin before it was more than half full, and this item fits in one of the previously opened bins, say the kth bin. Clearly, in that case, i cannot be the first item assigned to the jth bin since BF would not have opened a new bin if i fits in one of the previously opened bins. Let the levels of bins k and j, just before the time item i was packed by BF, be α_k and α_j and let item h be the first item in bin j. Hence $w_h \leq \alpha_j \leq \frac{1}{2}$ by the hypothesis. Since BF assigns an item to the bin where it fits with the largest content, and item i would have fit in bin k, we have $\alpha_j > \alpha_k$. Thus, $\alpha_k < \frac{1}{2}$ meaning that item H would have fit in bin k, a contradiction.   ∎

We use Lemma 2.2.3 to construct a lower bound on the minimum number of bins. For this purpose, we introduce the following procedure. For a given integer v, $2 \leq v \leq b^{\text{XF}}(L)$, select v bins from those produced by XF. Index the v bins in the order they are opened starting with 1 and ending with v. Let X_j be the set of items assigned by XF to the jth bin before it was more than half full, $j = 1, 2, \ldots, v$. Let S_j be the set of items assigned by XF to the jth bin, $j = 1, 2, \ldots, v$. Observe that $X_j \subseteq S_j$ for all $j = 1, 2, \ldots, v$.

Procedure LBBP (Lower Bound Bin-Packing)

Step 1: Let $X'_i = X_i, i = 1, 2, \ldots, v$.

Step 2: For $i = 1$ to $v - 1$ do
    Let $j = \max\{k : X'_k \neq \emptyset\}$.
    If $j = i$, stop.
    Else, let u be the smallest item in X'_j.
    Set $S_i \leftarrow S_i \cup \{u\}$ and $X'_j \leftarrow X'_j \setminus \{u\}$.

In view of Lemma 2.2.3 it is clear that Procedure LBBP generates nonempty subsets $S_1, S_2, \ldots, S_m$, for some $m \leq v$, such that $\sum_{i \in S_j} w_i > 1$ for $j \leq m - 1$ and possibly for $j = m$. This is true since by Lemma 2.2.3 item u (as defined in the LBBP procedure), originally assigned to bin j before it was more than half full, does not fit in any bin i with $i < j$. Then the following must hold.

Lemma 2.2.4 $\max\left\{|\bigcup_{j=m+1}^{v} X_j|,\ m - 1\right\} < \sum_{j=1}^{v} \sum_{i \in S_j} w_i.$

Proof. Since bins $1, 2, \ldots, m - 1$ generated by Procedure LBBP are not feasible, we have $\sum_{j=1}^{v} \sum_{i \in S_j} w_i > m - 1$. Note that every item in $\bigcup_{j=m+1}^{v} X_j$ is moved by Procedure LBBP to exactly one S_j, $j = 1, 2, \ldots, m - 1$ and possibly to S_m. Thus, if S_m is feasible, that is, no (additional) item is assigned by Procedure LBBP to S_m, then $|\bigcup_{j=m+1}^{v} X_j| \leq m - 1 < \sum_{j=1}^{v} \sum_{i \in S_j} w_i$. On the other hand, if an item is assigned by Procedure LBBP to S_m, then none of the subsets S_j, $j = 1, 2, \ldots, m$, are feasible and therefore $m = |\bigcup_{j=m+1}^{v} X_j| < \sum_{j=1}^{v} \sum_{i \in S_j} w_i$. ∎

We are now ready to prove the first part of Theorem 2.2.2, that is, establish the upper bound on the absolute performance ratio of the XF heuristic. Let c be the number of large items in the list L. Without loss of generality, assume $b^{XF}(L) > c$ since otherwise the solution produced by XF is optimal. So, $b^{XF}(L) - c > 0$ is the number of type I bins produced by XF. We consider the following two cases.

Case 1: c is even. In this case we partition the bins produced by XF into two sets. The first set includes only type I bins while the second set includes the remaining bins produced by XF, that is, all the type II bins. Index the bins in the first set in the order they are opened, from 1 to $b^{XF}(L) - c$. Let $v = b^{XF}(L) - c$, and apply Procedure LBBP to the set of type I bins, producing m bins out of which at least $m - 1$ are infeasible. Then:

Lemma 2.2.5 *If c is even,*

$$\max\left\{\frac{c}{2} + m,\ 2(b^{XF}(L) - m) - \frac{3c}{2}\right\} \leq b^*(L).$$

Proof. Combining Lemma 2.2.4 with the fact that no two large items fit in the same bin we have $\sum_{i \in L} w_i > m - 1 + \frac{c}{2}$. On the other hand, every bin in an optimal solution is feasible and therefore $\sum_{i \in L} w_i \leq b^*(L)$. Since c is even, $m + \frac{c}{2} \leq b^*(L)$. Since we applied Procedure LBBP only to the type I bins produced by XF, each one of these bins has at least two items except possibly one which may have only one item. Hence, $2(b^{\mathrm{XF}}(L) - m - c - 1) + 1 \leq |\bigcup_{j=m+1}^{v} X_j|$ and therefore, using Lemma 2.2.4,

$$2(b^{\mathrm{XF}}(L) - m - c - 1) + \frac{c}{2} + 1 < \sum_{i \in L} w_i \leq b^*(L),$$

or

$$2(b^{\mathrm{XF}}(L) - m - c - 1) + \frac{c}{2} + 2 \leq b^*(L).$$

Rearranging the left-hand side gives the second lower bound. ∎

Theorem 2.2.6 *If c is even,*

$$b^{\mathrm{XF}}(L) \leq \frac{7}{4} b^*(L).$$

Proof. From Lemma 2.2.5 we have $2(b^{\mathrm{XF}}(L) - m) - \frac{3c}{2} \leq b^*(L)$. Hence,

$$b^{\mathrm{XF}}(L) \leq \frac{b^*(L)}{2} + \frac{3c}{4} + m$$

$$= \frac{b^*(L)}{2} + (m + \frac{c}{2}) + \frac{c}{4}$$

$$\leq \frac{7}{4} b^*(L),$$

since $m + \frac{c}{2}$, $b^*(L)$ and c are lower bounds. ∎

<u>Case 2:</u> c is odd. In this case we partition the set of all bins generated by the XF heuristic in a slightly different way. The first set of bins, called B_1, comprise all the type I bins except the last type I bin opened by XF. The second set is made up of the remaining bins; that is, these are all the type II bins together with the type I bin not included in B_1. We now apply procedure LBBP to the bins in B_1 (with $v = b^{\mathrm{XF}}(L) - c - 1$), producing m bins out of which at least $m - 1$ bins are not feasible.

Lemma 2.2.7 *If c is odd,*

$$\max \left\{ \frac{c}{2} + m + \frac{1}{2}, \ 2(b^{\mathrm{XF}}(L) - m) - \frac{3c}{2} - \frac{1}{2} \right\} \leq b^*(L).$$

Proof. Take one of the type II bins and "match" it with the only type I bin not in B_1; the total weight of these two bins is more than 1. Thus, using Property 2.2, we have $\frac{c-1}{2} + 1 + (m - 1) < \sum_{i \in L} w_i \leq b^*(L)$ which proves the first lower bound. To prove the second lower bound, we use the fact that every bin in B_1 has at least 2 items and therefore $2(b^{\mathrm{XF}}(L) - m - c - 1) \leq |\bigcup_{j=m+1}^{v} X_j|$. Using Property 2.2, we get

$$2(b^{\mathrm{XF}}(L) - m - c - 1) + \frac{c-1}{2} + 1 < \sum_{i \in L} w_i \leq b^*(L),$$

or

$$2(b^{\text{XF}}(L) - m - c - 1) + \frac{c-1}{2} + 2 \le b^*(L).$$

Rearranging the left-hand side gives the second lower bound.   ∎

Theorem 2.2.8 *If c is odd,*

$$b^{\text{XF}}(L) \le \frac{7}{4}b^*(L) - \frac{1}{4}.$$

Proof. From Lemma 2.2.7 we have $2(b^{\text{XF}}(L) - m) - \frac{3c}{2} - \frac{1}{2} \le b^*(L)$. Hence,

$$\begin{aligned}
b^{\text{XF}}(L) &\le \frac{b^*(L)}{2} + m + \frac{3c}{4} + \frac{1}{4} \\
&= \frac{b^*(L)}{2} + \left(m + \frac{c}{2} + \frac{1}{2}\right) + \frac{c}{4} - \frac{1}{4} \\
&\le \frac{7}{4}b^*(L) - \frac{1}{4}.
\end{aligned}$$
    ∎

2.2.2 First-Fit Decreasing and Best-Fit Decreasing

The proof of the worst-case bounds for FFD and BFD is based on Lemma 2.2.3. This lemma states that if a bin produced by these heuristics contains only items of size at most $\frac{1}{2}$, then the first two items assigned to the bin cannot fit in any bin opened prior to it.

Let XFD denote either FFD or BFD. Index the bins produced by XFD in the order they are opened. We consider three cases. First, suppose $b^{\text{XFD}}(L) = 3p$ for some integer $p \ge 1$. Consider the bin with index $2p + 1$. If this bin contains a large item we are done, since in that case $b^*(L) > 2p = \frac{2}{3}b^{\text{XFD}}(L)$. Otherwise, bins $2p + 1$ through $3p$ must contain at least $2p - 1$ small items, none of which can fit in the first $2p$ bins. Hence, the total sum of the item sizes exceeds $2p - 1$, meaning that $b^*(L) \ge 2p = \frac{2}{3}b^{\text{XFD}}(L)$.

Suppose $b^{\text{XFD}}(L) = 3p + 1$. If bin $2p + 1$ contains a large item we are done. Otherwise, bins $2p + 1$ through $3p + 1$ contain at least $2p + 1$ small items, none of which can fit in the first $2p$ bins, implying that the total sum of the item sizes exceeds $2p$ and hence $b^*(L) \ge 2p + 1 > \frac{2}{3}b^{\text{XFD}}(L)$.

Similarly, suppose $b^{\text{XFD}}(L) = 3p + 2$. If bin $2p + 2$ contains a large item we are done. Otherwise, bins $2p + 2$ through $3p + 2$ contain at least $2p + 1$ small items, none of which can fit in the first $2p + 1$ bins, implying the sum of the item sizes exceeds $2p + 1$ and hence $b^*(L) \ge 2p + 2 > \frac{2}{3}b^{\text{XFD}}(L)$.

2.3   The Traveling Salesman Problem

Interesting worst-case results have been obtained for another combinatorial problem that plays an important role in the analysis of logistics systems: the Traveling Salesman Problem (TSP). The problem can be defined as follows: Let $G = (V, E)$ be a complete undirected graph with vertices V, $|V| = n$, and edges E and let d_{ij} be the *length* of edge (i, j). (We use the term *length* to designate the "cost" of using edge (i, j). The most general formulation of the TSP allows for completely arbitrary "lengths" and, in fact, in many applications the physical distance is irrelevant and the d_{ij} simply represents the *cost* of sequencing j immediately after i.) The objective in the TSP is to find a tour that visits each vertex exactly once and whose total length is as small as possible. The problem has been analyzed extensively in the last three decades; see Lawler et al. (1985) for an excellent survey and, in particular, the chapter written by Johnson and Papadimitriou (1985) which includes some of the worst-case results presented here.

We shall examine a variety of heuristics for the TSP and show that, for an important special case of this problem, heuristics with strong worst-case bounds exist. We start however with a negative result, due to Sahni and Gonzalez (1976), which states that in general finding a heuristic for the TSP with a constant worst-case bound is as hard as solving any $\mathcal{NP}$-Complete problem, no matter what the bound.

To present the result, let I be an instance of the TSP. Let $L^*(I)$ be the length of the optimal traveling salesman tour through V. Given a heuristic H, let $L^H(I)$ be the length of the tour generated by H.

Theorem 2.3.1 *Suppose there exists a polynomial time heuristic H for the TSP and a constant R^H such that for all instances I*

$$\frac{L^H(I)}{L^*(I)} \leq R^H;$$

then $\mathcal{P} = \mathcal{NP}$.

Proof. The proof is in the same spirit as the proof of Lemma 2.2.1. Suppose such a heuristic exists. We will use it to solve the $\mathcal{NP}$-Complete Hamiltonian Cycle Problem in polynomial time. The Hamiltonian Cycle Problem is defined as follows. Given a graph $G = (V, E)$, does there exist a *simple cycle* (a cycle that does not visit a point more than once) in G that includes all of V? To answer this question we construct an instance I of the TSP and apply H to it; the length of the tour generated by H will tell us whether G has a Hamiltonian cycle.

The instance I is defined on a complete graph whose set of vertices is V and the length of each edge $\{i, j\}$ is

$$d_{ij} = \begin{cases} 1, & \text{if } \{i, j\} \in E; \\ |V|R^H, & \text{otherwise.} \end{cases}$$

We distinguish between two cases depending on whether G contains a Hamiltonian cycle. If G does not contain a Hamiltonian cycle, then any traveling salesman tour in I must contain at least one edge with length $|V|R^H$ and hence the length of the tour generated by H is at least $|V|R^H + |V| - 1$.

On the other hand, if G has a Hamiltonian cycle, then I must have a tour of length $|V|$. This is true since we can use the Hamiltonian cycle as a traveling salesman tour for the instance I in which the vertices appear on the traveling salesman tour in the same order they appear in the Hamiltonian cycle. Thus, if G has a Hamiltonian cycle, heuristic H applied to I must provide a tour of length no more than $|V|R^H$.

Consequently, we have a method for solving the Hamiltonian Cycle Problem: apply H to the TSP defined on the instance I. If $L^H(I) \leq |V|R^H$, then there exists a Hamiltonian cycle in G. Otherwise, there is no such cycle in G. Finally, since H is assumed to be polynomial, we conclude that $\mathcal{P} = \mathcal{NP}$. ∎

The theorem thus implies that it is very unlikely that a polynomial time heuristic for the TSP with a constant absolute worst-case bound exists. However, there is an important version of the Traveling Salesman Problem that excludes the above negative result. This is when the distance matrix $\{d_{ij}\}$ satisfies *the triangle inequality assumption*.

Definition 2.3.2 *A distance matrix satisfies the triangle inequality assumption if for all $i, j, k \in V$ we have $d_{ij} \leq d_{ik} + d_{kj}$.*

In many logistics environments, the triangle inequality assumption is not a very restrictive one. It merely states that traveling directly from point (vertex) i to point (vertex) j is at most the cost of traveling from i to j through the point k.

In the next four sections we describe and analyze different heuristics developed for the TSP. To simplify presentation in what follows, we write L^* instead of $L^*(I)$; this should cause no confusion.

2.3.1   A Minimum Spanning Tree Based Heuristic

The following algorithm provides a simple example of how a fixed worst-case bound is possible for the TSP when the distance matrix satisfies the triangle inequality assumption. In this case, the bound is 2; that is, the heuristic provides a solution with total length at most 100% above the length of an optimal tour.

A *spanning tree* of a graph $G = (V, E)$ is a connected subgraph with $|V| - 1$ edges spanning all of V. The cost (or weight) of a tree is the sum of the length of the edges in the tree. A minimum spanning tree (MST) is a spanning tree with minimum cost. It is well known and easy to show that a minimum spanning tree can be found in polynomial time (see, for example, Papadimitriou and Steiglitz (1982)). If W^* denotes the weight (cost) of the minimum spanning tree, then we must have $W^* \leq L^*$ since deleting any edge from the optimal tour results in a spanning tree.

The minimum spanning tree can be used to find a feasible traveling salesman tour in polynomial time. The idea is to perform a depth-first search (see Aho et al. (1974)) over the minimum spanning tree and then to do simple improvements on this solution. Formally, this is done as follows (Johnson and Papadimitriou, 1985).

A Minimum Spanning Tree Based Heuristic

Step 1: Construct a minimum spanning tree and color its edges white, and all other edges black.

Step 2: Let the *current vertex* (denoted v) be an arbitrary vertex.

Step 3: If one of the edges adjacent to v in the MST is white, color it black and proceed to the vertex at the other end of this edge. Else (all edges from v are black), go back along the edge by which the current vertex was originally reached.

Step 4: Let this vertex be v. Stop if v is the vertex you started with and all edges of MST are black. Otherwise go to *Step 3*.

Observe that the above strategy produces a tour that starts and ends at one of the vertices and visits all other vertices in the graph covering each arc twice. This is not a very efficient tour since some vertices may be visited more than once. To improve on this tour, we can modify the above strategy as follows: instead of going back to a visited vertex, we can use a *shortcut* strategy in which we skip this vertex, and go directly to the next unvisited vertex. The triangle inequality assumption implies that the above modification will not increase the length of the tour, and in fact may reduce it.

Let L^{MST} be the length of the traveling salesman tour generated by the above strategy. We clearly have

$$L^{\text{MST}} \leq 2W^* \leq 2L^*,$$

where the first inequality follows since without shortcuts the length of the tour is exactly $2W^*$. This proves that the worst case bound of the algorithm is at most 2. It remains to verify that the worst case bound of this heuristic cannot be improved. For this purpose consider Figure 2.1, the example constructed by Johnson and Papadimitriou (1985). Here, $W^* = \frac{n}{3} + \frac{n}{3}(1 - \epsilon) + 2\epsilon - 1$, $L^{\text{MST}} \approx \frac{2n}{3} + \frac{2n}{3}(1 - \epsilon)$, and $L^* = \frac{2n}{3}$.

2.3.2   The Nearest Insertion Heuristic

Before describing this heuristic, consider the following intuitively appealing strategy, called the *Nearest Neighbor Heuristic*. Given an instance I of the TSP, start with an arbitrary vertex and find the vertex not yet visited that is closest to the current vertex. Travel to this vertex. Repeat this until all vertices are visited; then go back to the starting vertex.

Unfortunately, Rosenkrantz et al. (1977) show the existence of a family of instances for the TSP with arbitrary n with the following property. The length of the tour generated by the Nearest Neighbor Heuristic on each instance in the family is

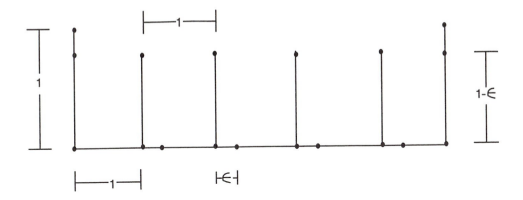

The minimum spanning tree

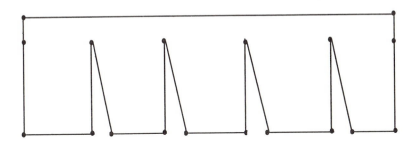

The tour generated by the
Minimum Spanning Tree Based Algorithm

FIGURE 2.1. An example for the minimum spanning tree based algorithm with $n = 18$.

$O(\log n)$ times the length of the optimal tour. Thus, the Nearest Neighbor Heuristic does not have a bounded worst-case performance.

This comes as no surprise since the algorithm obviously suffers from one major weakness. This "greedy" strategy tends to begin well, inserting very short arcs into the path, but ultimately it ends with arcs that are quite long. For instance, the last edge added, the one connecting the last node to the starting node, may be very long due to the fact that at no point does the heuristic consider the location of the starting vertex and possible ending vertices.

One way to improve the performance of the Nearest Neighbor Heuristic is presented in the following variant, called the *Nearest Insertion* (NI) Heuristic, developed and analyzed by Rosenkrantz et al. Informally, the heuristic works as follows: at each iteration of the heuristic a Hamiltonian cycle containing a subset of the vertices is constructed. The heuristic then selects a new vertex not yet in the cycle that is "closest" in a specific sense and inserts it between two adjacent vertices in the cycle. The process stops when all vertices are in the cycle. Formally, this is done as follows.

The Nearest Insertion Heuristic

Step 1: Choose an arbitrary node v and let the cycle C consist of only v.

Step 2: Find a node outside C closest to a node in C; call it k.

Step 3: Find an edge $\{i, j\}$ in C such that $d_{ik} + d_{kj} - d_{ij}$ is minimal.

Step 4: Construct a new cycle C by replacing $\{i, j\}$ with $\{i, k\}$ and $\{k, j\}$.

Step 5: If the current cycle C contains all the vertices, stop. Otherwise, go to *Step 2*.

Let L^{NI} be the length of the solution obtained by the Nearest Insertion Heuristic. Then:

Theorem 2.3.3 *For all instances of the TSP satisfying the triangle inequality,*

$$L^{NI} \leq 2L^*.$$

We start by proving the following interesting result. Let T be a spanning tree of G and let $W(T)$ be the weight (cost) of that tree; that is, $W(T)$ is the sum of the length of all edges in the tree T. Then:

Lemma 2.3.4 *For every spanning tree T,*

$$L^{NI} \leq 2W(T).$$

Proof. We prove the lemma by matching each vertex we insert during the execution of the algorithm with a single edge of the given tree T. To do that we describe a procedure that will be carried out in parallel to the Nearest Insertion Heuristic.

The Dual Nearest Insertion Procedure

Step 1: Start with a family $\mathcal{T}$ of trees that, at first, consists of only the tree T.

Step 2: Given k (the vertex selected in *Step 2* of NI), find the unique tree in $\mathcal{T}$ containing k. Let this tree be T_k.

Step 3: Let ℓ be the unique vertex in T_k that is in the current cycle.

Step 4: Let h be the vertex adjacent to ℓ on the unique path from ℓ to k. Replace T_k in $\mathcal{T}$ by two trees obtained from T_k by deleting edge $\{\ell, h\}$.

Step 5: If $\mathcal{T}$ contains n trees, stop. Otherwise, go to *Step 2*.

The Dual Nearest Insertion procedure is carried out in parallel to the Nearest Insertion Heuristic in the sense that each time *Step 1* is performed in the latter procedure, *Step 1* is performed in the former procedure. Each time *Step 2* is performed in the latter, *Step 2* is performed in the former, etc.

Observe that each time *Step 4* of the Dual Nearest Insertion procedure is performed, the set of trees $\mathcal{T}$ is updated so that each tree in $\mathcal{T}$ has exactly one vertex from the current cycle and each vertex of the current cycle belongs to exactly one tree. This is true since when edge $\{\ell, h\}$ is deleted, two subtrees are constructed, one containing the vertex ℓ and the other containing the vertex k. Edge $\{\ell, h\}$ is the one we associate with the insertion of vertex k.

Let m be the vertex in the current cycle to which vertex k (not in the cycle) was closest. That is, m is the vertex such that d_{km} is the smallest among all d_{uv} where u is in the cycle and v outside the cycle. Let $m + 1$ be one of the vertices on the cycle adjacent to m. Finally, let edge $\{i, j\}$ be the edge deleted from the current cycle. Clearly, inserting k into the current cycle increases the length of the tour by

$$d_{ik} + d_{kj} - d_{ij} \leq d_{mk} + d_{k,m+1} - d_{m,m+1} \leq 2d_{mk},$$

where the left-hand inequality holds because of *Step 3* of the Nearest Insertion Heuristic and the right-hand inequality holds in view of the triangle inequality assumption. This of course is true only when the cycle contains at least two vertices. When it contains exactly one vertex, that is, when the Nearest Insertion algorithm enters *Step 2* for the first time, inserting k to the current cycle increases the length of the tour by exactly $2d_{mk}$.

Since ℓ is in the current cycle and h is not, $d_{mk} \leq d_{\ell h}$. Hence, the increase in the cost of the current cycle is no more than $2d_{\ell h}$. Finally, since this relationship holds for every edge of T and the corresponding inserted vertex, we have

$$L^{\text{NI}} \leq 2W(T). \qquad \blacksquare$$

To finish the proof of Theorem 2.3.3, apply Theorem 2.3.4 with T^*; thus,

$$W^* = W(T^*) < L^* \leq L^{\text{NI}} \leq 2W(T^*).$$

This completes the proof of the Theorem.

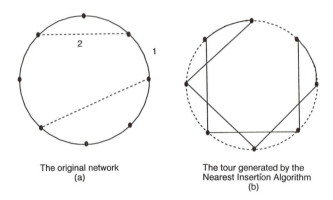

The original network
(a)

The tour generated by the
Nearest Insertion Algorithm
(b)

FIGURE 2.2. An example for the nearest insertion algorithm with $n = 8$.

To see that the bound is tight consider the example (constructed by Rosenkrantz et al., 1977) depicted in Figure 2.2. In this example, the length of every edge connecting two consecutive vertices on the perimeter is 1 while all other edges have length 2. Thus, the optimal traveling salesman tour visits the vertices according to their appearance on the circle and therefore $L^* = n$. It is easy to see that the Nearest Insertion Heuristic generates the tour depicted in Figure 2.2(b) with cost $L^{NI} = 2n - 2$.

2.3.3   Christofides' Heuristic

In 1976, Christofides presented a very simple algorithm that currently has the best known worst-case performance bound for the TSP. To present the algorithm we need to state several properties of graphs.

Lemma 2.3.5 *Given a graph with at least two vertices, the number of vertices with odd degree is even.*

Definition 2.3.6 *A Eulerian Tour is a tour that traverses all edges of a graph exactly once.*

Definition 2.3.7 *A Eulerian Graph is a graph that has a Eulerian Tour.*

Then it is a simple exercise to show the following.

Lemma 2.3.8 *A connected graph is Eulerian if and only if the degree of each vertex is even.*

Christofides' algorithm starts with a minimum spanning tree. Of course, this tree (as any other tree) is not Eulerian since some of the vertices have odd degree. We can augment the graph (by adding suitably chosen arcs) so that it becomes Eulerian. In fact, we would like to add a number of arcs connecting odd degree vertices so that they then have even degree. To do this, we will find a *minimum weight matching* among the odd degree vertices.

Given a graph with an even number of vertices, a *matching* is a subset of edges with the property that every vertex is the end-point of exactly one edge of the subset. In the minimum weight matching problem the objective is to find a matching whose total length of all its edges is minimum. This problem can be solved in $O(n^3)$ where n is the number of vertices in the graph (see Lawler (1976)).

Lemma 2.3.5 tells us that the number of vertices with odd degree in the MST is even. Thus, adding the edges of a matching defined on those odd degree vertices clearly increases the degree of each of these vertices by one. The resulting graph is Eulerian, by Lemma 2.3.8. Of course, to minimize the total cost, we would like to select the edges of a minimum weight matching. Finally, the Eulerian tour generated is transformed into a traveling salesman tour using shortcuts, similarly to what was done in the minimum spanning tree based heuristic of Section 2.3.1.

Let L^C be the length of the tour generated by Christofides' Heuristic. We prove:

Theorem 2.3.9 *For all instances of the TSP satisfying the triangle inequality, we have*

$$L^C \le \frac{3}{2} L^*.$$

Proof. Recall that $W^* \doteq W(T^*)$ is the cost of the MST and let $W(M^*)$ be the weight of the minimum weight matching, that is, the sum of edge length of all edges in the optimal matching. Because of the triangle inequality assumption,

$$L^C \le W(T^*) + W(M^*).$$

We already know that $W(T^*) \le L^*$. It remains to show that $W(M^*) \le \frac{1}{2} L^*$. For this purpose index the vertices of odd degree in the minimum spanning tree $i_1, i_2, \ldots, i_{2k}$ according to their appearance on an optimal traveling salesman tour. Consider two feasible solutions for the minimum weight matching problem defined on these vertices. The first matching, denoted M^1, consists of edges $\{i_1, i_2\}, \{i_3, i_4\}, \ldots, \{i_{2k-1}, i_{2k}\}$. The second matching, denoted M^2, consists of edges $\{i_2, i_3\}, \{i_4, i_5\}, \ldots, \{i_{2k}, i_1\}$.

We clearly have $W(M^*) \le \frac{1}{2}[W(M^1) + W(M^2)]$. The triangle inequality assumption tells us that $W(M^1) + W(M^2) \le L^*$; see Figure 2.3. Hence $W(M^*) \le \frac{1}{2} L^*$ and consequently,

$$L^* \le W(T^*) + W(M^*) \le \frac{3}{2} L^*. \qquad \blacksquare$$

As in the two previous heuristics, this bound is tight. Consider the example depicted in Figure 2.4 for which $L^* = n$ while $L^C = n - 1 + \frac{n-1}{2}$.

2.3.4   Local Search Heuristics

Some of the oldest and, by far, the most extensively used heuristics developed for the traveling salesman problem are the so-called k-opt procedures ($k \ge 2$). These heuristics, part of the extensive class of *local search* procedures, can be described

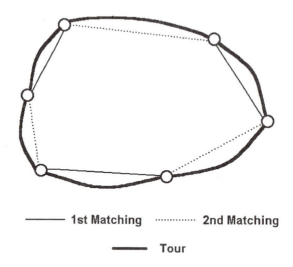

1st Matching   ⋯⋯⋯⋯ 2nd Matching

Tour

FIGURE 2.3. The matching and the optimal traveling salesman tour.

FIGURE 2.4. An example for Christofides' algorithm with $n = 7$.

as follows. Given a traveling salesman tour through the set of vertices V, say the sequence

$$\{i_1, i_2 \ldots, i_{u_1}, i_{u_2}, \ldots, i_{v_1}, i_{v_2}, \ldots, i_n\},$$

an $\ell-exchange$ is a procedure that replaces ℓ edges currently in the tour by ℓ new edges so that the result is again a traveling salesman tour. For instance, a 2-exchange procedure replaces edges $\{i_{u_1}, i_{u_2}\}$ and $\{i_{v_1}, i_{v_2}\}$ with $\{i_{u_1}, i_{v_1}\}$ and $\{i_{u_2}, i_{v_2}\}$ and results in a new tour

$$\{i_1, i_2 \ldots, i_{u_1}, i_{v_1}, i_{v_1-1}, \ldots, i_{u_2}, i_{v_2}, i_{v_2+1}, \ldots, i_n\}.$$

An *improving* ℓ-exchange is an ℓ-exchange that results in a tour whose total length (cost) is smaller than the cost of the original tour.

A k-opt procedure starts from an arbitrary traveling salesman tour and, using improving ℓ-exchanges, for $\ell \le k$, successively generates tours of smaller and smaller length. The procedure terminates when no improving ℓ-exchange is found for all $\ell \le k$. Let $L^{\text{OPT}(k)}$ be the length of the tour generated by a k-opt heuristic, for $k \ge 2$.

Recently, Chandra et al. (1995) obtained interesting results on the worst-case performance of the k-opt heuristic. They show

Theorem 2.3.10 *For all instances of the TSP satisfying the triangle inequality we have*

$$\frac{L^{\text{OPT}(2)}}{L^*} \le 4\sqrt{n}.$$

In addition, there exists an infinitely large family of TSP instances satisfying the triangle inequality assumption for which

$$\frac{L^{\text{OPT}(2)}}{L^*} \ge \frac{1}{4}\sqrt{n}.$$

They also provide a lower bound on the worst-case performance of k-opt for all $k \ge 3$.

Theorem 2.3.11 *There exists an infinitely large family of TSP instances satisfying the triangle inequality assumption with*

$$\frac{L^{\text{OPT}(k)}}{L^*} \ge \frac{1}{4}n^{\frac{1}{2k}}$$

for any $k \ge 2$.

Thus, the above results indicate that the worst-case performances of k-opt heuristics are quite poor. By contrast, many researchers and practitioners have reported that k-opt heuristics can be highly effective; see, for instance, Golden and Stewart (1985).

This raises a fundamental dilemma. Although worst-case analysis provides a rigid guarantee on a heuristic's performance, it suffers from being highly determined by certain pathological examples. Is there a more appropriate measure to assess the effectiveness of a particular heuristic, one that would assess the effectiveness on an *average* or realistic example? We will try to address this question in the next chapter.

2.4 Exercises

Exercise 2.1. Prove Lemma 2.3.8.

Exercise 2.2. The 2-TSP is the problem of designing two tours that together visit each of the customers and use the same starting point. Show that any algorithm for the TSP can solve this problem as well.

Exercise 2.3. (Papadimitriou and Steiglitz, 1982) Consider the n-city TSP in which the triangle inequality assumption holds. Let $c^* > 0$ be the length of an optimal tour, and let c' be the length of the second best tour. Prove: $(c' - c^*)/c^* \leq \frac{2}{n}$.

Exercise 2.4. Prove that in every completely connected directed graph (a graph in which between every pair of vertices there is a directed edge in one of the two possible directions) there is a directed Hamiltonian Path.

Exercise 2.5. Let Z^C be the length of the tour provided by Christofides' Heuristic, and let Z^* be the length of the optimal tour. Construct an example with $Z^C = \frac{3}{2} Z^*$.

Exercise 2.6. Prove that for any graph G there exists an even number of nodes with odd degree.

Exercise 2.7. Let G be a tree with $n \geq 2$ nodes. Show that:

(a) There exist at least two nodes with degree one.

(b) The number of arcs is $n - 1$.

Exercise 2.8. Consider the n-city TSP defined with distances d_{ij}. Assume that there exist $a, b \in I\!R^n$ such that for each i and j, $d_{ij} = a_i + b_j$. What is the length of the optimal traveling salesman tour? Explain your solution.

Exercise 2.9. Consider the TSP with the triangle inequality assumption and two prespecified nodes s and t. Assume that the traveling salesman tour has to include edge (s, t) (that is, the salesman has to travel from s directly to t). Modify Christofides' Heuristic for this model and show that the worst-case bound is $\frac{3}{2}$.

Exercise 2.10. Show that a minimum spanning tree T satisfies the following property. When T is compared with any other spanning tree T', the kth shortest edge of T is no longer than the kth shortest edge of T', for $k = 1, 2, \ldots, n - 1$.

Exercise 2.11. (Papadimitriou and Steiglitz, 1982) The Wandering Salesman Problem (WSP) is a Traveling Salesman Problem except that the salesman can start wherever he or she wishes and does not have to return to the starting city after visiting all cities.

(a) Describe a heuristic for the WSP with worst-case bound $\frac{3}{2}$.

(b) Show that the same bound can be obtained for the problem when one of the end-points of the path is specified in advance.

Exercise 2.12. (Papadimitriou and Steiglitz, 1982) Which of the following problems remain essentially unchanged (complexity-wise) when they are transformed from minimization to maximization problems? Why?

(a) Traveling Salesman Problem.

(b) Shortest Path from s to t.

(c) Minimum Weight Matching.

(d) Minimum Spanning Tree.

Exercise 2.13. Suppose there are n jobs that require processing on m machines. Each job must be processed by machine 1, then by machine 2, ..., and finally by machine m. Each machine can work on at most one job at a time and once it begins work on a job it must work on it until completion, without interruption. The amount of time machine j must process job i is denoted $p_{ij} \geq 0$ (for $i = 1, 2, \ldots, n$ and $j = 1, 2, \ldots, m$). Further suppose that once the processing of a job is completed on machine j, its processing must begin *immediately* on machine $j+1$ (for $j \leq m-1$). This is a *flow shop* with no wait-in-process.

Show that the problem of sequencing the jobs so that the last job is completed as early as possible can be formulated as an $(n + 1)$-city TSP. Specifically, show how the d_{ij} values for the TSP can be expressed in terms of the p_{ij} values.

Exercise 2.14. Consider the Bin-Packing Problem with items of size w_i, $i = 1, 2, \ldots, n$, such that $0 < w_i \leq 1$. The objective is find the minimum number of unit size bins b^* needed to pack all the items without violating the capacity constraint.

(a) Show that $\sum_{i=1}^{n} w_i$ is a lower bound on b^*.

(b) Define a *locally optimal* solution to be one where no two bins can be feasibly combined into one. Show that any locally optimal solution uses no more than twice the minimum number of bins, that is, no more than $2b^*$ bins.

(c) The Next-Fit Heuristic is the following. Start by packing the first item in bin 1. Then, each subsequent item is packed in the last opened bin if possible, or else a new bin is opened and it is placed there. Show that the Next-Fit Heuristic produces a solution with at most $2b^*$ bins.

Exercise 2.15. (Anily et al., 1994) Consider the Bin-Packing Problem and the Next-Fit Increasing heuristic. In this strategy items are ordered in a nondecreasing order according to their size. Start by packing the first item in bin 1. Then each subsequent item is packed in the last opened bin if possible, or else a new bin is opened and it is placed there. Show that the number of bins produced by this strategy is no more than $\frac{7}{4}$ times the optimal number of bins. For this purpose, consider the following two steps.

(a) Consider the following procedure. First order the items in nondecreasing order of their size. When packing bin $i \geq 1$, follow the packing rule: if the bin is currently feasible (i.e., total load is no more than 1), then assign the next item to this bin; otherwise, close this bin, open bin $i + 1$ and put this item in bin $i + 1$. Show that the number of bins generated by this procedure is a lower bound on the minimal number of bins needed.

(b) Relate this lower bounding procedure to the number of bins produced by the Next-Fit Increasing heuristic.

Exercise 2.16. Given a network $G = (V, E)$, and edge length l_e for every $e \in E$, assume that edge (u, v) has a variable length x. Find an expression for the length of the shortest path from s to t as a function of x.

Exercise 2.17. A complete directed network $G = (V, A)$ is a directed graph such that for every pair of vertices $u, v \in V$, there are arcs $u \to v$ and $v \to u$ in A with nonnegative arc lengths $d(u, v)$ and $d(v, u)$, respectively. The network $G = (V, A)$ satisfies the triangle inequality if for all $u, v, w \in V$, $d(u, v) + d(v, w) \geq d(u, w)$.

A directed cycle is a sequence of vertices $v_1 \to v_2 \to \cdots \to v_\ell \to v_1$ without any repeated vertex other than the first and last ones. If the cycle contains all the vertices in G, then it is said to be a *directed Hamiltonian cycle*. To keep notation simple, let $d_{ij} \doteq d(v_i, v_j)$.

A directed cycle containing exactly k vertices is called a k-cycle. The length of a cycle is defined as the sum of arc lengths used in the cycle. A directed network $G = (V, A)$ with $|V| \geq k$ is said to be k-symmetric if for every k-cycle $v_1 \to v_2 \to \cdots \to v_k \to v_1$ in G,

$$d_{12} + d_{23} + \cdots + d_{k-1,k} + d_{k1} = d_{1k} + d_{k,k-1} + \cdots + d_{32} + d_{21}.$$

In other words, a k-symmetric network is a directed network in which the length of every k-cycle remains unchanged if its orientation is reversed.

(a) Show that the asymmetric Traveling Salesman Problem on a $|V|$-symmetric network (satisfying the triangle inequality) can be solved via solving a corresponding symmetric Traveling Salesman Problem. In particular, show that any heuristic with fixed worst-case bound for the symmetric Traveling Salesman Problem can be used for the asymmetric Traveling Salesman Problem on a $|V|$-symmetric network to obtain a result with the same worst-case bound.

(*b*) Prove that any 3-symmetric network is k-symmetric for $k = 4, 5, \ldots, |V|$.

Thus part (*a*) can be used if we have a 3-symmetric network. Argue that a 3-symmetric network can be identified in polynomial time.

3

Average-Case Analysis

3.1 Introduction

Worst-case performance analysis is one method of characterizing the effectiveness of a heuristic. It provides a guarantee on the maximum relative difference between the solution generated by the heuristic and the optimal solution for any possible problem instance, even those that are not likely to appear in practice. Thus, a heuristic that works well in practice may have a weak worst-case performance, if, for example, it provides very bad solutions for one (or more) pathological instance(s).

To overcome this important drawback, researchers have recently focused on *probabilistic analysis* of algorithms with the objective of characterizing the average performance of a heuristic under specific assumptions on the distribution of the problem data. As pointed out, for example, by Coffman and Lueker (1991), probabilistic analysis is frequently quite difficult and even the analysis of simple heuristics can often present a substantial challenge. Therefore, usually the analysis is *asymptotic*. That is, the average performance of a heuristic can only be quantified when the problem size is extremely large.

As we demonstrate in Parts II and IV, an asymptotic probabilistic analysis is useful for several reasons:

1. It can foster new insights into which algorithmic approaches will be effective for solving large size problems. That is, the analysis provides a framework where one can analyze and compare the performance of heuristics on large size problems.

2. For problems with fast rates of convergence, the analysis can sometimes

explain the observed empirical behavior of heuristics for more reasonable size problems.

3. The approximations derived from the analysis can be used in other models and may lead to a better understanding of the tradeoffs in more complex problems integrating vehicle routing with other issues important to the firm, such as inventory control.

In this chapter we present some of the basic tools used in the analysis of the average performance of heuristics. Again we use the Bin-Packing Problem and the Traveling Salesman Problem as the "raw materials" on which to present them.

3.2   The Bin-Packing Problem

The Bin-Packing Problem provides a very well studied example for which to demonstrate the benefits of a probabilistic analysis.

Without loss of generality, we scale the bin capacity q so that it is 1. Consider the item sizes $w_1, w_2, w_3 \ldots$ to be independently and identically distributed on $(0, 1]$ according to some general distribution Φ. In this section we demonstrate two elegant and powerful techniques that can be used in the analysis of b_n^*, the random variable representing the optimal solution value on the items $w_1, w_2, \ldots, w_n$. The first is the theory of *subadditive processes* and the second is the theory of *martingale inequalities*.

Subaddtive Processes

Let $\{a_n\}$, $n \geq 1$, be a sequence of positive real numbers. We say that the sequence is *subadditive* if for all n and m we have $a_n + a_m \geq a_{n+m}$. The following important result was proved by Kingman (1976) and Steele (1990) whose proof we follow.

Theorem 3.2.1 *If the sequence $\{a_n\}$, $n \geq 1$ is subadditive, then there exists a constant γ such that*

$$\lim_{n \to \infty} \frac{a_n}{n} = \gamma.$$

Proof. Let $\gamma = \underline{\lim}_{n \to \infty} \frac{a_n}{n}$. For a given ϵ select n such that $\frac{a_n}{n} \leq \gamma + \epsilon$. Since the sequence $\{a_n\}$ is subadditive we have

$$a_{nm} \leq a_n + a_{n(m-1)}.$$

Making a repeated use of this inequality we get $a_{nm} \leq ma_n$ which implies

$$\frac{a_{nm}}{nm} \leq \gamma + \epsilon.$$

For any k, $0 \leq k \leq n$, define $\ell \doteq nm + k$. Using subadditivity again, we have

$$a_\ell = a_{nm+k} \leq a_{nm+k-1} + a_1$$

$$\leq a_{nm} + ka_1$$

$$\leq a_{nm} + na_1$$

where the second inequality is obtained by repeating the first one k times. Thus,

$$\frac{a_\ell}{\ell} = \frac{a_{nm+k}}{nm+k} \leq \frac{a_{nm} + na_1}{nm+k} \leq \frac{a_{nm}}{nm} + \frac{a_1}{m} \leq \gamma + \epsilon + \frac{a_1}{m}.$$

Taking the limit with respect to m we have

$$\overline{\lim_{\ell \to \infty}} \frac{a_\ell}{\ell} \leq \gamma + \epsilon + \overline{\lim_{m \to \infty}} \frac{a_1}{m} = \gamma + \epsilon.$$

The proof is therefore complete since ϵ was chosen arbitrarily. ∎

It is clear that the optimal solution of the Bin-Packing Problem possesses the subadditivity property; that is,

$$\forall n, m, \quad b_{n+m}^* \leq b_n^* + b_m^*.$$

The above analysis implies that there exists a constant γ such that the optimal solution to the Bin-Packing Problem b_n^* satisfies

$$\lim_{n \to \infty} \frac{b_n^*}{n} = \gamma.$$

In addition, γ is dependent only on the item size distribution Φ.

The Uniform Model

To illustrate the concepts just developed, consider the case where Φ is the uniform distribution on $[0, 1]$. In order to pack a set of n items drawn randomly from this distribution, we use the following Sliced Interval Partitioning heuristic with parameter r ($SIP(r)$). It works as follows. For any *fixed* positive integer $r \geq 1$, the set of items N is partitioned into the following $2r$ disjoint subsets, some of which may be empty:

$$N_j = \left\{ k \in N \, \middle| \, \frac{1}{2}\left(1 - \frac{j+1}{r}\right) < w_k \leq \frac{1}{2}\left(1 - \frac{j}{r}\right) \right\} \qquad j = 1, 2, \ldots, r-1,$$

and

$$N^j = \left\{ k \in N \, \middle| \, \frac{1}{2}\left(1 + \frac{j-1}{r}\right) < w_k \leq \frac{1}{2}\left(1 + \frac{j}{r}\right) \right\} \qquad j = 1, 2, \ldots, r-1.$$

Also

$$N_0 = \left\{ k \in N \, \middle| \, \frac{1}{2}\left(1 - \frac{1}{r}\right) < w_k \leq \frac{1}{2} \right\},$$

and

$$N^r = \left\{ k \in N \,\middle|\, \frac{1}{2}\left(1 + \frac{r-1}{r}\right) < w_k \right\}.$$

The number of items in each N_j (respectively, N^j) is denoted by n_j (respectively, n^j) for all possible values of j.

Note that for any $j = 1, 2, \ldots, r - 1$, one bin can hold an item from N_j together with exactly one item from N^j. The $SIP(r)$ heuristic generates pairs of items, one item from N_j and one from N^j, for every $j = 1, 2, \ldots, r - 1$. The items in $N_0 \cup N^r$ are put in individual bins; one bin is assigned to each of these items.

For any $j = 1, 2, \ldots, r - 1$, we arbitrarily match one item from N_j with exactly one item from N^j; one bin holds each such pair. If $n_j = n^j$, then all the items in $N_j \cup N^j$ are matched. If, however, $n_j \neq n^j$, then we can match exactly $\min\{n_j, n^j\}$ pairs of items. The remaining $|n_j - n^j|$ items in $N_j \cup N^j$ that have not yet been matched are put one per bin. Thus, the total number of bins used is

$$n_0 + n^r + \sum_{j=1}^{r-1} \max\{n_j, n^j\}.$$

The heuristic clearly generates a feasible solution to the Bin-Packing Problem. Since

$$\lim_{n \to \infty} \frac{n_j}{n} = \lim_{n \to \infty} \frac{n^j}{n} = \frac{1}{2r} \quad (a.s.) \quad \text{for all } j = 1, 2, \ldots, r,$$

we have

$$\gamma = \lim_{n \to \infty} \frac{b_n^*}{n} \leq \lim_{n \to \infty} \frac{1}{n}\left[n_0 + n^r + \sum_{j=1}^{r-1} \max\{n_j, n^j\} \right] = \frac{1}{2} + \frac{1}{2r} \quad (a.s.).$$

Since this holds for any $r > 1$, we see that $\gamma \leq \frac{1}{2}$. Since $\gamma \geq E(w)$ (see Exercise 3.4), then $\gamma \geq \frac{1}{2}$ and we conclude that $\gamma = \frac{1}{2}$ for the uniform distribution on $[0, 1]$.

Using this idea, we can actually devise an *asymptotically optimal* heuristic for instances where the item sizes are uniformly distributed on $[0, 1]$. To formally define this property, let Z_n^* be the cost of the optimal solution to the problem on a problem of size n, and let Z_n^H be the cost of the solution provided by a heuristic H. Let the relative error of a heuristic H on a particular instance of n points be

$$e_n^H = \frac{Z_n^H - Z_n^*}{Z_n^*}.$$

Definition 3.2.2 *Let* Ψ *be a probability measure on the set of instances* $\mathcal{I}$. *A heuristic H is asymptotically optimal for* Ψ *if almost surely*

$$\lim_{n \to \infty} e_n^H = 0,$$

where the problem data are generated randomly from Ψ.

That is, under certain assumptions on the distribution of the data, H generates solutions whose relative error tends to zero as n, the number of points, tends to infinity. The above $SIP(r)$ heuristic is not asymptotically optimal since for any fixed r, the relative error converges to $\frac{1}{r}$.

A truly asymptotically optimal heuristic can easily be constructed. The following heuristic is called MATCH. First, sort the items in nonincreasing order of the item sizes. Then take the largest item, say item i, and match it with the largest item with which it will fit. If no such item exists, then put item i in a bin alone. Otherwise, put item i and the item it was matched with in a bin together. Now repeat this until all items are packed. The proof of asymptotic optimality is given as an exercise (Exercise 3.11).

An additional use for the bin-packing constant γ is as an approximation for the number of bins needed. When n is large, the number of bins required to pack n random items from Φ is very close to $n\gamma$. How close the random variable representing the number of bins is to $n\gamma$ is discussed next.

Martingale Inequalities

Consider the stochastic processes $\{X_n\}$ and $\{Y_n\}$ with $n \geq 0$. We say that the stochastic process $\{X_n\}$ is a *martingale* with respect to $\{Y_n\}$ if for every $n \geq 0$ we have

$$(i) \quad E[X_n] < +\infty, \text{ and}$$

$$(ii) \quad E[X_{n+1}|Y_1, \ldots, Y_n] = X_n.$$

To get some insight into the definition of a martingale consider someone playing a sequence of fair games. Let $X_n = Y_n$ be the amount of money the player has at the end of the nth game. If $\{X_n\}$ is a martingale with respect to $\{Y_n\}$, then this says that the expected amount of money the player will have at the end of the $(n + 1)^{\text{st}}$ game is equal to what the player had at the beginning of that game X_n, regardless of the game's history prior to state n. See Karlin and Taylor (1975) for details.

Consider now the random variable:

$$D_n \doteq E[X_{n+1}|Y_1, \ldots, Y_n] - E[X_{n+1}|Y_1, \ldots, Y_{n-1}].$$

The sequence $\{D_n\}$ is called a *martingale difference sequence* if $E[D_n] = 0$ for every $n \geq 0$. Azuma (1967) developed the following interesting inequality for martingale difference sequences; see also Stout (1974) or Rhee and Talagrand (1987).

Lemma 3.2.3 *Let $\{D_i\}, i = 1, 2, \ldots, n$ be a martingale difference sequence. Then for every $t > 0$ we have*

$$Pr\left\{\left|\sum_{i \leq n} D_i\right| > t\right\} \leq 2\exp\left\{-t^2 / \left(2\sum_{i \leq n} ||D_i||_\infty^2\right)\right\},$$

where $||D_i||_\infty$ is a uniform upper bound on the D_i's.

The Lemma can be used to establish upper bounds on the probable deviations of both

- b_n^* from its mean $E[b_n^*]$, and

- $\frac{b_n^*}{n}$ from its asymptotic value γ.

For this purpose, define

$$
D_i = \begin{cases} E[b_n^*|w_1,\ldots,w_i] - E[b_n^*|w_1,\ldots,w_{i-1}], & \text{if } i \geq 2; \\ E[b_n^*|w_1] - E[b_n^*|\emptyset], & \text{if } i = 1. \end{cases}
$$

where $E[b_n^*|w_1,\ldots,w_i]$ is the random variable that represents the expected optimal solution value of the Bin-Packing Problem obtained by fixing the sizes of the first i items and averaging on all other item sizes. Clearly, $E[b_n^*|w_1,\ldots,w_n] = b_n^*$ while $E[b_n^*|\emptyset] = E[b_n^*]$. Hence, $\sum_{i=1}^{n} D_i = b_n^* - E[b_n^*]$. Furthermore, the sequence D_i defines a martingale difference sequence with the property that $D_i \leq 1$ for every $i \geq 1$.

Applying Lemma 3.2.3 we obtain the following upper bound.

$$
Pr\left\{|b_n^* - E[b_n^*]| > t\right\} = Pr\left\{\left|\sum_{i=1}^{n} D_i\right| > t\right\} \leq 2\exp\left\{-t^2/(2n)\right\}.
$$

This bound can now be used to construct an upper bound on the likelihood that $\frac{b_n^*}{n}$ differs from its asymptotic value by more than some fixed amount.

Theorem 3.2.4 *For every $\epsilon > 0$ there exists an integer n_0 such that for all $n \geq n_0$,*

$$
Pr\left\{\left|\frac{b_n^*}{n} - \gamma\right| > \epsilon\right\} < 2\exp\left(-\frac{n\epsilon^2}{2}\right).
$$

Proof. Lemma 3.2.1 implies that $\lim_{n\to\infty} E[\frac{b_n^*}{n}] = \gamma$ and therefore for every $\epsilon > 0$ and $k \geq 2$ there exists n_0 such that for all $n \geq n_0$ we have

$$
\left|E\left[\frac{b_n^*}{n}\right] - \gamma\right| < \frac{\epsilon}{k}.
$$

Consequently,

$$
Pr\left\{\left|\frac{b_n^*}{n} - \gamma\right| > \epsilon\right\} \leq Pr\left\{\left|\frac{b_n^*}{n} - \frac{E[b_n^*]}{n}\right| + \left|\frac{E[b_n^*]}{n} - \gamma\right| > \epsilon\right\}
$$

$$
\leq Pr\left\{\left|\frac{b_n^*}{n} - \frac{E[b_n^*]}{n}\right| + \frac{\epsilon}{k} > \epsilon\right\}
$$

$$
\leq Pr\left\{\left|b_n^* - E[b_n^*]\right| > \frac{n\epsilon(k-1)}{k}\right\}
$$

$$
\leq 2\exp\left\{-\frac{n\epsilon^2(k-1)^2}{2k^2}\right\}.
$$

Since this last inequality holds for arbitrary $k \geq 2$, this completes the proof. ∎

These results demonstrate that b_n^* is in fact very close to $n\gamma$, and this is true for any distribution of the item sizes. Therefore, it suggests that $n\gamma$ may serve as a good approximation for b_n^* in other, more complex, combinatorial problems.

3.3   The Traveling Salesman Problem

In this section we demonstrate an important use for the tools presented above. Our objective is to show how probabilistic analysis can be used to construct effective algorithms with certain attractive theoretical properties.

Let $x_1, x_2, \ldots, x_n$ be a sequence of points in the Euclidean plane ($I\!R^2$) and let L_n^* be the length of the optimal traveling salesman tour through these n points. We start with a deterministic upper bound on L_n^* developed by Few (1955). We follow Jaillet's (1985) presentation.

Theorem 3.3.1 *Let $a \times b$ be the size of the smallest rectangle that contains* $x_1, x_2 \ldots, x_n$, *then*

$$L_n^* \leq \sqrt{2(n-2)ab} + 2(a+b).$$

Proof. For an integer m (to be determined), partition the rectangle of size $a \times b$ (where a is the length and b is the height) into $2m$ equal width horizontal strips. This creates $2m+1$ horizontal lines and two vertical lines (counting the boundaries of the rectangle). Label the horizontal lines $1, 2, \ldots, 2m+1$ moving downwards. Now temporarily delete all horizontal lines with an even label. Connect each point x_i, $i = 1, 2 \ldots, n$, with two vertical segments, to the closest (odd-labeled) horizontal line. A path through $x_1, \ldots, x_n$ can now be constructed by proceeding from, say the upper left-hand corner of the $a \times b$ rectangle and moving from left to right on the first horizontal line picking up all points that are connected (with the two vertical segments) to this line. Then we proceed downwards and cover the third horizontal line from right to left. This continues until we reach the end of the $2m + 1^{\text{st}}$ line. This path can be extended to a traveling salesman tour by returning from the last point to the first by adding at most one vertical and one horizontal line (we avoid diagonal movements for the sake of simplicity). Now repeat this procedure with the even labeled horizontal lines and, in a similar manner, create a path through all the customers. Extend this path to a traveling salesman tour by adding one horizontal line and one vertical segment of length $b - \frac{b}{m}$. See Figure 3.1.

Clearly, the sum of length of the two traveling salesman tours is

$$a(2m+1) + \frac{nb}{m} + 2b + a + 2\left(b - \frac{b}{m}\right).$$

Since L_n^* is no larger than either of these two tours, we have

$$L_n^* \leq a + 2b + ma + (n-2)\frac{b}{2m}.$$

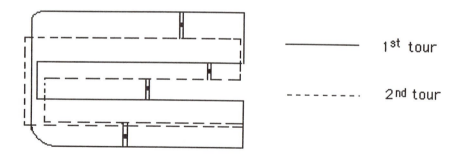

FIGURE 3.1. The two traveling salesman tours constructed by the partitioning algorithm.

The right-hand side is convex in m; hence, we minimize on m. That is, we choose:

$$m^* = \left\lceil \sqrt{\frac{b(n-2)}{2a}} \right\rceil,$$

then

$$L_n^* \le a + 2b + m^*a + \frac{b(n-2)}{2m^*}$$

$$\le a + 2b + a\left(\sqrt{\frac{b(n-2)}{2a}} + 1\right) + \frac{b(n-2)}{2}\sqrt{\frac{2a}{(n-2)b}}$$

$$= \sqrt{2(n-2)ab} + 2(a+b).$$

The above result implies that the length of the optimal traveling salesman tour is at most $O(\sqrt{n})$. In 1959, Beardwood et al. showed that the rate of growth of L^*, when customer locations are independent and identically distributed, is $\Theta(\sqrt{n})$. Specifically, they prove the following result.

Theorem 3.3.2 *Let $x_1, x_2, \ldots, x_n$ be a sequence of independent random variables having a distribution μ with compact support in $\mathbb{R}^2$. Then there exists a constant $\beta > 0$, independent of the distribution μ, such that with probability one,*

$$\lim_{n\to\infty} \frac{L_n^*}{\sqrt{n}} = \beta \int_{\mathbb{R}^2} f^{1/2}(x)dx,$$

where f is the density of the absolutely continuous part of the distribution μ.

Since Beardwood et al. proved this result many researchers have proved it using a variety of techniques. One of these methods is based on the concept of Euclidean subadditive processes (Steele, 1981) which is a generalization of the concept of subadditive processes described earlier.

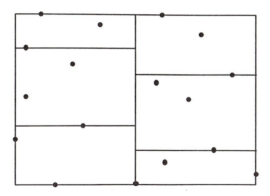

FIGURE 3.2. Region partitioning example with $n = 17$, $q = 3$, $h = 2$ and $t = 1$.

In this subsection we are not going to prove the result, but rather concentrate on its algorithmic implications. Specifically, we will describe the following polynomial time algorithm which is *asymptotically optimal*. The heuristic was suggested by Karp (1977), although we have modified it in several places for the purpose of clarifying the presentation.

A Region Partitioning Heuristic

In the Region Partitioning heuristic, the region containing the points is subdivided into subregions such that each subregion contains exactly q customers (except possibly for one) and where q is to be determined later. The heuristic then constructs an optimal traveling salesman tour on the set of points within each subregion and then connects these tours to form a traveling salesman tour through all the points.

To generate subregions each with exactly q points, except for possibly one subregion where there may be fewer points, we use the following strategy: the smallest rectangle with sides a and b containing the set of points $x_1, x_2, \ldots, x_n$ is partitioned by means of horizontal and vertical lines. First, the region is divided by t vertical lines such that each subregion contains exactly $(h + 1)q$ points except possibly the last one. This is done precisely as follows: temporarily index the customers in increasing order of their horizontal coordinate. Place the vertical lines so that the jth vertical line (for $j \leq t$) goes through the customer with index $j(h + 1)q$. Each of these $t + 1$ subregions is then partitioned by means of h horizontal lines into $h + 1$ smaller subregions such that each contains exactly q points except possibly the last one. More precisely, this is done as follows: in each vertical strip index the customers in increasing order of their vertical coordinates. Place the horizontal lines so that the jth horizontal line (for $j \leq h$) goes through the customer with index jq. See Figure 3.2 for an example.

To solve the Traveling Salesman Problems within each subregion, we use a dynamic programming algorithm developed by Held and Karp (1962). It finds an optimal traveling salesman tour through q points in running time which is $O(q^2 2^q)$. If we choose $q = \lceil \log n \rceil$ then solving the Traveling Salesman Problem

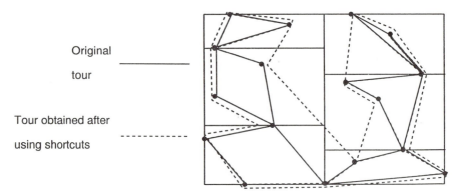

Original

tour

Tour obtained after

using shortcuts

FIGURE 3.3. The tour generated by the region partitioning algorithm.

for a single region takes $O(n \log^2 n)$, and since the number of subregions is no more than $1 + n/\log n$, the total time spent solving these Traveling Salesman Problems is $O(n^2 \log n)$.

After finding optimal traveling salesman tours within each subregion, observe that this collection of traveling salesman tours can be easily transformed into a single traveling salesman tour through all the points. This is true since this collection of tours along with the lines added as above, defines an Eulerian graph where the degree of each point (node) is either two or four (a point that is on the boundary of two subregions will have degree four). Thus, this tour can be transformed into a single traveling salesman tour, and using shortcuts its length can be further reduced. See Figure 3.3.

To guarantee that each subregion has exactly q points, except for maybe one, h and t must satisfy

$$t = \left\lceil \frac{n}{(h+1)q} \right\rceil - 1,$$

and

$$t(h+1)q < n \le (t+1)(h+1)q.$$

This is achieved by choosing $h = \lceil \sqrt{\frac{n}{q}} - 1 \rceil$.

Let L^{RP} be the length of the tour generated by the above Region Partitioning heuristic. To establish the quality of the heuristic we need to find an upper bound on L^{RP}; this is provided by the following.

Lemma 3.3.3

$$L^{RP} \le L^* + \frac{3}{2} P^{RP},$$

where P^{RP} is the sum of the perimeters of all subregions generated by the Region Partitioning heuristic.

Proof. Let L_j be the length of the optimal traveling salesman tour in subregion $j = 1, 2, \ldots, \lceil \frac{n}{q} \rceil$. Similarly, let L_j^* be the sum of the lengths of all segments of

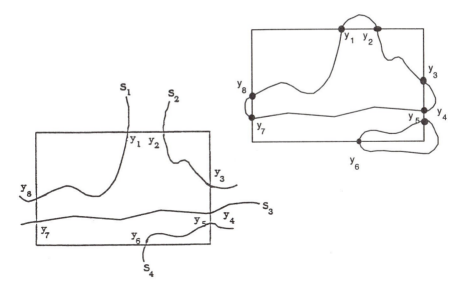

FIGURE 3.4. The segments $S_1, \ldots, S_k$ and the corresponding Eulerian graph.

the optimal traveling salesman tour through all n customers that are contained in the jth subregion, for $j \geq 1$. Since the collection of tours and lines constructed above defines an Eulerian graph, we have $L^{RP} \leq \sum_j L_j$. Also, by definition we have $L^* = \sum_j L_j^*$. Thus, it is sufficient to show that

$$L_j \leq L_j^* + \frac{3}{2}P_j, \qquad (3.1)$$

where P_j is the perimeter of subregion j.

To prove inequality (3.1), assume there are exactly k continuous segments $S_1, \ldots, S_k$, of the globally optimal traveling salesman tour, in subregion j; see Figure 3.4. Let the $2k$ end-points of these segments be $y_1, y_2, \ldots, y_{2k}$ ordered consecutively around the boundary of subregion j. Without loss of generality we assume that

$$\ell(y_1 y_2) + \ell(y_3 y_4) + \cdots + \ell(y_{2k} y_{2k-1}) \leq \ell(y_2 y_3) + \ell(y_4 y_5) + \cdots + \ell(y_{2k} y_1),$$

where $\ell(y_i y_{i+1})$ is the distance between point y_i and y_{i+1} along the perimeter of the jth subregion. We construct a feasible solution for the Traveling Salesman Problem defined by the points x_i that are in the jth subregion. The tour is based on (i) the segments $S_1, \ldots, S_k$; (ii) two copies of each segment $y_1 y_2, y_3 y_4, \ldots, y_{2k-1} y_{2k}$; and ($iii$) one copy of each segment $y_2 y_3, y_4 y_5, \ldots, y_{2k} y_1$.

Observe (Figure 3.4) that the above three components define an Eulerian graph whose set of vertices is the points x_i that belong to the jth subregion plus all the points y_i, for $i = 1, 2, \ldots, 2k$. This implies that the graph has an Eulerian tour whose cost is no more than

$$L_j^* + \frac{3}{2} P_j.$$

This tour can be converted into a traveling salesman tour, using shortcuts, and therefore

$$L_j \le L_j^* + \frac{3}{2} P_j.$$

Summing these up on j completes the proof. ∎

We can now prove the following result due to Karp.

Theorem 3.3.4 *Under the conditions of Theorem 3.3.2, with probability one,*

$$\lim_{n \to \infty} \frac{L^*}{\sqrt{n}} = \lim_{n \to \infty} \frac{L^{\mathrm{RP}}}{\sqrt{n}}.$$

Proof. Lemma 3.3.3 implies

$$L^* \le L^{\mathrm{RP}} \le L^* + \frac{3}{2} P^{\mathrm{RP}}.$$

Hence, we need to evaluate the quantity P^{RP}. Note that the number of vertical lines added in the construction of the subregions is $t \le \sqrt{\frac{n}{q}}$. Each of these lines is counted twice in the quantity P^{RP}.

In the second step of the RP heuristic we add h horizontal lines where $h \le \sqrt{\frac{n}{q}}$. These horizontal lines are also counted twice in P^{RP}. It follows that

$$P^{\mathrm{RP}} \le 2\sqrt{\frac{n}{q}}(a+b) + 2(a+b) \le 2\sqrt{\frac{n}{\log n}}(a+b) + 2(a+b),$$

where the right-hand side inequality is justified by the definition of q.

Consequently,

$$\frac{L^{\mathrm{RP}}}{\sqrt{n}} \le \frac{L^*}{\sqrt{n}} + \frac{3}{2} \frac{P^{\mathrm{RP}}}{\sqrt{n}}$$

$$\le \frac{L^*}{\sqrt{n}} + \frac{3(a+b)}{\sqrt{\log n}} + \frac{3(a+b)}{\sqrt{n}}.$$

Taking the limit as n goes to infinity proves the theorem. ∎

3.4 Exercises

Exercise 3.1. *A lower bound on β.* Let $X(n) = \{x_1, x_2, \ldots, x_n\}$ be a set of points uniformly and independently distributed in the unit square. Let ℓ_j be the distance from $x_j \in X(n)$ to the nearest point in $X(n) \setminus x_j$. Let $L(X(n))$ be the length of the optimal traveling salesman tour through $X(n)$. Clearly $E(L(X(n))) \ge n E(\ell_1)$. We evaluate a lower bound on β in the following way.

(a) Find $\Pr(\ell_1 \geq \ell)$.

(b) Use (a) to calculate a lower bound on $E(\ell_1) = \int_0^\infty \Pr(\ell_1 \geq \ell)d\ell$.

(c) Use Stirling's formula to approximate the bound when n is large.

(d) Show that $\frac{1}{2}$ is a lower bound on β.

Exercise 3.2. *An upper bound on β.* (Karp and Steele, 1985) The *strips method* for constructing a tour through n random points in the unit square dissects the square into $\frac{1}{\Delta}$ horizontal strips of width Δ, and then follows a zigzag path, visiting the points in the first strip in left-to-right order, then the points in the second strip in right-to-left order, etc., finally returning to the initial point from the final point of the last strip. Prove that, when Δ is suitably chosen, the expected length of the tour produced by the strips method is at most $1.16\sqrt{n}$.

Exercise 3.3. Consider the TSP defined on a set of points N indexed $1, 2, \ldots, n$. Let Z^* be the length of the optimal tour. Consider now the following strategy: starting with point 1, the salesman moves to the closest point in the set $N \setminus \{1\}$, say point 2. The salesman then constructs an optimal traveling salesman tour defined on this set of $n-1$ points $(N \setminus \{1\})$ and then returns to point 1 through point 2. Show that the length of this tour is no larger then $3Z^*/2$. Is the bound tight?

Exercise 3.4. Prove that the bin-packing constant γ satisfies $1 \leq \gamma/E(w) \leq 2$ where $E(w)$ is the expected item size.

Exercise 3.5. The Harmonic heuristic with parameter M, denoted $H(M)$, is the following. For each $k = 1, 2, \ldots, M - 1$, items of size $\frac{1}{k+1} < w_i \leq \frac{1}{k}$ are packed separately, at most k items per bin. That is, items of size greater than $\frac{1}{2}$ are packed one per bin, items of size $\frac{1}{3} < w_i \leq \frac{1}{2}$ are packed two per bin, etc. Finally, items of size $w_i \leq \frac{1}{M}$ are packed separately from the rest using First-Fit.

Given n items drawn randomly from the uniform distribution on $(\frac{1}{6}, 0]$, what is the asymptotic number of bins used by $H(5)$?

Exercise 3.6. Suggest a method to pack n items drawn randomly from the uniform distribution on $[\frac{1}{3}, 1]$. Can you prove that your method is asymptotically optimal? What is the bin-packing constant (γ) for this distribution?

Exercise 3.7. Suggest a method to pack n items drawn randomly from the uniform distribution on $[0, \frac{5}{12}]$. Can you prove that your method is asymptotically optimal? What is the bin-packing constant (γ) for this distribution?

Exercise 3.8. Suggest a method to pack n items drawn randomly from the uniform distribution on $[\frac{1}{40}, \frac{59}{120}]$. Can you prove that your method is asymptotically optimal? What is the bin-packing constant (γ) for this distribution?

Exercise 3.9. (Dreyfus and Law, 1977) The following is a dynamic programming procedure to solve the TSP. Let city 1 be an arbitrary city. Define the following function.

$$f_i(j, S) = \text{the length of the shortest path from city 1 to}$$

$$\text{city } j \text{ visiting cities in the set } S, \text{ where } |S| = i.$$

Determine the recursive formula and solve the following instance.

The distances between cities.

d_{ij}	1	2	3	4	5
1	0	3	1	5	4
2	1	0	5	4	3
3	5	4	0	2	1
4	3	1	3	0	3
5	5	2	4	1	0

Exercise 3.10. What is the complexity of the dynamic program developed in the previous exercise?

Exercise 3.11. (Coffman and Leuker, 1991) Consider flipping a fair coin n times in succession. Let X_n represent the random variable denoting the maximum excess of the number of heads over tails at any point in the sequence of n flips. It is known that $E(X_n)$ is $\Theta(\sqrt{n})$. From this, argue that

$$E[Z_n^{\text{MATCH}}] = \frac{n}{2} + \Theta(\sqrt{n}).$$

Exercise 3.12. Assume n cities are uniformly distributed in the unit disc. Consider the following heuristic for the n-city TSP. Let d_i be the distance from city i to the depot. Order the points so that $d_1 \leq d_2 \leq \cdots \leq d_n$. For each $i = 1, 2, \ldots, n$, draw a circle of radius d_i centered at the depot; call this circle i. Starting at the depot travel directly to city 1. From city 1 travel to circle 2 in a direction along the ray through city 1 and the depot. When circle 2 is reached, follow circle 2 in the direction (clockwise or counterclockwise) that results in a shorter route to city 2. Repeat this same step until city n is reached; then return to the depot. Let Z_n^H be the length of this traveling salesman tour. What is the asymptotic rate of growth of Z_n^H? Is this heuristic asymptotically optimal?

4

Mathematical Programming Based Bounds

4.1 Introduction

An important method of assessing the effectiveness of any heuristic is to compare it to the value of a lower bound on the cost of an optimal solution. In many cases this is not an easy task; constructing strong lower bounds on the optimal solution may be as difficult as solving the problem. An attractive approach for generating a lower bound on the optimal solution to an $\mathcal{NP}$-Complete problem is the following mathematical programming approach. First, formulate the problem as an integer program; then relax the integrality constraint and solve the resulting linear program.

What problems do we encounter when we try to use this approach? One difficulty is deciding on a integer programming formulation. There are myriad possible formulations from which to choose. Another difficulty may be that in order to formulate the problem as an integer program, a large (sometimes exponential) number of variables are required. That is, the resulting linear program may be very large, so that it is not possible to use standard linear programming solvers. The third problem is that it is not clear how tight the lower bound provided by the linear relaxation will be. This depends on the problem and the formulation.

In the sections below we demonstrate how a general class of formulations can provide tight lower bounds on the original integer program. In later chapters we show that these and similar linear programs can be solved effectively and implemented in algorithms that solve logistics problems to optimality or near optimality.

4.2   An Asymptotically Tight Linear Program

Again, consider the Bin-Packing Problem. There are many ways to formulate the problem as an integer program. The one we use here is based on formulating it as a Set-Partitioning Problem. The idea is as follows. Let F be the collection of all sets of items that can be feasibly packed into one bin; that is,

$$F \doteq \{S \subseteq N : \sum_{i \in S} w_i \leq 1\}.$$

For any $i \in N$ and $S \in F$, let

$$\alpha_{iS} = \begin{cases} 1, & \text{if } i \in S, \\ 0, & \text{otherwise.} \end{cases}$$

Let

$$y_S = \begin{cases} 1, & \text{if the set of items } S \text{ are placed in a single bin,} \\ 0, & \text{otherwise.} \end{cases}$$

Then the set-partitioning formulation of the Bin-Packing Problem is the following integer program.

$$\text{Problem } P: \quad Min \sum_{S \in F} y_S$$

$$s.t.$$

$$\sum_{S \in F} \alpha_{iS} y_S = 1, \quad \forall i \in N \tag{4.1}$$

$$y_S \in \{0, 1\}, \quad \forall S \in F.$$

In this section we prove that the relative difference between the optimal solution of the linear relaxation of problem P and the optimal solution of problem P (the integer solution) tends to zero as $|N| = n$, the number of items, increases. First we need the following definition.

Definition 4.2.1 *A function ϕ is Lipschitz continuous of order q on a set $A \subseteq \mathbb{R}$ if there exists a constant K such that*

$$|\phi(x) - \phi(y)| \leq K|x - y|^q, \forall x, y \in A.$$

Our first result of this section is the following.

Theorem 4.2.2 *Let the item sizes be independently and identically distributed according to a distribution Φ which is Lipschitz continuous of order $q \geq 1$ on $[0, 1]$. Let b_n^{LP} be the value of the optimal solution to the linear relaxation of P, and let b_n^* be the value of the optimal integer solution to P; that is, the value of the optimal solution to the Bin-Packing Problem. Then, with probability one,*

$$\lim_{n \to \infty} \frac{1}{n} b_n^{LP} = \lim_{n \to \infty} \frac{1}{n} b_n^*.$$

To prove the theorem we consider a related model. Consider a *discretized* Bin-Packing Problem in which there are a finite number W of item sizes. Each different size defines an *item type*. Let n_i be the number of items of type i, for $i = 1, 2, \ldots, W$, and let $n = \sum_{i=1}^{W} n_i$ be the total number of items. Clearly, this discretized Bin-Packing Problem can be solved by formulating it as the set-partitioning problem P. To obtain some intuition about the linear relaxation of P, we first introduce another formulation closely related to P.

Let a *bin assignment* be a vector $(a_1, a_2, \ldots, a_W)$, where $a_i \geq 0$ are integers, and such that a single bin can contain a_1 items of type 1, along with a_2 items of type 2, $\ldots$, along with a_W items of size W, without violating the capacity constraint. Index all the possible bin assignments $1, 2, \ldots, R$, and note that R is independent of n. The Bin-Packing Problem can be formulated as follows. Let

$$A_{ir} = \text{number of items of type } i \text{ in bin assignment } r,$$

for each $i = 1, 2, \ldots, W$ and $r = 1, 2, \ldots, R$. Let

$$y_r = \text{number of times bin assignment } r \text{ is used in the optimal solution.}$$

The new formulation of the discretized Bin-Packing Problem is:

$$\text{Problem } P_D : \quad Min \quad \sum_{r=1}^{R} y_r$$

$$s.t.$$

$$\sum_{r=1}^{R} y_r A_{ir} \geq n_i, \quad \forall i = 1, 2, \ldots, W,$$

$$y_r \geq 0 \text{ and integer}, \quad \forall r = 1, 2, \ldots, R.$$

Let b_D^* be the value of the optimal solution to Problem P_D and let b_D^{LP} be the optimal solution to the linear relaxation of Problem P_D. Clearly, Problem P and Problem P_D have the same optimal solution values; that is, $b^* = b_D^*$. On the other hand, b^{LP} is not necessarily equal to b_D^{LP}. However, it is easy to see that any feasible solution to the linear relaxation of Problem P can be used to construct a feasible solution to the linear relaxation of Problem P_D and therefore,

$$b^{LP} \geq b_D^{LP}. \tag{4.2}$$

The following is the crucial lemma needed to prove Theorem 4.2.2.

Lemma 4.2.3
$$b^{LP} \leq b^* \leq b_D^{LP} + W \leq b^{LP} + W.$$

Proof. The left-most inequality is trivial while the right-most inequality is due to equation (4.2). To prove the central inequality note that in Problem P_D there are W constraints, one for each item type. Let $\bar{y}_r$, for $r = 1, 2, \ldots, R$, be an optimal solution to the linear relaxation of Problem P_D and observe that there exists such an optimal solution with at most W positive variables; one for each constraint. We construct a feasible solution to Problem P_D by rounding the linear solution up; that is, for each $r = 1, 2, \ldots, R$ with $\overline{y}_r > 0$ we make $y_r = \lceil \overline{y}_r \rceil$ and for each $r = 1, 2, \ldots, R$ with $\overline{y}_r = 0$ we make $y_r = 0$. Hence, the increase in the objective function is no more than W. ∎

Observe that the upper bound on b^* obtained in Lemma 4.2.3 consists of two terms. The first, b^{LP}, is a lower bound on b^*, which clearly grows with the number of items n. The second term (W) is independent of n. Therefore, the upper bound on b^* of Lemma 4.2.3 is dominated by b^{LP} and consequently we see that for large n, $b^* \approx b^{LP}$, exactly what is implied by Theorem 4.2.2.

We can now use the intuition developed in the above analysis of the discrete Bin-Packing Problem to prove Theorem 4.2.2.

Proof. It is clear that $b^{LP} \leq b^*$ and therefore $\overline{\lim}_{n \to \infty} b^{LP}/n \leq \overline{\lim}_{n \to \infty} b^*/n$. To prove the upper bound, partition the interval $(0, 1]$ into $k \geq 2$ subintervals of equal length. Let N_j be the set of items whose size w satisfies $\frac{j-1}{k} < w \leq \frac{j}{k}$ and let $|N_j| = n_j$, $j = 1, 2, \ldots, k$. We construct a new Bin-Packing Problem where item sizes take only the values $\frac{j}{k}$, $j = 1, 2, \ldots, k$ and where the number of items of size $\frac{j}{k}$ is $\min\{n_j, n_{j+1}\}$, $j = 1, 2, \ldots, k - 1$. We refer to this instance of the Bin-Packing Problem as the *reduced instance*. For this reduced instance, define $\underline{b}^*$, $\underline{b}^{LP}$ and $\underline{b}_D^{LP}$ to be the obvious quantities.

It is easy to see that we can always construct a feasible solution to the original Bin-Packing Problem by solving the Bin-Packing Problem defined on the reduced instance and then assigning each of the remaining items to a single bin. This results in:

$$b^* \leq \underline{b}^* + \sum_{j=1}^{k-1} |n_j - n_{j+1}|$$

$$\leq \underline{b}_D^{LP} + k + \sum_{j=1}^{k-1} |n_j - n_{j+1}| \qquad \text{(using Lemma 4.2.3)}$$

$$\leq \underline{b}^{LP} + k + \sum_{j=1}^{k-1} |n_j - n_{j+1}|.$$

We now argue that $\underline{b}^{LP} \leq b^{LP}$. This must be true since every item in the reduced instance can be associated with a unique item in the original instance whose size is at least as large. Thus, every feasible solution to the linear relaxation of the set-partitioning problem defined on the original instance is feasible for the same problem on the reduced instance. Hence,

$$b^* \leq b^{LP} + k + \sum_{j=1}^{k-1} |n_j - n_{j+1}|.$$

The Strong Law of Large Numbers and the Mean Value Theorem imply that for a given $j = 1, \ldots, k - 1$, there exists s_j such that

$$\lim_{n \to \infty} \frac{n_j}{n} = \frac{1}{k} \phi(s_j),$$

where ϕ is the density of item sizes. Hence,

$$\varlimsup_{n \to \infty} \frac{1}{n} |n_j - n_{j+1}| = \frac{1}{k} |\phi(s_j) - \phi(s_{j+1})|$$

$$\leq \frac{1}{k} K (s_{j+1} - s_j)^q \qquad \text{(by Lipschitz continuity)}$$

$$\leq \frac{2}{k^{q+1}} K \qquad \left(\text{since } s_{j+1} - s_j \leq \frac{2}{k} \right)$$

$$\leq \frac{2}{k^2} K \qquad \text{(since } q \geq 1\text{)}.$$

Consequently,

$$\varlimsup_{n \to \infty} \frac{b^*}{n} \leq \varlimsup_{n \to \infty} \frac{b^{\text{LP}}}{n} + \frac{2K(k-1)}{k^2}.$$

Since this holds for arbitrary k, this completes the proof.   ∎

In fact, it appears that the linear relaxation of the set-partitioning formulation may be extremely close to the optimal solution in the case of the Bin-Packing Problem. Recently Chan et al. (1995) show that the worst-case effectiveness of the set-partitioning lower bound (the linear relaxation), that is, the maximum ratio of the optimal integer solution (b^*) to the optimal linear relaxation b^{LP}, is $\frac{4}{3}$. They also provide an example achieving this bound. That is, for any number of items and any set of item weights, the linear program is at least 75% of the optimal solution.

4.3   Lagrangian Relaxation

In 1971, Held and Karp applied a mathematical technique known as *Lagrangian relaxation* to generate a lower bound on a general integer (linear) program. Our discussion of the method follows the elegant presentation of Fisher (1981). We start with the following integer program.

$$\text{Problem } P: \quad Z = Min \qquad cx$$

$$s.t.$$

$$Ax = b, \qquad (4.3)$$

$$Dx \leq e, \qquad (4.4)$$

$$x \geq 0 \text{ and integer,}$$

where x is an n-vector, b is an m-vector, e is a k-vector, A is an $m \times n$ matrix and D is a $k \times n$ matrix. Let the optimal solution to the linear relaxation of Problem P

be Z_{LP}. The Lagrangian relaxation of constraints (4.3) with multipliers $u \in \mathbb{R}^m$ is:

$$\text{Problem } LR_u: \quad Z_D(u) = Min \quad cx + u(Ax - b)$$

$$s.t.$$

$$Dx \leq e, \qquad\qquad (4.5)$$

$$x \geq 0 \qquad \text{and integer.}$$

The following is a simple observation.

Lemma 4.3.1 *For all $u \in \mathbb{R}^m$, $Z_D(u) \leq Z$.*

Proof. Let x be any feasible solution to Problem P. Clearly, x is also feasible for LR_u and since $Z_D(u)$ is its optimal solution value, we get

$$Z_D(u) \leq cx + u(Ax - b) = cx.$$

Consequently, $Z_D(u) \leq Z$. ∎

Remark: If the constraints $Ax = b$ in Problem P are replaced with the constraints $Ax \leq b$, then Lemma 4.3.1 holds for $u \in \mathbb{R}^m_+$.

Since $Z_D(u) \leq Z$ holds for all u, we are interested in the vector u that provides the largest possible lower bound. This is achieved by solving Problem D, called the *Lagrangian dual*, defined as follows.

$$\text{Problem D}: \quad Z_D = max_u Z_D(u).$$

Problem D has a number of important and interesting properties.

Lemma 4.3.2 *The function $Z_D(u)$ is a piecewise linear concave function of u.*

This implies that $Z_D(u)$ attains its maximum at a nondifferentiable point. This maximal point can be found using a technique called *subgradient optimization* which can be described as follows: given an initial vector u^0 the method generates a sequence of vectors $\{u^k\}$ defined by

$$u^{k+1} = u^k + t_k(Ax^k - b), \qquad\qquad (4.6)$$

where x^k is an optimal solution to Problem LR_{u^k} and t_k is a positive scalar called the *step size*. Polyak (1967) shows that if the step sizes $t_1, t_2, \ldots$, are chosen such that $\lim_{k \to \infty} t_k = 0$ and $\sum_{k \geq 0} t_k$ is unbounded, then $Z_D(u^k)$ converges to Z_D.

The step size commonly used in practice is

$$t_k = \frac{\lambda_k(UB - Z_D(u^k))}{\sum_{i=1}^{n}(a_i x^k - b_i)^2},$$

where UB is an upper bound on the optimal integer solution value (found using a heuristic), $a_i x^k - b_i$ is the difference between the left-hand side and the right-hand side of the ith constraint in $Ax^k \leq b$, and λ_k is a scalar satisfying $0 < \lambda_k \leq 2$. Usually, one starts with $\lambda_0 = 2$ and cuts it in half every time $Z_D(u)$ fails to increase after a number of iterations.

It is now interesting to compare the Lagrangian relaxation lower bound (Z_D) to the lower bound achieved by solving the linear relaxation of the set-partitioning formulation (Z_{LP}).

Theorem 4.3.3
$$Z_{LP} \leq Z_D.$$

Proof.

$$Z_D = \max_u \left\{ \min_x cx + u(Ax - b) \middle| Dx \leq e, x \geq 0 \text{ and integer} \right\}$$

$$\geq \max_u \left\{ \min_x cx + u(Ax - b) \middle| Dx \leq e, x \geq 0 \right\}$$

$$= \max_u \max_v \left\{ ve - ub \middle| vD \leq c + uA, v \leq 0 \right\} \qquad \text{(by strong duality)}$$

$$= \max_{u,v} \left\{ ve - ub \middle| vD \leq c + uA, v \leq 0 \right\}$$

$$= \min_y \left\{ cy \middle| Ay = b, Dy \leq e, y \geq 0 \right\} \qquad \text{(by strong duality)}$$

$$= Z_{LP}. \qquad\blacksquare$$

We say a mathematical program P possesses the *integrality property* if the solution to the linear relaxation of P always provides an integer solution. Inspection of the above proof reveals the following corollary.

Corollary 4.3.4 *If Problem LR_u possesses the integrality property, then $Z_D = Z_{LP}$.*

4.4 Lagrangian Relaxation and the Traveling Salesman Problem

Held and Karp (1970, 1971) developed the Lagrangian relaxation technique in the context of the Traveling Salesman Problem. They show some interesting relationships between this method and a graph-theoretic problem called the *minimum weight 1-tree problem*.

4.4.1 The 1-Tree Lower Bound

We start by defining a 1-tree. For a given choice of vertex, say vertex 1, a 1-tree is a tree having vertex set $\{2, 3, \ldots, n\}$ together with two distinct edges connected to vertex 1. Therefore, a 1-tree is a graph with exactly one cycle. Define the weight of a 1-tree to be the sum of the costs of all its edges. In the minimum weight 1-tree problem the objective is to find a 1-tree of minimum weight. Such a 1-tree can be constructed by finding a minimum spanning tree on the entire network excluding vertex 1 and its corresponding edges, and by adding to the minimum spanning tree the two edges incident to vertex 1 of minimum cost.

We observe that any traveling salesman tour is a 1-tree tour in which each vertex has a degree 2. Moreover, if a minimum weight 1-tree is a tour, then it is an optimal traveling salesman tour. Thus, the minimum weight 1-tree provides a lower bound on the length of the optimal traveling salesman tour.

Unfortunately, this bound can be quite weak. However, there are ways to improve it. For this purpose consider the vector $\pi = \{\pi_1, \pi_2, \ldots, \pi_n\}$ and the following transformation of the distances $\{d_{ij}\}$:

$$d'_{ij} \doteq d_{ij} + \pi_i + \pi_j.$$

Let L^* be the length of the optimal tour with respect to the distance matrix $\{d_{ij}\}$. It is clear that the same tour is also optimal with respect to the distance matrix $\{d'_{ij}\}$. To see that observe that any traveling salesman tour S of cost L with respect to $\{d_{ij}\}$ has a cost $L + 2\sum_{i=1}^{n} \pi_i$ with respect to $\{d'_{ij}\}$. Thus, the difference between the length of any traveling salesman tour in $\{d_{ij}\}$ and $\{d'_{ij}\}$ is constant, independent of the tour.

Observe also that the above transformation of the distances *does* change the minimum 1-tree. How can this idea be used? First, enumerate all possible 1-trees and let d_i^k be the degree of vertex i in the kth 1-tree. Let T_k be the weight (cost) of that 1-tree (before transforming the distances). This implies that the cost of that 1-tree after the transformation is exactly

$$T_k + \sum_{i \in V} d_i^k \pi_i.$$

Thus, the minimum weight 1-tree on the transformed distance matrix is obtained by solving

$$\min_k \left\{ T_k + \sum_{i \in V} d_i^k \pi_i \right\}.$$

Since, in the transformed distance matrix, the optimal traveling salesman tour does not change while the 1-tree provides a lower bound, we have

$$L^* + 2\sum_{i \in V} \pi_i \geq \min_k \left\{ T_k + \sum_{i \in V} d_i^k \pi_i \right\},$$

which implies

$$L^* \geq \min_k \left\{ T_k + \sum_{i \in V} (d_i^k - 2)\pi_i \right\} \doteq w(\pi).$$

Consequently, the best lower bound is obtained by maximizing the function $w(\pi)$ over all possible values of π. How can we find the best value of π? Held and Karp

(1970, 1971) use the subgradient method described in the previous section. That is, starting with some arbitrary vector π^0, in step k the method updates the vector π^k according to

$$\pi_i^{k+1} = \pi_i^k + t_k(d_i^k - 2),$$

where π_i^k is the ith element in the vector π^k and t_k, the step size, equals

$$t_k = \frac{\lambda_k(UB - w(\pi^k))}{\sum_{i=1}^n (d_i^k - 2)^2}.$$

4.4.2   The 1-Tree Lower Bound and Lagrangian Relaxation

We now relate the 1-tree lower bound to a Lagrangian relaxation associated with the following formulation of the Traveling Salesman Problem. For every $e \in E$, let d_e be the cost of the edge and let x_e be a variable that takes on the value 1 if the optimal tour includes the edge and the value zero, otherwise. Given a subset $S \subset V$, let $E(S)$ be the set of edges from E such that each edge has its two endpoints in S. Let $\delta(S)$ be the collection of edges from E in the cut separating S from $V \backslash S$. The Traveling Salesman Problem can be formulated as follows:

Problem P' : $Z^* = Min \sum_{e \in E} d_e x_e$

s.t.

$$\sum_{e \in \delta(i)} x_e = 2, \quad \forall i = 1, 2, \ldots, n \qquad (4.7)$$

$$\sum_{e \in E(S)} x_e \le |S| - 1, \quad \forall S \subseteq V \backslash \{1\}, \ S \ne \emptyset \qquad (4.8)$$

$$0 \le x_e \le 1, \quad \forall e \in E \qquad (4.9)$$

$$x_e \quad \text{integer}, \quad \forall e \in E. \qquad (4.10)$$

Constraints (4.7) ensure that each vertex has an edge going in and an edge going out. Constraints (4.8), called *subtour elimination* constraints, forbid integral solutions consisting of a set of disjoint cycles.

Observe that constraints (4.7) can be replaced by the following constraints.

$$\sum_{e \in \delta(i)} x_e = 2, \quad \forall i = 1, \ldots, n - 1 \qquad (4.11)$$

$$\sum_{e \in E} x_e = n. \qquad (4.12)$$

This is true since constraints (4.11) are exactly constraints (4.7) for $i = 1, \ldots, n-1$. The only missing constraint is $\sum_{e \in \delta(n)} x_e = 2$. Therefore, it is sufficient to show that (4.12) holds if and only if this one holds. To see this:

$$\sum_{e \in E} x_e = \frac{1}{2} \sum_{i=1}^{n} \sum_{e \in \delta(i)} x_e$$

$$= \frac{1}{2} \sum_{i=1}^{n-1} \sum_{e \in \delta(i)} x_e + \frac{1}{2} \sum_{e \in \delta(n)} x_e$$

$$= (n-1) + \frac{1}{2} \sum_{e \in \delta(n)} x_e.$$

Thus, $\sum_{e \in E} x_e = n$ if and only if $\sum_{e \in \delta(n)} x_e = 2$.

The resulting formulation of the Traveling Salesman Problem is

$$\left\{ Min \sum_{e \in E} d_e x_e \,\middle|\, (4.8), (4.9), (4.10), (4.11) \text{ and } (4.12) \right\}.$$

We can now use the Lagrangian relaxation technique described in Section 4.3 and get the following lower bound on the length of the optimal tour.

$$\max_{u} \left\{ \min_{x} \sum_{i,j \in V} (d_{ij} + u_i + u_j) x_{ij} \,\middle|\, (4.8), (4.9), (4.10) \text{ and } (4.12) \right\}.$$

Interestingly enough, Edmonds (1971) showed that the extreme points of the polyhedron defined by constraints (4.8), (4.9), (4.10) and (4.12) is the set of all 1-trees; that is, the optimal solution to a linear program defined on these constraints must be integral. Thus, we can apply Corollary 4.3.4 to see that, the lower bound obtained from the 1-tree approach is the same as the linear relaxation of Problem P'.

4.5   The Worst-Case Effectiveness of the 1-tree Lower Bound

We conclude this chapter by demonstrating that the Held and Karp (1970, 1971) 1-tree relaxation provides a lower bound that is not far from the length of the optimal tour. For this purpose, we show that the Held and Karp lower bound can be written as follows.

$$\text{Problem HK : } \quad Z_{LP} = Min \sum_{e \in E} d_e x_e$$

$$s.t.$$

$$\sum_{e \in \delta(i)} x_e = 2, \quad \forall i = 1, 2, \ldots, n \qquad (4.13)$$

$$\sum_{e \in \delta(S)} x_e \geq 2, \ \forall S \subseteq V \setminus \{1\}, \ S \neq \emptyset \qquad (4.14)$$

$$0 \leq x_e \leq 1, \quad \forall e \in E. \qquad (4.15)$$

Lemma 4.5.1 *The linear relaxation of Problem P' is equivalent to Problem HK.*

Proof. We first show that any feasible solution $\bar{x}$ to the linear relaxation of Problem P' is feasible for Problem HK. Since $\sum_{e \in S} \bar{x}_e \leq |S| - 1$, $\sum_{e \in E(V \setminus S)} \bar{x}_e \leq n - |S| - 1$ and $\sum_{e \in E(V)} x_e = n$ (why?) we get $\sum_{e \in \delta(S)} \bar{x}_e \geq 2$.

Similarly, we show that any feasible solution $\tilde{x}$ to Problem HK is feasible for the linear relaxation of Problem P'. The feasibility of $\tilde{x}$ in Problem HK implies that $\sum_{i \in S} \sum_{e \in \delta(i)} \tilde{x}_e = 2|S|$. However,

$$\sum_{i \in S} \sum_{e \in \delta(i)} \tilde{x}_e = 2 \sum_{e \in E(S)} \tilde{x}_e + \sum_{e \in \delta(S)} \tilde{x}_e = 2|S|,$$

and since $\sum_{e \in \delta(S)} \tilde{x}_e \geq 2$, we get $\sum_{e \in E(S)} \tilde{x}_e \leq |S| - 1$.   ∎

Shmoys and Williamson (1990) have shown that the Held and Karp lower bound (Problem HK) has a particular monotonicity property, and as a consequence, they obtain a new proof of an old result from Wolsey (1980) who showed:

Theorem 4.5.2 *For every instance of the TSP for which the distance matrix satisfies the triangle inequality, we have $Z^* \leq \frac{3}{2} Z_{LP}$.*

The proof presented here is based on the monotonicity property established by Shmoys and Williamson (1990). However, we use a powerful tool discovered by Goemans and Bertsimas (1993), called the *parsimonious property*. This is a property that holds for a general class of network design problems.

To present the property consider the following linear program defined on the complete graph $G = (V, E)$. Associated with each vertex $i \in V$ is a given number r_i which is either zero or two. Let $V_2 = \{i \in V \mid r_i = 2\}$.

We will analyze the following linear program (here ND stands for *network design*).

$$\text{Problem ND} : \quad Min \quad \sum_{e \in E} d_e x_e$$

$$\text{s.t.}$$

$$\sum_{e \in \delta(i)} x_e = r_i, \quad \forall i = 1, 2, \ldots, n \qquad (4.16)$$

$$\sum_{e \in \delta(S)} x_e \geq 2, \quad \forall S \subset V, \ V_2 \cap S \neq \emptyset,$$

$$V_2 \cap (V \setminus S) \neq \emptyset \qquad (4.17)$$

$$0 \leq x_e \leq 1, \quad \forall e \in E. \qquad (4.18)$$

It is easy to see that when $V_2 = V$ this linear program is equivalent to the linear program Problem HK. We now provide a short proof of the following result.

Lemma 4.5.3 *The optimal solution value to Problem ND is unchanged if we omit constraint (4.16).*

Our proof is similar to the proof presented in Bienstock and Simchi-Levi (1993); see also Bienstock et al. (1993), which uses a result of Lovasz (1979). In his book of problems, (Exercise 6.51) Lovasz presents the following result, together with a short proof. But first, we need a definition.

Definition 4.5.4 *An undirected graph G is k-connected between two vertices i and j if there are k (node) disjoint paths between i and j.*

Lemma 4.5.5 *Let G be an Eulerian multigraph and $s \in V(G)$, such that G is k-connected between any two vertices different from s. Then, for any neighbor u of s, there exists another neighbor w of s, such that the multigraph obtained from G by removing $\{s, u\}$ and $\{s, w\}$, and adding a new edge $\{u, w\}$ (the splitting-off operation) is also k-connected between any two vertices different from s.*

Lovasz's proof of Lemma 4.5.5 can be easily modified to yield the following.

Lemma 4.5.6 *Let G be an Eulerian multigraph, $Y \subseteq V(G)$ and $s \in V(G)$, such that G is k-connected between any two vertices of Y different from s. Then, for any neighbor u of s, there exists another neighbor w of s, such that the multigraph obtained from G by removing $\{s, u\}$ and $\{s, w\}$, and adding a new edge $\{u, w\}$ is also k-connected between any two vertices of Y different from s.*

We can now prove Lemma 4.5.3.

Proof. Let $V_0 = V \setminus V_2$; that is, $V_0 = \{i \in V \mid r_i = 0\}$. Let Problem ND' be Problem ND without (4.16). Finally, let $\tilde{x}$ be a rational vector feasible for Problem ND', chosen such that (i) $\tilde{x}$ is optimal for Problem ND', and (ii) subject to (i), $\sum_{e \in E} \tilde{x}_e$ is minimized.

Let M be a positive integer, large enough so that $\tilde{v} = 2M\tilde{x}$ is a vector of even integers. We may regard $\tilde{v}$ (with a slight abuse of notation) as the incidence vector of the edge-set $\tilde{E}$ of a multigraph $\tilde{G}$ with vertex set V. Clearly, $\tilde{G}$ is Eulerian, and by (4.17), it is $4M$-connected between any two elements of V_2.

Now suppose that for some vertex s, $\sum_{e \in \delta(\{s\})} \tilde{x}_e > r_s$ (i.e., s has a degree larger than $2Mr_s$ in $\tilde{G}$). Let us apply Lemma 4.5.6 to s and any neighbor u of s (where $Y = V_2$), and let $\tilde{H}$ be the resulting multigraph, with incidence vector $\tilde{z}$.

Clearly,

$$\sum_{e \in E} d_e \tilde{z}_e \leq \sum_{e \in E} d_e \tilde{v}_e,$$

and so

$$\sum_{e \in E} d_e \frac{\tilde{z}_e}{2M} \leq \sum_{e \in E} d_e \tilde{x}_e.$$

Moreover,

$$\sum_{e \in E} \frac{\tilde{z}_e}{2M} = \sum_{e \in E} \tilde{x}_e - \frac{1}{2M}.$$

Hence, by the choice of $\tilde{x}$, $z = \frac{\tilde{z}}{2M}$ cannot be feasible for Problem ND'.

If $s \in V_0$, then by Lemma 4.5.6, z is feasible for Problem ND'. Thus, we must have $s \in V_2$ and, in fact, $\sum_{e \in \delta(\{t\})} \tilde{x}_e = 0$ for all $t \in V_0$. In other words, $\tilde{E}$ spans precisely V_2, $\tilde{G}$ is $4M$−connected and $\sum_{e \in \delta(\{s\})} \geq 4M + 2$. But we claim now that the multigraph $\tilde{H}$ is $4M$−connected. For by Lemma 4.5.6, it could only fail to be $4M$−connected between s and some other vertex, but the only possible cut of size less than $4M$ is the one separating s from $V \backslash \{s\}$. Since this cut has at least $4M$ edges, the claim is proved. Consequently, again we obtain that z is feasible for Problem ND', a contradiction. In other words, $\sum_{e \in E} \tilde{v}_e = 2Mr_i$ for all i; that is, (4.16) holds.   ∎

An immediate consequence of Lemma 4.5.3 is that in Problem HK, one can ignore constraint (4.13) without changing the value of its optimal solution. This new formulation reveals the following monotonocity property of the Held and Karp lower bound: let $A \subseteq V$ and consider the Held and Karp lower bound on the length of the optimal traveling salesman tour through the vertices in A; that is,

$$\text{Problem HK}(A) \; : \quad Z_{LP}(A) = \text{Min} \sum_{e \in E} d_e x_e$$

$$s.t.$$

$$\sum_{e \in \delta(S)} x_e \geq 2, \quad \forall S \subset A, \quad (4.19)$$

$$0 \leq x_e \leq 1, \quad \forall e \in E. \quad (4.20)$$

Since any feasible solution to problem HK(V) is feasible for problem HK(A), the cost of this linear program is monotone with respect to the set of nodes A.

We are ready to prove Theorem 4.5.2.

Proof. Section 2.3.3 presents and analyzes the heuristic developed by Christofides for the TSP which is based on constructing a minimum spanning tree plus a matching on the nodes of odd degree. Observe that a similar heuristic can be obtained if we start from a 1-tree, instead of a minimum spanning tree. Thus, the length of the optimal tour is bounded by $W(T_1^*) + W(M^*(A))$ where $W(T_1^*)$ is the weight (cost) of the best 1-tree and $W(M^*(A))$ is the weight of the optimal weighted matching defined on the set of odd degree nodes in the best 1-tree, denoted by A.

We argue that $W(M^*(A)) \leq \frac{1}{2} Z_{LP}(A)$. Let $\overline{x}$ be an optimal solution to Problem HK(A). It is easy to see that the vector $\frac{1}{2}\overline{x}$ is feasible for the following constraints.

$$\sum_{e \in \delta(i)} x_e = 1, \quad \forall i \in A \qquad (4.21)$$

$$\sum_{e \in E(S)} x_e \leq \frac{1}{2}(|S| - 1), \quad \forall S \subset A, S \neq \emptyset, |S| \geq 3, |S| \text{ is odd} \qquad (4.22)$$

$$0 \leq x_e \leq 1, \quad \forall e \in E. \qquad (4.23)$$

A beautiful result of Edmonds (1965) tells us that these constraints are sufficient to formulate the matching problem as a linear program. Consequently,

$$W(M^*(A)) \le \frac{1}{2} Z_{LP}(A) \le \frac{1}{2} Z_{LP}(V) = \frac{1}{2} Z_{LP}$$

and therefore,

$$L^* \le W(T_1^*) + W(M^*(A))$$

$$\le Z_{LP} + \frac{1}{2} Z_{LP}$$

$$\le \frac{3}{2} Z_{LP}.$$

∎

4.6   Exercises

Exercise 4.1. Prove Lemma 4.3.2.

Exercise 4.2. Show that a lower bound on the cost of the optimal traveling salesman tour can be given by:

$$\frac{2}{|N|} \max_{i \in N} \sum_{j \in N} d_{ij},$$

where N is the set of cities and d_{ij} is the distance from city i to city j.

Exercise 4.3. Consider an instance of the Bin-Packing Problem where there are m_j items of size $w_j \in (0, 1]$ for $j = 1, 2, \ldots, n$. Define a *bin configuration* to be a vector $\bar{c} = (c_1, c_2, \ldots, c_n)$ with the property that $c_i \ge 0$ for $i = 1, 2, \ldots, n$ and $\sum_{j=1}^{n} c_j w_j \le 1$. Enumerate all possible bin configurations. Let there be M such configurations. Define C_{jk} to be the number of items of size w_j in bin configuration k, for $k = 1, 2, \ldots, M$ and $j = 1, 2, \ldots, n$.

Formulate an integer program to solve this Bin-Packing Problem using the following variables: x_k is the number of times configuration k is used, for $k = 1, 2, \ldots, M$.

Exercise 4.4. A function $u : [0, 1] \to [0, 1]$ is *dual-feasible* if for any sets of numbers $w_1, w_2, \ldots, w_k$, we have

$$\sum_{i=1}^{k} w_i \le 1 \implies \sum_{i=1}^{k} u(w_i) \le 1.$$

(a) Given an instance of the Bin-Packing Problem with item sizes $w_1, w_2, \ldots, w_n$ and a dual-feasible function u, prove that $\sum_{i=1}^{n} u(w_i) \le b^*$.

(*b*) Assume n is even. Let half of the items be of size $\frac{2}{3}$ and the other half of size $\frac{1}{2}$. Find a dual-feasible function u that satisfies:

$$\sum_{i=1}^{n} u(w_i) = b^*.$$

Exercise 4.5. Consider a list L of n items of sizes in $(\frac{1}{3}, \frac{1}{2}]$. Let b^{LP} be the optimal fractional solution to the set-partitioning formulation of the Bin-Packing Problem, and let b^* be the optimal integer solution to the same formulation. Prove that

$$b^* \leq b^{LP} + 1.$$

Exercise 4.6. Prove that if a graph has exactly $2k$ vertices of odd degree, then the set of edges can be partitioned into k paths such that each edge is used exactly once.

Part II

VEHICLE ROUTING

MODELS

5

The Capacitated VRP with Equal Demands

5.1 Introduction

A large part of many logistics systems involves the management of a fleet of vehicles used to serve warehouses, retailers and/or customers. In order to control the costs of operating the fleet, a dispatcher must continuously make decisions on how much to load on each vehicle and where to send it. These types of problems fall under the general class of Vehicle Routing Problems mentioned in Chapter 1.

The most basic Vehicle Routing Problem (VRP) is the single-depot Capacitated Vehicle Routing Problem (CVRP). It can be described as follows: a set of customers has to be served by a fleet of identical vehicles of limited capacity. The vehicles are initially located at a given depot. The objective is to find a set of routes for the vehicles of minimal total length. Each route begins at the depot, visits a subset of the customers and returns to the depot without violating the capacity constraint.

Consider the following scenario. A customer requests w units of product. If we allow this load to be *split* between more than one vehicle (i.e., the customer gets several deliveries which together sum up to the total load requested), then we can view the demand for w units as w different customers each requesting *one* unit of product located at the same point. The capacity constraint can then be viewed as simply the maximum number of customers (in this new problem) that can be visited by a single vehicle. This is the capacity $Q \geq 1$. Therefore, if we allow this splitting of demands, and this may not be a desirable property (we investigate the unsplit demand case in Chapter 6), there is no loss in generality in assuming that each customer has the same demand, namely, one unit, and the vehicle can visit at most Q of these customers on a route. Therefore, this model is sometimes called the CVRP with *splittable* demands or the ECVRP.

We denote the depot by x_0 and the set of customers by $N = \{x_1, x_2, \ldots, x_n\}$. The set $N_0 \doteq N \cup \{x_0\}$ designates all customers and the depot. The customers and the depot are represented by a set of nodes on an undirected graph $G = (N_0, E)$. We denote by d_i the distance between customer i and the depot, $d_{\max} \doteq \max_{i \in N} d_i$ the distance from the depot to the furthest customer, and d_{ij} the distance between customer i and customer j. The distance matrix $\{d_{ij}\}$ is assumed to be symmetric and satisfy the triangle inequality; that is, $d_{ij} = d_{ji}$ for all i, j and $d_{ij} \leq d_{ik} + d_{kj}$ for all i, k, j. We denote the optimal solution value of the CVRP by Z^* and the solution provided by a heuristic H by Z^H.

In what follows, the optimal traveling salesman tour plays an important role. So, for any set $S \subseteq N_0$, let $L^*(S)$ be the length of the optimal traveling salesman tour through the set of points S. Also, let $L^\alpha(S)$ be the length of an α-optimal traveling salesman tour through S, that is, one whose length is bounded from above by $\alpha L^*(S), \alpha \geq 1$.

The graph depicted in Figure 5.1 , which is denoted by $\mathcal{G}(t, s)$, also plays an important role in our worst-case analyses. It consists of s groups of Q nodes and another $s - 1$ nodes, called *white nodes*, separating the groups. The nodes within the same group have zero interdistance and each group is connected to the depot by an arc of unit length. The white nodes are of *zero distance apart* and t units distance away from the depot. Each white node is connected to the two groups of nodes it separates by an arc of unit length. Note that when $0 \leq t \leq 2$, $\mathcal{G}(t, s)$ satisfies the triangle inequality (if an edge (i, j) is not shown in the graph, then the distance between node i and node j is defined as the length of the shortest path from i to j). Also note that whenever $0 \leq t \leq 2$, the tour depicted in Figure 5.2 is an optimal traveling salesman tour of length $2s$.

In this chapter, we analyze this problem using the two tools developed earlier, worst-case and average-case analyses. Later, in Chapter 6, we will analyze a more general model of the CVRP.

5.2   Worst-Case Analysis of Heuristics

A simple heuristic for the CVRP, suggested by Haimovich and Rinnooy Kan (1985) and later modified by Altinkemer and Gavish (1990), is to partition a traveling salesman tour into segments, such that each segment of customers is served by a single vehicle; that is, each segment has no more than Q points. The heuristic, called the Iterated Tour Partitioning (ITP) heuristic, starts from a traveling salesman tour through all $n = |N|$ customers and the depot. Starting at the depot and following the tour in an arbitrary orientation, the customers and the depot are numbered $x^{(0)}, x^{(1)}, x^{(2)}, \ldots, x^{(n)}$ where $x^{(0)}$ is the depot. We partition the path from $x^{(1)}$ to $x^{(n)}$ into $\lceil \frac{n}{Q} \rceil$ disjoint segments, such that each one contains no more than Q customers, and connect the end-points of each segment to the depot. The first segment contains only customer $x^{(1)}$. All the other segments contain exactly Q customers, except maybe the last one. This defines one feasible solution to the

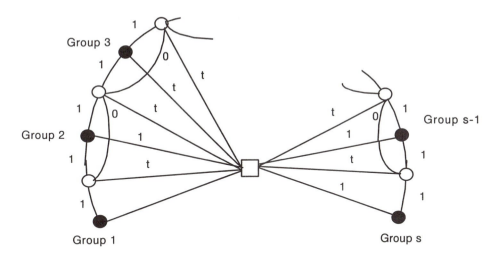

FIGURE 5.1. Every group contains Q customers with interdistance zero.

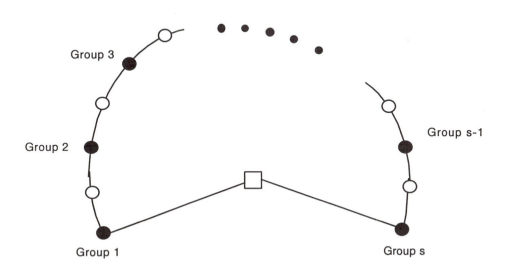

FIGURE 5.2. An optimal traveling salesman tour in $\mathcal{G}(t, s)$.

problem. We can repeat the above construction by shifting the end-points of all but the first and last segments up by one position in the direction of the orientation. This can be repeated $Q - 1$ times producing a total of Q different solutions. We then choose the best of the set of Q solutions generated.

It is easy to see that, for a given traveling salesman tour, the running time of the ITP heuristic is $O(nQ)$. The performance of this heuristic clearly depends on the quality of the initial traveling salesman tour chosen in the first step of the algorithm. Hence, when the ITP heuristic partitions an α-optimal traveling salesman tour, it is denoted ITP(α). To establish the worst-case behavior of the algorithm, we first find a lower bound on Z^*, and then calculate an upper bound on the cost of the solution produced by the ITP(α) heuristic.

Lemma 5.2.1 $Z^* \geq \max\{L^*(N_0), \frac{2}{Q} \sum_{i \in N} d_i\}$.

Proof. Clearly, $Z^* \geq L^*(N_0)$ by the triangle inequality. To prove $Z^* \geq \frac{2}{Q} \sum_{i \in N} d_i$, consider an optimal solution in which N is partitioned into subsets $\{N_1, N_2, \ldots, N_m\}$ where each set N_j is served by a single vehicle. Clearly,

$$Z^* = \sum_j L^*(N_j \cup \{x_0\}) \geq \sum_j 2 \max_{i \in N_j} d_i \geq \sum_j \frac{2}{|N_j|} \sum_{i \in N_j} d_i$$

$$\geq \sum_j \frac{2}{Q} \sum_{i \in N_j} d_i = \frac{2}{Q} \sum_{i \in N} d_i.$$

∎

Lemma 5.2.2 $Z^{\text{ITP}(\alpha)} \leq \frac{2}{Q} \sum_{i \in N} d_i + (1 - \frac{1}{Q})\alpha L^*(N_0)$.

Proof. We prove the lemma by finding the cumulative length of the Q solutions generated by the ITP heuristic. The ith solution consists of the segments:

$$\{x^{(1)}, x^{(2)}, \ldots, x^{(i)}\}, \{x^{(i+1)}, x^{(i+2)}, \ldots, x^{(i+Q)}\}, \ldots, \{x^{(i+1+\lfloor \frac{n-i}{Q} \rfloor Q)}, \ldots, x^{(n)}\}.$$

Thus, among the Q solutions generated, each customer $x^{(i)}$, $2 \leq i \leq n - 1$ appears exactly once as the first point of a segment and exactly once as the last point. Therefore, in the cumulative length of the Q solutions the term $2d_{x^{(i)}}$ is incurred for each i, $2 \leq i \leq n - 1$. Customer $x^{(1)}$ is the first point of a segment in each of the Q solutions, and in the first one it is also the last point. Thus, the term $d_{x^{(1)}}$ appears $Q + 1$ times in the cumulative length. Similarly, $x^{(n)}$ is always the last point of a segment in each of the Q solutions, and once the first point. Thus, the term $d_{x^{(n)}}$ appears $Q + 1$ times in the cumulative length as well. Finally, each one of the arcs $(x^{(i)}, x^{(i+1)})$ for $1 \leq i \leq n - 1$ appears in exactly $Q - 1$ solutions since it is excluded from only one solution. These arcs, together with the $Q - 1$ arcs connecting the depot to $x^{(1)}$ and $Q - 1$ arcs connecting the depot to $x^{(n)}$, form $Q - 1$ copies of the initial traveling salesman tour selected in the first step of the heuristic. Thus, if the initial traveling salesman tour is an α-optimal tour, the cumulative length of all Q tours is

$$2 \sum_{i \in N} d_i + (Q - 1)L^{\alpha}(N_0)$$

$$\leq 2 \sum_{i \in N} d_i + (Q - 1)\alpha L^*(N_0).$$

Hence,

$$Z^{\text{ITP}(\alpha)} \leq \frac{2}{Q} \sum_{i \in N} d_i + (1 - \frac{1}{Q})\alpha L^*(N_0). \qquad\blacksquare$$

Combining upper and lower bounds, we obtain the following result.

Theorem 5.2.3

$$\frac{Z^{\text{ITP}(\alpha)}}{Z^*} \leq 1 + \left(1 - \frac{1}{Q}\right)\alpha. \qquad (5.1)$$

For example, if Christofides' polynomial-time heuristic ($\alpha = 1.5$) is used to obtain the initial traveling salesman tour, we have

$$\frac{Z^{\text{ITP}(1.5)}}{Z^*} \leq \frac{5}{2} - \frac{3}{2Q}.$$

The proof of the worst-case result for the ITP(α) heuristic suggests that if we can improve the bound in (5.1) for $\alpha = 1$, then the bound can be improved for any $\alpha > 1$. However, the following theorem, proved by Li and Simchi-Levi (1990), says that this is impossible; that is, the bound

$$\frac{Z^{\text{ITP}(1)}}{Z^*} \leq 2 - \frac{1}{Q}$$

is sharp.

Theorem 5.2.4 *For any integer $Q \geq 1$, there exists a problem instance with* $Z^{\text{ITP}(1)}/Z^* = 2 - \frac{1}{Q}$.

Proof. Let us consider the graph $\mathcal{G}(0, q)$. A solution obtained by the ITP heuristic is shown in Figure 5.3. In this solution,

$$Z^{\text{ITP}(1)} = 2 + 2 + \underbrace{4 + 4 + \cdots + 4}_{Q-2 \text{ times}} + 2 = 4Q - 2.$$

One can construct a solution that has Q vehicles serve the Q groups of customers and the $(Q + 1)^{\text{st}}$ vehicle serve the other $Q - 1$ nodes. Thus,

$$Z^* \leq 2Q.$$

Hence,

$$\frac{Z^{\text{ITP}(1)}}{Z^*} \geq 2 - \frac{1}{Q}.$$

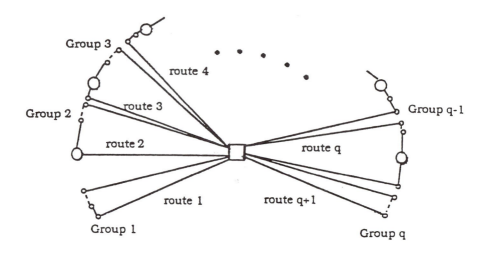

Group 3

route 4

Group 2

route 3

Group q-1

route 2

route q

route 1

route q+1

Group 1

Group q

FIGURE 5.3. Solution obtained by the ITP heuristic

This together with the upper bound of (5.1) completes the proof.   ∎

Another variant of the tour partitioning heuristic is the Optimal Partitioning (OP) heuristic described by Beasley (1983). The algorithm takes a traveling salesman tour and optimally partitions it into a set of feasible routes; that is, each route contains at most Q customers.

Given a traveling salesman tour through the customers and the depot, the points are numbered $x^{(0)}, x^{(1)}, \ldots, x^{(n)}$ in order of appearance on the tour, where $x^{(0)}$ is the depot. Define

$$C_{jk} = \begin{cases} \text{the distance traveled by a vehicle that starts at } x^{(0)} \text{ visits,} \\ \text{customers } x^{(j+1)}, x^{(j+2)}, \ldots, x^{(k)} \text{ and returns to } x^{(0)}, & \text{if } k - j \le Q; \\ \infty, & \text{otherwise.} \end{cases}$$

If we find the shortest path from $x^{(0)}$ to $x^{(n)}$ in the acyclic graph (with nodes $x^{(i)}$, $0 \le i \le n$, and arcs $(x^{(i)}, x^{(j)})$ for $0 \le i < j \le n$) where the distance between $x^{(j)}$ and $x^{(k)}$ is C_{jk}, we will have an optimal partition of the traveling salesman tour into feasible routes. For example, if the shortest path from $x^{(0)}$ to $x^{(n)}$ is $x^{(0)} \rightarrow x^{(t)} \rightarrow x^{(u)} \rightarrow x^{(n)}$ then three tours are formed, namely, $(x^{(0)}, x^{(1)}, \ldots, x^{(t)}, x^{(0)})$, $(x^{(0)}, x^{(t+1)}, x^{(t+2)}, \ldots, x^{(u)}, x^{(0)})$ and $(x^{(0)}, x^{(u+1)}, x^{(u+2)}, \ldots, x^{(n)}, x^{(0)})$.

For a given traveling salesman tour, the above shortest path problem can be solved in $O(nQ)$ time including the time required to evaluate the costs C_{jk}.

When the OP heuristic partitions an α-optimal traveling salesman tour, it is denoted OP(α). The partitions considered by the OP(α) heuristic include all Q of the partitions generated by the ITP(α) heuristic. Therefore, $Z^{OP(\alpha)} \le Z^{ITP(\alpha)}$ and hence its worst-case bound is at least as good; that is,

$$\frac{Z^{\mathrm{OP}(\alpha)}}{Z^*} \leq 1 + \left(1 - \frac{1}{Q}\right)\alpha.$$

The next theorem implies that for $\alpha = 1$ this bound is asymptotically sharp; that is, $Z^{\mathrm{OP}(1)}/Z^*$ tends to 2 when Q approaches infinity.

Theorem 5.2.5 *For any integer $Q \geq 1$, there exists a problem instance with $Z^{\mathrm{OP}(1)}/Z^*$ arbitrarily close to $2 - \frac{2}{Q+1}$.*

Proof. Consider the graph $\mathcal{G}(1, Kq + 1)$, where K is a positive integer. It is easy to check that

$$Z^{\mathrm{OP}(1)} = 2(KQ + 1) + 2KQ.$$

On the other hand, consider the solution in which $KQ+1$ vehicles serve the $KQ+1$ groups of customers and another K vehicles serve the other nodes. Hence,

$$Z^* \leq 2(KQ + 1) + 2K,$$

and therefore,

$$\lim_{K \to \infty} \frac{Z^{\mathrm{OP}(1)}}{Z^*} \geq 2 - \frac{2}{Q + 1}. \qquad \blacksquare$$

5.3 The Asymptotic Optimal Solution Value

In the following two sections, we assume that the customers are points in the plane and that the distance between any pair of customers is given by the Euclidean distance. Assume without loss of generality that the depot is the point $(0, 0)$ and $||x||$ designates the distance from the depot to the point $x \in \mathbb{R}^2$. The results discussed in this section and the next are mainly based on Haimovich and Rinnooy Kan (1985).

The upper bound of Lemma 5.2.2 has two cost components; the first component is proportional to the total "radial" cost between the depot and the customers. The second component is proportional to the "circular" cost: the cost of traveling between customers. This cost is related to the cost of the optimal traveling salesman tour. As discussed in Chapter 2, for large n, the cost of the optimal traveling salesman tour grows like $\sqrt{n}$, while the total radial cost between the depot and the customers grows like n. Therefore, it is intuitive that when the number of customers is large enough the first cost component will dominate the second. This observation is now formally proven.

Theorem 5.3.1 *Let x_k, $k = 1, 2, \ldots, n$ be a sequence of independent random variables having a distribution μ with compact support in $\mathbb{R}^2$. Let*

$$E(d) = \int_{\mathbb{R}^2} ||x|| d\mu(x).$$

Then, with probability one,

$$\lim_{n \to \infty} \frac{Z^*}{n} = \frac{2}{Q} E(d).$$

Proof. Lemma 5.2.1 and the strong law of large numbers tell us that

$$\lim_{n \to \infty} \frac{Z^*}{n} \geq \frac{2}{Q} E(d) \qquad (a.s.). \tag{5.2}$$

On the other hand, from Lemma 5.2.2,

$$\frac{Z^*}{n} \leq \frac{Z^{\text{ITP}(1)}}{n} \leq \frac{2}{nQ} \sum_{i \in N} d_i + \left(1 - \frac{1}{Q}\right) \frac{L^*(N_0)}{n}.$$

From Chapter 3, we know that there exists a constant $\beta > 0$, independent of the distribution μ, such that with probability one,

$$\lim_{n \to \infty} \frac{L^*(N_0)}{\sqrt{n}} = \beta \int_{I\!R^2} f^{1/2}(x) dx,$$

where f is the density of the absolutely continuous part of the distribution μ. Hence,

$$\lim_{n \to \infty} \frac{Z^*}{n} \leq \frac{2}{Q} E(d) \qquad (a.s.).$$

This together with (5.2) proves the Theorem. ∎

The following observation is in order. Haimovich and Rinnooy Kan prove Theorem 5.3.1 merely assuming $E(d)$ is finite rather than the stronger assumption of a compact support. However, the restriction to a compact support seems to be satisfactory for all practical purposes. The following is another important generalization of Theorem 5.3.1. Assume that a *cluster* of w_k customers (rather than a single customer) is located at point $x_k, k = 1, 2, \ldots, n$. The theorem then becomes

$$\lim_{n \to \infty} \frac{Z^*}{n} = \frac{2}{Q} E(w) E(d), \tag{5.3}$$

where $E(w)$ is the expected cluster size, provided that the cluster size is independent of the location. This follows from a straightforward adaptation of Lemma 5.2.1 and Lemma 5.2.2.

5.4   Asymptotically Optimal Heuristics

The proof of the previous Theorem (Theorem 5.3.1) reveals that the ITP(α) heuristic provides a solution whose cost approaches the optimal cost when n tends to infinity. Indeed, replacing ITP(1) by ITP(α) in the previous proof gives the following theorem.

Theorem 5.4.1 *Under the conditions of Theorem 5.3.1 and for any fixed $\alpha \geq 1$, the ITP(α) heuristic is asymptotically optimal.*

As is pointed out by Haimovich and Rinnooy Kan (1985), iterated tour partitioning heuristics, although asymptotically optimal, hardly exploit the special topological structure of the Euclidean plane in which the points are located. It is therefore natural to consider *Region Partitioning* (RP) heuristics that are more geometric in nature.

Haimovich and Rinnooy Kan consider three classes of regional partitioning schemes. In *Rectangular Region Partitioning* (RRP), one starts with a rectangle containing the set of customers N and cuts it into smaller rectangles. In *Polar Region Partitioning* (PRP) and *Circular Region Partitioning* (CRP), one starts with a circle centered at the depot and partitions it by means of circular arcs and radial lines. We shall shortly discuss each one of these in detail.

In each case the RP heuristics construct subregions of the plane, where subregion j contains a set of customers $N(j)$. These subregions are constructed so that each one of them has exactly Q customers except possibly one.

Since every subset $N(j)$ has no more than Q customers, each of these RP heuristics allocates one vehicle to each subregion. The vehicles then use the following routing strategy. The first customer visited is the one closest to the depot among all the customers in $N(j)$. The rest are visited in the order of an α-optimal traveling salesman tour through $N(j)$. After visiting all the customers in the subregion the vehicle returns to the depot through the first (closest) customer. It is therefore natural to call these heuristics $RP(\alpha)$ heuristics. In particular we have $RRP(\alpha)$, $PRP(\alpha)$ and $CRP(\alpha)$.

Lemma 5.4.2 $Z^{RP(\alpha)} \leq \frac{2}{Q} \sum_{i \in N} d_i + 2d_{\max} + \alpha \sum_j L^*(N(j)).$

Proof. We number the subsets $N(j)$ constructed by the $RP(\alpha)$ heuristic so that $|N(j)| = Q$ for every $j \geq 2$ and $|N(1)| \leq Q$. It follows that the total distance traveled by the vehicle that visits subset $N(j)$, for $j \geq 2$, is

$$\leq 2 \min_{i \in N(j)} d_i + \alpha L^*(N(j))$$

$$\leq \frac{2}{Q} \sum_{i \in N(j)} d_i + \alpha L^*(N(j)),$$

while the total distance traveled by the vehicle that visits $N(1)$ is no more than

$$2d_{\max} + \alpha L^*(N(1)).$$

Taking the sum over all subregions we obtain the desired result.   ∎

The quality of the upper bound of Lemma 5.4.2 depends, of course, on the quantity $\sum_j L^*(N(j))$. This value was analyzed in Chapter 3 where it was shown that for any RP heuristic

$$\sum_j L^*(N(j)) \leq L^*(N) + \frac{3}{2} P^{RP}, \tag{5.4}$$

where P^{RP} is the sum of perimeters of the subregions generated by the RP heuristic. For this reason we analyze the quantity P^{RP} in each of the three region partitioning heuristics.

Rectangular Region Partitioning (RRP)

This heuristic is identical to the one introduced for the Traveling Salesman Problem in Section 3.3. The smallest rectangle with sides a and b containing the set of customers N is partitioned by means of horizontal and vertical lines. First, the region is subdivided by t vertical lines such that each subregion contains exactly $(h + 1)Q$ points except possibly the last one. Each of these $t + 1$ subregions is then partitioned by means of h horizontal lines into $h + 1$ smaller subregions such that each contains exactly Q points except possibly for the last one.

As before, h and t should satisfy

$$t = \left\lceil \frac{n}{(h + 1)Q} \right\rceil - 1,$$

and

$$t(h + 1)Q < n \le (t + 1)(h + 1)Q.$$

The unique integer that satisfies these conditions is $h = \lceil \sqrt{\frac{n}{Q}} - 1 \rceil$. Note that the number of vertical lines added is $t \le \sqrt{\frac{n}{Q}}$, and each of these lines is counted twice in the quantity P^{RRP}.

In the second step of the RRP we add h horizontal lines where $h \le \sqrt{\frac{n}{Q}}$. These horizontal lines are also counted twice in P^{RRP}. It follows that

$$P^{RRP} \le 2\sqrt{\frac{n}{Q}}(a + b) + 2(a + b) \le 8d_{max}\sqrt{\frac{n}{Q}} + 8d_{max}.$$

Polar Region Partitioning (PRP)

The circle with radius d_{max} containing the set N and centered at the depot is partitioned in exactly the same way as in the previous partitioning scheme, with the exception that circular arcs and radial lines replace vertical and horizontal lines. Using the same analysis, one can show:

$$P^{PRP} \le 6\pi d_{max}\sqrt{\frac{n}{Q}} + 2\pi d_{max} + 2d_{max}. \tag{5.5}$$

Circular Region Partitioning (CRP)

This scheme partitions the circle centered at the depot with radius d_{max} into h equal sectors, where h is to be determined. Each sector is then partitioned into subregions by means of circular arcs, such that each subregion contains exactly Q customers except possibly the one closest to the depot. Thus, at most h subregions, each from one sector, have less than Q customers. These subregions (with the depot on their boundary) are then repartitioned by means of radial cuts such that at most $h - 1$ of them have exactly Q customers each except for possibly the last one.

The total length of the initial radial lines is $h d_{max}$. The length of an inner circular arc bounding a subregion containing a set $N(j)$ is no more than

$$\frac{2\pi}{h} \min_{i \in N(j)} d_i \leq \frac{2\pi}{h} \frac{\sum_{i \in N(j)} d_i}{|N(j)|} = \frac{2\pi \sum_{i \in N(j)} d_i}{hQ},$$

while the length of the outer circle is $2\pi d_{max}$. Finally, the repartitioning of the central subregions adds no more than $\frac{h d_{max}}{2}$. Thus,

$$P^{CRP} \leq 2\left(h d_{max} + \frac{2\pi \sum_{i \in N} d_i}{hQ} + \frac{h d_{max}}{2}\right) + 2\pi d_{max}.$$

Taking $h = \left\lceil \sqrt{\frac{4\pi \sum_{i \in N} d_i}{3Q d_{max}}} \right\rceil$, we obtain the following upper bound on P^{CRP},

$$P^{CRP} \leq 4\sqrt{3\pi d_{max} \frac{1}{Q} \sum_{i \in N} d_i} + (3 + 2\pi)d_{max}.$$

The reader should be aware that all of these partitioning schemes can be implemented in $O(n \log n)$ time. We now have all the necessary ingredients for an asymptotic analysis of the performance of these partitioning heuristics.

Theorem 5.4.3 *Under the conditions of Theorem 5.3.1 and for any fixed $\alpha \geq 1$, $RRP(\alpha)$, $PRP(\alpha)$ and $CRP(\alpha)$ are asymptotically optimal.*

Proof. Lemma 5.4.2 together with equation (5.4) provide the following upper bound on the total distance traveled by all vehicles in the solution produced by the above RP heuristics.

$$Z^{RP(\alpha)} \leq \frac{2}{Q} \sum_{i \in N} d_i + 2d_{max} + \alpha L^*(N) + \frac{3}{2}\alpha P^{RP}.$$

By the strong law of large numbers and the fact that the distribution has compact support, $\frac{1}{n} \sum_{i \in N} d_i$ converges almost surely to $E(d)$ while $\frac{d_{max}}{n}$ converges almost surely to 0. Furthermore, $\frac{L^*(N)}{n}$ converges to 0 almost surely; see the proof of Theorem 5.3.1. Finally, from the analysis of each of the region partitioning heuristics and the fact that the points are in a compact region, $\frac{P^{RP}}{n}$ converges almost surely to zero as well. ∎

In conclusion, we see that the CVRP with equal demands is asymptotically solvable via several different region partitioning schemes. In fact, since each customer has the same demand, the packing of the customers' demands into the vehicles is a trivial problem. Any Q customers can fit. The more difficult problem, when demands are of different sizes, presents complicating bin-packing features which will prove to be more difficult.

5.5   Exercises

Exercise 5.1. Consider the following version of the Capacitated Vehicle Routing Problem (CVRP). You are given a network $G = (V, A)$ with positive arc lengths. Assume that $E \subseteq A$ is a given set of edges that have to be "covered" by vehicles. The vehicles are initially located at a depot $p \in V$. Each vehicle has a "capacity" q; that is, each vehicle can cover no more than q edges from E. Once a vehicle starts an edge in E it has to cover all of it. The objective is to design tours for vehicles so that all edges in E are covered, vehicles' capacities are not violated and total distance traveled is as small as possible.

(*a*) Suppose we want first to find a single tour that starts at the depot p, traverses all edges in E and ends at p whose total cost (length) is as small as possible. Generalize Christofides' heuristic for this case.

(*b*) Consider now the version of the CVRP described above and suggest two possible lower bounds on the optimal cost of the CVRP.

(*c*) Describe a heuristic algorithm based on a tour partitioning approach using, as the initial tour, the tour you found in part (*a*). What is the worst-case bound of your algorithm?

Exercise 5.2. Derive equation (5.3).

Exercise 5.3. Consider an n customer instance of the CVRP with equal demands. Assume there are m depots and at each depot is an unlimited number of vehicles of limited capacity. Suggest an asymptotically optimal region partitioning scheme for this case.

Exercise 5.4. Consider an n customer instance of the CVRP with equal demands. There are K customer types: a customer is of type k with independent probability $p_k > 0$. Customers of different types cannot be served together in the same vehicle. Devise an asymptotically optimal heuristic for this problem. If K is a function of n, what conditions on $K(n)$ are necessary to ensure that this same heuristic is asymptotically optimal?

Exercise 5.5. Derive equation (5.5).

6
The Capacitated VRP with Unequal Demands

6.1 Introduction

In this chapter we consider the Capacitated Vehicle Routing Problem with unequal demands (UCVRP). In this version of the problem, each customer i has a demand w_i and the capacity constraint stipulates that the total amount delivered by a single vehicle cannot exceed Q. We let Z_u^* denote the optimal solution value of UCVRP, that is, the minimal total distance traveled by all vehicles.

In this version of the problem, the demand of a customer *cannot be split* over several vehicles; that is, each customer must be served by a single vehicle. This, more general version of the model, is sometimes called the CVRP with *unsplit* demands. The version where demands may be split is dealt with in Chapter 5. Splitting a customer's demand is often physically impossible or managerially undesirable due to customer service or accounting considerations.

6.2 Heuristics for the CVRP

A great deal of work has been devoted to the development of heuristics for the UCVRP; see, for example, Christofides (1985), Fisher (1995), Federgruen and Simchi-Levi (1995) or Bertsimas and Simchi-Levi (1996). Following Christofides, we classify these heuristics into the 4 categories:

- Constructive Methods

- Route First-Cluster Second Methods

- Cluster First-Route Second Methods

- Incomplete Optimization Methods.

We will describe the main characteristics of each of these classes and give examples of heuristics that fall into each.

Constructive Methods

The *Savings Algorithm* suggested by Clarke and Wright (1964) is the most important member of this class. This heuristic, which is the basis for a number of commercial vehicle routing packages, is one of the earliest heuristics designed for this problem and, without a doubt, the most widely known. The idea of the savings algorithm is very simple: consider the depot and n demand points. Suppose that initially we assign a separate vehicle to each demand point. The total distance traveled by a vehicle that visits demand point i is $2d_i$, where d_i is the distance from the depot to demand point i. Therefore, the total distance traveled in this solution is $2 \sum_{i=1}^{n} d_i$.

If we now combine two routes, say we serve i and j on a single trip (with the same vehicle), the total distance traveled by this vehicle is $d_i + d_{ij} + d_j$, where d_{ij} is the distance between demand points i and j. Thus, the *savings* obtained from combining demand points i and j, denoted s_{ij}, is:

$$s_{ij} = 2d_i + 2d_j - (d_i + d_j + d_{ij}) = d_i + d_j - d_{ij}.$$

The larger the savings s_{ij}, the more desirable it is to combine demand points i and j. Based on this idea, Clarke and Wright suggest the following algorithm.

The Savings Algorithm

Step 1: Start with the solution that has each customer visited by a separate vehicle.

Step 2: Calculate the *savings* $s_{ij} = d_{0i} + d_{j0} - d_{ij} \geq 0$ for all pairs of customers i and j.

Step 3: Sort the savings in nonincreasing order.

Step 4: Find the first feasible arc (i, j) in the savings list where
       1) i and j are on different routes,
       2) both i and j are either the first or last visited on their respective routes, and
       3) the sum of demands of routes i and j is no more than Q.

Add arc (i, j) to the current solution and delete arcs $(0, i)$ and $(j, 0)$. Delete arc (i, j) from the savings list.

Step 5: Repeat step 4 until no more arcs satisfy the conditions.

Additional constraints, which might be present, can easily be incorporated into Step 4. Usually a simple check can be performed to see whether combining the tours containing i and j violates any of these constraints.

Other examples of heuristics that fall into this class are the heuristics of Gaskel (1967), Yellow (1970) and Russell (1977). In particular the first two are modifications of the Savings algorithm.

Route First-Cluster Second Methods

Traditionally, this class has been defined as follows. The class consists of those heuristics that first construct a traveling salesman tour through all the customers (route first) and then partition the tour into segments (cluster second). One vehicle is assigned to each segment and visits the customers according to their appearance on the traveling salesman tour.

As we shall see in the next section some strong statements can be made about the performance of heuristics of this class. For this purpose, we give a more precise definition of the class here.

Definition 6.2.1 *A heuristic is a route first-cluster second heuristic if it first orders the customers according to their locations, disregarding demand sizes, and then partitions this ordering to produce feasible clusters. These clusters consist of sets of customers that are consecutive in the initial order. Customers are then routed within their cluster depending on the specific heuristic.*

This definition of the class is more general than the traditional definition given above. The disadvantage of this class, of which we will give a rigorous analysis, can be highlighted by the following simple example. Consider a routing strategy that orders the demands in such a way that the sequence of demand sizes in the order is $(9, 2, 9, 2, 9, 2, 9, 2, \ldots)$. If the vehicle capacity is 10, then any partition of this tour *must* assign one vehicle to each customer. This solution would consist of half of the vehicles going to pick up two units (using 20% of the vehicle capacity) and returning to the depot; not a very efficient strategy. By contrast, a routing strategy that looks at the demands at the same time as it looks at customer locations would clearly find a more intelligent ordering of the customers: one that sequences demands efficiently to decrease total distance traveled.

The route first-cluster second class includes classical heuristics such as the Optimal Partitioning heuristic introduced by Beasley (1983), and the Sweep algorithm suggested by Gillett and Miller (1974).

In the Optimal Partitioning heuristic, one tries to find an optimal traveling salesman tour, or, if this is not possible, a tour that is close to optimal. This provides the initial ordering of the demand points. The ordering is then partitioned in an efficient way into segments. This step can be done by formulating a shortest path problem. See Section 5.2 for details.

In the Sweep algorithm, an arbitrary demand point is selected as the starting point. The other customers are ordered according to the angle made between them, the depot and the starting point. Demands are then assigned to vehicles following this initial order. In effect, the points are "swept" in a clockwise direction around the depot and assigned to vehicles. Then efficient routes are designed for each vehicle. Specifically, the Sweep algorithm is the following.

The Sweep Algorithm

Step 1: Calculate the polar coordinates of all customers where the center is the depot and an arbitrary customer is chosen to be at angle 0. Reorder the customers so that

$$0 = \theta_1 \leq \theta_2 \leq \cdots \leq \theta_n.$$

Step 2: Starting from the unrouted customer i with smallest angle θ_i construct a new cluster by sweeping consecutive customers $i + 1, i + 2 \ldots$ until the capacity constraint will not allow the next customer to be added.

Step 3: Continue *Step 2* until all customers are included in a cluster.

Step 4: For each cluster constructed, solve the TSP on the subset of customers and the depot.

In both of these methods additional constraints can easily be incorporated into the algorithm.

We note that, traditionally, researchers have classified the Sweep algorithm as a cluster first-route second method and *not* as a route first-cluster second method. Our opinion is that the essential part of any vehicle routing algorithm is the clustering phase of the algorithm, that is, how the customers are *clustered* into groups that can be served by individual vehicles. The specific sequencing within a cluster can and, for most problems, should be done once these clusters are determined. Therefore, a classification of algorithms for the CVRP should be solely based on how the clustering is performed. Thus, the Sweep algorithm can be viewed as an algorithm of the route first-cluster second class since the clustering is performed on a fixed ordering of the nodes.

Cluster First-Route Second Methods

In this class of heuristics, the clustering is the most important phase. Customers are first clustered into feasible groups to be served by the same vehicle (cluster first) without regard to any preset ordering and then efficient routes are designed for each cluster (route second).

Heuristics of this class are usually more technically sophisticated than the previous class, since determining the clusters is often based on a *mathematical programming* approach. This class includes the following three heuristics:

- The Two-Phase Method (Christofides et al., 1978)

- The Generalized Assignment Heuristic (Fisher and Jaikumar, 1981)

- The Location-Based Heuristic (Bramel and Simchi-Levi, 1995)

The first two heuristics use, in a first step, the concept of *seed* customers. The seed customers are customers that will be in separate vehicles in the solution, and around which tours are constructed. In both cases, the performance of the algorithm depends highly on the choice of these seeds. Placing the CVRP in the framework of a different combinatorial problem, the Location-Based Heuristic selects the seeds in an *optimal* way and creates, at the same time, tours around these seeds. Thus, instead of decomposing the process into two steps, as done in the Two-Phase Method and the Generalized Assignment Heuristic, the Location-Based Heuristic simultaneously picks the seeds and designs tours around them. We will discuss this heuristic in detail in Section 6.7.

Incomplete Optimization Methods

These methods are optimization algorithms that, due to the prohibitive computing time involved in reaching an optimal solution, are terminated prematurely. Examples of these include:

- Cutting Plane Methods (Cornuéjols and Harche, 1993)

- Minimum K-Tree Methods (Fisher, 1994).

The disadvantage of incomplete optimization methods is that they still require large amounts of processing time; they can handle problems with usually no more than 100 customers.

6.3   Worst-Case Analysis of Heuristics

In the worst-case analysis presented here, we assume that the customer demands $w_1, w_2, \ldots, w_n$ and the vehicle capacity Q are rationals. Hence, without loss of generality, Q and w_i are assumed to be integers. Furthermore, we may assume that Q is even; otherwise one can double Q as well as each w_i, $i = 1, 2, \ldots, n$, without affecting the problem. The following two-phase route first-cluster second heuristic was suggested by Altinkemer and Gavish (1987). In the first phase, we relax the requirement that the demand of a customer cannot be split. Each customer i is replaced by w_i unit demand points that are zero distance apart. We then apply the ITP(α) heuristic (see Section 5.3) using a vehicle capacity of $\frac{Q}{2}$. In the second phase, we convert the solution obtained in Phase I to a feasible solution to the original problem without increasing the total cost. This heuristic is called the Unequal-Weight Iterated Tour Partitioning (UITP(α)) heuristic.

   We now describe the second phase procedure. Our notation follows the one suggested by Haimovich et al. (1988). Let $m = \sum_{i \in N} w_i$ be the number of demand points in the expanded problem. Recall that in the first phase an arbitrary orientation of the tour is chosen. The customers are then numbered $x^{(0)}, x^{(1)}, x^{(2)}, \ldots, x^{(n)}$ in order of their appearance on the tour, where $x^{(0)}$ is the depot. The ITP(α) heuristic partitions the path from $x^{(1)}$ to $x^{(n)}$ into $\lceil \frac{2m}{Q} \rceil$ disjoint segments such that each one contains no more than $\frac{Q}{2}$ demand points and connects the end-points of each segment to the depot. The segments are indexed by $j = 1, 2, \ldots, \lceil \frac{2m}{Q} \rceil$, such that the first customer of the jth segment is $x^{(b_j)}$ and the last customer is $x^{(e_j)}$. Hence, the jth segment, denoted by S_j, includes customers $\{x^{(b_j)}, \cdots, x^{(e_j)}\}$. Obviously, if $x^{(e_j)} = x^{(b_{j+1})}$ for some j, then the demand of customer $x^{(e_j)}$ is split between the jth and $(j+1)^{th}$ segments; therefore, these are not feasible routes. On the other hand, if $x^{(e_j)} \neq x^{(b_{j+1})}$ for all j, then the set of routes is feasible.

We now transform the solution obtained in the first phase into a feasible solution without increasing the total distance traveled. We use the following procedure.

The Phase Two Procedure

Step 1: Set $S'_j = \emptyset$, for $j = 1, 2, \ldots, \lceil \frac{2m}{Q} \rceil$

Step 2: For $j = 1$ to $\lceil \frac{2m}{Q} \rceil - 1$ do
  If $x^{(e_j)} = x^{(b_{j+1})}$ then
    If $\sum_{i=b_j}^{b_{j+1}} w_{x^{(i)}} \leq Q$ then let $S'_j = \{x^{(b_j)}, \cdots, x^{(e_j)}\}$ and
      let $x^{(b_{j+1})} = x^{(b_{j+1}+1)}$
    else let $S'_j = \{x^{(b_j)}, \cdots, x^{(e_j-1)}\}$ and $x^{(b_{j+1})} = x^{(e_j)}$
  else, let $S'_j = \{x^{(b_j)}, \cdots, x^{(e_j)}\}$.

We argue that the procedure generates feasible sets S'_j for $j = 1, 2, \ldots, \lceil \frac{2m}{Q} \rceil$. Note that the jth set can be enlarged only in the $(j-1)^{st}$ and j^{th} iterations (if at all). Moreover if it is enlarged in the jth iteration, it is clearly done feasibly in view of the test $\sum_{i=b_j}^{b_{j+1}} w_{x^{(i)}} \leq Q$. On the other hand, if S_j is enlarged in the $(j-1)^{st}$ iteration, at most $\frac{Q}{2}$ demand points are added thus ensuring feasibility. This can be verified as follows. Assume to the contrary that in the $(j-1)^{st}$ iteration more than $\frac{Q}{2}$ demand points are transferred from S'_{j-1} to S_j so that in the $(j-1)^{st}$ iteration $x^{(e_{j-1})} = x^{(b_j)}$. Since the original set S_{j-1} contains at most $\frac{Q}{2}$ demand points we must have shifted demand points in the $(j-2)^{nd}$ iteration from S_{j-2} to S_{j-1} (and in particular $x^{(b_{j-1})} = x^{(e_{j-2})}$), part of which are now being transferred to S_j. This implies that $x^{(*)} \doteq x^{(e_{j-2})} = x^{(b_{j-1})} = x^{(e_{j-1})} = x^{(b_j)}$, where $e_{j-2}, b_{j-1}, e_{j-1}$ and b_j refer to the original sets S_{j-2}, S_{j-1} and S_j. In other words at the beginning of the $(j-1)^{st}$ iteration the set S'_{j-1} contains a single customer $x^{(*)}$. But then, shifting $x^{(b_j)} = x^{(*)}$ backwards to S'_{j-1} is feasible, contradicting the fact that more than $\frac{Q}{2}$ demand points need to be shifted forward from S'_{j-1} to S'_j. Therefore, the procedure generates feasible sets and we have the following worst case bound.

Theorem 6.3.1 $\frac{Z^{UITP(\alpha)}}{Z_u^*} \leq 2 + (1 - \frac{2}{Q})\alpha$.

Proof. Recall that in the first phase the vehicle capacity is set to $\frac{Q}{2}$. Hence, using the bound of Lemma 5.2.2 we obtain the following upper bound on the length of the tours generated in Phase I of the UITP(α) heuristic,

$$\frac{4}{Q}\sum_{i \in N} d_i w_i + \left(1 - \frac{2}{Q}\right)\alpha L^*(N_0). \tag{6.1}$$

In the second phase of the algorithm, the tour obtained in the first phase is converted into a feasible solution with total length no more than (6.1). To verify this, we need only to analyze those segments whose end-points are modified by the procedure.

Suppose that S_j and S'_j differ in their starting point; then S'_j must start with $x^{(b_j+1)}$. This implies that arc $(x^{(b_j)}, x^{(b_j+1)})$, which is part of the Phase I solution, does not appear in the jth route. The triangle inequality ensures that the sum of the length of arcs $(x^{(0)}, x^{(b_j)})$ and $(x^{(b_j)}, x^{(b_j+1)})$ is no smaller than the length of arc $(x^{(0)}, x^{(b_j+1)})$. A similar argument can be applied if S_j and S'_j differ in their terminating point. Consequently, for every segment j, for $j = 1, 2, \ldots, \lceil \frac{2m}{Q} \rceil$, the length of the jth route according to the new partition is no longer than the length of the jth route according to the old partition. Hence,

$$Z^{\text{UITP}(\alpha)} \leq \frac{4}{Q} \sum_{i \in N} d_i w_i + \left(1 - \frac{2}{Q}\right) \alpha L^*(N_0).$$

Clearly, $Z_u^* \geq Z^*$, and therefore using the lower bound on Z^* developed in Lemma 5.2.1 completes the proof. ∎

The UITP heuristic was divided into two phases to prove the above worst-case result. However, if the Optimal Partitioning heuristic is used in the unequal weight model, the actual implementation is a one-step process. This is done as follows. Given a traveling salesman tour through the set of customers and the depot, we number the nodes $x^{(0)}, x^{(1)}, \ldots, x^{(n)}$ in order of their appearance on the tour where $x^{(0)}$ is the depot. We then define a distance matrix with cost C_{jk}, where

$$C_{jk} = \begin{cases} \text{the distance traveled by a vehicle that starts} \\ \text{at } x^{(0)}, \text{ visits customers } x^{(j+1)}, x^{(j+2)}, \ldots, x^{(k)} \\ \text{and returns to } x^{(0)}, & \text{if } \sum_{i=j+1}^{k} w_{x^{(i)}} \leq Q; \\ \\ \infty, & \text{otherwise.} \end{cases}$$

As in the equal demand case (see Section 5.2), it follows that a shortest path from $x^{(0)}$ to $x^{(n)}$ in the directed graph with distance cost C_{jk} corresponds to an optimal partition of the traveling salesman tour. This version of the heuristic, developed by Beasley and called the Unequal-Weight Optimal Partitioning (UOP) heuristic, also has $Z^{\text{UOP}(\alpha)}/Z^* \leq 2 + (1 - \frac{2}{Q})\alpha$. The following theorem, proved by Li and Simchi-Levi (1990), implies that when $\alpha = 1$, this bound is asymptotically tight as Q approaches infinity.

Theorem 6.3.2 *For any integer $Q \geq 1$, there exists a problem instance with $Z^{\text{UOP}(1)}/Z_u^*$ (and therefore $Z^{\text{UITP}(1)}/Z_u^*$) arbitrarily close to $3 - \frac{6}{Q+2}$.*

Proof. We modify the graph $\mathcal{G}(2, Kq+1)$, where K is a positive integer, as follows. Every group now, instead of containing Q customers, contains only one customer with demand Q. The other KQ customers have unit demand. The optimal traveling salesman tour is again as shown in Figure 5.2, and the solution obtained by the

UOP(1) heuristic is to have $2KQ + 1$ vehicles, each one of them serving only one customer. Thus

$$Z^{\mathrm{UOP}(1)} = 2(KQ + 1) + 4KQ.$$

The optimal solution to this problem has $KQ + 1$ vehicles serve those customers with demand Q, and K other vehicles serve the unit demand customers. Hence,

$$Z_u^* = 2(KQ + 1) + 4K.$$

Therefore,

$$\lim_{K \to \infty} \frac{Z^{\mathrm{UOP}(1)}}{Z_u^*} = \lim_{K \to \infty} \frac{2(KQ + 1) + 4KQ}{2(KQ + 1) + 4K} = 3 - \frac{6}{Q + 2}. \qquad \blacksquare$$

6.4   The Asymptotic Optimal Solution Value

In the probabilistic analysis of the UCVRP we assume, without loss of generality, that the vehicles' capacity Q equals 1, and the demand of each customer is no more than 1. Thus, vehicles and demands in a capacitated vehicle routing problem correspond to bins and item sizes (respectively) in a Bin-Packing Problem. Hence, for every routing instance there is a unique corresponding bin-packing instance.

Assume the demands $w_1, w_2, \ldots, w_n$ are drawn independently from a distribution Φ defined on $[0, 1]$. Assume customer locations are drawn independently from a probability measure μ with compact support in $\mathbb{R}^2$. We assume that $d_i > 0$ for each $i \in N$ since customers at the depot can be served at no cost. In this section we find the asymptotic optimal solution value for *any* Φ and *any* μ. This is done by showing that an asymptotically optimal algorithm for the Bin-Packing Problem, with item sizes distributed like Φ, can be used to solve, in an asymptotic sense, the UCVRP.

Given the demands $w_1, w_2, \ldots, w_n$, let b_n^* be the number of bins used in the optimal solution to the corresponding Bin-Packing Problem. As demonstrated in Theorem 3.2.4 there exists a constant $\gamma > 0$ (depending only on Φ) such that

$$\lim_{n \to \infty} \frac{b_n^*}{n} = \gamma \qquad (a.s.). \qquad (6.2)$$

We shall refer to the constant γ as the *bin-packing constant* and omit the dependence of γ on Φ in the notation.

The following theorem was proved by Simchi-Levi and Bramel (1990). Recall, without loss of generality the depot is positioned at $(0, 0)$ and $||x||$ represents the distance from the point $x \in \mathbb{R}^2$ to the depot.

Theorem 6.4.1 *Let x_k, $k = 1, 2, \ldots, n$ be a sequence of independent random variables having a distribution μ with compact support in $\mathbb{R}^2$. Let*

$$E(d) = \int_{\mathbb{R}^2} ||x|| d\mu(x).$$

Let the demands w_k, $k = 1, 2, \ldots, n$ be a sequence of independent random variables having a distribution Φ with support on $[0, 1]$ and assume that the demands and the locations of the customers are independent of each other. Let γ be the bin-packing constant associated with the distribution Φ; then, almost surely,

$$\lim_{n \to \infty} \frac{1}{n} Z_u^* = 2\gamma E(d).$$

Thus, the theorem fully characterizes the asymptotic optimal solution value of the UCVRP, for any reasonable distributions Φ and μ. An interesting observation concerns the case where the distribution of the demands allows *perfect packing*, that is, when the wasted space in the bins tends to become a small fraction of the number of bins used. Formally, Φ is said to allow *perfect packing* if almost surely $\lim_{n \to \infty} \frac{b_n^*}{n} = E(w)$. Karmarkar (1982) proved that a nonincreasing probability density function (with some mild regularity conditions) allows perfect packing. Rhee (1988) completely characterizes the class of distribution functions Φ which allow perfect packing. Clearly, in this case $\gamma = E(w)$. Thus, Theorem 6.4.1 indicates that allowing the demands to be split or not does not change the asymptotic objective function value. That is, the UCVRP and the ECVRP can be said to be *asymptotically equivalent* when Φ allows perfect packing.

To prove Theorem 6.4.1, we start by presenting in Section 6.4.1 a lower bound on the optimal objective function value. In Section 6.4.2, we present a heuristic for the UCVRP based on a simple region partitioning scheme. We show that the cost of the solution produced by the heuristic converges to our lower bound for any Φ and μ, thus proving the main theorem of the section.

6.4.1   A Lower Bound

We introduce a lower bound on the optimal objective function value Z_u^*. Let $A \subset I\!R^2$ be the compact support of μ and define $d_{\max} \doteq \sup_{x \in A} \{||x||\}$. For a given fixed positive integer $r \geq 1$, partition the circle with radius $d_{\max}$ centered at the depot into r rings of equal width. Let $\underline{d}_j \doteq (j - 1)\frac{d_{\max}}{r}$ for $j = 1, 2, \ldots, r, r + 1$, and construct the following $2r$ sets of customers:

$$S_j = \left\{ x_k \in N \middle| \underline{d}_j < d_k \leq \underline{d}_{j+1} \right\} \qquad \text{for } j = 1, \ldots, r,$$

and

$$F_j = \bigcup_{i=j}^{r} S_i \qquad \text{for } j = 1, 2, \ldots, r.$$

Note that $F_r \subseteq F_{r-1} \subseteq \cdots \subseteq F_1 = N$ since $d_k > 0$ for all $y_k \in N$.

In the lemma below, we show that $|F_r|$ grows to infinity almost surely as n grows to infinity. This implies that $|F_j|$ also grows to infinity almost surely for $j = 1, 2, \ldots, r$, since $|F_{j+1}| \leq |F_j|$, for $j = 1, 2, \ldots, r - 1$. The proof follows from the definitions of compact support and $d_{\max}$.

Lemma 6.4.2

$$\lim_{n \to \infty} \frac{|F_r|}{n} = p \ (a.s.) \ for \ some \ constant \ p > 0.$$

For any set of customers $T \subseteq N$, let $b^*(T)$ be the minimum number of vehicles needed to serve the customers in T; that is, $b^*(T)$ is the optimal solution to the Bin-Packing Problem defined by item sizes equal to the demands of the customers in T. We can now present a family of lower bounds on Z_u^* that hold for different values of $r \geq 1$.

Lemma 6.4.3

$$Z_u^* > 2 \frac{d_{\max}}{r} \sum_{j=2}^{r} b^*(F_j) \qquad for \ any \ r \geq 1.$$

Proof. Given an optimal solution to the UCVRP, let K_r^* be the number of vehicles in the optimal solution that serve at least one customer from S_r, and for $j = 1, 2, \ldots, r-1$, let K_j^* be the number of vehicles in the optimal solution that serve at least one customer in the set S_j, but do not serve any customers in F_{j+1}. Also, let V_j^* be the number of vehicles in the optimal solution that serve at least one customer in F_j. By these definitions, $V_j^* = \sum_{i=j}^{r} K_i^*$, for $j = 1, 2, \ldots, r$; hence, $K_j^* = V_j^* - V_{j+1}^*$ for $j = 1, 2, \ldots, r-1$ and $K_r^* = V_r^*$.

Note that $V_j^* \geq b^*(F_j)$, for $j = 1, 2, \ldots, r$, since V_j^* represents the number of vehicles used in a feasible packing of the demands of customers in F_j, while $b^*(F_j)$ represents the number of bins used in an optimal packing.

By the definition of K_j^* and $\underline{d}_j$, $Z_u^* > 2 \sum_{j=1}^{r} \underline{d}_j K_j^*$ and therefore,

$$Z_u^* > 2\underline{d}_r V_r^* + \sum_{j=1}^{r-1} 2\underline{d}_j \left(V_j^* - V_{j+1}^* \right)$$

$$= 2\underline{d}_1 V_1^* + \sum_{j=2}^{r} 2(\underline{d}_j - \underline{d}_{j-1}) V_j^*$$

$$= 2 \sum_{j=2}^{r} (\underline{d}_j - \underline{d}_{j-1}) V_j^* \qquad (\text{since } \underline{d}_1 = 0)$$

$$\geq 2 \sum_{j=2}^{r} (\underline{d}_j - \underline{d}_{j-1}) b^*(F_j) \qquad (\text{since } V_j^* \geq b^*(F_j))$$

$$= 2 \sum_{j=2}^{r} \frac{d_{\max}}{r} b^*(F_j). \qquad \blacksquare$$

Note that Lemma 6.4.3 provides a deterministic lower bound; that is, no probabilistic assumptions are involved. Lemma 6.4.2 and Lemma 6.4.3 are both required to provide a lower bound on $\frac{1}{n} Z_u^*$ that holds almost surely.

Lemma 6.4.4 *Under the conditions of Theorem 6.4.1, we have*

$$\lim_{n \to \infty} \frac{1}{n} Z_u^* \geq 2\gamma E(d) \qquad (a.s.).$$

Proof. Lemma 6.4.3 implies that

$$\lim_{n \to \infty} \frac{1}{n} Z_u^* \geq 2 \frac{d_{\max}}{r} \lim_{n \to \infty} \sum_{j=2}^{r} \frac{b^*(F_j)}{n}$$

$$= 2 \frac{d_{\max}}{r} \sum_{j=2}^{r} \lim_{n \to \infty} \frac{b^*(F_j)}{|F_j|} \lim_{n \to \infty} \frac{|F_j|}{n}.$$

From Lemma 6.4.2, $|F_j|$ grows to infinity almost surely as n grows to infinity, for $j = 1, 2, \ldots, r$. Moreover, since demands and locations are independent of each other, the demands in F_j, $j = 1, 2, \ldots, r$ are distributed like Φ. Therefore,

$$\lim_{n \to \infty} \frac{b^*(F_j)}{|F_j|} = \lim_{|F_j| \to \infty} \frac{b^*(F_j)}{|F_j|} = \gamma \qquad (a.s.).$$

Hence, almost surely

$$\lim_{n \to \infty} \frac{1}{n} Z_u^* \geq 2 \frac{d_{\max}}{r} \sum_{j=2}^{r} \gamma \lim_{n \to \infty} \frac{|F_j|}{n}$$

$$= 2 \frac{d_{\max}}{r} \gamma \lim_{n \to \infty} \frac{1}{n} \sum_{j=2}^{r} |F_j|.$$

Since

$$F_j = \bigcup_{i=j}^{r} S_i \qquad \text{for } j = 1, 2, \ldots, r,$$

we have $|F_j| = \sum_{i=j}^{r} |S_i|$; hence, almost surely

$$\lim_{n \to \infty} \frac{1}{n} Z_u^* \geq 2 \frac{d_{\max}}{r} \gamma \lim_{n \to \infty} \frac{1}{n} \sum_{j=2}^{r} \sum_{i=j}^{r} |S_i|$$

$$= 2 \frac{d_{\max}}{r} \gamma \lim_{n \to \infty} \frac{1}{n} \sum_{j=2}^{r} (j - 1) |S_j|.$$

By the definition of $\underline{d}_j$,

$$\lim_{n \to \infty} \frac{1}{n} Z_u^* \geq 2\gamma \lim_{n \to \infty} \frac{1}{n} \sum_{j=2}^{r} \underline{d}_j |S_j| = 2\gamma \lim_{n \to \infty} \frac{1}{n} \sum_{j=1}^{r} \underline{d}_j |S_j|,$$

since $\underline{d}_1 = 0$ and $|S_1| \leq n$. By the definition of $\underline{d}_j$ and S_j, $\underline{d}_j \geq d_k - \frac{d_{max}}{r}$, for all $x_k \in S_j$. Then almost surely

$$\lim_{n\to\infty} \frac{1}{n} Z_u^* \geq 2\gamma \lim_{n\to\infty} \frac{1}{n} \sum_{x_k \in N} (d_k - \frac{d_{max}}{r})$$

$$= 2\gamma \lim_{n\to\infty} \frac{1}{n} \sum_{x_k \in N} d_k - 2\gamma \frac{d_{max}}{r}$$

$$= 2\gamma E(d) - 2\gamma \frac{d_{max}}{r}.$$

This lower bound holds for arbitrarily large r; hence,

$$\lim_{n\to\infty} \frac{1}{n} Z_u^* \geq 2\gamma E(d) \qquad (a.s.). \qquad \blacksquare$$

In the next section we show that this lower bound is tight by presenting an upper bound on the cost of the optimal solution that asymptotically approaches the same value.

6.4.2   An Upper Bound

We prove Theorem 6.4.1 by analyzing the cost of the following three-step heuristic which provides an upper bound on Z_u^*. In the first step, we partition the area A into subregions. Then, for each of these subregions, we find the optimal packing of the customers' demands in the subregion, into bins of unit size. Finally, for each subregion, we allocate one vehicle to serve the customers in each bin.

The Region Partitioning Scheme

For a *fixed* $h > 0$, let $G(h)$ be an infinite grid of squares with side $\frac{h}{\sqrt{2}}$ and edges parallel to the system coordinates. Recall that A is the compact support of the distribution function μ, and let $A_1, A_2, \ldots, A_{t(h)}$ be the intersection of the squares of $G(h)$ with the compact support A that have $\mu(A_i) > 0$. Note $t(h) < \infty$ since A is compact and $t(h)$ is independent of n.

Let $N(i)$ be the set of customers located in subregion A_i, and define $n(i) \doteq |N(i)|$. For every $i = 1, 2, \ldots, t(h)$, let $b^*(i)$ be the minimum number of bins needed to pack the demands of customers in $N(i)$. Finally, for each subregion $A_i, i = 1, 2, \ldots, t(h)$, let $n_j(i)$ be the number of customers in the jth bin of this optimal packing, for each $j = 1, 2, \ldots, b^*(i)$.

We now proceed to find an upper bound on the value of our heuristic. Recall that for each bin produced by the heuristic, we send a single vehicle to serve all the customers in the bin. First, the vehicle visits the customer closest to the depot in the subregion to which the bin belongs, then serves all the customers in the bin in any order, and the vehicle returns to the depot through the closest customer again. Let $\underline{d}(i)$ be the distance from the depot to the closest customer in $N(i)$, that is, in subregion A_i. Note that since each subregion A_i is a subset of a square of side $\frac{h}{\sqrt{2}}$, the distance between any two customers in A_i is no more than h. Consequently, using the method just described, the distance traveled by the vehicle that serves all the customers in the jth bin of subregion A_i is no more than

$$2\underline{d}(i) + h(n_j(i) + 1).$$

Therefore,

$$Z_u^* \leq \sum_{i=1}^{t(h)} \sum_{j=1}^{b^*(i)} \left[2\underline{d}(i) + h(n_j(i) + 1) \right] \leq 2\sum_{i=1}^{t(h)} b^*(i)\underline{d}(i) + 2nh. \tag{6.3}$$

This inequality will be coupled with the following lemma to find an almost sure upper bound on the cost of this heuristic.

Lemma 6.4.5 *Under the conditions of the Theorem 6.4.1, we have*

$$\overline{\lim_{n\to\infty}} \frac{1}{n} \sum_{i=1}^{t(h)} b^*(i)\underline{d}(i) \leq \gamma E(d) \qquad (a.s.).$$

Proof. Let $p_i \doteq \mu(A_i)$ be the probability that a given customer x_k falls in subregion A_i. Since $p_i > 0$, by the strong law of large numbers, $\lim_{n\to\infty} \frac{n(i)}{n} = p_i$ almost surely and therefore $n(i)$ grows to infinity almost surely as n grows to infinity. Thus, we have

$$\lim_{n\to\infty} \frac{b^*(i)}{n(i)} = \lim_{n(i)\to\infty} \frac{b^*(i)}{n(i)} = \gamma \qquad (a.s.).$$

Hence,

$$\overline{\lim_{n\to\infty}} \frac{1}{n} \sum_{i=1}^{t(h)} b^*(i)\underline{d}(i) = \overline{\lim_{n\to\infty}} \frac{1}{n} \sum_{i=1}^{t(h)} \frac{b^*(i)}{n(i)} n(i)\underline{d}(i)$$

$$\leq \overline{\lim_{n\to\infty}} \frac{1}{n} \sum_{i=1}^{t(h)} \frac{b^*(i)}{n(i)} \sum_{x_k \in N(i)} d_k \qquad (\text{since } \underline{d}(i) \leq d_k, \forall x_k \in N(i))$$

$$= \sum_{i=1}^{t(h)} \overline{\lim_{n\to\infty}} \frac{b^*(i)}{n(i)} \overline{\lim_{n\to\infty}} \frac{1}{n} \sum_{x_k \in N(i)} d_k$$

$$= \gamma \overline{\lim_{n\to\infty}} \frac{1}{n} \sum_{x_k \in N} d_k.$$

Using the strong law of large numbers, we have

$$\overline{\lim_{n\to\infty}} \frac{1}{n} \sum_{i=1}^{t(h)} b^*(i)\underline{d}(i) \leq \gamma E(d) \qquad (a.s.),$$

which completes the proof of this lemma. ∎

Remark: A simple modification of the proof of Lemma 6.4.5 shows that the inequality that appears in the statement of the lemma can be replaced by equality (see Exercise 6.5).

We can now finish the proof of the Theorem 6.4.1. From equation (6.3) we have

$$\frac{1}{n}Z_u^* \le \frac{2}{n}\sum_{i=1}^{t(h)} b^*(i)\underline{d}(i) + 2h.$$

Taking the limits and using Lemma 6.4.5, we obtain

$$\overline{\lim_{n\to\infty}} \frac{1}{n}Z_u^* \le 2\gamma E(d) + 2h \qquad (a.s.).$$

Since this inequality holds for arbitrarily small $h > 0$, we have

$$\overline{\lim_{n\to\infty}} \frac{1}{n}Z_u^* \le 2\gamma E(d) \qquad (a.s.).$$

This upper bound combined with the lower bound of Lemma 6.4.4 proves the main theorem.

6.5   Probabilistic Analysis of Classical Heuristics

Recently, Bienstock et al. (1993) analyze the average performance of heuristics that belong to the route first-cluster second class. Recall our definition of this class: all those heuristics that first order the customers according to their locations and then partition this ordering to produce feasible clusters.

It is clear that the UITP(α) and UOP(α) heuristics described in Section 6.3 belong to this class. As mentioned in Section 6.2, the Sweep algorithm suggested by Gillett and Miller can also be viewed as a member of this class.

Bienstock et al. show that the performance of any heuristic in this class is strongly related to the performance of a nonefficient bin-packing heuristic called Next-Fit (NF). The Next-Fit bin-packing heuristic can be described in the following manner. Given a list of n items, start with item 1 and place it in bin 1. Suppose we are packing item j; let bin i be the highest indexed nonempty bin. If item j fits in bin i, then place it there; else place it in a new bin indexed $i + 1$. Thus, NF is an online heuristic; that is, it assigns items to bins according to the order in which they appear without using any knowledge of subsequent items in the list.

The NF heuristic possesses some interesting properties that will be useful in the analysis of the class route first-cluster second. Assume the items are indexed $1, 2, \ldots, n$ and let a *consecutive* heuristic be one that assigns items to bins such that items in any bin appear consecutively in the sequence. The following is a simple observation.

Property 6.5.1 *Among all consecutive heuristics, NF uses the least number of bins.*

The next property is similar to a property developed in Section 3.2 for b_n^*, the optimal solution to the Bin-Packing Problem.

Property 6.5.2 *Let the item sizes* $w_1, w_2, \ldots, w_n, \ldots$ *in the Bin-Packing Problem be a sequence of independent random variables and let* b_n^{NF} *be the number of bins produced by NF on the items* $1, 2, \ldots, n$. *For every* $t \geq 0$

$$Pr\left\{|b_n^{NF} - E(b_n^{NF})| > t\right\} \leq 2\exp(-t^2/8n). \tag{6.4}$$

A direct result of this property is the following. The proof is left as an exercise (Exercise 6.2).

Corollary 6.5.3 *For any* $n \geq 1$,

$$b_n^{NF} \leq E(b_n^{NF}) + 4\sqrt{n \log n} \quad (a.s.).$$

The next property is a simple consequence of the theory of subadditive processes (see Section 3.2) and the structure of solutions generated by NF.

Property 6.5.4 *For any distribution of item sizes, there exists a constant* $\gamma^{NF} > 0$ *such that* $\lim_{n \to \infty} \frac{b_n^{NF}}{n} = \gamma^{NF}$ *almost surely, where* b_n^{NF} *is the number of bins produced by the NF packing and* γ^{NF} *depends only on the distribution of the item sizes.*

These properties are used to prove the following theorem, the main result of this section.

Theorem 6.5.5 *(i) Let H be a route first-cluster second heuristic. Then, under the assumptions of Theorem 6.4.1, we have*

$$\lim_{n \to \infty} \frac{1}{n} Z^H \geq 2\gamma^{NF} E(d) \quad (a.s.).$$

(ii) The UOP(α) heuristic is the best possible heuristic in this class; that is, for any fixed $\alpha \geq 1$ *we have*

$$\lim_{n \to \infty} \frac{1}{n} Z^{UOP(\alpha)} = 2\gamma^{NF} E(d) \quad (a.s.).$$

In view of Theorems 6.4.1 and 6.5.5 it is interesting to compare γ^{NF} to γ since the asymptotic error of any heuristic H in the class of route first-cluster second satisfies

$$\lim_{n \to \infty} Z^H/Z_u^* \geq \lim_{n \to \infty} Z^{UOP(\alpha)}/Z_u^* = \gamma^{NF}/\gamma.$$

Although in general the ratio is difficult to characterize, Karmarkar was able to characterize it for the case when the item sizes are uniformly distributed on an interval $(0, a]$ for $0 < a \leq 1$. For instance, for a satisfying $\frac{1}{2} < a \leq 1$, we have

$$\gamma^{NF}/\gamma = \frac{2}{a}\left\{\frac{1}{12a^3}(15a^3 - 9a^2 + 3a - 1) + \sqrt{2}\left(\frac{1-a}{2a}\right)\tanh\left(\frac{1-a}{\sqrt{2}a}\right)\right\},$$

so that when the item sizes are uniform $(0, 1]$ the above ratio is $\frac{4}{3}$ which implies that UOP(α) converge to a value which is 33.3 % more than the optimal cost, a very disappointing performance for the best heuristic currently available in terms of worst-case behavior.

Moreover, heuristics in the route first-cluster second class can never be asymptotically optimal for the UCVRP, except in some trivial cases (e.g., demands are all the same size). In fact, Theorem 6.5.5 clearly demonstrates that the route first-cluster second class suffers from misplaced priorities. The routing (in the first phase) is done without any regard to the customer demands and thus this leads to a packing of demands into vehicles that is *at best* like the Next-Fit bin-packing heuristic. This is clearly suboptimal in all but trivial cases, one being when customers have equal demands, and thus we see the connection with the results of the previous chapter. Therefore, this theorem shows that an asymptotically optimal heuristic for the UCVRP must use an asymptotically optimal bin-packing heuristic to pack the customer demands into the vehicles.

In the next two subsections we prove Theorem 6.5.5 by developing a lower bound (Section 6.5.1) on Z^H and an upper bound on $Z^{UOP(\alpha)}$ (Section 6.5.2).

6.5.1   A Lower Bound

In this section, we present a lower bound on the solution produced by these heuristics. Let H denote a route first-cluster second heuristic.

As in Section 6.4.1, let A be the compact support of the distribution μ, and define $d_{max} \doteq \sup_{x \in A}\{||x||\}$. Given a fixed integer $r \geq 1$, define $\underline{d}_j = (j-1)\frac{d_{max}}{r}$ for $j = 1, 2, \ldots, r$, and construct the following r sets of customers:

$$F_j = \left\{ x_k \in N \middle| \underline{d}_j < d_k \right\} \qquad \text{for } j = 1, \ldots, r.$$

Note that $F_r \subseteq F_{r-1} \subseteq \ldots \subseteq F_1$, and $F_1 = N$ since, without loss of generality, $d_k > 0$ for all $x_k \in N$.

Let the customers be indexed $x_1, x_2, \ldots, x_n$ according to the order determined by the heuristic H in the route-first phase.

For any set of customers $T \subseteq N$, let $b^{NF}(T)$ be the number of bins generated by the Next-Fit heuristic when applied to the Bin-Packing Problem defined by item sizes equal to the demands of the customers in T, packed in the order of increasing index.

Lemma 6.5.6 *For any $r \geq 1$,*

$$Z_n^H > 2\frac{d_{max}}{r} \sum_{j=2}^{r} b^{NF}(F_j).$$

Proof. For a given solution constructed by H, let $V(F_j)$ be the number of vehicles that serve at least one customer in F_j, for $j = 1, 2, \ldots, r$. By this definition, $V(F_j) - V(F_{j+1})$, $j = 1, 2, \ldots, r-1$ is exactly the number of vehicles whose farthest customer visited is in F_j but not in F_{j+1}, and trivially $V(F_r)$ is the number of vehicles whose farthest customer visited is in F_r. Hence,

$$Z_n^H > 2\underline{d}_r V(F_r) + \sum_{j=1}^{r-1} 2\underline{d}_j \left(V(F_j) - V(F_{j+1})\right)$$

$$= 2\underline{d}_1 V(F_1) + \sum_{j=2}^{r} 2(\underline{d}_j - \underline{d}_{j-1})V(F_j).$$

For a given subset of customers F_j, $j = 1, 2, \ldots, r$, the $V(F_j)$ vehicles that contain these customer demands (in the solution produced by H) can be ordered in such a way that the customer indices are in increasing order. Disregarding the demands of customers in these vehicles that are not in F_j, this represents the solution produced by a consecutive packing heuristic on the demands of customers in F_j. By Property 6.5.1 we must have $V(F_j) \geq b^{NF}(F_j)$, for every $j = 1, 2, \ldots, r$. This, together with $\underline{d}_1 = 0$, $\underline{d}_j - \underline{d}_{j-1} = \frac{d_{max}}{r}$, imply that

$$Z_n^H > 2 \sum_{j=2}^{r} \frac{d_{max}}{r} b^{NF}(F_j). \qquad \blacksquare$$

This lemma is used to derive an asymptotic lower bound on the cost of the solution produced by H that holds almost surely. The proof of the lemma is identical to the proof of Lemma 6.4.4.

Lemma 6.5.7 *Under the conditions of Theorem 6.4.1, we have*

$$\lim_{n \to \infty} \frac{1}{n} Z_n^H \geq 2\gamma^{NF} E(d) \qquad (a.s.).$$

In the next section we show that this lower bound is asymptotically tight in the case of UOP(α) by presenting an upper bound that approaches the same value.

6.5.2 The UOP(α) Heuristic

We prove Theorem 6.5.5 by finding an upper bound on $Z_n^{UOP(\alpha)}$. Let L^α be the length of the α-optimal tour selected by UOP(α). Starting at the depot and following the tour in an arbitrary orientation, the customers and the depot are numbered $x^{(0)}, x^{(1)}, x^{(2)}, \ldots, x^{(n)}$, where $x^{(0)}$ is the depot. Select an integer $m \doteq \lceil n^\beta \rceil$ for some fixed $\beta \in (\frac{1}{2}, 1)$ and note that for each such β we have $\lim_{n \to \infty} \frac{m}{n} = 0$ (i.e., $m = o(n)$) and $\lim_{n \to \infty} \frac{\sqrt{n}}{m} = 0$ (i.e., $\sqrt{n} = o(m)$). We partition the path from $x^{(1)}$ to $x^{(n)}$ into $m + 1$ segments, such that each one contains exactly $\lfloor \frac{n}{m} \rfloor$ customers, except possibly the last one.

Number the segments $1, 2, \ldots, m + 1$ according to their appearance on the traveling salesman tour, where each segment has exactly $\lfloor \frac{n}{m} \rfloor$ customers except possibly segment $m + 1$. Let L_i (respectively, N_i) be the length of (respectively, subset of customers in) segment i, $1 \leq i \leq m + 1$. Finally, let $n_i = |N_i|$, $i = 1, 2, \ldots, m + 1$.

To obtain an upper bound on the cost of $\text{UOP}(\alpha)$, we apply the Next-Fit heuristic to each segment separately, where items are packed in bins in the same order they appear in the segment. This gives us a partition of the tour that must provide an upper bound on the cost produced by $\text{UOP}(\alpha)$. Let b_i^{NF} be the number of bins produced by the Next-Fit heuristic when applied to the customer demands in segment i. We assign a single vehicle to each bin produced by the above procedure, each of which starts at the depot, visits the customers assigned to its corresponding bin in the same order as they appear on the traveling salesman tour, and then returns to the depot. Let $\bar{d}_i$ be the distance from the depot to the farthest customer in N_i. Clearly, the total distance traveled by all the vehicles that serve the customers in segment i, $1 \leq i \leq m + 1$, is no more than

$$2b_i^{\text{NF}} \bar{d}_i + L_i.$$

Hence,

$$Z^{\text{UOP}(\alpha)} \leq 2 \sum_{i=1}^{m+1} b_i^{\text{NF}} \bar{d}_i + L^{\alpha}$$

$$\leq 2 \sum_{i=1}^{m} b_i^{\text{NF}} \bar{d}_i + 2b_{m+1}^{\text{NF}} d_{\max} + \alpha L^*. \qquad (6.5)$$

Lemma 6.5.8 *Under the conditions of Theorem 6.4.1, we have*

$$\overline{\lim_{n \to \infty}} \frac{1}{n} \sum_{i=1}^{m} b_i^{\text{NF}} \bar{d}_i \leq \gamma^{\text{NF}} E(d) \qquad (a.s.).$$

Proof. Since the number of customers in every segment i, $1 \leq i \leq m$, is exactly $n_i = \lfloor \frac{n}{m} \rfloor$ and $\lim_{n \to \infty} \frac{m}{n} = 0$, we have for a given i, $1 \leq i \leq m$,

$$b_i^{\text{NF}} \leq E(b_i^{\text{NF}}) + \sqrt{9Kn_i \log n_i} \qquad (a.s.),$$

for any $K \geq 2$.

We now show that, for sufficiently large n, these m inequalities hold simultaneously almost surely. To prove this, note that Property 6.5.2 tells us that, for n_i large enough, the probability that one such inequality does not hold is no more than $2 \exp(-K \log n_i) = 2n_i^{-K}$. Thus, the probability that at least one of these inequalities is violated is no more than $2m(\frac{n}{m} - 1)^{-K}$. By the Borel-Cantelli Lemma, these m inequalities hold almost surely if $\sum_n m(\frac{m}{n-m})^K < \infty$. Choosing $K > \frac{1+\beta}{1-\beta} > 3$ shows that this holds for any $m = \lceil n^{\beta} \rceil$ where $\frac{1}{2} < \beta < 1$.

Thus,

$$\overline{\lim_{n \to \infty}} \frac{1}{n} \sum_{i=1}^{m} b_i^{\text{NF}} \bar{d}_i \leq \gamma^{\text{NF}} \overline{\lim_{n \to \infty}} \sum_{i=1}^{m} \frac{1}{m} \bar{d}_i \qquad (a.s.).$$

Clearly, $\overline{d}_i \leq d_k + L_i$ for every $x_k \in N_i$ and every $i = 1, 2, \ldots, m$. Thus,

$$\overline{d}_i \leq \left(\left\lfloor \frac{n}{m} \right\rfloor^{-1} \sum_{x_k \in N_i} d_k \right) + L_i \quad \text{for every } i = 1, 2 \ldots, m.$$

Hence,

$$\overline{\lim_{n \to \infty}} \sum_{i=1}^{m} \frac{1}{m} \overline{d}_i \leq \overline{\lim_{n \to \infty}} \frac{1}{n - m} \sum_{x_k \in N} d_k + \overline{\lim_{n \to \infty}} \frac{1}{m} L^{\alpha}$$

$$\leq \overline{\lim_{n \to \infty}} \frac{1}{n - m} \sum_{x_k \in N} d_k + \alpha \overline{\lim_{n \to \infty}} \frac{1}{m} L^{*}.$$

Applying the strong law of large numbers and using $\lim_{n \to \infty} \frac{m}{n} = 0$, we have

$$\overline{\lim_{n \to \infty}} \frac{1}{n - m} \sum_{x_k \in N} d_k = E(d) \qquad (a.s.).$$

Now from Chapter 3, we know that the length of the optimal traveling salesman tour through a set of k points independently and identically distributed in a given region grows almost surely like $\sqrt{k}$. This together with $\lim_{n \to \infty} \frac{\sqrt{n}}{m} = 0$ implies that

$$\lim_{n \to \infty} \frac{L^{*}}{m} = 0 \qquad (a.s.).$$

These facts complete the proof. ∎

We can now complete the proof of Theorem 6.4.1. From (6.5) and Lemma 4.1 we have

$$\overline{\lim_{n \to \infty}} \frac{1}{n} Z_n^{\mathrm{UOP}(\alpha)} \leq 2\gamma^{\mathrm{NF}} E(d) + 2d_{\max} \overline{\lim_{n \to \infty}} \frac{1}{n} b_{m+1}^{\mathrm{NF}} + \alpha \overline{\lim_{n \to \infty}} \frac{1}{n} L^{*} \qquad (a.s.).$$

Finally, using Beardwood et al.'s (1959) result (see Theorem 3.3.2), and the fact that the number of points in segment $m + 1$ is at most $\frac{n}{m}$, we obtain the desired result.

6.6 The Uniform Model

To our knowledge, no polynomial time algorithm that is asymptotically optimal is known for the UCVRP for general Φ. We now describe such a heuristic for the case where Φ is uniform on the interval $[0, 1]$. In the unit interval, it is known that there exists an asymptotically optimal solution to the Bin-Packing Problem with at most two items per bin. This forms the basis for the heuristic for the UCVRP, called Optimal Matching of Pairs (OMP). It considers only feasible solutions in which each vehicle visits no more than two customers. Among all such feasible solutions, the heuristic finds the one with minimum cost. This can be done by formulating the following integer linear program.

For every $x_k, x_l \in N$, let

$$c_{kl} = \begin{cases} d_k + d_{kl} + d_l, & \text{if } k \neq l \text{ and } w_k + w_l \leq 1; \\ 2d_k, & \text{if } k = l; \\ \infty, & \text{otherwise.} \end{cases}$$

The integer program to solve is

Problem P : Min $\displaystyle\sum_{k \leq l} c_{kl} X_{kl}$

s.t.

$$\sum_{l \geq k} X_{kl} + \sum_{l < k} X_{lk} = 1, \quad \forall k = 1, 2, \ldots, n \quad (6.6)$$

$$X_{kl} \in \{0, 1\}, \quad \forall k \leq l. \quad (6.7)$$

For $k < l$, X_{kl} is 1 if a vehicle delivers items to customers x_k and x_l and is 0 otherwise. Constraint (6.6) ensures that each customer is visited.

It is not hard to see that P can be solved in polynomial time since it is no more than a classical weighted matching problem defined on a specific graph. Define the following graph $\overline{G} = (\overline{N}, \overline{E})$, where each customer x_k is represented by two nodes v_k and v'_k, for $k = 1, 2, \ldots, n$. The set of edges of $\overline{G}$ is defined as follows.

$$\overline{E} = \{(v_k, v'_k) | x_k \in N\}$$

$$\cup \{(v_k, v_l) | x_k \in N, x_l \in N, k \neq l, w_k + w_l \leq 1\}$$

$$\cup \{(v'_k, v'_l) | x_k \in N, x_l \in N, k \neq l, w_k + w_l \leq 1\}.$$

Thus, $\overline{G}$ has $2n$ vertices. The length of edge (v_k, v_l), for $k \neq l$, is c_{kl}, of edge (v_k, v'_k) is c_{kk} and of edge (v'_k, v'_l) is 0, for all k and l.

Note that any given feasible solution to P can be transformed into a feasible solution to the matching problem on $\overline{G}$ with the same cost. For any feasible solution to P, choose edge (v_k, v'_k) if customer k is served by a vehicle that does not serve any other customer and choose edges (v_k, v_l) and (v'_k, v'_l) if customers x_k and x_l are visited together. Similarly, any feasible solution to the matching problem can be transformed into a feasible solution to P with the same cost. Hence, the two problems are equivalent.

An optimal matching in $\overline{G}$ can be found in $O(n^3)$ using Lawler's (1976) algorithm.

The main result of this section is the following.

Theorem 6.6.1 *Let* x_k, $k = 1, 2, \ldots, n$ *be a sequence of independent random variables having a distribution* μ *with compact support in* $\mathbb{R}^2$. *Let*

$$E(d) = \int_{\mathbb{R}^2} ||x|| d\mu(x).$$

Let the demands w_k, $k = 1, 2, \ldots, n$ *be a sequence of independent random variables having a uniform distribution on* [0, 1] *and assume that the demands and the location of the customers are independent of each other. Then, the OMP heuristic is asymptotically optimal. That is, with probability one,*

$$\lim_{n \to \infty} \frac{Z_u^*}{n} = \lim_{n \to \infty} \frac{Z^{OMP}}{n} = E(d).$$

To prove that the *OMP* heuristic is asymptotically optimal, we approximate its performance by that of the Sliced Region Partitioning heuristic with parameters h and r ($SRP(h, r)$). For any *fixed* positive integer $r \geq 1$, the set N is partitioned into the following $2r$ disjoint subsets, some of which may be empty.

$$N_j = \left\{ x_k \in N \Big| \frac{1}{2}\left(1 - \frac{j+1}{r}\right) < w_k \leq \frac{1}{2}\left(1 - \frac{j}{r}\right) \right\} \qquad j = 1, 2, \ldots, r-1,$$

and

$$N^j = \left\{ x_k \in N \Big| \frac{1}{2}\left(1 + \frac{j-1}{r}\right) < w_k \leq \frac{1}{2}\left(1 + \frac{j}{r}\right) \right\} \qquad j = 1, 2, \ldots, r-1.$$

Also

$$N_0 = \left\{ x_k \in N \Big| \frac{1}{2}\left(1 - \frac{1}{r}\right) < w_k \leq \frac{1}{2} \right\},$$

and

$$N^r = \left\{ x_k \in N \Big| \frac{1}{2}\left(1 + \frac{r-1}{r}\right) < w_k \right\}.$$

The number of customers in each N_j (respectively, N^j) is denoted by n_j (respectively, n^j) for all possible values of j.

Note that for any $j = 1, 2, \ldots, r-1$, one vehicle can deliver the demand of a customer from N_j together with the demand of exactly one customer from N^j. The $SRP(h, r)$ heuristic generates pairs of customers, one customer from N_j and one from N^j, for every $j = 1, 2, \ldots, r-1$, using the same region partitioning scheme used in the proof of Theorem 6.4.1 (Section 6.4.2). The customers in $N_0 \cup N^r$ are served separately; a single vehicle is assigned to each of these customers.

For every subregion A_i, $i = 1, 2, \ldots, t(h)$, generated by the grid $G(h)$ (see Section 6.4.2) and for every $j = 1, 2, \ldots, r-1$, let $N_j(i)$ (respectively, $N^j(i)$) be the subset of points in N_j (respectively, N^j) that fall in subregion A_i. Also, let $n_j(i) = |N_j(i)|$ and $n^j(i) = |N^j(i)|$.

In each subregion A_i, $i = 1, 2, \ldots, t(h)$, and for any $j = 1, 2, \ldots, r-1$, we arbitrarily match one customer from $N_j(i)$ with exactly one customer from $N^j(i)$; one vehicle serves each such pair. If $n_j(i) = n^j(i)$, then all customers in $N_j(i) \cup N^j(i)$ are matched and therefore visited in pairs. If, however, $n_j(i) \neq n^j(i)$, then we can match exactly $\min\{n_j(i), n^j(i)\}$ pairs of customers. The remaining $|n_j(i) - n^j(i)|$ customers in $N_j(i) \cup N^j(i)$ that have not yet been matched are each served by one vehicle. Thus the total number of vehicles used in subregion A_i is

$$n_0(i) + n^r(i) + \sum_{j=1}^{r-1} \max\{n_j(i), n^j(i)\}.$$

The heuristic clearly generates a feasible solution to the UCVRP. Moreover, this solution is feasible for P, as each vehicle visits at most two customers. Thus,

$$Z^{OMP} \leq Z^{SRP(h,r)} \qquad \text{for any } r \geq 1 \text{ and } h > 0.$$

We now proceed by finding an upper bound on $Z^{SRP(h,r)}$. Essentially the same analysis as in Section 6.4.2 shows that the total distance traveled by all vehicles is no more than

$$2 \sum_{i=1}^{t(h)} \underline{d}(i) \left[n_0(i) + n^r(i) + \sum_{j=1}^{r-1} \max\{n_j(i), n^j(i)\} \right] + 2nh.$$

Since

$$\lim_{n(i)\to\infty} \frac{n_j(i)}{n(i)} = \lim_{n(i)\to\infty} \frac{n^j(i)}{n(i)} = \frac{1}{2r} \qquad (a.s.) \qquad \text{for all } j = 1, 2, \ldots, r,$$

we have

$$\lim_{n(i)\to\infty} \frac{1}{n(i)} \left[n_0(i) + n^r(i) + \sum_{j=1}^{r-1} \max\{n_j(i), n^j(i)\} \right] = \frac{1}{2} + \frac{1}{2r} \qquad (a.s.).$$

The remainder of the proof is identical to the proof of the upper bound of Theorem 6.4.1.

Therefore, the OMP is asymptotically optimal when demands are uniformly distributed between 0 and 1. In fact, the proof can be extended to a larger class of demand distributions. For example, for any demand distribution with symmetric density, one with $f(x) = f(1-x)$ for $x \in [0, 1]$, one can show that the same result holds.

6.7   The Location-Based Heuristic

Recently, Bramel and Simchi-Levi (1995) used the insight obtained from the analysis of the asymptotic optimal solution value (see Theorem 6.4.1 above and the discussion that follows it) to develop a new and effective class of heuristics for the UCVRP called Location-Based Heuristics. Specifically, this class of heuristics was motivated by the following observations.

A byproduct of the proof of Theorem 6.4.1 is that the region partitioning scheme used to find an upper bound on Z_u^* is asymptotically optimal. Unfortunately, the scheme is not polynomial since it requires, among other things, optimally solving the Bin-Packing Problem. But, the scheme suggests that, asymptotically, the tours in an optimal solution will be of a very simple structure consisting of two parts. The first is the round trip the vehicle makes from the depot to the subregion (where the customers are located); we call these the *simple tours*. The second is the additional distance (we call this *insertion cost*) accrued by visiting each of the customers it serves in the subregion. Our goal is therefore to construct a heuristic that assigns customers to vehicles so as to minimize the sum of the length of all simple tours plus the total insertion costs of customers into each simple tour. If done carefully, the solution obtained is asymptotically optimal.

To construct such a heuristic we formulate the routing problem as another combinatorial problem commonly called (see, e.g., Pirkul (1987)) the single-source Capacitated Facility Location Problem (CFLP). This problem can be described as follows: given m possible sites for facilities of fixed capacity Q, we would like to locate facilities at a subset of these m sites and assign n retailers, where retailer i demands w_i units of a facility's capacity, in such a way that each retailer is assigned to *exactly one* facility, the facility capacities are not exceeded and the total cost is minimized. A site-dependent cost is incurred for locating each facility; that is, if a facility is located at site j, the *set-up* cost is v_j, for $j = 1, 2, \ldots, m$. The cost of assigning retailer i to facility j is c_{ij} (the *assignment* cost), for $i = 1, 2, \ldots, n$ and $j = 1, 2, \ldots, m$.

The single-source CFLP can be formulated as the following integer linear program. Let

$$y_j = \begin{cases} 1, & \text{if a facility is located at site } j, \\ 0, & \text{otherwise,} \end{cases}$$

and let

$$x_{ij} = \begin{cases} 1, & \text{if retailer } i \text{ is assigned to a facility at site } j, \\ 0, & \text{otherwise.} \end{cases}$$

Problem CFLP : Min $\displaystyle\sum_{i=1}^{n} \sum_{j=1}^{m} c_{ij} x_{ij} + \sum_{j=1}^{m} v_j y_j$

$$s.t. \qquad \sum_{j=1}^{m} x_{ij} = 1, \qquad \forall i \qquad (6.8)$$

$$\sum_{i=1}^{n} w_i x_{ij} \leq Q, \qquad \forall j \qquad (6.9)$$

$$x_{ij} \leq y_j, \qquad \forall i, j \qquad (6.10)$$

$$x_{ij} \in \{0, 1\}, \qquad \forall i, j \qquad (6.11)$$

$$y_j \in \{0, 1\}, \qquad \forall j. \qquad (6.12)$$

Constraints (6.8) ensure that each retailer is assigned to exactly one facility, and constraints (6.9) ensure that the facility's capacity constraint is not violated. Constraints (6.10) guarantee that if a retailer is assigned to site j, then a facility is located at that site. Constraints (6.11) and (6.12) ensure the integrality of the variables.

In formulating the UCVRP as an instance of the CFLP, we set every customer x_j in the UCVRP as a possible facility site in the location problem. The length of the simple tour that starts at the depot visits customer x_j and then goes back to the depot is the set-up cost in the location problem (i.e., $v_j = 2d_j$). Finally, the cost of inserting a customer into a simple tour in the UCVRP is the assignment cost in the location problem (i.e., $c_{ij} = d_i + d_{ij} - d_j$). This cost should represent the added cost of inserting customer i into a simple tour through the depot and customer j. Consequently, when i is added to a tour with j, the added cost is $c_{ij} = d_i + d_{ij} - d_j$, so that $v_j + c_{ij} = d_i + d_{ij} + d_j$. However, when a third customer is added, the calculation is not so simple, and therefore the values of c_{ij} should in fact represent an *approximation* to the cost of adding i to a tour that goes through customer j and the depot. Hence, finding a solution for the CVRP is obtained by solving the CFLP with the data as described above. The solution obtained from the CFLP is transformed (in an obvious way) to a solution to the CVRP.

Although $\mathcal{NP}$-Hard, the CFLP can efficiently, but approximately, be solved by the familiar Lagrangian relaxation technique (see Chapter 12), as described in Pirkul or Bramel and Simchi-Levi (1995) or by a cutting-plane algorithm, as described in Deng and Simchi-Levi (1992).

We can now describe the Location-Based Heuristic (LBH):

The Location-Based Heuristic

Step 1: Formulate the UCVRP as an instance of the CFLP.

Step 2: Solve the CFLP.

Step 3: Transform the solution obtained in Step 2 into a solution for the UCVRP.

Variations of the LBH can also be applied to other problems; we discuss this and related issues in the next chapter where we consider a more general vehicle routing problem.

The LBH algorithm was tested on a set of 11 standard test problems taken from the literature. The problems are in the Euclidean plane and they vary in size from 15 to 199 customers. The performance of the algorithm on these test problems was found to be comparable to the performance of most published heuristics. This includes both the running time of the algorithm as well as the quality (value) of the solutions found; see Bramel and Simchi-Levi (1995) for a detailed discussion.

One way to explain the excellent performance of the LBH is by analyzing its average performance. Indeed, a proof similar to the proof of Theorem 6.4.1 reveals (see also Bramel and Simchi-Levi (1995)) that,

Theorem 6.7.1 *Under the assumptions of Theorem 6.4.1, there are versions of the LBH that are asymptotically optimal; that is,*

$$\lim_{n \to \infty} \frac{1}{n} Z^{\text{LBH}} = 2\gamma E(d) \qquad (a.s).$$

Finally, we observe that the Generalized Assignment Heuristic due to Fisher and Jaikumar (1981) can be viewed as a special case of the LBH in which the seed customers are selected by a dispatcher. In the second step, customers are assigned to the seeds in an efficient way by solving a generalized assignment problem. The advantage of the LBH is that the selection of the seeds and the assignment of customers to seeds are done simultaneously, and not sequentially as in the Generalized Assignment Heuristic. Note that neither of these heuristics (the LBH or the Generalized Assignment Heuristic) requires that potential seed points be customer locations; both can be easily implemented to start with seed points that are simply points on the plane. A byproduct of the analysis, therefore, is that when the Generalized Assignment Heuristic is carefully implemented (i.e., "good" seeds are selected), it is asymptotically optimal as well.

6.8   Rate of Convergence to the Asymptotic Value

While the results in the two previous sections completely characterize the asymptotic optimal solution value of the UCVRP, they do not say anything about the rate of convergence to the asymptotic solution value. See Psaraftis (1984) for an informal discussion of this issue.

To get some intuition on the rate of convergence, it is interesting to determine the expected difference between the optimal solution for a given number of customers n, and the asymptotic solution value (i.e., $2\gamma E[d]$). This can be done for the uniform model discussed in Section 6.6.

In this case, Bramel et al. (1991) and, independently, Rhee (1991) proved the following strong result.

Theorem 6.8.1 *Let x_k $k = 1, 2, \ldots, n$ be a sequence of independent random variables uniformly distributed in the unit square $[0, 1]^2$. Let the demands w_k, $k = 1, 2, \ldots, n$ be drawn independently from a uniform distribution on $(0, 1]$. Then*

$$E[Z_n^*] = nE[d] + \Theta(n^{2/3}).$$

The proof of Theorem 6.8.1 relies heavily on the theory of three-dimensional stochastic matching which is outside the scope of our survey. We refer the reader to Coffman and Lueker (1991, Chapter 3) for an excellent review of matching problems.

Rhee has also found an upper bound on the rate of convergence to the asymptotic solution value, for general distribution of the customers' locations and their demands. Using a new matching theorem developed together with Talagrand, she proved:

Theorem 6.8.2 *Under the assumptions of Theorem 6.4.1, we have*

$$2n\gamma E[d] \leq E[Z_n^*] \leq 2n\gamma E[d] + O((n \log n)^{2/3}).$$

6.9   Exercises

Exercise 6.1. Consider the following heuristic for the CVRP with unequal demands. All customers of demand $w_i > \frac{1}{2}$ are served individually, one customer per vehicle. To serve the rest, apply the UITP heuristic with vehicle capacity Q. Prove that this solution can be transformed into a feasible solution to the CVRP with unequal demands. What is the worst-case bound of this heuristic?

Exercise 6.2. Prove Corollary 6.5.3.

Exercise 6.3. Given a seed point i, assume you must estimate the cost of the optimal traveling salesman tour through a set of points $S \cup \{i\}$ using the following cost approximation. Starting with $2d_i$, when each point j is added to the tour, add the cost $c_{ij} = d_j + d_{ij} - d_i$. That is, show that for any $r \geq 1$ there is an example where the approximation is r times the optimal cost.

Exercise 6.4. Construct an example of the single-source CFLP where each facility is a potential site (and vice versa) in which an optimal solution chooses a facility but the demand of that facility is assigned to another chosen site.

Exercise 6.5. Show that Lemma 6.4.5 can be replaced by an equality instead of an inequality.

Exercise 6.6. Prove that the version of the LBH with set-up costs $v_j = 2d_j$ and assignment costs $c_{ij} = d_i + d_{ij} - d_j$ is asymptotically optimal.

Exercise 6.7. Explain why the following constraints can or cannot be integrated into the Savings Algorithm.

(a) *Distance constraint.* Each route must be at most λ miles long.

(b) *Minimum route size.* Each route must pick up at least m points.

(c) *Mixing constraints.* Even indexed points cannot be on the same route as odd indexed points.

Exercise 6.8. Consider an instance of the CVRP with n customers. A customer is red with probability p and blue with probability $1 - p$, for some $p \in [0, 1]$. Red customers have loads of size $\frac{2}{3}$, while blue customers have loads of size $\frac{1}{3}$. What is $\lim_{n \to \infty} \frac{Z^*}{n}$ as a function of p?

7

The VRP with Time Window Constraints

7.1 Introduction

In many distribution systems each customer specifies, in addition to the load that has to be delivered to it, a period of time, called a *time window*, in which this delivery must occur. The objective is to find a set of routes for the vehicles, where each route begins and ends at the depot, serves a subset of the customers without violating the vehicle capacity and time window constraints, while minimizing the total length of the routes. We call this model the Vehicle Routing Problem with Time Windows (VRPTW).

Due to the wide applicability and the economic importance of the problem, variants of it have been extensively studied in the vehicle routing literature; for a review see Solomon and Desrosiers (1988). Most of the work on the problem has focused on an empirical analysis while very few papers have studied the problem from an analytical point of view. This is done in an attempt to characterize the theoretical behavior of heuristics and to use the insights obtained to construct effective algorithms. Some exceptions are the recent works of Federgruen and van Ryzin (1992) and Bramel and Simchi-Levi (1996). Below we describe the results of the latter paper.

7.2 The Model

To formally describe the model we analyze here, let the index set of the n customers be denoted $N = \{1, 2, \dots, n\}$. Let $x_k \in I\!\!R^2$ be the location of customer $k \in N$.

Assume, without loss of generality, that the depot is at the origin and, by rescaling, that the vehicle capacity is 1 and that the length of the working day is 1. We assume vehicles can leave and return to the depot at any time. Associated with customer k is a quadruplet (w_k, e_k, s_k, l_k), called the customer *parameters*, which represents, respectively, the load that must be picked up, the earliest starting time for service, the time required to complete the service, called the *service time*, and the latest time service can end. Clearly, feasibility requires that $e_k + s_k \leq l_k$ and $w_k, e_k, l_k \in [0, 1]$, for each $k \in N$.

For any point $x \in I\!R^2$, let $\|x\|$ denote the Euclidean distance between x and the depot. Let $d_k \doteq \|x_k\|$ be the distance between customer k and the depot. Also, let $d_{jk} \doteq \|x_j - x_k\|$ be the distance between customer j and customer k. Let Z_t^* be the total distance traveled in an optimal solution to the VRPTW, and let Z_t^H be the total distance traveled in the solution provided by a heuristic H.

Consider the customer locations to be distributed according to a distribution μ with compact support in $I\!R^2$. Let the customer parameters $\{(w_k, e_k, s_k, l_k) : k \in N\}$ be drawn from a joint distribution Φ with a continuous density ϕ. Let C be the support of ϕ; that is, C is a subset of $\{(a_1, a_2, a_3, a_4) \in [0, 1]^4 : a_2 + a_3 \leq a_4\}$. Each customer is therefore represented by its location in the Euclidean plane along with a point in C. Finally, we assume that a customer's location and its parameters are *independent* of each other.

In our analysis we associate a *job* with each customer. The parameters of job k are the parameters of customer k, that is, (w_k, e_k, s_k, l_k), where w_k is referred to as the *load* of job k and, using standard scheduling terminology, e_k represents the earliest time job k can begin processing, s_k represents the processing time and l_k denotes the latest time the processing of the job can end. The value of e_k can be thought of as the *release time* of job k, that is, the time it is available for processing. The value of l_k represents the *due date* for the job. Each job can be viewed abstractly as simply a point in C. Occasionally, we will refer to customers and jobs interchangeably; this convenience should cause no confusion.

To any set of customers $T \subseteq N$ with parameters $\{(w_k, e_k, s_k, l_k) : k \in T\}$, we associate a corresponding *machine scheduling problem* as follows. Consider the set of jobs T and an infinite sequence of *parallel* machines. Job k becomes available for processing at time e_k and must be finished processing by time l_k. The objective in this scheduling problem is to assign each job to a machine such that (*i*) each machine has at most one job being processed on it at a given time, (*ii*) the processing time of each job starts no earlier than its release time and ends no later than its due date and (*iii*) the total load of all jobs assigned to a machine is no more than 1, and the number of machines used is minimized. In our discussion we refer to (*ii*) as the *job time window constraint* and to (*iii*) as the *machine load constraint*.

Scheduling problems have been widely studied in the operations research literature; see Lawler et al. (1993) and Pinedo (1995). Unfortunately, no paper has considered the scheduling problem in its general form with the objective function of minimizing the number of machines used.

Observe that in the absence of time window constraints, the scheduling problem is no more than a Bin-Packing Problem. Indeed, in that case the VRPTW reduces to the model analyzed in the previous chapter, the CVRP. Thus, our strategy is to try to relate the machine scheduling problem to the VRPTW in much the same way as we used results obtained for the Bin-Packing Problem in the analysis of the CVRP. As we shall shortly see, this is much more complex.

Let $M^*(S)$ be the minimum number of machines needed to schedule a set S of jobs. It is clear that this machine scheduling problem possesses the subadditivity property, described in Section 3.2. This implies that if M_n^* is the minimum number of machines needed to schedule a set of n jobs whose parameters are drawn independently from a distribution Φ, then there exists a constant $\gamma > 0$ (depending only on Φ) such that $\lim_{n\to\infty} M_n^*/n = \gamma$ (a.s.).

In this chapter we relate the solution to the VRPTW to the solution to the scheduling problem defined by the customer parameters. That is, we show that asymptotically the VRPTW is no more difficult to solve than the corresponding scheduling problem. Our main result is the following.

Theorem 7.2.1 *Let $x_1, x_2, \ldots, x_n$ be independently and identically distributed according to a distribution μ with compact support in $\mathbb{R}^2$, and define*

$$E(d) = \int_{\mathbb{R}^2} \|x\| d\mu(x).$$

Let the customer parameters $\{(w_k, e_k, s_k, l_k) : k \in N\}$ be drawn independently from Φ. Let M_n^* be the minimum number of machines needed to feasibly schedule the n jobs corresponding to these parameters, and $\lim_{n\to\infty} \frac{M_n^*}{n} = \gamma$ (a.s.). Then

$$\lim_{n\to\infty} \frac{1}{n} Z_t^* = 2\gamma E(d) \quad (a.s.).$$

We prove this theorem (in Section 7.3) by introducing a lower bound on the optimal solution value and then developing an upper bound that converges to the same value. The lower bound uses a similar technique to the one developed in Chapter 6. The upper bound can be viewed as a *randomized* algorithm that is guaranteed to generate a feasible solution to the problem. That is, different runs of the algorithm on the same data may generate different feasible solutions. In Section 7.4, we show that the analysis leads, in a natural way, to the development of a new deterministic algorithm which is asymptotically optimal for the VRPTW. Though not polynomial, computational evidence shows that the algorithm works very well on a set of standard test problems.

7.3 The Asymptotic Optimal Solution Value

We start the analysis by introducing a lower bound on the optimal objective function value Z_t^*. First, let A be the compact support of μ, and define $d_{\max} \doteq \sup\{\|x\| : x \in A\}$. Pick a fixed integer $r \geq 1$, and define $\underline{d}_j \doteq (j-1)\frac{d_{\max}}{r}$, for $j = 1, 2, \ldots, r$. Now define the sets:

$$F_j = \left\{ k \in N \mid \underline{d}_j < d_k \right\} \qquad \text{for } j = 1, 2, \ldots, r.$$

For any set $T \subseteq N$, let $M^*(T)$ be the minimum number of machines needed to feasibly schedule the set of jobs $\{(w_k, e_k, s_k, l_k) : k \in T\}$. The next lemma provides a deterministic lower bound on Z_t^* and is analogous to Lemma 6.4.3 developed for the VRP with capacity constraints.

Lemma 7.3.1

$$Z_t^* > 2 \frac{d_{max}}{r} \sum_{j=2}^{r} M^*(F_j).$$

Proof. Let V_j^* be the number of vehicles in an optimal solution to the VRPTW that serve a customer from F_j, for $j = 1, 2, \ldots, r$. By this definition, V_r^* is exactly the number of vehicles whose farthest customer visited is in F_r, and $V_j^* - V_{j+1}^*$ is exactly the number of vehicles whose farthest customer visited is in $F_j \setminus F_{j+1}$. Observe that if $V_j^* = V_{j+1}^*$, then there are no vehicles whose farthest customer visited is in $F_j \setminus F_{j+1}$. Consequently,

$$Z_t^* > 2\underline{d}_r V_r^* + \sum_{j=1}^{r-1} 2\underline{d}_j (V_j^* - V_{j+1}^*)$$

$$= 2\underline{d}_1 V_1^* + \sum_{j=2}^{r} 2(\underline{d}_j - \underline{d}_{j-1}) V_j^*$$

$$= 2 \frac{d_{max}}{r} \sum_{j=2}^{r} V_j^*.$$

We now claim that for each $j = 1, 2, \ldots, r$, $V_j^* \geq M^*(F_j)$. This should be clear from the fact that the set of jobs in F_j can be feasibly scheduled on V_j^* machines by scheduling the jobs at the times they are served in the VRPTW solution. ∎

We can now determine the asymptotic value of this lower bound. This can be done in a similar manner to that of Chapter 6, and hence we omit the proof here.

Lemma 7.3.2 *Under the conditions of Theorem 7.2.1*

$$\lim_{n \to \infty} \frac{1}{n} Z_t^* \geq 2\gamma E(d) \quad (a.s.).$$

We prove Theorem 7.2.1 by approximating the optimal cost from above by that of the following four-step heuristic. In the first step, we partition the region where the customers are distributed into subregions. In the second step, we randomly separate the customers of each subregion into two sets. Then for each subregion, we solve a machine scheduling problem defined on the customers in one of these sets. Finally, we use this schedule to specify how to serve all the customers in the subregion.

Pick an $\epsilon > 0$, and let δ be given by the definition of continuity of ϕ, that is, $\delta > 0$ is such that for all $x, y \in C$ with $||x - y|| < \delta$, we have $|\phi(x) - \phi(y)| < \epsilon$. Finally, pick a $\Delta < \min\{\frac{\delta}{\sqrt{2}}, \epsilon\}$.

Let $G(\Delta)$ be an infinite grid of squares of *diagonal* Δ, that is, of side $\frac{\Delta}{\sqrt{2}}$, with edges parallel to the system coordinates. Recall that A is the compact support of μ and let $A_1, A_2, \ldots, A_{t(\Delta)}$ be the subregions of $G(\Delta)$ that intersect A and have $\mu(A_i) > 0$.

Let $N(i)$ be the indices of the customers located in subregion A_i, and define $n(i) = |N(i)|$. For each customer $k \in N(i)$, with parameters (w_k, e_k, s_k, l_k), we associate a job with parameters $(w_k, e_k, s_k + \Delta, l_k + \Delta)$. For any set $T \subseteq N$ of customers, let $M_\Delta^*(T)$ be the minimum number of machines needed to feasibly schedule the set of jobs $\{(w_k, e_k, s_k + \Delta, l_k + \Delta) : k \in T\}$. In addition, for any set T of customers, let $T(i) = N(i) \cap T$, for $i = 1, 2, \ldots, t(\Delta)$.

For the given grid partition and for any set $T \subseteq N$ of customers, the following is a feasible way to serve the customers in N. All subregions are served separately; that is, no customers from different subregions are served by the same vehicle. In subregion A_i, we solve the machine scheduling problem defined by the jobs $\{(w_k, e_k, s_k + \Delta, l_k + \Delta) : k \in T(i)\}$. Then, for each machine in this scheduling solution, we associate a vehicle that serves the customers corresponding to the jobs on that machine. The customers are visited in the exact order they are processed on the machine, and they are served in exactly the same interval of time as they are processed. This is repeated for each machine of the scheduling solution. The customers of the set $N(i) \setminus T(i)$ are served one vehicle per customer. This strategy is repeated for every subregion, thus providing a solution to the VRPTW.

We will show that for a suitable choice of the set T, this routing strategy is asymptotically optimal for the VRPTW. An interesting fact about the set T is that it is a randomly generated set; that is, each time the algorithm is run it results in different sets T.

The first step is to show that, for any set $T \subseteq N$ (possibly empty), the solution produced by the above-mentioned strategy provides a feasible solution to the VRPTW. This should be clear from the fact that having an extra Δ units of time to travel between customers in a subregion is enough since all subregions have diagonal Δ. Therefore, any sets of customers scheduled on a machine together can be served together by one vehicle. Customers of $N(i) \setminus T$ can clearly be served within their time windows since they are served individually, one per vehicle.

We now proceed to find an upper bound on the value of this solution. For each subregion A_i, let $n_j(i)$ be the number of jobs on the jth machine in the optimal schedule of the jobs in $T(i)$, for each $j = 1, 2, \ldots, M_\Delta^*(T(i))$. Let $\underline{d}(i)$ be the distance from the depot to the closest customer in $N(i)$, that is, in subregion A_i. Using the routing strategy described above, the distance traveled by the vehicle serving the customers whose job was assigned to the jth machine of subregion A_i is no more than

$$2\underline{d}(i) + \Delta(n_j(i) + 1).$$

Therefore,

$$Z_t^* \le \sum_{i=1}^{t(\Delta)} \sum_{j=1}^{M_\Delta^*(T(i))} \left[2\underline{d}(i) + \Delta(n_j(i) + 1) \right] + \sum_{k \notin T} 2d_k$$

$$\le 2 \sum_{i=1}^{t(\Delta)} M_\Delta^*(T(i))\underline{d}(i) + 2n\Delta + \sum_{k \notin T} 2d_k.$$

Dividing by n and taking the limit we have

$$\overline{\lim_{n \to \infty}} \frac{1}{n} Z_t^* \le 2 \sum_{i=1}^{t(\Delta)} \overline{\lim_{n \to \infty}} \frac{1}{n} M_\Delta^*(T(i))\underline{d}(i) + 2\Delta + \overline{\lim_{n \to \infty}} \frac{1}{n} \sum_{k \notin T} 2d_k$$

$$= 2 \sum_{i=1}^{t(\Delta)} \overline{\lim_{n \to \infty}} \frac{n(i)}{n} \frac{M_\Delta^*(T(i))}{n(i)} \underline{d}(i) + 2\Delta + \overline{\lim_{n \to \infty}} \frac{1}{n} \sum_{k \notin T} 2d_k$$

$$\le 2 \sum_{i=1}^{t(\Delta)} \overline{\lim_{n \to \infty}} \frac{n(i)}{n} \overline{\lim_{n \to \infty}} \frac{M_\Delta^*(T(i))}{n(i)} \underline{d}(i) +$$

$$2\Delta + \overline{\lim_{n \to \infty}} \frac{1}{n} \sum_{k \notin T} 2d_k. \qquad (7.1)$$

In order to relate this quantity to the lower bound of Lemma 7.3.2, we must choose the set T appropriately. For this purpose, we make the following observation. Recall that ϕ is the continuous density associated with the distribution Φ. The customer parameters (w_k, e_k, s_k, l_k) of each of the customers of N are drawn randomly from the density ϕ. Associated with each customer is a job whose parameters are perturbed by Δ in the third and fourth coordinates, that is, $(w_k, e_k, s_k + \Delta, l_k + \Delta)$. This is equivalent to randomly drawing the job parameters from a density which we call ϕ'. The density ϕ' can be found simply by translating ϕ by Δ in the third and fourth coordinates, that is, for each $x = (\theta_1, \theta_2, \theta_3, \theta_4) \in I\!\!R^4$, $\phi'(x) = \phi'(\theta_1, \theta_2, \theta_3, \theta_4) = \phi(\theta_1, \theta_2, \theta_3 - \Delta, \theta_4 - \Delta)$. Finally, for each $x \in I\!\!R^4$, define $\psi(x) \doteq \min\{\phi(x), \phi'(x)\}$ and let $q \doteq \int_{I\!\!R^4} \psi < 1$.

The n jobs (or customer parameters) $\{y_k \doteq (w_k, e_k, s_k + \Delta, l_k + \Delta) : k \in N\}$ are drawn randomly from the density ϕ' and our task is to select the set $T \subseteq N$. To simplify presentation, we refer interchangeably to the index set of jobs and to the set of jobs itself; that is, $k \in N$ will have the same interpretation as $y_k \in N$ where $y_k \doteq (w_k, e_k, s_k + \Delta, l_k + \Delta)$.

For each job y_k, generate a random value, call it u_k, uniformly in $[0, \phi'(y_k)]$. The point $(y_k, u_k) \in I\!\!R^5$ is a point below the *graph* of ϕ'; that is, $u_k \le \phi'(y_k)$. Define T as the set of indices of jobs whose u_k value falls below the graph of ϕ; that is, $T \doteq \{k \in N : u_k \le \phi(y_k)\}$. Then the set of jobs $\{y_k : k \in T\}$ can be viewed as a random sample of $|T|$ jobs drawn randomly from the density $\frac{\psi}{q}$.

In order to relate this upper bound to the lower bound we need to present the following lemma.

Lemma 7.3.3 *For T generated as above and for each subregion A_i, $i = 1, 2, \ldots,$ $t(\Delta)$,*

$$\varlimsup_{n \to \infty} \frac{M_\Delta^*(T(i))}{n(i)} \leq \gamma, \qquad (a.s.).$$

Proof. To prove the result for a given subregion A_i, we construct a feasible schedule for the set of jobs $\{y_k = (w_k, e_k, s_k + \Delta, l_k + \Delta) : k \in T(i)\}$. Generate $n(i) - |T(i)|$ jobs randomly from the density

$$\frac{1}{1 - q}[\phi - \psi].$$

Call this set of jobs D, for *dummy* jobs. From the construction of the sets D and $T(i)$, it is a simple exercise to show that the parameters of the jobs in $D \cup T(i)$ are distributed like ϕ.

A feasible schedule of the jobs in $T(i)$ is obtained by optimally scheduling the jobs in $D \cup T(i)$ using, say M_i machines. The number of machines needed to schedule the jobs in $T(i)$ is obviously no more than M_i, since the jobs in D can simply be ignored. Thus we have the bound

$$M_\Delta^*(T(i)) \leq M_i.$$

Now dividing by $n(i)$ and taking the limits, we get

$$\varlimsup_{n \to \infty} \frac{M_\Delta^*(T(i))}{n(i)} \leq \varlimsup_{n \to \infty} \frac{M_i}{n(i)} = \gamma, \ (a.s.),$$

since the set of jobs $D \cup T(i)$ is just a set of $n(i)$ jobs whose parameters are drawn independently from the density ϕ. ∎

Lemma 7.3.3 thus reduces equation (7.1) to

$$\varlimsup_{n \to \infty} \frac{1}{n} Z_t^* \leq 2 \sum_{i=1}^{t(\Delta)} \gamma \varlimsup_{n \to \infty} \frac{n(i)}{n} \underline{d}(i) + 2\Delta + \varlimsup_{n \to \infty} \frac{1}{n} \sum_{k \notin T} 2d_k$$

$$= 2\gamma \varlimsup_{n \to \infty} \frac{1}{n} \sum_{i=1}^{t(\Delta)} n(i) \underline{d}(i) + 2\Delta + \varlimsup_{n \to \infty} \frac{1}{n} \sum_{k \notin T} 2d_k$$

$$\leq 2\gamma \varlimsup_{n \to \infty} \frac{1}{n} \sum_{k \in N} d_k + 2\Delta + \varlimsup_{n \to \infty} \frac{1}{n} \sum_{k \notin T} 2d_k$$

$$= 2\gamma E(d) + 2\Delta + \varlimsup_{n \to \infty} \frac{1}{n} \sum_{k \notin T} 2d_k$$

$$\leq 2\gamma E(d) + 2\Delta + 2d_{max} \varlimsup_{n \to \infty} \frac{1}{n} |N \setminus T|.$$

The next lemma determines an upper bound on $\varlimsup_{n \to \infty} \frac{1}{n} |N \setminus T|$.

Lemma 7.3.4 *Given $\epsilon > 0$ and T generated as above,*

$$\varlimsup_{n \to \infty} \frac{1}{n} |N \setminus T| < (1 + \epsilon)^2 \epsilon \qquad (a.s.).$$

Proof. By the Strong Law of Large Numbers, the limit is equal to the probability that a job of N is not in the set T. The probability of a particular job y_k *not* being in T is simply

$$
\begin{cases}
\frac{\phi'(y_k) - \phi(y_k)}{\phi'(y_k)}, & \text{if } \phi'(y_k) \geq \phi(y_k), \\
0, & \text{otherwise.}
\end{cases}
$$

Hence, almost surely

$$
\varlimsup_{n \to \infty} \frac{1}{n} |N \setminus T| = \int_{\mathbb{R}^4} \max\left\{ \frac{\phi'(x) - \phi(x)}{\phi'(x)}, 0 \right\} \phi'(x) dx
$$

$$
\leq \int_{\mathbb{R}^4} \left| \frac{\phi'(x) - \phi(x)}{\phi'(x)} \right| \phi'(x) dx
$$

$$
= \int_{\mathbb{R}^4} |\phi'(x) - \phi(x)| dx
$$

$$
= \int_{\mathbb{R}^4} |\phi'(\theta_1, \theta_2, \theta_3, \theta_4) - \phi(\theta_1, \theta_2, \theta_3, \theta_4)| d(\theta_1, \theta_2, \theta_3, \theta_4)
$$

$$
= \int_{\mathbb{R}^4} |\phi(\theta_1, \theta_2, \theta_3 - \Delta, \theta_4 - \Delta) - \phi(\theta_1, \theta_2, \theta_3, \theta_4)| d(\theta_1, \theta_2, \theta_3, \theta_4)
$$

$$
< (1 + \Delta)^2 \epsilon
$$

$$
< (1 + \epsilon)^2 \epsilon,
$$

where the second to last inequality follows from $\|(\theta_1, \theta_2, \theta_3 - \Delta, \theta_4 - \Delta) - (\theta_1, \theta_2, \theta_3, \theta_4)\| \leq \Delta \sqrt{2} < \delta$ and the continuity of ϕ. ∎

We now have all the necessary ingredients to finish the proof of Theorem 7.2.1; thus

$$
\varlimsup_{n \to \infty} \frac{1}{n} Z_t^* \leq 2\gamma E(d) + 2d_{\max}(1 + \epsilon)^2 \epsilon + 2\Delta \qquad (a.s.).
$$

Since ϵ was arbitrary and recalling that $\Delta < \epsilon$, we have

$$
\varlimsup_{n \to \infty} \frac{1}{n} Z_t^* \leq 2\gamma E(d) \qquad (a.s.).
$$

This upper bound combined with the lower bound proves Theorem 7.2.1.

7.4   An Asymptotically Optimal Heuristic

In this section we generalize the LBH heuristic developed for the CVRP (see Chapter 6) to handle time window constraints. Similarly to the original LBH we prove that the generalized version is asymptotically optimal for the VRPTW. We refer to this more general version of the heuristic also as the Location-Based Heuristic; this should cause no confusion.

7.4.1   The Location-Based Heuristic

The LBH can be viewed as a three-step algorithm. In the first step, the parameters of the VRPTW are transformed into data for a location problem called the Capacitated Vehicle Location Problem with Time Windows (CVLPTW), described below. This location problem is solved in the second step. In the final step, we transform the solution to the CVLPTW into a feasible solution to the VRPTW.

The Capacitated Vehicle Location Problem with Time Windows

The Capacitated Vehicle Location Problem with Time Windows (CVLPTW) is a generalization of the single-source Capacitated Facility Location Problem (see Section 6.7) and can be described as follows: we are given m possible sites to locate vehicles of capacity Q. There are n customers geographically dispersed in a given region, where customer i has w_i units of product that must be picked up by a vehicle. The pickup of customer i takes s_i units of time and must occur in the time window between times e_i and l_i; that is, the service of customer i can start at any time $t \in [e_i, l_i - s_i]$. The objective is to select a subset of the possible sites, to locate one vehicle at each site, and to assign the customers to the vehicles. Each vehicle must leave its site, pick up the load of customers assigned to it in such a way that the vehicle capacity is not exceeded and all pickups occur within the customer's time window, and then return to its site. The costs are as follows: a site-dependent cost is incurred for locating each vehicle; that is, if a vehicle is located at site j, the *set-up* cost is v_j, for $j = 1, 2, \ldots, m$. The cost of assigning customer i to the vehicle at site j is c_{ij} (the *assignment* cost), for $i = 1, 2, \ldots, n$ and $j = 1, 2, \ldots, m$. We assume that there are enough vehicles and sites so that a feasible solution exists.

The CVLPTW can be formulated as the following mathematical program. Let

$$y_j = \begin{cases} 1, & \text{if a vehicle is located at site } j, \\ 0, & \text{otherwise,} \end{cases}$$

and let

$$x_{ij} = \begin{cases} 1, & \text{if customer } i \text{ is assigned to the vehicle at site } j, \\ 0, & \text{otherwise.} \end{cases}$$

For any set $S \subseteq N$, let $f_j(S) = 1$ if the set of customers S can be feasibly served in their time windows by one vehicle that starts and ends at site j (disregarding the capacity constraint), and 0 otherwise.

$$\text{Problem } P : Min \quad \sum_{i=1}^{n} \sum_{j=1}^{m} c_{ij} x_{ij} + \sum_{j=1}^{m} v_j y_j$$

$$s.t. \quad \sum_{j=1}^{m} x_{ij} = 1, \qquad \forall i \qquad (7.2)$$

$$\sum_{i=1}^{n} w_i x_{ij} \leq Q, \qquad \forall j \qquad (7.3)$$

$$x_{ij} \leq y_j, \qquad \forall i, j \qquad (7.4)$$

$$f_j(\{i : x_{ij} = 1\}) = 1, \quad \forall j \qquad (7.5)$$

$$x_{ij}, y_j \in \{0, 1\}, \qquad \forall i, j. \qquad (7.6)$$

Constraints (7.2) ensure that each customer is assigned to exactly one vehicle, and constraints (7.3) ensure that the vehicle's capacity constraint is not violated. Constraints (7.4) guarantee that if a customer is assigned to the vehicle at site j, then a vehicle is located at that site. Constraints (7.5) ensure that the time window constraints are not violated. Constraints (7.6) ensure the integrality of the variables.

The Heuristic

To relate the CVLPTW to the VRPTW, consider each customer in the VRPTW to be a potential site for a vehicle; that is, the set of potential sites is exactly the set of customers, and therefore $m = n$. Picking a subset of the sites in the CVLPTW corresponds to picking a subset of the customers in the VRPTW; we call this set of selected customers the *seed* customers. These customers are those that will form simple tours with the depot.

In order for the LBH to perform well, the costs of the CVLPTW should approximate the costs of the VRPTW. The set-up cost for locating a vehicle at site j (v_j) or, in other words, of picking customer j as a seed customer, should be the cost of sending a vehicle from the depot to customer j and back (i.e., the length of the simple tour). Hence, we set $v_j = 2d_j$ for each $j \in N$. The assignment cost c_{ij} is the cost of assigning customer i to the vehicle at site j. Therefore, this cost should represent the added cost of inserting customer i into the simple tour through the depot and customer j. Consequently, when i is added to a tour with j, the added cost is $c_{ij} = d_i + d_{ij} - d_j$, so that $v_j + c_{ij} = d_i + d_{ij} + d_j$. This cost is exact for two and sometimes three customers. However, as the number of customers increases, the values of c_{ij} in fact represent an *approximation* to the cost of adding i to a tour that goes through customer j and the depot. In Section 7.4.3 we present values of c_{ij} that we have found to work well in practice.

Once these costs are determined the second step of the LBH consists of solving CVLPTW. The solution provided is a set of sites (seed customers) and a set of customers assigned to each of these sites (to each seed). This solution can then be easily transformed into a solution to the VRPTW, since a set of customers that can be feasibly served starting from site j can also be feasibly served starting from the depot.

7.4.2   A Solution Method for CVLPTW

The computational efficiency of the LBH depends on the efficiency with which CVLPTW can be solved. We therefore present a method to solve the CVLPTW.

As discussed earlier, the CVLPTW without constraints (7.5) is simply the single-source Capacitated Facility Location Problem (CFLP) for which efficient solution methods exist based on the celebrated Lagrangian relaxation technique; see Section 4.3. For the CVLPTW, we use a similar method, although the specifics are more complex in view of the existence of these time window constraints.

In this case, for a given multiplier vector $\lambda \in \mathbb{R}^n$, constraints (7.2) are relaxed and put into the objective function with the multiplier vector. The resulting problem can be separated into n subproblems (one for each of the n sites), since constraints (7.2) are the only constraints that relate the sites to one another. The subproblem for site j is:

$$\text{Problem } P_j : Min \quad \sum_{i=1}^{n} \overline{c}_{ij} x_{ij} + v_j y_j$$

$$s.t. \quad \sum_{i=1}^{n} w_i x_{ij} \leq Q$$

$$x_{ij} \leq y_j, \qquad \forall i$$

$$f_j(\{i : x_{ij} = 1\}) = 1$$

$$x_{ij} \in \{0, 1\} \ \forall i \text{ and } y_j \in \{0, 1\},$$

where $\overline{c}_{ij} \doteq c_{ij} + \lambda_i$, for each $i \in N$.

In the optimal solution to problem P_j, y_j is either 0 or 1. If $y_j = 0$, then $x_{ij} = 0$ for all $i \in N$, and the objective function value is 0. If $y_j = 1$, then the problem reduces to a different, but simpler, routing problem. Consider a vehicle of capacity Q initially located at site j. The driver gets a profit of $p_{ij} \doteq -\overline{c}_{ij}$ for picking up the w_i items at customer i in the time window (e_i, l_i). The pickup operation takes s_i units of time. The objective is to choose a subset of the customers, to pick up their loads in their time windows, without violating the capacity constraint, using a vehicle which must begin and end at site j, while maximizing the driver's profit. Let G_j^* be the maximum profit attainable at site j; that is, G_j^* is the optimal solution to the problem just described for site j. This implies that $v_j - G_j^*$ is the optimal solution value of Problem P_j given that $y_j = 1$. Therefore, we can write the optimal solution to Problem P_j as simply $\min\{0, v_j - G_j^*\}$.

Unfortunately, in general, determining the values G_j^* for $j \in N$ is $\mathcal{NP}$-Hard. We can, however, determine upper bounds on G_j^*; call them G_j. This provides a *lower bound* on the optimal solution to problem P_j which is equal to $\min\{0, v_j - G_j\}$. We use the simple bound given by $G_j \doteq \sum_{\{i:p_{ij}>0\}} p_{ij}$. Consequently, $\sum_{j=1}^{n} \min\{0, v_j - G_j\} - \sum_{i=1}^{n} \lambda_i$ is a lower bound on the optimal solution to the CVLPTW.

To generate a feasible solution to the VRPTW at each iteration of the procedure, we use information from the upper bounds on profit G_j for $j \in N$. After every iteration of the lower bound (for each multiplier) we renumber the sites so that $G_1 \geq G_2 \geq \cdots \geq G_n$. The upper bounds on profit are used as an estimate of the profitability of placing a vehicle at a particular site. For example, site 1 is considered to be a "good" site (or seed customer), since a large profit is possible there. A large profit for site j corresponds to a seed customer where neighboring customers can be feasibly served from it at *low cost*. Therefore, a site with large profit is selected as a seed customer since it will tend to have neighboring customers around it that can be feasibly served by a vehicle starting at that site.

To generate a feasible solution to CVLPTW, we do the following: starting with $j = 1$ in the new ordering of the sites (customers), we locate a vehicle at site j. For every customer still not assigned to a site, we first determine if this customer can be feasibly served with the customers that are currently assigned to site j. Then, of the customers that can be served from this site, we determine the one that will cause the least increase in cost, that is, the one with minimum c_{ij} over all customers i that can be served from this site. We then assign this customer to the site. We continue until no more customers can be assigned to site j, due to capacity or time constraints. We then increment j to 2 and continue with site 2. After all customers have been feasibly assigned to a site, we obtain a feasible solution whose cost is compared to the cost of the current best solution.

As we find solutions to the CVLPTW, we also generate feasible solutions to the VRPTW, using the information from the lower bound to CVLPTW. Starting with $j = 1$, pick customer j as a seed customer. Then, for every customer that can be feasibly served with this seed, we determine the added distance this would entail; that is, we determine the best place to insert the customer into the current tour through the customers assigned to seed j. We choose the customer that causes the least increase in distance traveled as the one to assign to seed j. This idea is similar to the Nearest Insertion heuristic discussed in Section 2.3.2. We then continue trying to add customers in this way to seed j. Once no more can be added to this tour (due to capacity or time constraints), we increment j to 2, select seed customer 2 and continue. Once every customer appears in a tour, that is, every customer is assigned to a seed, we have a feasible solution to the VRPTW corresponding to the current set of multipliers. The cost of this solution is compared to the cost of the current best solution.

Multipliers are updated using (4.6). The step size is initially set to 2 and halved after the lower bound has not improved in a series of 30 iterations. After the step size has reached a preset minimum (0.05), the heuristic is terminated.

7.4.3 Implementation

It is clear that many possible variations of the LBH can be implemented depending on the type of assignment costs (c_{ij}) used. In the computational results discussed below, the following have been implemented.

$$direct\ cost:\ c_{ij} = 2d_{ij}, \quad and$$

$$nearest\ insertion\ cost:\ c_{ij} = d_i + d_{ij} - d_j.$$

Direct cost c_{ij} has the advantage that, when several customers are added to the seed, the resulting cost, which is the sum of the set-up costs and these direct costs, is an upper bound on the length of any efficient route through the customers. On the other hand, the nearest insertion cost works well because it is accurate at least for tours through two customers, and often for tours through three customers as well.

Several versions of the LBH have been implemented and tested. In the first, the Star-Tours (ST) heuristic, the direct assignment cost is used, while in the second, the Seed-Insertion (SI) heuristic, the nearest insertion assignment cost is applied. Observe that the LBH is not a polynomial-time heuristic. However, as we shall shortly demonstrate, the running times reported on standard test problems are very reasonable and are comparable to the running times of many heuristics for the vehicle routing problem.

The ST heuristic is of particular interest because it is asymptotically optimal as demonstrated in the following lemma. The proof is similar to the previous proofs and is therefore omitted.

Lemma 7.4.1 *Let n customers, indexed by N, be independently and identically distributed according to a distribution μ with compact support in $\mathbb{R}^2$. Define*

$$E(d) = \int_{\mathbb{R}^2} ||x|| d\mu(x).$$

Let the customer parameters $\{(w_k, e_k, s_k, l_k) : k \in N\}$ be jointly distributed like Φ. In addition, let M_n^* be the minimum number of machines needed to feasibly schedule the jobs $\{(w_k, e_k, s_k, l_k) : k \in N\}$ and let $\lim_{n\to\infty} M_n^*/n = \gamma$, (a.s.). Then

$$\lim_{n\to\infty} \frac{1}{n} Z^{ST} = \lim_{n\to\infty} \frac{1}{n} Z_t^* = 2\gamma E(d) \qquad (a.s.).$$

7.4.4 Numerical Study

Tables 1 and 2 summarize the computational experiments with the standard test problems of Solomon (1986). The problem set consists of 56 problems of various types. All problems consist of 100 customers and one depot, and the distances are Euclidean. Problems with the "R" prefix are problems where the customer locations are randomly generated according to a uniform distribution. Problems with the "C" prefix are problems where the customer locations are clustered. Problems with the "RC" prefix are a mixture of both random and clustered. In addition, all the problems have a constraint on the latest time T_0 at which a vehicle can return to the depot. For a full description of these problems we refer the reader to Solomon.

We compare the performance of the LBH against the heuristics of Solomon and the column generation approach of Desrochers et al. (1992). The latter method was able to solve effectively 7 of the 56 test problems; we describe this approach in the next chapter.

Table 1

Problem	Alg. ST	CPU Time	Alg. SI	CPU Time	Solomon's Best Solution
C201	591.6	245.9s	591.6	260.5s	591
C202	* 652.8	276.1s	* 640.8	262.7s	731
C203	* 692.2	309.2s	* 741.1	308.9s	786
C204	* 721.6	335.9s	782.3	340.6s	758
C205	713.8	250.8s	699.9	258.8s	606
C206	770.8	257.3s	* 722.8	283.3s	730
C207	767.2	265.7s	708.9	275.8s	680
C208	736.2	287.7s	660.2	272.4s	607
R201	*1665.3	207.1s	*1533.4	209.6s	1741
R202	*1485.3	276.4s	*1484.3	248.5s	1730
R203	*1371.5	406.5s	*1349.3	389.0s	1567
R204	1096.7	532.0s	1077.0	538.2s	1059
R205	1472.3	287.0s	*1329.4	312.6s	1471
R206	*1237.0	412.2s	*1283.7	374.2s	1405
R207	*1217.7	484.8s	*1162.9	453.9s	1241
R208	* 966.1	587.8s	* 959.9	612.6s	1046
R209	*1276.1	394.8s	*1262.8	355.7s	1418
R210	*1312.5	380.7s	*1340.6	388.6s	1425
R211	1080.9	474.7s	1141.3	488.7s	1016
RC201	*1873.8	203.5s	*1841.7	185.8s	1880
RC202	*1742.1	227.8s	*1705.1	241.0s	1799
RC203	*1417.5	331.5s	*1471.1	300.1s	1550
RC204	*1139.6	437.7s	*1190.3	411.5s	1208
RC205	*1830.5	233.0s	*1878.9	214.0s	2080
RC206	1640.1	259.0s	1607.5	248.2s	1582
RC207	*1566.4	294.2s	*1557.3	272.3s	1632
RC208	1254.8	345.7s	1298.7	317.3s	1194

(* indicates that the LBH improves upon the best solution known.)

To compare the LBH to these solution methods, a time window reduction phase was implemented before the start of the heuristic. Here, the earliest time for service e_k is replaced by $\max\{e_k, d_k\}$; in that way, vehicles leave the depot no earlier than time 0. In addition, the latest time service can end l_k is replaced by $\min\{l_k, T_0 - d_k\}$. The LBH can then be run as it is described in Section 7.4.1.

As can be seen in the tables, both the ST and the SI heuristics have been implemented. CPU times are in seconds on a Sun SPARC Station II. In Tables 1 and 2, the column "Solomon's Best Solution" corresponds to the best solution found by Solomon. Solomon tested eight different heuristics on problem sets R1 and C1,

Table 2

Problem	Alg. ST	CPU Time	Alg. SI	CPU Time	Solomon's Best Solution	DDS Solution Value
C101	828.9	74.1s	828.9	67.0s	829	827.3
C102	982.8	82.9s	1043.4	73.1s	968	827.3
C103	*1015.1	95.9s	1232.9	88.4s	1026	
C104	* 980.9	105.4s	* 976.1	114.5s	1053	
C105	* 828.9	79.7s	860.8	67.3s	829	
C106	852.9	82.8s	880.1	66.7s	834	827.3
C107	828.9	83.1s	841.2	74.7s	829	827.3
C108	852.9	88.6s	853.6	80.9s	829	827.3
C109	991.0	88.6s	1014.5	83.1s	829	
R101	1983.7	57.2s	2071.2	39.9s	1873	1607.7
R102	1789.0	70.8s	1821.4	57.4s	1843	1434.0
R103	1594.5	88.6s	1599.1	67.9s	1484	
R104	1242.0	106.2s	1237.3	81.0s	1188	
R105	1604.4	67.0s	1696.2	52.0s	1502	
R106	1606.9	78.0s	1589.2	70.0s	1460	
R107	*1324.9	92.4s	1361.2	70.4s	1353	
R108	1202.6	107.5s	1205.5	101.1s	1134	
R109	1504.7	78.5s	1491.8	69.6s	1412	
R110	1380.9	92.0s	1434.4	69.4s	1211	
R111	1422.1	91.7s	1432.4	69.5s	1202	
R112	1248.1	105.2s	1284.6	79.4s	1086	
RC101	2045.1	60.6s	2014.4	45.0s	1867	
RC102	1806.6	68.7s	1969.5	52.2s	1760	
RC103	1708.9	81.7s	1716.3	69.6s	1641	
RC104	1372.1	93.5s	1458.8	79.5s	1301	
RC105	*1826.3	68.9s	2036.8	51.3s	1922	
RC106	1710.8	68.0s	1804.8	50.5s	1611	
RC107	1593.2	76.4s	1630.9	64.9s	1385	
RC108	1421.0	84.7s	1493.8	65.5s	1253	

(* indicates that the LBH improves upon the best solution known.)

and six heuristics on problems RC1, R2, C2 and RC2. We see that the ST heuristic provides a better solution than Solomon's heuristics in 25 of the 56 problems, while the SI heuristic provides a better solution in 21 of the 56 problems. In Table 2, the column "DDS Solution Value" corresponds to the value of the solution found using the column generation approach of Desrochers et al.

7.5 Exercises

Exercise 7.1. You are given a network $G = (V, A)$ where $|V| = n$, $d(i, j)$ is the length of edge (i, j) and a specified vertex $a \in V$. One service unit is located at a and has to visit each vertex in V so that total waiting time of all vertices is as small as possible. Assume the waiting time of a vertex is proportional to the total distance traveled by the server from a to the vertex. The total waiting time (summed up over all customers) is then:

$$(n - 1)d(a, 2) + (n - 2)d(2, 3) + (n - 3)d(3, 4) + \cdots + d(n - 1, n).$$

The Delivery Man Problem (DMP) is the problem of determining the tour that minimizes the total waiting time.

Assume that G is a tree with $d(i, j) = 1$ for every $(i, j) \in A$. Show that any tour that follows a depth-first search starting from a is optimal.

Exercise 7.2. Consider the Delivery Man Problem described in Exercise 7.1. A delivery man currently located at the depot must visit each of n customers. Let Z^{DM} be the total waiting time in the optimal delivery man tour through the n points. Let Z^* be the total time required to travel the optimal traveling salesman tour through the n points.

(a) Prove that

$$Z^{DM} \leq \left(\frac{n}{2}\right) Z^*.$$

(b) One heuristic proposed for this problem is the Nearest Neighbor (NN) Heuristic. In this heuristic, the vehicle serves the closest unvisited customer next. Provide a family of examples to show that the heuristic does not have a fixed worst-case bound.

Exercise 7.3. Consider the Vehicle Routing Problem with Distance Constraints. Formally, a set of customers has to be served by vehicles that are all located at a common depot. The customers and the depot are presented as the nodes of an undirected graph $G = (N, E)$. Each customer has to be visited by a vehicle. The jth vehicle starts from the depot and returns to the depot after visiting a subset $N_j \subseteq N$. The total distance traveled by the jth vehicle is denoted by T_j. Each vehicle has a distance constraint λ: no vehicle can travel more than λ units of distance (i.e., $T_j \leq \lambda$). We assume that the distance matrix satisfies the triangle inequality assumption. Also, assume that the length of the optimal traveling salesman tour through all the customers and the depot is greater than λ.

(a) Suppose the objective function is to minimize the total distance traveled. Let K^* be the number of vehicles in an optimal solution to this problem. Show that there always exists an optimal solution with total distance traveled $> \frac{1}{2} K^* \lambda$. Does this lower bound hold for any optimal solution?

(b) Consider the following greedy heuristic: start with the optimal traveling salesman tour through all the customers and the depot. In an arbitrary orientation of this tour, the nodes are numbered $(i_0, i_1, \ldots, i_n) \equiv S$ in order of appearance, where n = the number of customers, i_0 is the depot and $i_1, i_2, \ldots, i_n$ are the customers. We break the tour into K^H segments and connect the end-points of each segment to the depot. This is done in the following way. Each vehicle j, $1 \le j < K^H$ starts by traveling from the depot to the first customer i_q not visited by the previous $j - 1$ vehicles and then visits the maximum number of customers according to S without violating the distance constraint upon returning to the depot.

Show that $K^H \le \min\{n, \lceil \frac{T - 2d_m}{\lambda - 2d_m} \rceil\}$ where T is the length of the optimal traveling salesman tour and d_m is the distance from the depot to the farthest customer.

Exercise 7.4. Consider the Pickup and Delivery Problem. Here customers are pickup customers with probability p and delivery customers with probability $1 - p$. Assume a vehicle capacity of 1. If customer i is a pickup customer, then a load of size $w_i \le 1$ must be picked up at the customer and brought to the depot. If customer i is a delivery customer, then a load of size $w_i \le 1$ must be brought from the depot to the customer. Assume pickup sizes are drawn randomly from a distribution with bin-packing constant γ_P and delivery sizes are drawn randomly from a distribution with bin-packing constant γ_D. A pickup and a delivery can be in the vehicle at the same time.

(a) Develop a heuristic H for this problem and determine $\lim_{n \to \infty} \frac{Z^H}{n}$ as a function of p, γ_P and γ_D.

(b) Assume all pickups are of size $\frac{1}{3}$ and deliveries are of size $\frac{2}{3}$. Suggest a better heuristic for this case. What is $\lim_{n \to \infty} \frac{Z^H}{n}$ as a function of p for this heuristic?

8

Solving the VRP Using a Column Generation Approach

8.1 Introduction

A classical method, first suggested by Balinski and Quandt (1964), for solving the VRP with capacity and time window constraints is based on formulating the problem as a set-partitioning problem. (See Chapter 4 for a general discussion of set partitioning.) The idea is as follows: let the index set of all feasible routes be $\{1, 2, \ldots, R\}$ and let c_r be the length of route r. Define

$$\alpha_{ir} = \begin{cases} 1, & \text{if customer } i \text{ is served in route } r, \\ 0, & \text{otherwise,} \end{cases}$$

for each customer $i = 1, 2, \ldots, n$ and each route $r = 1, 2, \ldots, R$. Also, for every $r = 1, 2, \ldots, R$, let

$$y_r = \begin{cases} 1, & \text{if route } r \text{ is in the optimal solution,} \\ 0, & \text{otherwise.} \end{cases}$$

In the *Set-Partitioning formulation* of the VRP, the objective is to select a minimum cost set of feasible routes such that each customer is included in some route. It is:

$$\text{Problem } S: \quad Min \quad \sum_{r=1}^{R} c_r y_r$$

$$s.t. \quad \sum_{r=1}^{R} \alpha_{ir} y_r \geq 1, \quad \forall i = 1, 2, \ldots, n \qquad (8.1)$$

$$y_r \in \{0, 1\}, \quad \forall r = 1, 2, \ldots, R.$$

Observe that we have written constraints (8.1) as inequality constraints instead of equality constraints. The formulation with equality constraints is equivalent if we assume the distance matrix $\{d_{ij}\}$ satisfies the triangle inequality and therefore each customer will be visited *exactly* once in the optimal solution. The formulation with inequality constraints will prove to be easier to work with from an implementation point of view.

This formulation was first used successfully by Cullen et al. (1981) to design heuristic methods for the VRP. Recently, Desrochers et al. (1992) have used it in conjunction with a branch and bound method to generate optimal or near optimal solutions to the VRP. Similar methods have been used to solve crew scheduling problems, such as Hoffman and Padberg (1993).

Of course, the set of all feasible routes is extremely large and one cannot expect to generate it completely. Even if this set is given, it is not clear how to solve the set-partitioning problem since it is a large-scale integer program. Any method based on this formulation must overcome these two obstacles. We start, in Section 8.2, by showing how the linear relaxation of the set-partitioning problem can be solved to optimality without enumerating all possible routes. In Section 8.3, we combine this method with a polyhedral approach that generates an optimal or near-optimal solution to the VRP. Finally, in Section 8.4, we provide a probabilistic analysis that helps explain why a method of this type will be effective.

To simplify the presentation, we assume *no time window constraints exist*; the extension to the more general model is, for the most part, straightforward. The interested reader can find some of these extensions in Desrochers et al.

8.2   Solving a Relaxation of the Set-Partitioning Formulation

To solve the linear relaxation of Problem S without enumerating all the routes, Desrochers et al. use the celebrated column generation technique. A thorough explanation of this method is given below, but the general idea is as follows. A portion of all possible routes is enumerated, and the resulting linear relaxation with this partial route set is solved. The solution to this linear program is then used to determine if there are any routes not included that can reduce the objective function value. This is the *column generation* step. Using the values of the optimal dual variables (with respect to the partial route set), a new route is generated and the linear relaxation is resolved. This is continued until one can show that an optimal solution to the linear program is found, one that is optimal for the complete route set.

Specifically, this is done by enumerating a partial set of routes, $1, 2, \ldots, R'$, and formulating the corresponding linear relaxation of the set-partitioning problem with respect to this set:

$$\text{Problem } S' : \quad Min \quad \sum_{r=1}^{R'} c_r y_r$$

s.t.

$$\sum_{r=1}^{R'} \alpha_{ir} y_r \geq 1, \quad \forall i = 1, 2, \dots, n \quad (8.2)$$

$$y_r \geq 0, \quad \forall r = 1, 2, \dots, R'.$$

Let $\bar{y}$ be the optimal solution to Problem S', and let $\bar{\pi}$ be the corresponding optimal dual variables. We would like to know whether $\bar{y}$ (or equivalently, $\bar{\pi}$) is optimal for the linear relaxation of Problem S (respectively, the dual of the linear relaxation of Problem S). To answer this question observe that the dual of the linear relaxation of Problem S is

$$\text{Problem } S_D : \quad Max \quad \sum_{i=1}^{n} \pi_i$$

s.t.

$$\sum_{i=1}^{n} \alpha_{ir} \pi_i \leq c_r, \quad \forall r = 1, 2, \dots, R \quad (8.3)$$

$$\pi_i \geq 0, \quad \forall i = 1, 2, \dots, n.$$

Clearly, if $\bar{\pi}$ satisfies every constraint (8.3) then it is optimal for Problem S_D and therefore $\bar{y}$ is optimal for the linear programming relaxation of Problem S. How can we check whether $\bar{\pi}$ satisfies every constraint in Problem S_D? Observe that the vector $\bar{\pi}$ is not feasible in Problem S_D if we can identify a single constraint, r, such that

$$\sum_{i=1}^{n} \alpha_{ir} \bar{\pi}_i > c_r.$$

Consequently, if we can find a column r minimizing the quantity $c_r - \sum_i^n \alpha_{ir} \bar{\pi}_i$ and this quantity is negative, then a violated constraint is found. In that case the current vector $\bar{\pi}$ is not optimal for Problem S_D. The corresponding column just found can be added to the formulation of Problem S_P, which is solved again. The process repeats itself until no violated constraint (column) is found; in this case we have found the optimal solution to the linear relaxation of Problem S (the vector $\bar{y}$) and the optimal solution to Problem S_D (the vector $\bar{\pi}$).

Our task is then to find a column, or a route, r minimizing the quantity:

$$c_r - \sum_i^n \alpha_{ir} \bar{\pi}_i. \quad (8.4)$$

We can look at this problem in a different way. Suppose we replace each distance d_{ij} with a new distance d'_{ij} defined by

$$d'_{ij} \doteq d_{ij} - \frac{\bar{\pi}_i}{2} - \frac{\bar{\pi}_j}{2}.$$

Then a tour $u_1 \rightarrow u_2 \rightarrow \ldots \rightarrow u_\ell$ whose length using $\{d_{ij}\}$ is $\sum_{i=1}^{\ell-1} d_{u_i u_{i+1}} + d_{u_\ell u_1}$ has, using $\{d'_{ij}\}$, a length

$$\sum_{i=1}^{\ell-1} d'_{u_i u_{i+1}} + d'_{u_\ell u_1} = \sum_{i=1}^{\ell-1} d_{u_i u_{i+1}} + d_{u_\ell u_1} - \sum_{i=1}^{\ell} \pi_{u_i}.$$

Hence, finding a route r that minimizes (8.4) is the same as finding a tour of minimum length using the distance matrix $\{d'_{ij}\}$ that starts and ends at the depot, visits a subset of the customers, and has a total load no more than Q. Unfortunately, this itself is an $\mathcal{NP}$-Hard problem and so we are left with a method that is not attractive computationally.

To overcome this difficulty, the set-partitioning formulation, Problem S, is modified so as to allow routes visiting the same customer more than once. The purpose of this modification will be clear in a moment. This model, call it Problem S_M (where M stands for the "modified" formulation), is defined as follows. Enumerate all feasible routes, satisfying the capacity constraint, that may visit the same customer a number of times; each such visit increases the total load by the demand of that customer. Let the number of routes (columns) be R_M, and let c_r be the total distance traveled in route r. For each customer $i = 1, 2, \ldots, n$ and route $r = 1, 2, \ldots, R_M$, let

$$\xi_{ir} = \text{number of times customer } i \text{ is visited in route } r.$$

Also, for each $r = 1, 2, \ldots, R_M$, define

$$y_r = \begin{cases} 1, & \text{if route } r \text{ is in the optimal solution,} \\ 0, & \text{otherwise.} \end{cases}$$

The VRP can be formulated as:

$$\text{Problem } S_M : \quad \text{Min} \sum_{r=1}^{R_M} c_r y_r$$

$$\text{s.t.}$$

$$\sum_{r=1}^{R_M} \xi_{ir} y_r \geq 1, \quad \forall i = 1, 2, \ldots, n \qquad (8.5)$$

$$y_r \in \{0, 1\}, \quad \forall r = 1, 2, \ldots, R_M.$$

This is the set-partitioning problem solved by Desrochers et al. and therefore it is not exactly Problem S. Clearly, the optimal integer solution to Problem S_M is the optimal solution to the VRP. However, the optimal solution values of the linear relaxations of Problem S_M and Problem S may be different. Of course, the linear relaxation of Problem S_M provides a lower bound on the linear relaxation of Problem S.

To solve the linear relaxation of Problem S_M we use the method described above (for solving Problem S). We enumerate a partial set of R'_M routes; solve Problem

S'_M which is the linear relaxation of Problem S_M defined only on this partial list; use the dual variables to see whether there exists a column not in the current partial list with $\sum_{i=1}^{n} \xi_{ir} \overline{\pi}_i > c_r$. If there exists such a column(s), we add it (them) to the formulation and solve the resulting linear program again. Otherwise, we have the optimal solution to the linear relaxation of Problem S_M.

The modification we have made makes the column generation step computationally easier. This can now be found in pseudopolynomial time using dynamic programming.

For this purpose, we need the following definitions. Given a path $P = \{0, u_1, u_2, \ldots, u_\ell\}$, where it is possible that $u_i = u_j$ for $i \neq j$, let the load of this path be $\sum_{i=1}^{\ell} w_{u_i}$. That is, the load of the path is the sum, over all customers in P, of the demand of a customer multiplied by the number of times that customer appears in P. Let $f_q(i)$ be the cost (using $\{d'_{ij}\}$) of the least cost path that starts at the depot and terminates at vertex i with total load q. This can be calculated using the recursion

$$f_q(i) = \min_{j \neq i} \left\{ f_{q-w_i}(j) + d'_{ij} \right\}, \tag{8.6}$$

with the initial conditions

$$f_q(i) = \begin{cases} d'_{0i} & \text{if } q = w_i, \\ +\infty & \text{otherwise.} \end{cases}$$

Finally, let $f_q^0(i) = f_q(i) + d'_{0i}$. Thus, $f_q^0(i)$ is the length of a least cost tour that starts at the depot, visits a subset of the customers, of which customer i is the last to be visited, has a total load q and terminates at the depot. Observe that finding $f_q^0(i)$ for every q, $1 \leq q \leq Q$, and every i, $i \in N$, requires $O(n^2 Q)$ calculations. The recursion chooses the predecessor of i to be a node $j \neq i$. This requires repeat visits to the same customer to be separated by at least one visit to another customer. In fact, expanding the state space of this recursion can eliminate *two-loops*: loops of the type $\ldots i, j, i \ldots$. This forces repeat visits to the same customer to be separated by visits to at least *two* other customers. This can lead to a stronger relaxation of the set-partitioning model. For a more detailed discussion of this recursion, see Christofides et al. (1981).

If there exists a q, $1 \leq q \leq Q$ and i, $i \in N$ with $f_q^0(i) < 0$, then the current vectors $\overline{y}$ and $\overline{\pi}$ are not optimal for the linear relaxation of Problem S_M. In such a case we add the column corresponding to this tour (the one with negative $f_q^0(i)$) to the set of columns in Problem S'_M. If, on the other hand, $f_q^0(i) \geq 0$ for every q and i, then the current $\overline{y}$ and $\overline{\pi}$ are optimal for S_M.

To summarize, the column generation algorithm can be described as follows.

The Column Generation Procedure

Step 1: Generate an initial set of R'_M columns.

Step 2: Solve Problem S'_M and find $\overline{y}$ and $\overline{\pi}$.

Step 3: Construct the distance matrix $\{d'_{ij}\}$ and find $f_i^0(q)$ for all $i \in N$ and $1 \leq q \leq Q$.

Step 4: For every i and q with $f_i^0(q) < 0$, add the corresponding column to R'_M and go to *Step 2*.

Step 5: If $f_i^0(q) \geq 0$ for all i and q, stop.

The procedure produces a vector $\bar{y}$ which is the optimal solution to the linear relaxation of Problem S_M. This is a *lower bound* on the optimal solution to the VRP.

8.3   Solving the Set-Partitioning Problem

In the previous section we introduced an effective method for solving the linear relaxation of the set-partitioning formulation of the VRP, Problem S_M. How can we use this solution to the linear program to find an optimal or near-optimal integer solution?

Starting with the set of columns present at the end of the column generation step (the set E), one approach to generating an integer solution to the set-partitioning formulation is to use the method of *branch and bound*. This method consists of splitting the problem into easier subproblems by fixing the value of a *branching* variable. The variable (in this case a suitable choice is y_r for some route r) is either set to 1 or 0. Each of these subproblems is solved using the same method; that is, another variable is branched. At each step, tests are performed to see if the entire branch can be eliminated; that is, no better solution than the one currently known can be found in this branch. The solution found by this method will be the best integer solution among all the solutions in E. This solution will not necessarily be the optimal solution to the VRP, but it may be close.

Another approach that will generate the same integer solution as the branch and bound method is the following. Given a fractional solution to S_M, we can generate a set of constraints that will cut off this fractional solution. Then we can resolve this linear program and if it is integer, we have found the optimal integer solution (among the columns of E). If it is still fractional, then we can continue generating constraints and resolving the linear program until an integer solution is found. Again, the best integer solution found using this method may be close to optimal. This is the method successfully used by Hoffman and Padberg (1993) to solve crew-scheduling problems.

Formally, the method is as follows.

The Cutting Plane Algorithm

Step 1: Generate an initial set of R'_M columns.

Step 2: Solve, using column generation, Problem S'_M.

Step 3: If the optimal solution to Problem S'_M is integer, stop.
    Else, generate cutting planes separating this solution.
        Add these cutting planes to the linear program S'_M.

Step 4: Solve the linear program S'_M. Goto *Step 3*.

To illustrate this constraint generation step (*Step 3*), we make use of a number of observations. First, let E be the set of routes at the end of the column generation procedure. Clearly, we can split E into two subsets. One subset E_m includes every column r for which there is at least one i with $\xi_{ir} \geq 2$; these columns are called *multiple visit columns*. The second subset E_s includes the remaining columns; these columns are referred to as *single visit columns*. It is evident that an optimal solution to the VRP will use no columns from E_m. That is, there always exists a single visit column of at most the same cost that can be used instead. We therefore can immediately add the following constraint to the linear relaxation of Problem S_M.

$$\sum_{r \in E_m} y_r = 0. \tag{8.7}$$

To generate more constraints, construct the *intersection* graph G. The graph G has a node for each column in E_s. Two nodes in G are connected by an edge if the corresponding columns have at least one customer in common. Observe that a solution to the VRP where no customer is visited more than once can be represented by an *independent set* in this graph. That is, it is a collection of nodes on the graph G such that no two nodes are connected by an edge.

These observations give rise to two inequalities that can be added to the formulation.

1. We select a subset of the nodes of G, say K, such that every pair of nodes $i, j \in K$ are connected by an edge of G. Each set K, called a *clique*, must satisfy the following condition.

$$\sum_{r \in K} y_r \leq 1. \tag{8.8}$$

Clearly, if there is a node $j \notin K$ such that j is adjacent to every $i \in K$, then we can replace K with $K \cup \{j\}$ in inequality (8.8) to strengthen it (this is called *lifting*). In that sense we would like to use inequality (8.8) when the set of nodes K is *maximal* in that sense.

2. Define a cycle $C = \{u_1, u_2, \ldots, u_\ell\}$ in G, such that node u_i is adjacent to u_{i+1}, for each $i = 1, 2, \ldots, \ell - 1$, and node u_ℓ is adjacent to node u_1. A cycle C is called an odd cycle if the number of nodes in C, $|C| = \ell$, is odd. An odd cycle is called an *odd hole* if there is no arc connecting two nodes of the cycle except the ℓ arcs defining the cycle. It is easy to see that in any optimal solution to the VRP each odd hole must satisfy the following property.

$$\sum_{r \in C} y_r \leq \frac{|C| - 1}{2}. \tag{8.9}$$

8.3.1 Identifying Violated Clique Constraints

Hoffman and Padberg suggest several procedures for clique identification, one of which is based on the fact that small size problems can be solved quickly by enumeration. For this purpose, select v to be the node with minimum degree among all nodes of G. Clearly, every clique of G containing v is a subset of the neighbors of v, denoted by $neigh(v)$. Thus, starting with v as a temporary clique, that is, $K = \{v\}$, we add an arbitrary node w from $neigh(v)$ to K. We now delete from $neigh(v)$ all nodes that are not connected to a node of K, in this case either v or w. Continue adding nodes in this manner from the current set $neigh(v)$ to K until either there is no node in $neigh(v)$ connected to all nodes in K, or $neigh(v) = \emptyset$. In the end, K will be a maximal clique. We can then calculate the *weight* of this clique, that is, the sum of the values (in the linear program) of the columns in the clique. If the weight is more than one, then the corresponding clique inequality is violated. If not, then we continue the procedure with a new starting node. The method can be improved computationally by, for example, always choosing the "heaviest" among those nodes eligible to enter the clique.

8.3.2 Identifying Violated Odd Hole Constraints

Hoffman and Padberg use the following procedure to identify violated odd hole constraints. Suppose $\bar{y}$ is the current optimal solution to the linear program and G is the corresponding intersection graph. Starting from an arbitrary node $v \in G$, construct a *layered graph* $G_\ell(v)$ as follows. The node set of $G_\ell(v)$ is the same as the node set of G. Every neighbor of v in G is connected to v by an edge in $G_\ell(v)$. We refer to v as the root, or level 0 node, and we refer to the neighbors of v as level 1 nodes. Similarly, nodes at level $k \geq 2$ are those nodes in G that are connected (in G) to a level $k - 1$ node but are not connected to any node at level $< k - 1$. Finally, each edge (u_i, u_j) in $G_\ell(v)$ is assigned a length of $1 - \bar{y}_{u_i} - \bar{y}_{u_j} \geq 0$.

Now pick a node u in $G_\ell(v)$ at level $k \geq 2$ and find the shortest path from u to v in $G_\ell(v)$. Delete all nodes at levels i ($1 \leq i < k$) that are either on the shortest path or adjacent to nodes along this shortest path (other than nodes that are adjacent to v). Now pick another node w that is adjacent (in G) to u in level k. Find the shortest path from w to v in the current graph $G_\ell(v)$. Combining these two paths with the arc (u, w) creates an odd hole. If the total length of this cycle is less than 1, then we have found a violated odd hole inequality. If not, we continue with another neighbor of u and repeat the process. We can then choose a node different from u at level k. If no violated odd hole inequality is found at level k, we proceed to level $k + 1$. This subroutine can be repeated for different starting nodes (v) as well.

8.4   The Effectiveness of the Set-Partitioning Formulation

The effectiveness of this algorithm depends crucially on the quality of the initial lower bound; this lower bound is the optimal solution to the linear relaxation of Problem S_M. If this lower bound is not very tight, then the branch and bound or the constraint generation methods will most likely not be computationally effective. On the other hand, when the gap between the lower bound and the best integer solution is small, the procedure will probably be effective.

Fortunately, many researchers have reported that the linear relaxation of the set-partitioning problem, Problem S_M, provides a solution close to the optimal integer solution (see, e.g., Desrochers et al. (1992)). That is, the solution to the linear relaxation of Problem S_M provides a very tight lower bound on the solution of the VRP. For instance, in their paper, Desrochers et al. report an average relative gap between the optimal solution to the linear relaxation and the optimal integer solution of only 0.733%. A possible explanation for this observation is embodied in the following theorem which states that asymptotically the relative error between the optimal solution to the linear relaxation of the set-partitioning model and the optimal integer solution goes to zero as the number of customers increases. Consider again the general VRP with capacity and time window constraints.

Theorem 8.4.1 *Let the customer locations $x_1, x_2, \ldots, x_n$ be a sequence of independent random variables having a distribution μ with compact support in $\mathbb{R}^2$. Let the customer parameters (see Chapter 7) be independently and identically distributed like Φ. Let Z^{LP} be the value of the optimal fractional solution to S, and let Z^* be the value of the optimal integer solution to S; that is, the value of the optimal solution to the VRP. Then*

$$\lim_{n \to \infty} \frac{1}{n} Z^{LP} = \lim_{n \to \infty} \frac{1}{n} Z^* \quad (a.s.).$$

The theorem thus implies that the optimal solution value of the linear programming relaxation of Problem S tends to the optimal solution of the vehicle routing problem as the number of customers tends to infinity. This is important since, as shown by Bramel and Simchi-Levi (1994) other classical formulations of the VRP can lead to diverging linear and integer solution values (see Exercise 8.8).

In the next section we motivate Theorem 8.4.1 by presenting a simplified model which captures the essential ideas of the proof. Finally, in Section 8.4.2 we provide a formal proof of the theorem. Again, to simplify the presentation, we assume no time window constraints exist; for the general case, the interested reader is referred to Bramel and Simchi-Levi (1994).

8.4.1   Motivation

Define a customer type to be a location $x \in \mathbb{R}^2$ and a customer demand w; that is, a customer type defines the customer location and a value for the customer demand.

Consider a *discretized* vehicle routing model in which there is a finite number W of customer types, and a finite number m of distinct customer locations. Let n_i be the number of customers of type i, for $i = 1, 2, \ldots, W$ and let $n = \sum_{i=1}^{W} n_i$ be the total number of customers. Clearly, this discretized vehicle routing problem can be solved by formulating it as a set-partitioning problem. To obtain some intuition about the linear relaxation of S, we introduce another formulation of the vehicle routing problem closely related to S.

Let a *vehicle assignment* be a vector $(a_1, a_2, \ldots, a_W)$, where $a_i \geq 0$ are integers, and such that a single vehicle can feasibly serve a_1 customers of type 1, and a_2 customers of type $2, \ldots,$ and a_W customers of type W together without violating the vehicle capacity constraint. Index all the possible vehicle assignments $1, 2, \ldots, R_a$ and let c_r be the total length of the shortest feasible route serving the customers in vehicle assignment r. (Note that R_a is independent of n.) The vehicle routing problem can be formulated as follows. Let

$$A_{ir} = \text{number of customers of type } i \text{ in vehicle assignment } r,$$

for each $i = 1, 2, \ldots, W$ and $r = 1, 2, \ldots, R_a$. Let

$$y_r = \text{number of times vehicle assignment } r \text{ is used in the optimal solution.}$$

The new formulation of this discretized VRP is:

$$\text{Problem } S_N: \quad Min \quad \sum_{r=1}^{R_a} y_r c_r$$

$$s.t.$$

$$\sum_{r=1}^{R_a} y_r A_{ir} \geq n_i, \quad \forall i = 1, 2, \ldots, W,$$

$$y_r \geq 0 \text{ and integer}, \quad \forall r = 1, 2, \ldots, R_a.$$

Let Z_N^* be the value of the optimal solution to Problem S_N and let Z_N^{LP} be the optimal solution to the linear relaxation of Problem S_N. Clearly, Problem S and Problem S_N have the same optimal solution values; that is, $Z^* = Z_N^*$ while their linear relaxations may be different. Define $\bar{c} \doteq \max_{r=1,2,\ldots,R_a}\{c_r\}$; that is, $\bar{c}$ is the length of the longest route among the R_a vehicle assignments. Using an analysis identical to the one in Section 4.2, we obtain:

Lemma 8.4.2

$$Z^{\text{LP}} \leq Z^* \leq Z_N^{\text{LP}} + W\bar{c} \leq Z^{\text{LP}} + W\bar{c}.$$

Observe that the upper bound on Z^* obtained in Lemma 8.4.2 consists of two terms. The first, Z^{LP}, is a lower bound on Z^*, which clearly grows with the number of customers n. The second term ($W\bar{c}$) is the product of two numbers that are fixed and independent of n. Therefore, the upper bound on Z^* of Lemma 8.4.2 is dominated by Z^{LP} and consequently we see that for large n, $Z^* \approx Z^{\text{LP}}$, exactly what is implied by Theorem 8.4.1. Indeed, much of the proof of the following section is concerned with approximating the distributions μ (customer locations) and Φ (customer demands) with discrete distributions and forcing the number of different customer types to be independent of n.

8.4.2   Proof of Theorem 8.4.1

It is clear that $Z^{LP} \leq Z^*$ and therefore $\underline{\lim}_{n \to \infty} \frac{1}{n}(Z^* - Z^{LP}) \geq 0$. The interesting part is to find an upper bound on Z^* that involves Z^{LP} and use this upper bound to show that $\overline{\lim}_{n \to \infty} \frac{1}{n}(Z^* - Z^{LP}) \leq 0$. We do this in essentially the same way as in Section 8.4.1. We successively discretize the problem by introducing a sequence of vehicle routing problems whose optimal solutions are "relatively" close to Z^*. The last vehicle routing problem is a discrete problem which therefore, as in Section 8.4.1, can be directly related to the linear relaxation of its set-partitioning formulation. This linear program is also shown to have an optimal solution close to Z^{LP}.

To prove the upper bound, let N be the index set of customers, with $|N| = n$, and let problem P be the original VRP. Let A be the compact support of the distribution of the customer locations (μ), and define $d_{\max} \doteq \sup\{\|x\| : x \in A\}$, where $\|x\|$ is the distance from point $x \in A$ to the depot. Finally, pick a fixed $k > 1$.

Discretization of the Locations

We start by constructing the following vehicle routing problem with discrete locations. Define $\Delta \doteq \frac{1}{k}$ and let $G(\Delta)$ be an infinite grid of squares of *diagonal* Δ, that is, of side $\frac{\Delta}{\sqrt{2}}$, with edges parallel to the system coordinates. Let $A_1, A_2, \ldots, A_{m(\Delta)}$ be the subregions of $G(\Delta)$ that intersect A and have $\mu(A_i) > 0$. Since A is bounded, $m(\Delta)$ is finite for each $\Delta > 0$. For convenience, we omit the dependence of m on Δ in the notation. For each subregion, let X_i be the *centroid* of subregion A_i, that is, the point at the center of the grid square containing A_i. This defines m points $X_1, X_2, \ldots, X_m$ and note that a customer is at most $\frac{\Delta}{2}$ units from the centroid of the subregion in which it is located.

Construct a new VRP, called $P(m)$, defined on the customers of N. Each of the customers in N is moved to the centroid of the subregion in which it is located. Let $Z^*(m)$ be the optimal solution to $P(m)$. We clearly have

$$Z^* \leq Z^*(m) + n\Delta. \tag{8.10}$$

Discretization of the Customer Demands

We now describe a VRP where the customer demands are also discretized in much the same way as it is done in Section 4.2. Partition the interval $(0, 1]$ into subintervals of size $\Delta(= \frac{1}{k})$. This produces k segments and $I \doteq k - 1$ points in the interval $(0, 1)$ which we call *corners*.

We refer to each centroid–corner pair as a customer type; each centroid defines a customer location and each corner defines the customer demand. It is clear that there are mI possible customer types. An instance of a fully discretized vehicle routing problem is then defined by specifying the number of customers of each of the mI types.

For each centroid $j = 1, 2, \ldots, m$, and corner $i = 1, 2, \ldots, I$, let

$$N_{ji} = \left\{ h \in N : \frac{i-1}{k} < w_h \leq \frac{i}{k} \text{ and } x_h \in A_j \right\}.$$

Finally, for every $j = 1, 2, \ldots, m$, and $i = 1, 2, \ldots, I$, let $n_{ji} = |N_{ji}|$.

We now define a fully discretized vehicle routing problem $P_k(m)$, whose optimal solution value is denoted $Z_k^*(m)$. The vehicle routing problem $P_k(m)$ is defined as having $\min\{n_{ji}, n_{j,i+1}\}$ customers located at centroid j with customer demand equal to $\frac{i}{k}$, for each $i = 1, 2, \ldots, I$ and $j = 1, 2, \ldots, m$.

We have the following result.

Lemma 8.4.3

$$Z^*(m) \leq Z_k^*(m) + 2d_{\max} \sum_{j=1}^{m} \sum_{i=1}^{I} |n_{ji} - n_{j,i+1}|.$$

Proof. Observe:

(i) In $P_k(m)$, the number of customers at centroid j and with demand defined by corner i is $\min\{n_{ji}, n_{j,i+1}\}$.

(ii) In $P(m)$ each customer belongs to exactly one of the subsets N_{ji}, for $j = 1, 2, \ldots, m$ and $i = 1, 2, \ldots, I$.

(iii) In $P(m)$ the customers in N_{ji} have smaller loads than the customers of $P_k(m)$ at centroid j with demand defined by corner i.

Given an optimal solution to $P_k(m)$, let us construct a solution to $P(m)$. For each centroid $j = 1, 2, \ldots, m$ and corner $i = 1, 2, \ldots, I$, we pick any $\max\{n_{ji} - n_{j,i+1}, 0\}$ customers from N_{ji} and serve them in individual vehicles. The remaining $\min\{n_{ji}, n_{j,i+1}\}$ customers in N_{ji} can be served with exactly the same vehicle schedules as in $P_k(m)$. This can be done due to (iii) and therefore one can always serve customers with demand of $P(m)$ in the same vehicles that the customers of $P_k(m)$ are served. ∎

Now $P_k(m)$ is fully discrete and we can apply results as in Section 8.4.1. Let $Z_k^{\mathrm{LP}}(m)$ be the optimal solution to the linear relaxation of the set-partitioning formulation of the routing problem $P_k(m)$. Let $\bar{c}$ be defined as in Section 8.4.1; that is, it is the cost of the most expensive tour among all the possible routes in $P_k(m)$.

Lemma 8.4.4

$$Z_k^*(m) \leq Z_k^{\mathrm{LP}}(m) + mI\bar{c}.$$

Proof. Since the number of customer types is at most mI, we can formulate $P_k(m)$ as the integer program, like Problem S_N, described in Section 8.4.1, with mI constraints. The bound then follows from Lemma 8.4.2.   ∎

Recall that Z^{LP} is the optimal solution to the linear relaxation of the set-partitioning formulation of the VRP defined by problem P. Then

Lemma 8.4.5

$$Z_k^{\text{LP}}(m) \leq Z^{\text{LP}} + n\Delta.$$

Proof. Let $\{\overline{y}_r : r = 1, 2, \ldots, R\}$ be the optimal solution to the linear relaxation of the set-partitioning formulation of problem P. We can assume (see Exercise 8.3) that $\sum_{r=1}^{R} \overline{y}_r \alpha_{ir} = 1$, for each $i = 1, 2, \ldots, n$. We construct a feasible solution to the linear relaxation of the set-partitioning formulation of $P_k(m)$ using the values $\overline{y}_r$. Since every customer in $P_k(m)$ assigned to centroid j and corner i can be associated with a customer in P with $x_k \in A_j$ and whose demand is at least as large, each route r with $\overline{y}_r > 0$ can be used to construct a route r' feasible for $P_k(m)$. Since in $P_k(m)$ the customers are at the centroids instead of at their original locations, we modify the route so that the vehicle travels from the customer to its centroid and back. Thus, the length (cost) of route r' is at most the cost of route r in P plus $n_r \Delta$ where n_r is the number of customers in route r.

To create a feasible solution to the linear relaxation of the set-partitioning formulation to $P_k(m)$ we take the solution to the linear relaxation of P and create the routes r' as above. Therefore,

$$Z_k^{\text{LP}}(m) \leq Z^{\text{LP}} + \sum_{r=1}^{R} \overline{y}_r n_r \Delta \leq Z^{\text{LP}} + n\Delta. \qquad ∎$$

We can now prove Theorem 8.4.1.

$$Z^* \leq Z^*(m) + n\Delta$$

$$\leq Z_k^*(m) + 2d_{\max} \sum_{j=1}^{m} \sum_{i=1}^{I} |n_{ji} - n_{j,i+1}| + n\Delta$$

$$\leq Z_k^{\text{LP}}(m) + mI\overline{c} + 2d_{\max} \sum_{j=1}^{m} \sum_{i=1}^{I} |n_{ji} - n_{j,i+1}| + n\Delta$$

$$\leq Z^{\text{LP}} + mI\overline{c} + 2d_{\max} \sum_{j=1}^{m} \sum_{i=1}^{I} |n_{ji} - n_{j,i+1}| + 2n\Delta.$$

We now need to show that Z^{LP} is the dominant part of the last upper bound. We do that using the following lemma.

Lemma 8.4.6 *There exists a constant K such that*

$$\overline{\lim_{n \to \infty}} \frac{1}{n} \sum_{j=1}^{m} \sum_{i=1}^{I} |n_{ji} - n_{j,i+1}| \leq \frac{2K}{k}.$$

Proof. In Section 4.2 we prove that given i and j there exists a constant K such that

$$\varlimsup_{n\to\infty} \frac{1}{n} |n_{ji} - n_{j,i+1}| \leq \frac{2K}{k^2}.$$

Therefore, a similar analysis gives

$$\varlimsup_{n\to\infty} \frac{1}{n} \sum_{j=1}^{m} \sum_{i=1}^{l} |n_{ji} - n_{j,i+1}| \leq \sum_{j=1}^{m} \mu(A_j) \frac{2K}{k} = \frac{2K}{k}. \qquad \blacksquare$$

Finally observe that each tour in $P_k(m)$ has a total length no more than 1, since the truck travels at a unit speed and the length of each working day is 1. Hence, $m\bar{I}\bar{c} = O(1)$, and therefore,

$$\varlimsup_{n\to\infty} \frac{1}{n}(Z^* - Z^{LP}) \leq 4d_{\max} \frac{K}{k} + 2\Delta$$

$$= \frac{2}{k}(2Kd_{\max} + 1).$$

Since K is a constant and k was arbitrary, we see that the right-hand side can be made arbitrarily small. Therefore,

$$0 \leq \varliminf_{n\to\infty} \frac{1}{n}(Z^* - Z^{LP}) \leq \varlimsup_{n\to\infty} \frac{1}{n}(Z^* - Z^{LP}) \leq 0.$$

We conclude this chapter with the following observation. The proof of Theorem 8.4.1 also reveals an upper bound on the rate of convergence of Z^{LP} to its asymptotic value. Indeed (see Exercise 8.1), we have

$$E(Z^*) \leq E(Z^{LP}) + O(n^{3/4}). \qquad (8.11)$$

8.5 Exercises

Exercise 8.1. Prove the upper bound on the convergence rate (equation (8.11)).

Exercise 8.2. Consider an undirected graph $G = (V, E)$ where each edge (i, j) has a cost c_{ij} and each vertex $i \in V$ a nonnegative penalty π_i. In the Prize-Collecting Traveling Salesman Problem (PCTSP), the objective is to find a tour that visits a subset of the vertices such that the length of the tour plus the sum of penalties of all vertices not in the tour is as small as possible. Show that the problem can be formulated as a Longest Path Problem between two prespecified nodes of a new network.

Exercise 8.3. Consider the Bin-Packing Problem. Let w_i be the size of item i, $i = 1, \ldots, n$, and assume the bin capacity is 1. An important formulation of the

Bin-Packing Problem is as a set-covering problem. Let

$$F = \{S : \sum_{i \in S} w_i \leq 1\}.$$

Define

$$\alpha_{iS} = \begin{cases} 1, & \text{if item } i \text{ is in } S, \\ 0, & \text{otherwise,} \end{cases}$$

for each $i = 1, 2, \ldots, n$ and each $S \in F$. Finally, for any S, $S \in F$, let

$$y_S = \begin{cases} 1, & \text{if the items in } S \text{ are packed in a single bin with no other items,} \\ 0, & \text{otherwise.} \end{cases}$$

In the set-covering formulation of the Bin-Packing Problem, the objective is to select a minimum number of feasible bins such that each item is included in some bin. It is the following integer program.

$$\text{Problem P} : \quad Min \quad \sum_{S \in F} y_S$$

$$s.t.$$

$$\sum_{S \in F} y_S \alpha_{iS} \geq 1, \quad \forall i = 1, 2, \ldots, n \qquad (8.12)$$

$$y_S \in \{0, 1\}, \quad \forall S \in F.$$

Let Z^* be the optimal solution to problem P and let Z^{LP} be the optimal solution to the linear relaxation of Problem P. We want to prove that

$$Z^* \leq 2Z^{LP}. \qquad (8.13)$$

(a) Formulate the dual of the linear relaxation of Problem P.

(b) Show that $\sum_{i=1}^{n} w_i \leq Z^{LP}$.

(c) Argue that $Z^* \leq 2 \sum_{i=1}^{n} w_i$. Conclude that (8.13) holds.

(d) An alternative formulation to Problem P is obtained by replacing constraints (8.12) with equality constraints. Call the new problem Problem PE. Show that the optimal solution value of the linear relaxation of Problem P equals the optimal solution value of the linear relaxation of Problem PE.

Exercise 8.4. Recall the dynamic program given by equation (8.6). Let

$$\underline{f} = \min_{i \in N} \min_{w_i \leq q \leq Q} f_q(i).$$

Consider the function defined as follows.

$$g_q(i) = \min_{w_i \leq q' \leq q} \{f_{q'}(i) + f_{q-q'+w_i}(i)\},$$

for each $i \in N$ and $w_i \leq q \leq Q$. Now define $\underline{g} = \min_{i \in N} \min_{w_i \leq q \leq Q} g_q(i)$. Show that $\underline{f} = \underline{g}$.

Exercise 8.5. Develop a dynamic programming procedure for the column generation step similar to $f_q(i)$ that avoids two-loops (loops of the type $...i, j, i...$). What is the complexity of this procedure?

Exercise 8.6. Develop a dynamic programming procedure for the column generation step in the presence of time-window constraints. What is required of the time-window data in order for this to be possible? What is the complexity of your procedure?

Exercise 8.7. Develop a dynamic programming procedure for the column generation step in the presence of a distance constraint on the length of any route. What is required of the distance data in order for this to be possible? What is the complexity of your procedure?

Exercise 8.8. Consider an instance of the VRPTW with n customers. Given a subset of the customers S, let $b^*(S)$ be the minimum number of vehicles required to carry the demands of customers in S; that is, $b^*(S)$ is the solution to the Bin-Packing Problem defined on the demands of all customers in S. For $i = 1, 2, \ldots, n$ and $j = 1, 2, \ldots, n$, let

$$x_{ij} = \begin{cases} 1, & \text{if a vehicle travels directly between points } i \text{ and } j, \\ 0, & \text{otherwise.} \end{cases}$$

Let 0 denote the depot and define c_{ij} as the cost of traveling directly between points i and j, for $i, j = 0, 1, 2, \ldots, n$. Let t_i represent the time a vehicle arrives at the location of customer i and for every i and j, such that $i < j$, define $M_{ij} = \max\{l_i + d_{ij} - e_j, 0\}$ where $d_{ij} \equiv \|Y_i - Y_j\|$. Then the following is a valid formulation of the VRPTW.

Problem P' : $Min \quad \sum_{i<j} c_{ij} x_{ij}$

$s.t. \quad \sum_{i<j} x_{ij} + \sum_{i>j} x_{ji} = 2, \quad \forall i = 1, 2, \ldots, n,$

$\sum_{i,j \in S} x_{ij} \leq |S| - b^*(S), \quad \forall S \subset \{1, 2, \ldots, n\}, 2 \leq |S| \leq n - 1,$

$e_i \leq t_i \leq l_i - s_i, \quad 1 \leq i \leq n,$

$t_i + s_i + d_{ij} - t_j \leq M_{ij}(1 - x_{ij}), \quad 1 \leq i < j \leq n,$

$x_{ij} \in \{0, 1\}, \quad 1 \leq i < j \leq n,$ (8.14)

$x_{0j} \in \{0, 1, 2\}, \quad j = 1, 2, \ldots, n.$ (8.15)

The case $x_{0j} = 2$ corresponds to a vehicle serving only customer j. The linear programming relaxation of P' is obtained by replacing constraints (8.14) and (8.15) by their linear equivalents.

Construct an instance of the VRPTW in which the fractional and integer solutions to the above linear program do not approach the same value asymptotically.

Part III

INVENTORY MODELS

9

Economic Lot Size Models with Constant Demands

9.1   Introduction

Production planning is also an area where difficult combinatorial problems appear in day to day logistics operations. In this chapter, we analyze problems related to lot sizing when demands are constant and known in advance. Lot sizing in this deterministic setting is essentially the problem of balancing the fixed costs of ordering with the costs of holding inventory. In this chapter, we look at several different models of deterministic lot sizing. First we consider the most basic single-item model, the Economic Lot Size Model. Then we look at coordinating the ordering of several items with a warehouse of limited capacity. Finally, we look at a one-warehouse multiretailer system.

9.1.1   The Economic Lot Size Model

The classical Economic Lot Size Model, introduced by Harris (1915) (see Erlenkotter (1990) for an interesting historical discussion), is a framework where we can see the simple tradeoffs between ordering and storage costs. Consider a facility, possibly a warehouse or a retailer, that faces a constant demand for a *single* item and places orders for the item from another facility in the distribution network which is assumed to have an unlimited quantity of the product. The model assumes the following.

- Demand is constant at a rate of D items per unit time.

- Order quantities are fixed at Q items per order.

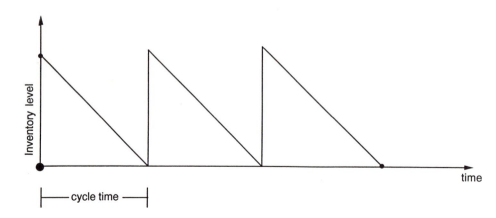

FIGURE 9.1. Inventory level as a function of time.

- A fixed set-up cost K is incurred every time the warehouse places an order.

- A linear inventory carrying cost h, also referred to as *holding cost*, is accrued for every unit held in inventory per unit time.

- The lead time, that is, the time that elapses between the placement of an order and its receipt, is zero.

- Initial inventory is zero.

- The planning horizon is infinite.

The objective is to find the optimal ordering policy minimizing total purchasing and carrying cost per unit of time without shortage.

Like all models, this is a simplified version of what might actually occur in practice. The assumption of a known fixed demand over the infinite horizon is clearly unrealistic. Lead time is most likely positive, and the requirement of a fixed order quantity is restrictive. As we shall see, all these assumptions can be easily relaxed while maintaining a relatively simple optimal policy. For the purposes of understanding the basic tradeoffs in the model, we keep the assumptions listed above.

It is easy to see that an optimal ordering policy must satisfy the *Zero Inventory Ordering Property* which says that every order is received precisely when the inventory level drops to zero. This can be seen by considering the case where an order is placed when the inventory level is not zero. In that case, cost is not increased if we simply wait until inventory is zero to order.

To find the optimal ordering policy in the Economic Lot Size Model, we consider the inventory level as a function of time (see Figure 9.1). This is the so-called *saw-toothed* inventory pattern. We refer to the time between two successive replenishments as a *cycle* time. Thus, total inventory cost in a cycle of length T is

$$K + \frac{hTQ}{2},$$

and since $Q = TD$, the average total cost per unit of time is

$$\frac{KD}{Q} + \frac{hQ}{2}.$$

Hence, the optimal order quantity is

$$Q^* \doteq \sqrt{\frac{2KD}{h}}.$$

This quantity is referred to as the Economic Order Quantity (EOQ) and it is the quantity at which inventory set-up cost per unit of time ($\frac{KD}{Q}$) equals inventory holding cost per unit of time ($\frac{hQ}{2}$).

We now see how some of our assumptions can be relaxed, without losing any of the simplicity of the model. Consider the case in which initial inventory is positive, say at level I_0; then the first order for Q^* items is simply delayed until time $\frac{I_0}{D}$. Further, the assumption of zero lead time can also be easily relaxed. In fact, the model can handle any deterministic lead time L. To do this simply place an order for Q^* items when the inventory level is DL. On the other hand, relaxing the assumptions of fixed demands and infinite planning horizon requires significant changes to the above solution.

9.1.2 The Finite Horizon Model

To make the model more realistic, we now introduce a finite horizon, say t. For instance, in the retail apparel industry, such a horizon may represent an 8–12 week period, for example, the "winter season," in which demand for the product might be assumed to be constant and known. We also relax the assumption that the order quantities are fixed. We seek an inventory policy on the interval $[0, t]$ that minimizes ordering and carrying costs.

For this purpose, consider any inventory policy, say $\mathcal{P}$, that places $m \geq 1$ orders in the interval $[0, t]$. Clearly, the first order must be placed at time zero and the last must be placed so that the inventory at time t is zero. For any i, $1 \leq i \leq m - 1$, let T_i be the time between the placement of the ith order and the $(i + 1)^{\text{st}}$ order and let T_m be the time between the placement of the last order and t. Thus, by definition, $t = \sum_{i=1}^{m} T_i$, and $\mathcal{P}$ places the jth order at time $\sum_{i=1}^{j} T_i$, for $1 \leq j \leq m$. Again, it is clear that the policy $\mathcal{P}$ must satisfy the Zero Inventory Ordering Property. Figure 9.2 illustrates the inventory level of the policy $\mathcal{P}$.

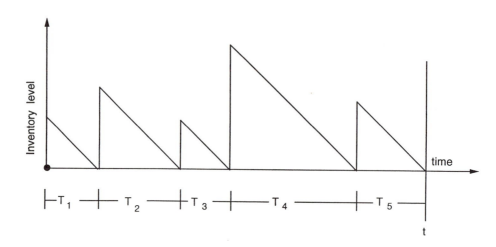

FIGURE 9.2. Inventory level as a function of time under policy $\mathcal{P}$.

For the policy $\mathcal{P}$, let $I(\tau)$ be the inventory level at time $\tau \in [0, t]$. Thus, the total cost per unit of time associated with $\mathcal{P}$ is

$$\frac{1}{t}\left[Km + h\int_0^t I(\tau)d\tau\right].$$

The only thing we know about the function $I(\tau)$ is that it decreases at a rate of D (a slope of $-D$) between orders and reaches zero exactly m times. Thus, we can express the total inventory up to time t as a function of the time between orders $\{T_i\}_{i=1,\ldots,m}$ as follows.

$$\sum_{i=1}^{m} \frac{T_i \cdot DT_i}{2} = \frac{D}{2}\sum_{i=1}^{m} T_i^2.$$

Consequently, if m orders are placed we can find the best times to place them by solving:

$$Min\left\{\sum_{i=1}^{m} T_i^2 \,\Big|\, \sum_{i=1}^{m} T_i = t, \; T_i \geq 0, \; \forall i = 1, 2, \ldots, m\right\}.$$

The optimal solution to this convex optimization problem is $T_i = \frac{t}{m}$ for each $i = 1, 2, \ldots, m$. Hence, an optimal policy must have the following property.

Property 9.1.1 *For a problem with one product over the interval $[0, t]$, the inventory policy with minimum cost that places m orders is achieved by placing orders of equal size at equally spaced points in time.*

The property thus implies that total purchasing and carrying cost per unit time associated with $\mathcal{P}$ is at least

$$\frac{Km}{t} + \frac{hDt}{2m}.$$

Consequently, by selecting the value of m that minimizes this value we can construct a policy of minimal cost. Let

$$\alpha = t\sqrt{\frac{hD}{2K}},$$

and thus the best value of m is either $\lfloor \alpha \rfloor$ or $\lceil \alpha \rceil$, depending on which yields smaller cost. Thus our policy in the finite horizon case is in fact very similar to the infinite horizon case. Orders are placed at regularly spaced intervals of time, and of course the orders are of the same size each time.

9.1.3   Power of Two Policies

Consider the infinite horizon model described in Section 9.1. For this model we know that average total cost per unit of time is

$$\frac{KD}{Q} + \frac{hQ}{2} = \frac{K}{T} + \frac{hTD}{2} \doteq f(T),$$

where T is the time between orders. In this subsection, following Muckstadt and Roundy (1993), we introduce a new class of policies called power-of-two policies.

To simplify the analysis, and in accordance with the notation used in the literature (see Roundy, 1985, and Muckstadt and Roundy, 1993), let $g \doteq \frac{hD}{2}$ and hence

$$f(T) = \frac{K}{T} + gT.$$

Observe that the function $f(T)$ motivates another interpretation of the model. We can consider the problem to be an Economic Lot Size model with unit demand rate, that is, $D = 1$, and inventory holding cost $2g$. The optimal reorder interval is $T^* = \sqrt{\frac{K}{g}}$ and total cost per unit time is $f(T^*) = 2\sqrt{Kg}$.

One difficulty with the Economic Lot Size Model is that the optimal reorder interval T^* may take on any value and thus might lead to highly impractical optimal policies. For instance, reorder intervals of $\sqrt{3}$ days, or $\sqrt{\pi}$ weeks would not be easy to implement. That is, the model might specify that orders be placed on Monday of one week, Thursday of the next, Tuesday of the next week etc., a schedule of orders that may not have an easily recognizable pattern. Therefore, it is natural to consider policies where the reorder interval T is restricted to values that would entail easily implementable policies. One such restriction is termed the *power of two* restriction. In this case, T is restricted to be a power of two multiple of some fixed base planning period T_B; that is,

$$T = T_B 2^k, \quad k \in \{0, 1, 2, 3, \ldots\}. \tag{9.1}$$

Such a policy is called a *power of two policy*. The base planning period T_B may represent a day, week, month, etc. and is usually fixed beforehand. It represents the minimum possible reorder interval.

Restricting ourselves to power of two policies requires addressing the following issues.

- How does one find the best power of two policy, the one minimizing the cost over all possible power of two policies?

- How far from optimal is the best policy of this type?

We start by answering the first question. Let $T^* = \sqrt{\frac{K}{g}}$ be the optimal (unrestricted) reorder interval and let T be the optimal power of two reorder interval. Since f is convex, the optimal k in (9.1) is the smallest integer k satisfying

$$f(T_B 2^k) \le f(T_B 2^{k+1}),$$

or

$$\frac{K}{T_B 2^k} + g T_B 2^k \le \frac{K}{T_B 2^{k+1}} + g T_B 2^{k+1}.$$

Hence, k is the smallest integer such that

$$\sqrt{\frac{K}{2g}} = \frac{1}{\sqrt{2}} T^* \le T_B 2^k = T.$$

Thus, finding the optimal power of two policy is straightforward.

Observe that by the definition of the optimal k, it must also be true that

$$T = T_B 2^k \le \sqrt{\frac{2K}{g}} = \sqrt{2} T^*,$$

and hence the optimal power of two policy, for a given base planning period T_B, must be in the interval $[\frac{1}{\sqrt{2}} T^*, \sqrt{2} T^*]$. It is easy to verify that

$$f\left(\frac{1}{\sqrt{2}} T^*\right) = f(\sqrt{2} T^*) = \frac{1}{2}\left(\frac{1}{\sqrt{2}} + \sqrt{2}\right) f(T^*),$$

and hence, since f is convex, we have

$$\frac{f(T)}{f(T^*)} \le \frac{1}{2}\left(\frac{1}{\sqrt{2}} + \sqrt{2}\right) \approx 1.06.$$

Consequently, the average inventory purchasing and carrying cost of the best power of two policy is guaranteed to be within 6% of the average cost of the overall minimum policy. The reader can see that this property is a result of the "flatness" of the function f around its minimum.

This restriction, to powers of two multiples of the base planning period, will also prove to be quite useful later in a more general setting.

9.2   Multi-Item Inventory Models

9.2.1   Introduction

The previous models established optimal inventory policies for single item models. It is simple to show that without the presence of joint order costs, a problem with several items each facing a constant demand can be handled by solving each item's replenishment problem separately. In reality, management of a single warehouse inventory system involves coordinating inventory orders to minimize cost without exceeding the *warehouse capacity*. The warehouse capacity limits the total volume held by the warehouse at any point in time. This constraint ties together the different items and necessitates careful coordination (or scheduling) of the orders. That is, it is not only important to know how often an item is ordered, but exactly the point in time at which each order takes place. This problem is called the Economic Warehouse Lot Scheduling Problem (EWLSP). The scheduling part, hereafter called the *Staggering* problem, is exactly the problem of time-phasing the placement of the orders to satisfy the warehouse capacity constraint. Unfortunately, this problem has no easy solution and consequently it has attracted a considerable amount of attention in the last three decades.

The earliest known reference to the problem appears in Churchman et al. (1957) and subsequently in Holt (1958) and Hadley and Whitin (1963). These authors were concerned with determining lot sizes that made an overall schedule satisfy the capacity constraint, and not with the possibility of phasing the orders to avoid holding the maximum volume of each item at the same time. Thus, they only considered what are called *Independent Solutions,* wherein every item is replenished without any regard for coordination with other items.

Several authors considered another class of policies called *Rotation Cycle* policies wherein all items share the same order interval. Homer (1966) showed how to optimally time-phase (stagger) the orders to satisfy the warehouse constraint for a given common order interval. Page and Paul (1976), Zoller (1977) and Hall (1988) independently rediscovered Homer's result. At the end of his paper devoted to Rotation Cycle policies, Zoller indicates the possibility of partitioning the items into disjoint subsets, or *clusters,* if the assumption of a Rotation Policy "proves to be too restrictive." This is precisely Page and Paul's partitioning heuristic. In their heuristic, all the items in a cluster share a common order interval. The orders are then optimally staggered within each cluster, but no attempt is made to time-phase the orders of different clusters. Goyal (1978) argued that such a time-phasing across the different clusters may lead to further reduction in warehouse space requirements. Hartley and Thomas (1982) and Thomas and Hartley (1983) considered the two-item case in detail.

Recently a number of studies have been concerned with the *strategic* version of the EWLSP in which the warehouse capacity is not a constraint but rather a decision variable. These include Hodgson and Howe (1982), Park and Yun (1985), Hall (1988), Rosenblatt and Rothblum (1990) and Anily (1991). In this model, the inventory carrying cost consists of two parts; one part is proportional to the average inventory while the second part is proportional to the peak inventory. A component of the latter cost, discussed in Silver and Peterson (1985), is the cost of *leasing* the storage space. This cost is typically proportional to the size of the warehouse, and not to the inventories actually stored in it.

Define a policy to be a *Stationary Order Size* policy if all replenishments of an item are of the same size. Likewise, a *Stationary Order Intervals* policy has all orders for an item equally spaced in time. It is easily verified that an optimal Stationary Order Size (respectively, Stationary Order Interval) policy is also a Stationary Order Interval (respectively, a Stationary Order Size) policy if every order of an item is received precisely when the inventory of that item drops to zero; that is, it also satisfies the Zero Inventory Ordering property. Thus, it is natural to consider policies that have all three properties: Stationary Order Size, Stationary Order Interval and Zero Inventory Ordering. We call such policies *Stationary Order Sizes and Intervals* policies, in short, *SOSI policies*. Two "extreme" cases of SOSI policies are the Independent Solutions and the Rotation Cycle policies defined above. All the authors cited above considered SOSI policies exclusively. Zoller claims that SOSI policies are the only rational alternative, and most authors agree that SOSI policies are much easier to implement in practice. In his Ph.D. thesis, however, Hariga (1988) investigated both time-variant and stationary order sizes. He was motivated to study time-variant order sizes by their successful application in resolving the feasibility issue in the Economic Lot Scheduling Problem (ELSP) (see Dobson (1987)).

The paper by Anily departs from earlier work on the EWLSP in its focus on worst-case performance of heuristics. In her paper, Anily restricts herself to the class of SOSI policies for the strategic model. She proves lower bounds on the minimum required warehouse size and on the total cost for this class of policies. She presents a partitioning heuristic of which the best Independent Solution and the best Rotation Cycle policies are special cases. This partitioning heuristic is similar to the one proposed by Page and Paul for the tactical model, although the precise methods for finding the partition are different. Anily proves that the ratio of the cost of the best Independent Solution to her lower bound is at most $\sqrt{2}$. She also provides a data-dependent bound for the best Rotation Cycle, derived from Jones and Inman's (1989) work on the Economic Lot Size Problem. As a result, her partitioning heuristic is at least as good as either special case, and thus has a worst case bound of $\sqrt{2}$ relative to SOSI policies.

In this section we determine easily computable lower bounds on the cost of the EWLSP as well as some simple heuristics for the problem. These bounds are used to determine the worst-case performance of these heuristics on different versions of the problem. First, in Section 9.2.2, we introduce notation, state assumptions and formally define the strategic and tactical versions of the EWLSP. In Section 9.2.3, we establish the worst-case results. The discussion in this section is based on the work of Gallego et al. (1996).

9.2.2 Notation and Assumptions

Let $N = \{1, 2, \ldots, n\}$ be a set of n items each facing a constant *unit* demand rate (this can be done without loss of generality). An ordering cost K_i is incurred each time an order for item i is placed. A linear holding cost $2h_i$ is accrued for each unit of item i held in inventory per unit of time. Demand for each item must be met over an infinite horizon without shortages or backlogging.

The volume of inventory of item i held at a given point in time is the product of its inventory level at that time and the volume usage rate of item i, denoted by $\gamma_i > 0$. The volume usage rate is defined as the volume displaced by one unit of item i. Without loss of generality, we select the unit of volume so that $\sum_{i=1}^n \gamma_i = 1$.

The objective in the strategic version of the EWLSP is to minimize the long-run average inventory carrying and ordering cost plus a cost proportional to the maximum volume held by the warehouse at any point in time. Formally, for any inventory policy $\mathcal{P}$, let $V(\mathcal{P})$ denote the maximum inventory volume held by the warehouse and let $C(\mathcal{P})$ be the long-run average inventory carrying and holding cost incurred by this policy. Then, the objective is to find a policy $\mathcal{P}$ minimizing

$$Z(\mathcal{P}) \doteq C(\mathcal{P}) + V(\mathcal{P}).$$

The tactical version of the EWLSP has also received much attention in the literature. There, the objective is to find a policy $\mathcal{P}$ minimizing the long-run average inventory carrying and holding costs subject to the inventory always being less than the warehouse capacity. Hence, the tactical version can be formulated as: find a policy $\mathcal{P}$ minimizing $C(\mathcal{P})$ subject to $V(\mathcal{P}) \leq v$, where v denotes the available warehouse volume.

9.2.3 Worst-Case Analyses

Preliminaries

We present here two simple results that are used in subsequent analyses.

Given a SOSI policy, let $T = \{T_1, T_2, \ldots, T_n\}$ be the vector of reorder intervals where T_i is the reorder interval of item i. For any such vector T, let $V(T)$ denote the maximum volume of inventory held by the warehouse over all points in time. The following provides a simple upper bound on $V(T)$.

Lemma 9.2.1 *For any vector* $T = \{T_1, T_2, \ldots, T_n\}$, *we have*

$$V(T) \leq \sum_{i=1}^n \gamma_i T_i.$$

Proof. Clearly, the inventory level of item i, at any moment in time, is no more than T_i (recall demand is 1 for all i).   ■

For the next result we need some additional notation. Consider any inventory policy $\mathcal{P}$ and any time interval $[0, t]$. Let $V(\mathcal{P}, t)$ be the maximum inventory held by the warehouse in policy $\mathcal{P}$ over the interval $[0, t]$ and $C(\mathcal{P}, t)$ be the average inventory holding and carrying cost incurred over $[0, t]$. Let m_i be the number of times the warehouse places an order for item i over the interval $[0, t]$. For $\tau \in [0, t]$, let $I_i(\tau)$ be the inventory level of item i at time τ. Let $v_i(\tau)$ be the volume of inventory held by item i at time τ; that is, $v_i(\tau) = \gamma_i I_i(\tau)$. Also, let $v(\tau) = \sum_{i=1}^{n} v_i(\tau)$ be the volume of inventory held by the warehouse at time τ.

Lemma 9.2.2 *For any inventory policy $\mathcal{P}$ and time interval $[0, t]$, we have*

$$\frac{1}{2} \sum_{i=1}^{n} \frac{\gamma_i t}{m_i} \leq \sum_{i=1}^{n} \frac{1}{t} \gamma_i \int_{\tau=0}^{t} I_i(\tau) d\tau \leq V(\mathcal{P}, t).$$

Proof. Clearly, $v(\tau) \leq V(\mathcal{P}, t)$ for all $\tau \leq t$. Taking the integral up to time $t > 0$ gives

$$V(\mathcal{P}, t) \geq \frac{1}{t} \int_{\tau=0}^{t} \sum_i v_i(\tau) d\tau$$

$$= \frac{1}{t} \int_{\tau=0}^{t} \sum_i \gamma_i I_i(\tau) d\tau$$

$$= \sum_i \frac{1}{t} \gamma_i \int_{\tau=0}^{t} I_i(\tau) d\tau$$

$$\geq \sum_i \frac{1}{2} \frac{\gamma_i t}{m_i},$$

where the last inequality follows from Property 9.1.1 which states that when m_i orders for a single item are placed over the interval $[0, t]$, the average inventory level is minimized by placing equal orders at equally spaced points in time. ∎

The Strategic Model

Consider the following heuristic for the strategic version of the EWLSP. Use the vector of reorder intervals T that solves

$$Z^H = \min_T \left\{ \sum_i \left(\frac{K_i}{T_i} + h_i T_i \right) + \sum_i \gamma_i T_i \right\}.$$

Clearly, the vector T can be found in $O(n)$ time by solving n separate Economic Lot Scheduling models, and

$$Z^H = 2 \sum_i \sqrt{K_i(h_i + \gamma_i)}. \tag{9.2}$$

By Lemma 9.2.1, Z^H must provide an upper bound on the optimal solution value of the strategic model.

We now construct a lower bound on the optimal solution value over all possible inventory policies. The lower bound is the cost of the optimal policy if the warehouse cost were based on average inventory rather than maximum inventory. This bound will be used to prove the worst-case result.

Lemma 9.2.3 *A lower bound on the optimal solution value over all possible inventory strategies is given by*

$$Z^{LB} = 2 \sum_i \sqrt{K_i(h_i + \gamma_i/2)}. \tag{9.3}$$

Proof. We show that $Z^{LB} \leq C(\mathcal{P}, t) + V(\mathcal{P}, t)$ for all possible inventory policies $\mathcal{P}$ and for all $t > 0$. Given an inventory policy $\mathcal{P}$, where m_i orders for item i are placed over a time interval $[0, t]$, then

$$C(\mathcal{P}, t) = \frac{1}{t} \sum_i \left(m_i K_i + 2h_i \int_{\tau=0}^{t} I_i(\tau)d\tau \right).$$

Combining this cost with the lower bound obtained in Lemma 9.2.2 on $V(\mathcal{P}, t)$ yields the following lower bound on $C(\mathcal{P}, t) + V(\mathcal{P}, t)$.

$$C(\mathcal{P}, t) + V(\mathcal{P}, t) \geq \frac{1}{t} \sum_i \left[m_i K_i + 2h_i \int_{\tau=0}^{t} I_i(\tau)d\tau \right] + \frac{1}{t} \sum_i \gamma_i \int_{\tau=0}^{t} I_i(\tau)d\tau$$

$$= \frac{1}{t} \sum_i \left[m_i K_i + (2h_i + \gamma_i) \int_{\tau=0}^{t} I_i(\tau)d\tau \right]$$

$$\geq \sum_i \left[K_i \left(\frac{m_i}{t} \right) + \frac{(2h_i + \gamma_i)}{2} \left(\frac{t}{m_i} \right) \right].$$

The last inequality again follows from Property 9.1.1. Minimizing the last expression with respect to $\frac{t}{m_i}$ for each $i \in N$ proves the result. ∎

We now show that this heuristic is effective in terms of worst-case performance.

Theorem 9.2.4

$$\frac{Z^H}{Z^{LB}} \leq \sqrt{2}.$$

Proof. Combining equations (9.2) and (9.3) we get

$$\frac{Z^H}{Z^{LB}} = \frac{2 \sum_i \sqrt{K_i(h_i + \gamma_i)}}{2 \sum_i \sqrt{K_i(h_i + \gamma_i/2)}} \leq \sqrt{2}. \quad ∎$$

Can this bound be improved? The following example shows that the bound is tight as the number of items grows to infinity. Consider an example n items with $K_i = K$, $h_i = 0$ and $\gamma_i = \gamma = \frac{1}{n}$ for all $i \in N$. Clearly,

$$Z^H = 2n\sqrt{K\gamma}.$$

We now construct a feasible solution whose cost approaches the lower bound Z^{LB} as n goes to infinity. Consider a feasible policy $\mathcal{P}$ with identical reorder intervals denoted by $\tilde{T}$. To reduce the maximum volume $V(\tilde{T})$, we stagger the orders such that item i is ordered at times $\tilde{T}[\frac{(i-1)}{n} + k]$ for $k \geq 0$. Then the maximum volume of inventory is $\frac{(n+1)}{2}\tilde{T}\gamma$. Hence, the cost of policy $\mathcal{P}$ is

$$Z(\mathcal{P}) = \frac{nK}{\tilde{T}} + \frac{n+1}{2}\tilde{T}\gamma.$$

Minimizing with respect to $\tilde{T}$ gives

$$Z(\mathcal{P}) = \sqrt{2n(n+1)K\gamma}.$$

Consequently,

$$\frac{Z^H}{Z^{LB}} \geq \frac{Z^H}{Z(\mathcal{P})} = \frac{2n\sqrt{K\gamma}}{\sqrt{2n(n+1)K\gamma}}.$$

The limit of this last quantity is $\sqrt{2}$ (as n goes to infinity) hence, along with Theorem 9.2.4, we see that an example can be constructed where the worst-case ratio is arbitrarily close to $\sqrt{2}$.

The Tactical Model

For the tactical version of the EWLSP, a simple heuristic denoted HW first proposed by Hadley and Whitin (1963) is to solve

Problem P^{HW} : $C^{HW} = Min \sum_i \left(h_i T_i + \frac{K_i}{T_i}\right)$

s.t.

$$\sum_i \gamma_i T_i \leq v,$$

$$T \geq 0.$$

We show that the HW heuristic has a worst-case performance bound of 2 with respect to all feasible policies. We do so by proving that the solution to the following nonlinear program provides a lower bound on the cost of any feasible policy.

Problem P^{LB} : $C^{LB} = Min \sum_i \left(h_i T_i + \frac{K_i}{T_i}\right)$

s.t.

$$\frac{1}{2}\sum_i \gamma_i T_i \leq v, \tag{9.4}$$

$$T \geq 0.$$

Lemma 9.2.5 C^{LB} *is a lower bound on the cost of any feasible inventory policy.*

Proof. Consider any feasible policy $\mathcal{P}$ over the interval $[0, t]$ that places m_i orders for item i in $[0, t]$. From Lemma 9.2.2 we have $\forall t > 0$,

$$v \geq V(\mathcal{P}, t) \geq \frac{1}{2} \sum_i \frac{\gamma_i}{m_i} t.$$

The average inventory holding and carrying cost incurred over the interval $[0, t]$ is

$$C(\mathcal{P}, t) = \frac{1}{t} \sum_i \left[m_i K_i + 2h_i \int_{\tau=0}^t I_i(\tau) d\tau \right]$$

$$\geq \sum_i \left[K_i \left(\frac{m_i}{t} \right) + h_i \left(\frac{t}{m_i} \right) \right]. \tag{9.5}$$

Again, the last inequality follows from Property 9.1.1.

Thus, by replacing $\frac{t}{m_i}$ with T_i for all $i \geq 1$, we see that minimizing (9.5) subject to $\frac{1}{2} \sum_i \gamma_i t / m_i \leq v$ provides a lower bound on $C(\mathcal{P}, t)$.   ∎

We now prove the worst-case bound.

Theorem 9.2.6
$$\frac{C^{HW}}{C^{LB}} \leq 2.$$

Proof. Let $T^{LB} = \{T_1^{LB}, T_2^{LB}, \ldots, T_n^{LB}\}$ be the optimal solution to P^{LB}. Obviously, $T_i' = \frac{1}{2} T_i^{LB}$ is feasible for P^{HW}. Hence,

$$C^{HW} \leq \sum_i \left(h_i T_i' + \frac{K_i}{T_i'} \right)$$

$$= \frac{1}{2} \sum_i h_i T_i^{LB} + 2 \sum_i \frac{K_i}{T_i^{LB}}$$

$$\leq 2C^{LB}. \qquad \blacksquare$$

As in the strategic version, the worst-case bound provided by the above theorem can be shown to be tight. To do so, consider the case where all items are identical with $K_i = K$, $h_i = 0$ and $\gamma_i = \gamma = \frac{1}{n}$ for all $i \in N$. The solution to problem P^{HW} is clearly $T_i = v$ for all $i \in N$, so $C^{HW} = \frac{nK}{v}$. Consider now a feasible policy $\mathcal{P}$ with identical reorder intervals denoted by $\tilde{T}$ such that an order for item i is placed at times $\tilde{T}[\frac{(i-1)}{n} + k]$ for $k \geq 0$. The maximum volume occupied by policy $\mathcal{P}$ is $\frac{(n+1)}{2} \tilde{T} \gamma$. So $\tilde{T} = \frac{2v}{(n+1)\gamma}$ is feasible and $C(\mathcal{P}) = \frac{K(n+1)}{2v}$. Hence,

$$\lim_{n \to \infty} \frac{C^{HW}}{C(\mathcal{P})} = \lim_{n \to \infty} \frac{nK/v}{K(n+1)/2v} = 2.$$

By performing a similar analysis one can obtain worst-case bounds on the performance of heuristics for other versions of the EWLSP. For instance, for the *Joint Replenishment* version of the strategic model, where an additional set-up cost K_0 is incurred whenever an order for one or more items is placed, the worst-case bound of a heuristic, similar to the one described for the EWLSP, can be shown to be $\sqrt{3}$. The worst-case bound on the tactical version of the Joint Replenishment model can be shown to be $2\sqrt{2}$.

9.3   A Single Warehouse Multi-Retailer Model

9.3.1   Introduction

Many distribution systems involve replenishing the inventories of geographically dispersed retailers. Consider a distribution system in which a single warehouse supplies a set of retailers with a single product. Each retailer faces a constant retailer-specific demand that must be met without shortage or backlogging. The warehouse faces orders for the product from the different retailers and in turn places orders to an outside supplier. A fixed, facility-dependent, set-up cost is charged each time the warehouse or the retailers receive an order and inventory carrying cost is accrued at each facility at a constant facility-dependent rate. The objective is to determine simultaneously the timing and sizes of retailer deliveries to the warehouse as well as replenishment strategies at the warehouse so as to minimize long-run average inventory purchasing and carrying costs.

In the absence of a fixed set-up cost charged when the warehouse places an order, the problem can be decomposed into an Economic Lot Size model for each retailer. That is, the existence of this cost ties together the different retailers requiring the warehouse to coordinate its orders and deliveries to the different retailers. It is well known that optimal policies can be very complex and thus the problem has attracted a considerable amount of attention in recent years (see Graves and Schwarz, 1977; Roundy, 1985). The latter paper presents the best approach currently available for this model; it suggests a set of power of two reorder intervals for each facility and show that the cost of this solution is within 6% of a lower bound on the optimal cost. In this section, we present this method along with the worst-case bound.

9.3.2   Notation and Assumptions

Consider a single warehouse (indexed by 0) which supplies n retailers, indexed $1, 2, \ldots, n$. We will use the term facility to designate either the warehouse or a retailer. We make the following assumptions.

- Each retailer faces a constant demand rate of D_i units, for $i = 1, 2, \ldots, n$.

- Set-up cost for an order at a facility is K_i, for $i = 0, 1, \ldots, n$.

- Holding cost is h'_0 at the warehouse and h'_i at retailer i, with $h'_i \geq h'_0$ for each $i = 1, 2, \ldots, n$.

- No shortages are allowed.

As demonstrated by several researchers, policies for this problem may be quite complex and thus it is of interest to restrict our attention to a subset of all feasible policies. A popular subset of policies is the set of *nested* and *stationary* policies. A nested policy is characterized by having each retailer place an order whenever the warehouse does. As in the previous section, stationarity implies that reorder intervals are constant for each facility. It is easy to show that any policy should satisfy the Zero Inventory Ordering Property. Roundy (1985) showed that, although appealing from a coordination point of view, nested policies may perform arbitrarily badly in one-warehouse multi-retailer systems. We therefore will not restrict ourselves to nested policies. We concentrate on policies where each retailer's reorder intervals are a powers of two multiple of a base planning period T_B. Below, we assume the base planning period is fixed. The worst-case bound reduces to 1.02 if it can be chosen optimally, although we omit this extension.

Let's first determine the cost of an arbitrary power of two policy $T = \{T_0, T_1, \ldots, T_n\}$ that satisfies the Zero Inventory Ordering Property. If we consider the inventory at the warehouse, then it does not have the saw-toothed pattern. To overcome this difficulty, it is convenient to introduce the notion of *system* inventory as well as *echelon* holding cost rates. Retailer i's system inventory is defined as the inventory at retailer i plus the inventory at the warehouse that is destined for retailer i. If we consider the *system* inventory of retailer i, then it has the saw-toothed pattern. Echelon holding cost rates are defined as $h_0 = h_0'$ and $h_i = h_i' - h_0'$. For simplicity, define $g_i = \frac{1}{2} h_i D_i$ and $g^i = \frac{1}{2} h_0 D_i$ for each $i = 1, 2, \ldots, n$. To compute the cost of such a policy, we separate each item in the warehouse's inventory into categories depending on the retailer for which the item is destined. Let $H_i(T_0, T_i)$ be the average cost of holding inventory for retailer i at the warehouse and at retailer i. We claim:

$$H_i(T_0, T_i) = g_i T_i + g^i \max\{T_0, T_i\}.$$

To prove this consider the two cases:

Case 1: $T_i \geq T_0$. Since T is a power of two policy, $T_i \geq T_0$ implies that the warehouse places an order every time the retailer does. Therefore, the warehouse never holds inventory for retailer i and average holding cost is

$$\frac{1}{2} h_i' T_i D_i = \frac{1}{2} (h_i + h_0) T_i D_i = (g_i + g^i) T_i.$$

Case 2: $T_i < T_0$. Consider the portion of the warehouse inventory that is destined for retailer i. Using the echelon holding cost rates, that is, inventory at retailer i is charged at a rate of h_i and system inventory is charged at a rate of h_0, we have

$$H_i(T_0, T_i) = \frac{1}{2} h_i D_i T_i + \frac{1}{2} h_0 D_i T_0 = g_i T_i + g^i T_0.$$

Therefore, the average cost of a power of two policy T is given by:

$$\sum_{i \geq 0} \frac{K_i}{T_i} + \sum_{i \geq 1} H_i(T_0, T_i). \tag{9.6}$$

Our objective then is to find the power of two policy T that minimizes (9.6).

Our approach to solving this problem is to first minimize the average cost over all vectors $T \geq 0$, that is, we solve this problem when the restriction to power of two vectors is relaxed. We then round the solution T to a vector whose elements are the powers of two multiple of T_B.

For a fixed value of T_0, we consider the following problem

$$b_i(T_0) = \inf_{T_i > 0} \left\{ \frac{K_i}{T_i} + H_i(T_0, T_i) \right\}. \tag{9.7}$$

To solve this problem, let $\tau_i' \doteq \sqrt{\frac{K_i}{g_i + g^i}}$ and let $\tau_i \doteq \sqrt{\frac{K_i}{g_i}}$ and note that $\tau_i' \le \tau_i$ for all $i \ge 1$. Then one can show that

$$b_i(T_0) = \begin{cases} 2\sqrt{K_i(g_i + g^i)} & \text{if } T_0 < \tau_i' \\ \frac{K_i}{T_0} + (g_i + g^i)T_0 & \text{if } \tau_i' \le T_0 \le \tau_i \\ 2\sqrt{K_i g_i} + g^i T_0 & \text{if } \tau_i < T_0. \end{cases}$$

That is, if $T_0 < \tau_i'$, it is best to choose $T_i^* = \tau_i'$. If $\tau_i' \le T_0 \le \tau_i$, then choose $T_i^* = T_0$. If $T_0 > \tau_i$, it is best to choose $T_i^* = \tau_i$.

We now consider minimizing

$$B(T_0) \doteq \frac{K_0}{T_0} + \sum_{i=1}^{n} b_i(T_0)$$

over all $T_0 > 0$. The function B is of the form

$$\frac{K(T_0)}{T_0} + M(T_0) + H(T_0)T_0$$

over any interval where $K()$, $M()$ and $H()$ are constant. For any T_0, define the sets $G(T_0) \doteq \{i : T_0 < \tau_i'\}$, $E(T_0) \doteq \{i : \tau_i' \le T_0 \le \tau_i'\}$ and $L(T_0) \doteq \{i : \tau_i < T_0\}$. Then $K()$, $M()$ and $H()$ are constant on those intervals where $G()$, $E()$ and $L()$ do not change. To find the minimum of B, consider the intervals induced by the $2n$ values τ_i' and τ_i for $i = 1, 2, \ldots, n$. Say T_0 falls in some specific interval; then we set

$$T_i^* = \begin{cases} \tau_i' & \text{if } i \in G(T_0) \\ T_0 & \text{if } i \in E(T_0) \\ \tau_i & \text{if } i \in L(T_0). \end{cases}$$

The sets G, E and L change only when T_0 crosses a *breakpoint* τ_i' or τ_i for some $i \ge 1$. Specifically, if T_0 moves from right to left across τ_i, retailer i moves from L to E. If T_0 moves from right to left across τ_i', retailer i moves from E to G. This suggests a simple algorithm to minimize $B(T_0)$. Start with T_0 larger than the largest breakpoint, and let $L = \{1, 2, \ldots, n\}$ and $G = E = \emptyset$. We then successively decrease T_0 moving from interval to interval. On each interval we need only check that $\sqrt{\frac{K(T_0)}{H(T_0)}}$ falls in the same subinterval as T_0. In this case we set $T_0^* = \sqrt{\frac{K(T_0)}{H(T_0)}}$. Let $B^* \doteq B(T_0^*) = \inf_{T_0 \ge 0}\{B(T_0)\}$; then this value is clearly a lower bound on the cost of any power of two policy.

We now want to prove that this value is a lower bound on the cost of any policy. For notational convenience, we abbreviate $G = G(T_0^*)$, $E = E(T_0^*)$ and $L = L(T_0^*)$.

Let $K = K_0 + \sum_{i \in E} K_i$, $G = \sum_{i \in E}(g_i + g^i) + \sum_{i \in L} g^i$ and $M = 2\sqrt{KG}$. We also define for each $i \geq 0$

$$G_i = \begin{cases} g_i + g^i, & \text{if } i \in G, \\ g_i, & \text{if } i \in L, \\ \frac{K_i}{(T_0^*)^2}, & \text{if } i \in E \cup \{0\}, \end{cases}$$

$G^i = g^i + g_i - G_i$, and $M_i = 2\sqrt{K_i G_i}$. In this way we can write B^* as

$$B^* = M + \sum_{i \in L \cup G} M_i. \tag{9.8}$$

We now prove that B^* is a lower bound on any policy. We first show that in fact $B^* = \sum_{i \geq 0} M_i$. From (9.8), we need only show that $M = \sum_{i \in E \cup \{0\}} M_i$,

$$M = 2\sqrt{KG} = 2\frac{K}{T_0^*}$$

$$= 2 \sum_{i \in E \cup \{0\}} \frac{K_i}{T_0^*}$$

$$= 2 \sum_{i \in E \cup \{0\}} \frac{K_i}{\sqrt{K_i / G_i}}$$

$$= 2 \sum_{i \in E \cup \{0\}} \sqrt{K_i G_i}$$

$$= \sum_{i \in E \cup \{0\}} M_i.$$

Consider any policy over an interval $[0, t']$ for $t' > 0$. We show that the total cost associated with this policy over $[0, t']$ is at least $B^* t'$. Let m_i be the number of orders placed by facility $i \geq 0$ in the interval $[0, t']$. Let $I_i(t)$ be the inventory at facility $i \geq 1$ at time t and let $S_i(t)$ be the system inventory of facility $i \geq 1$ at time t. Clearly, total inventory holding cost is

$$\sum_{i \geq 1} \int_0^{t'} \left(g_i I_i(t) + g^i S_i(t) \right) dt.$$

We will show that this is no smaller than

$$\sum_{i \geq 1} \int_0^{t'} \left(G_i I_i(t) + G^i S_i(t) \right) dt.$$

For this purpose consider the quantity $G_i I_i(t) + G^i S_i(t)$ for each $i \geq 1$. There are three cases to consider.

Case 1: $i \in G$. Then $G_i = g_i + g^i$ and $G^i = g_i + g^i - G_i = 0$ and since $S_i(t) \geq I_i(t)$ for all $t > 0$, we have

$$g_i I_i(t) + g^i S_i(t) \geq G_i I_i(t) + G^i S_i(t).$$

Case 2: $i \in L$. Then $G_i = g_i$ and $G^i = g_i + g^i - G_i = g^i$; hence

$$g_i I_i(t) + g^i S_i(t) = G_i I_i(t) + G^i S_i(t).$$

Case 3: $i \in E$. Then $G_i = \frac{K_i}{(T_0^*)^2}$ and $G^i = g_i + g^i - G_i$. Observe that by definition if $i \in E$, then $\tau_i' \leq T_0^* \leq \tau_i$ which implies $g_i \leq G_i \leq g_i + g^i$. Since $S_i(t) \geq I_i(t)$ for all $t \geq 0$, then

$$g_i I_i(t) + g^i S_i(t) = G_i I_i(t) + G^i S_i(t) + (G_i - g_i)(S_i(t) - I_i(t))$$
$$\geq G_i I_i(t) + G^i S_i(t). \qquad (9.9)$$

Finally, it is a simple exercise (see Exercise 9.7) to show that $G_0 = \sum_{i \geq 1} G^i$, and therefore our lower bound on the inventory holding cost can be written as

$$\sum_{i \geq 1} \int_0^{t'} \left(G_i I_i(t) + G^i S_i(t) \right) dt = \sum_{i \geq 0} \int_0^{t'} G_i I_i(t) dt,$$

where we have defined $I_0(t) = \frac{1}{G_0} \sum_{i \geq 1} G^i S_i(t)$.

Hence, total cost per unit of time under this policy is at least

$$\frac{1}{t'} \sum_{i \geq 0} \left(K_i m_i + \int_0^{t'} G_i I_i(t) dt \right) \geq \sum_{i \geq 0} \left(K_i \frac{m_i}{t'} + G_i \frac{t'}{m_i} \right) \quad \text{(by Property 9.1.1)}$$

$$\geq 2 \sum_{i \in L \cup G} \sqrt{K_i G_i} + 2 \sum_{i \in E \cup \{0\}} \sqrt{K_i G_i}$$

$$= \sum_{i \geq 0} M_i = B^*.$$

We have thus established that B^* is a lower bound on the total cost per unit time of any policy.

Finally, for each $i \in G \cup L$ select a power of two policy (a value of k) such that

$$\frac{1}{\sqrt{2}} T_i^* \leq T_B 2^k \leq \sqrt{2} T_i^*.$$

For each $i \in E \cup \{0\}$ select a power of two policy (a value of k) such that

$$\frac{1}{\sqrt{2}} T_0^* \leq T_B 2^k \leq \sqrt{2} T_0^*.$$

It is a simple exercise (Exercise 9.4) to show that the policy constructed in this manner has cost at most 1.06 times the cost of the lower bound.

9.4   Exercises

Exercise 9.1. Consider the Economic Lot Size Model and let K be the set-up cost, h be the holding cost per item per unit of time and D the demand rate. Shortage is not allowed and the objective is to find an order quantity so as to minimize the long-run average cost. That is, the objective is to minimize

$$C(Q) = \frac{KD}{Q} + \frac{hQ}{2},$$

where Q is the order quantity. Suppose the warehouse can order only an integer multiple of q units. That is, the warehouse can order q, or $2q$, or $3q$, etc.

(a) Prove that the optimal order quantity Q^* has the following property. There exists an integer m such that $Q^* = mq$ and

$$\sqrt{\frac{m-1}{m}} \le \frac{Q^e}{Q^*} \le \sqrt{\frac{m+1}{m}},$$

where Q^e, the Economic Order Quantity, is:

$$Q^e = \sqrt{\frac{2KD}{h}}.$$

(b) Suppose now that $m \ge 2$. Show that $C(Q^*) \le 1.06C(Q^e)$.

Exercise 9.2. (Zavi, 1976) Consider the Economic Lot Size Model with infinite horizon and deterministic demand D items per unit of time. When the inventory level is zero, production of Q items starts at a rate of P items per unit of time, $P \ge D$. The set-up cost is $K\$$ and holding cost is $h\$$/item/time. Every time production starts at a level of P items/time, we incur a cost of αP, $\alpha > 0$.

(a) What is the optimal production rate?

(b) Suppose that due to technological constraints, P must satisfy $2D \le P \le 3D$. What is the optimal production rate and the optimal order quantity?

Exercise 9.3. Consider the Economic Lot Size Model over the infinite horizon. Assume that when an order of size Q is placed the items are delivered by trucks of capacity q and thus the number of trucks used to deliver Q is $\lceil \frac{Q}{q} \rceil$, where $\lceil m \rceil$ is the smallest integer greater than or equal to m. The set-up cost is a linear function of the number of trucks used: it is $K_0 + \lceil \frac{Q}{q} \rceil K$. Holding cost is h \$/item/time and shortage is not allowed. What is the optimal reorder quantity?

Exercise 9.4. Prove that the heuristic for the Single Warehouse Multi-Retailer Model described in Section 9.3 provides a solution within 1.06 of the lower bound.

Exercise 9.5. Consider the power of two policies described in the single product model of Section 9.1.3. Describe how you could generate a power of three policy (a policy where each $T_i = 3^k T_B$ for some integer $k \geq 0$). What is the effectiveness (in terms of worst-case performance) of the best power of three policy?

Exercise 9.6. (Porteus, 1985) The Japanese concept of JIT (Just In Time) advocates reducing set up cost as much as possible. To analyze this concept, consider the Economic Lot Size model with constant demand of D items per year, holding cost h \$ per item per year and **current set up cost** K_0. Suppose **you can** lease a new technology that allows you to reduce the set up cost from K_0 to K at an annual leasing cost of $A - Bln(K)$ dollars. That is, reducing the set up cost from the current set up cost, K_0, to K will cost annually $A - Bln(K)$ dollars. Of course, we assume that $A - B\ln(K_0) = 0$ which implies that using the current set up cost requires no leasing cost. What is the optimal set up cost? What is the optimal order quantity in this case?

Exercise 9.7. Show that in the proof of the lower bound, B^*, for the single warehouse multi-retailer model we have $G_0 = \sum_{i \geq 1} G^i$.

Exercise 9.8. Prove equation (9.9).

10
Economic Lot Size Models with Varying Demands

Our analysis of inventory models so far has focused on situations where demand was both known in advance and constant over time. We now relax this latter assumption and turn our attention to systems where demand is known in advance, yet varies with time. This is possible, for example, if orders have been placed in advance, or contracts have been signed specifying deliveries for the next few months. In this case, a *planning horizon* is defined as those periods where demand is known. Our objective is to identify optimal inventory policies for single item models as well as heuristics for the multi-item case.

10.1   The Wagner-Whitin Model

Assume we must plan a sequence of orders, or production batches, over a T period planning horizon. In each period, a single decision must be made: the size of the order or production batch.

We make the following assumptions.

- Demand during period t is known and is denoted $d_t > 0$.

- The per unit order cost is c and a fixed order cost K is incurred every time an order is placed; that is, if y units are ordered, the order cost is $cy + K\delta(y)$ (where $\delta(y) = 1$ if $y > 0$, and 0 otherwise).

- The holding cost is $h > 0$ per unit per period.

- Initial inventory is zero.

- Leadtimes are zero; that is, an order arrives as soon as it is placed.

- All ordering and demand occurs at the start of the period. Inventory is charged on the amount on hand at the end of the period.

The problem is to decide how much to order in each period so that demands are met without backlogging and the total cost, including the cost of ordering and holding inventory, is minimized. This basic model was first analyzed by Wagner and Whitin (1958) and has now been called the Wagner-Whitin Model.

In this model, it is clear that the total variable order cost incurred will be fixed and independent of the schedule of orders, and thus this cost can be ignored. Let y_t be the amount ordered in period t, and I_t be the amount of product in inventory at the end of period t. Using these variables, the problem can be formulated as follows:

$$\text{Problem } WW: \quad Min \sum_{t=1}^{T} \left[K\delta(y_t) + hI_t \right]$$

$$s.t.$$

$$I_t = I_{t-1} + y_t - d_t, \quad t = 1, 2, \ldots, T \quad (10.1)$$
$$I_0 = 0 \quad (10.2)$$
$$I_t, y_t \geq 0, \quad t = 1, 2, \ldots, T. \quad (10.3)$$

Here constraints (10.1) are called the *inventory-balance* constraints, while (10.2) simply specifies initial inventory. Note that the inventory can also be rewritten as: $I_t = \sum_{i=1}^{t}(y_i - d_i)$ and therefore the I_t variables can be eliminated from the formulation.

Wagner and Whitin made the following important observation.

Theorem 10.1.1 *Any optimal policy is a zero-inventory ordering policy, that is, a policy in which*

$$y_t I_{t-1} = 0, \text{ for } t = 1, 2, \ldots, T.$$

Proof. The proof is quite simple. By contradiction, assume there is an optimal policy in which an order is placed in period t even though the inventory level at the beginning of the period (I_{t-1}) is positive. We will demonstrate the existence of another policy with lower total cost. Evidently, the I_{t-1} items of inventory were ordered in various periods prior to t. Thus, if we instead order these items in period t, we save all the holding cost incurred from the time they were each ordered. ∎

Thus, ordering only occurs when inventory is zero. A simple corollary is that in an optimal policy *an order is of size equal to satisfy demands for an integer number of subsequent periods*.

Using the above property, Wagner and Whitin developed a dynamic programming algorithm to determine those periods when ordering takes place. By constructing a simple acyclic network with nodes $V = \{1, 2, \ldots, T+1\}$, we can view the problem of determining a policy as a shortest path problem. Formally, let ℓ_{ij}, the length of arc (i, j) in this network, be the cost of ordering in period i to satisfy the demands in periods $i, i + 1, \ldots, j - 1$, for all $1 \le i < j \le T + 1$. That is,

$$\ell_{ij} = K + h \sum_{k=i}^{j-1} (k - i) d_k.$$

All other arcs have $\ell_{ij} = +\infty$. The length of the shortest path from node 1 to node $T + 1$ in this acyclic network is the minimal cost of satisfying the demands for periods 1 through T. The optimal policy, that is, a specification of the periods in which an order is placed, can be easily reconstructed from the shortest path itself. This procedure is clearly $O(T^2)$.

Most of the assumptions made above can be relaxed without changing the basic solution methodology. For example, one can consider problem data that are period dependent (e.g., c_t, h_t or K_t). The assumption of zero leadtimes can be relaxed if one assumes the leadtimes are known in advance and deterministic. In that case, if an order is required in period t, then it is ordered in period $t - L$, where L is the leadtime.

Researchers have also considered order costs that are general concave functions of the amount ordered, that is, $c_t(y)$. The problem can be formulated as a network flow problem with concave arc costs. This was the approach of Zangwill (1966) who also extended the model to handle backlogging, although the solution method is only computationally attractive for small size problems.

The Wagner-Whitin model can also be useful if demands during periods well into the future are not known. This idea is embodied in the following theorem.

Theorem 10.1.2 *Let t be the last period a set-up occurs in the optimal order policy associated with a T period problem. Then for any problem of length $T^* > T$ it is necessary to consider only periods $\{j : t \le j \le T^*\}$ as candidates for the last set-up. Furthermore, if $t = T$, the optimal solution to a T^* period problem has $y_t > 0$.*

This result is useful since it shows that if an order is placed in period t, the optimal policy for periods $1, 2, \ldots, t - 1$ does not depend on demands beyond period t.

Surprisingly, even though the Wagner-Whitin solution procedure is extremely efficient, often simple approximate, yet intuitive, heuristics may be more appealing to managers. For example, this may be the reason for the popularity of the Silver-Meal (1973) heuristic or the Part-Period Balancing heuristic of Dematteis (1968). One important reason is the sensitivity of the *optimal* strategy to changes in forecasted demands $d_t, t = 1, 2, \ldots, T$. Indeed, in practice these forecasted demands are typically modified "on-the-fly." These changes typically imply changes in the optimal strategy. Some of the previously mentioned heuristics are not as sensitive to these changes while producing optimal or near optimal strategies. For another approach, see Federgruen and Tzur (1991).

Recently researchers have shown that it is possible to take advantage of the special cost structure in the Wagner-Whitin model and use it to develop faster exact algorithms (i.e., $O(T)$). This includes the work of Aggarwal and Park (1990), Federgruen and Tzur (1991) and Wagelmans et al. (1992).

We sketch here the $O(T)$ algorithm of Wagelmans et al. which is the most intuitive of the ones proposed. It is a backwards dynamic programming approach. Define $d_{ij} = \sum_{t=i}^{j} d_t$ for $i, j = 1, 2, \ldots, T$, that is, the demand from period i to period j. To describe the algorithm, we will change slightly the way we account for the holding cost. If an item is ordered in period i to satisfy a demand in period $j \geq i$, then we are charged $H_i \doteq (T - i + 1)h$ per unit. That is, we incur the holding cost until the end of the time horizon. As long as we remember to subtract the constant $h \sum_{i=1}^{T} d_{1i}$ from our final cost, then we are charged exactly the right amount. With this in mind, define $G(i)$ to be cost of an optimal solution with a planning horizon from period i to period T, for $i = 1, 2, \ldots, T$. For convenience, define $G(T + 1) = 0$. Then,

$$G(i) = \min_{i < t \leq T+1} \{K + H_i d_{i,t-1} + G(t)\}$$

$$= K + \min_{i < t \leq T+1} \{H_i d_{i,t-1} + G(t)\}. \tag{10.4}$$

The final cost is then $G(1) - h \sum_{i=1}^{T} d_{1i}$. Using this recursion, which is just a reformulation of the shortest path recursion discussed earlier, it is clear that the complexity is $O(T^2)$. Wagelmans et al.'s $O(T)$ algorithm is based on the crucial observation that with careful implementation, the total amount of time spent finding the period that minimizes (10.4) over the entire running of the algorithm is $O(T)$.

Consider the calculation of $G(i)$. It is useful to plot the points $(d_{jT}, G(j))$ for $j = i+1, i+2, \ldots, T+1$, where the point $(d_{T+1,T}, G(T+1))$ is simply the origin. Let $\mathcal{E}$ be the lower convex envelope of these points; then define the function $g(x) = y$ if and only if $(x, y) \in \mathcal{E}$. It is clear that g is a piecewise linear convex function on $[0, d_{i+1,T}]$ with $g(d_{i+1,T}) = G(i + 1)$ and $g(0) = 0$. See Figure 10.1.

Define the breakpoints of g to be all the points x where g changes slope in addition to the points $x = 0$ and $x = d_{i+1,T}$. If x is a breakpoint, then $x = d_{jT}$ for some period $j \in \{i + 1, i + 2, \ldots, T + 1\}$. Let there be r breakpoints and let $i + 1 = t(1) < t(2) < \ldots < t(r) = T + 1$ denote the corresponding periods. These periods are called *efficient* because of the following.

Theorem 10.1.3

$$\min_{i < t \leq T+1} \{H_i d_{i,t-1} + G(t)\} = \min_{1 \leq p \leq r} \{H_i d_{i,t(p)-1} + G(t(p))\}.$$

Proof. Suppose that j (with $i + 1 < j < T + 1$) is not an efficient period and let k and ℓ (with $k < j < \ell$) be the two consecutive efficient periods straddling j. The slope of g on $[d_{\ell T}, d_{kT}]$ is equal to $[G(k) - G(\ell)]/d_{k,\ell-1}$, hence

$$g(d_{jT}) = G(\ell) + \frac{G(k) - G(\ell)}{d_{k,\ell-1}} d_{j,\ell-1}.$$

Furthermore, $G(j) \geq g(d_{jT})$.

There are two cases to consider.

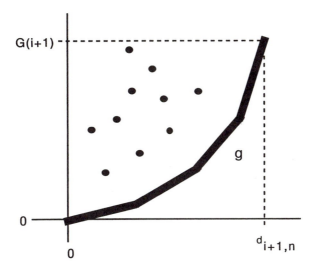

FIGURE 10.1. The plotted points and the function g.

Case 1: $H_i \geq \frac{G(k) - G(\ell)}{d_{k,\ell-1}}$. Then

$$H_i d_{i,j-1} + G(j) \geq H_i d_{i,k-1} + H_i d_{k,j-1} + g(d_{jT})$$

$$\geq H_i d_{i,k-1} + \frac{G(k) - G(\ell)}{d_{k,\ell-1}} d_{k,j-1} + G(\ell) + \frac{G(k) - G(\ell)}{d_{k,\ell-1}} d_{j,\ell-1}$$

$$= H_i d_{i,k-1} + G(k).$$

Case 2: $H_i < \frac{G(k) - G(\ell)}{d_{k,\ell-1}}$. Then

$$H_i d_{i,j-1} + G(j) \geq H_i d_{i,\ell-1} - H_i d_{j,\ell-1} + g(d_{jT})$$

$$\geq H_i d_{i,\ell-1} - \frac{G(k) - G(\ell)}{d_{k,\ell-1}} d_{j,\ell-1} + G(\ell) + \frac{G(k) - G(\ell)}{d_{k,\ell-1}} d_{j,\ell-1}$$

$$= H_i d_{i,\ell-1} + G(\ell).$$

In both cases, the minimum occurs at an efficient period. ∎

Being able to quickly find the efficient period p that achieves the minimum is therefore crucial to the complexity of the algorithm. This step is aided by the following result.

Lemma 10.1.4 *Let k and ℓ, $k < \ell$ be two consecutive efficient periods. If*

$$\frac{G(k) - G(\ell)}{d_{k,\ell-1}} < H_i,$$

then

$$H_i d_{i,k-1} + G(k) < H_i d_{i,\ell-1} + G(\ell);$$

otherwise

$$H_i d_{i,k-1} + G(k) \geq H_i d_{i,\ell-1} + G(\ell).$$

Proof. Suppose that $\frac{G(k)-G(\ell)}{d_{k,\ell-1}} < H_i$; then $G(k) < H_i d_{k,\ell-1}+G(\ell)$. Adding $H_i d_{i,k-1}$ to both sides results in $H_i d_{i,k-1} + G(k) < H_i d_{i,\ell-1} + G(\ell)$. The other case can be shown in a similar fashion. ∎

We now describe specifically how to find the efficient period achieving the minimum in (10.4). This is done by keeping an up-to-date list L of the current efficient periods. Let $\ell(p)$ be the index of the efficient period immediately following efficient period p; that is, $p < \ell(p)$. From Lemma 10.1.4 and the convexity of g it follows that the value of j that achieves the minimum of

$$\min_{i < j \leq T+1}\{H_i d_{i,j-1} + G(j)\}$$

corresponds to the period $q(i)$ defined by:

$$q(i) \doteq \min\left[T+1, \min\left\{p \in L \mid p < T+1 \text{ and } \frac{G(p) - G(\ell(p))}{d_{p,\ell(p)-1}} < H_i\right\}\right],$$

because then

$$H_i d_{i,p-1} + G(p) \geq H_i d_{i,\ell(p)-1} + G(\ell(p)), \quad \text{for } p \in L \text{ and } p < q(i),$$

and

$$H_i d_{i,p-1} + G(p) < H_i d_{i,\ell(p)-1} + G(\ell(p)), \quad \text{for } p \in L \text{ and } p \geq q(i).$$

In fact, it is easy to determine $q(i)$ from $q(i+1)$. Note that $q(i+1) \in L$ and as long as $q(i+1)$ is efficient it has the same successor $\ell(i+1)$ in L. Using the definition of $q(i+1)$ we obtain:

$$\frac{G(q(i+1)) - G(\ell(q(i+1)))}{d_{q(i+1),\ell(q(i+1))-1}} < H_{i+1} \leq H_i.$$

Hence, it follows that $q(i) \leq q(i+1)$; that is, *the values of $q(i)$ are decreasing in i.* Therefore, starting at $q(i+1)$ we successively decrement by one until we find $q(i)$. The total amount of time spent searching for $q(i)$ in the entire algorithm is therefore $O(T)$.

To complete the complexity result, we must be able to quickly update the list of efficient periods, that is, update the lower convex envelope. After calculating $G(i)$ and plotting the point $(d_{iT}, G(i))$, we search for the smallest efficient period $t(s)$ such that the slope of the line segment connecting $(d_{iT}, G(i))$ to $(d_{t(s),T}, G(t(s)))$ is greater than the slope of the line segment connecting $(d_{t(s+1),T}, G(t(s+1)))$ to $(d_{t(s),T}, G(t(s)))$ (thus maintaining convexity). Then the new efficient periods are i and the periods from $t(s)$ to $t(r) \equiv T+1$; the efficient periods between $i+1$ and $t(s)-1$ become inefficient. Since a period can become inefficient at most once, one can verify that the total amount of work spent updating the list L over the entire algorithm is $O(T)$.

10.2   Models with Capacity Constraints

An important generalization of the Wagner-Whitin model is the inclusion of upper bounds on the amount that can be ordered or produced in a given period. This corresponds to adding the following constraints to Problem WW.

$$y_t \leq C_t, \quad t = 1, 2, \ldots, T. \tag{10.5}$$

The values $C_t \geq 0$ correspond to the maximum amount that can be ordered (or produced) in period t due to, for example, limited production capacities.

In this case, the problem is not as simple as before; Florian et al. (1980) show that in general, the problem is $\mathcal{NP}$-Complete. Florian and Klein (1971) propose a dynamic programming approach which involves solving a sequence of acyclic shortest path problems for the special case where $C_t = C$ for all t. Love (1973) devises an algorithm based on characterizing the extreme points of the solution space for the general problem. The branch and bound algorithm of Baker et al. (1978) seems to be the most computationally effective, although it is not polynomial.

We sketch here the approach of Florian and Klein. For now assume unequal capacities; most of the structural results proved by Florian and Klein hold in this more general case. Clearly, a feasible solution exists if and only if

$$\sum_{j=1}^{i} C_j \geq \sum_{j=1}^{i} d_j, \quad \text{for } i = 1, 2, \ldots, T.$$

We therefore assume this is satisfied. Let

$$\mathcal{P} = \{y \in \mathbb{R}^T : y \text{ satisfies (10.1), (10.2), (10.3) and (10.5)}\},$$

and let D be the set of extreme points of $\mathcal{P}$. Since the objective function is concave (why?), we know an optimal solution will exist in D.

Florian and Klein prove the following *Inventory Decomposition Property*.

Theorem 10.2.1 *Suppose that the constraint*

$$I_k = 0, \text{ for some } k \in [1, \ldots, T - 1]$$

is added to Problem WW and

$$\sum_{j=k+1}^{i} C_j \geq \sum_{j=k+1}^{i} d_j, \quad \text{for } i = k+1, \ldots, T$$

holds. Then an optimal solution to the original problem can be found by independently finding solutions to the problems for the first k periods and for the last $T - k$ periods.

This is clearly a generalization of Theorem 10.1.2. Following this idea, call a period t a *regeneration point* if $I_t = 0$. Define a *production sequence* S_{ij}, where $0 \leq i < j \leq T$, to be:

$$S_{ij} = \{(y_{i+1}, y_{i+2}, \ldots, y_j) \mid I_i = I_j = 0, I_k > 0 \text{ for } i < k < j\}.$$

Clearly, any production plan can be decomposed into a set of production sequences. Define a production sequence S_{ij} to be *capacity constrained* if the production level in at most one period k, $(i + 1 \leq k \leq j)$ satisfies $0 < y_k < C_k$ and all other production levels are either zero or at their capacities.

The authors then characterize the extreme points of $\mathcal{P}$ in the following way.

Theorem 10.2.2

$y \in D \Longleftrightarrow y$ *consists of capacity constrained production sequences only.*

This characterization is done in several steps. First:

Lemma 10.2.3 *If* $y \in D$, *then* y *consists only of capacity constrained production sequences.*

Proof. Suppose $y \in D$ and S_{ij} is a production sequence of y that is not capacity constrained. This means there are at least two periods, say k and ℓ, $(i + 1 \leq k < \ell \leq j)$, in which $0 < y_k < C_k$ and $0 < y_\ell < C_\ell$. Without loss of generality we can assume there are only two periods of this type.
Let

$$\delta = \frac{1}{2} \min\{y_k, C_k - y_k, y_\ell, C_\ell - y_\ell, \min_{i+1 \leq t < j} I_t\},$$

and let e_n be the $(j - i)$ component vector with a one in the nth position and zeros everywhere else. Define two production sequences

$$S'_{ij} = S_{ij} - \delta e_k + \delta e_\ell,$$

and

$$S''_{ij} = S_{ij} + \delta e_k - \delta e_\ell.$$

Note that production sequence S'_{ij} simply represents a shifting of production from period k to period ℓ, while sequence S''_{ij} represents the opposite shift. They are clearly feasible, and since $\delta > 0$ they are distinct. However, $S_{ij} = \frac{1}{2}(S'_{ij} + S''_{ij})$, a contradiction. ∎

Lemma 10.2.4 *If* y' *and* y'' *are distinct feasible production plans and* $y = \frac{1}{2}(y' + y'')$, *then* y' *and* y'' *share all the regeneration points of* y.

Proof. Let period k be a regeneration point of y. Then

$$0 = \sum_{t=1}^{k}(y_t - d_t) = \frac{1}{2}\left[\sum_{t=1}^{k}(y'_t - d_t) + \sum_{t=1}^{k}(y''_t - d_t)\right] = \frac{1}{2}(I'_k + I''_k).$$

Since $I'_k, I''_k \geq 0$, both I'_k and I''_k must be zero. ∎

Lemma 10.2.5 *If a feasible plan y consists only of capacity constrained production sequences, then $y \in D$.*

Proof. Suppose by contradiction that $y \notin D$. Then there exist feasible plans y' and y'' such that $y = \frac{1}{2}(y' + y'')$.

From Lemma 10.2.4, y' and y'' share the regeneration points of y. Let i and j be two such successive regeneration points, and let S_{ij}, S'_{ij} and S''_{ij} be the associated distinct production sequences of y, y' and y'', respectively. Evidently,

$$S_{ij} = \frac{1}{2}(S'_{ij} + S''_{ij}).$$

We show that the only possibility is $S_{ij} = S'_{ij} = S''_{ij}$. For this purpose, consider any period k, $i + 1 \leq k \leq j$ and observe that y_k can take only three possible values. Either $y_k = 0$ in which case $y'_k = y''_k = 0$, or $y_k = C_k$ in which case $y'_k = y''_k = C_k$ or $0 < y_k < C_k$. Since S_{ij} is a capacity constrained sequence, at most one period, say period ℓ, $i + 1 \leq \ell \leq j$ has $0 < y_\ell < C_\ell$. But total production between period $i + 1$ and period j must be equal to total demands over the same periods, and hence $y_\ell = y'_\ell = y''_\ell$. Consequently, $S_{ij} = S'_{ij} = S''_{ij}$. ∎

This completes the proof of Theorem 10.2.2.

It is now clear that an optimal solution must be made up of a sequence of optimal capacity constrained production sequences. However, determining these sequences can be quite tedious and computationally expensive. To make the problem tractable, Florian and Klein consider the case where the capacity constraints are identical and equal to C. Demand between any two periods, say periods i and j, can then be written as $mC + p$ where m is an integer and $p < C$. Then:

Corollary 10.2.6 *If $C_t = C$ for all t, an optimal production sequence has a number of periods in which production levels are equal to C, at most one period where production level is $0 < p < C$, and the remaining periods have zero production levels.*

This simplifies the problem considerably; for example, consider determining the optimal production sequence between regeneration points i and j. From Corollary 10.2.6, in each period $k \in \{i + 1, i + 2, \ldots, j\}$ production is either 0, C or p for some $p \in (0, C)$. Let $Y_k = \sum_{\ell=i+1}^{k} y_k$, for $i < k \leq j$, that is, the amount produced between periods $i + 1$ and k in this production sequence. Then Y_k can only take on values in $\{0, p, C, C + p, 2C, \ldots, mC, mC + p\}$.

Thus, we can construct a network where the vertices correspond to the possible values of Y_k for each $i < k \leq j$ with directed edges (Y_k, Y_{k+1}) defined by:

- If $Y_k = \ell C$, $\ell = 0, 1, \ldots, m$, then there are three edges emanating from this vertex: one to $Y_{k+1} = \ell C$ (corresponding to no production in period k), one to $Y_{k+1} = \ell C + p$ (corresponding to production of p in period k) and one to $Y_{k+1} = (\ell + 1)C$ (corresponding to production of C in period k).

- If $Y_k = \ell C + p$, $\ell = 0, 1, \ldots, m$, then there are two edges emanating from this vertex: one to $Y_{k+1} = \ell C + p$ (corresponding to no production in period

k) and one to $Y_{k+1} = (\ell + 1)C + p$ (corresponding to production of C in period k).

After creating an artificial initial vertex Y_0, we see that every path from Y_0 to Y_j represents a feasible capacity constrained production sequence. Assigning arc costs equal to the cost of producing and storing the corresponding product amounts, it is clear that finding the optimal production sequence from i to j is no harder than solving the shortest path problem on this network. The complexity of this procedure is clearly proportional to $(j - i)^2$, thus determining that the optimal production sequence between all pairs of periods is $O(T^3)$.

To determine the optimal production plan over the entire planning horizon, Florian and Klein solve another shortest path problem on a network similar to the one formulated in Section 10.1. That is, length of an arc (i, j) in this network is the total cost of the optimal production sequence from i to j. After solving the shortest path problem, the optimal set of regeneration points can be found by checking the shortest path. This step is $O(T^2)$.

Unfortunately, Florian and Klein's approach cannot be extended to a computationally effective technique for the general case with unequal capacities. In that case, a more effective approach may be the one by Baker et al. We sketch this approach here. As in the uncapacitated case, the authors first identify special properties that an optimal solution must satisfy. They are the following.

Theorem 10.2.7 *If* $(y_1, y_2, \ldots, y_T)$ *represents an optimal solution, then for every* t:

$$I_{t-1}(C_t - y_t)y_t = 0.$$

This can be proven easily using the same technique as in Theorem 10.1.1. Though not quite as useful as the Zero Inventory Ordering property of the (uncapacitated) Wagner-Whitin model, this property does simplify the problem considerably. It states that if there is inventory carried into the period, then production in this period is either zero or at capacity. On the other hand, if production is positive, but less than capacity, the inventory must be zero.

A simple corollary of this result, and the key to the approach, is the following.

Theorem 10.2.8 *Let* $t = \max\{j : y_j > 0\}$. *If* $(y_1, y_2, \ldots, y_T)$ *represents an optimal solution, then*

$$y_t = \min\left\{C_t, \sum_{j=t}^{T} d_j\right\}.$$

To see how this might be useful, consider the two possible cases. If $y_t = \sum_{j=t}^{T} d_j < C_t$, then since $I_{t-1} = 0$ the problem becomes one of determining the best way to satisfy the demands of periods $1, 2, \ldots, t - 1$ with no final inventory. On the other hand, if $y_t = C_t \leq \sum_{j=t}^{T} d_j$, then the problem becomes one of determining the best way to satisfy the demands of periods $1, 2, \ldots, t - 1$ with final inventory equal to $d = \sum_{j=t}^{T} d_j - C_t$. This final inventory stipulation can easily be handled by considering it simply as extra demand in that last period. Therefore, starting from the end of the planning horizon, one can successively solve smaller and more manageable problems.

The authors therefore propose a tree-search solution method that works as follows. We start at the root of the tree, the one associated with the last period, period T. Production in this period is either $y_T = 0$ or $y_T = \min\{C_T, d_T\}$ (from Theorem 10.2.8). These two possibilities result in the creation of two subproblems (or subnodes in the tree). The authors explain how to continue in this manner, and, using some shortcuts to reduce the number of nodes that need to be fathomed, it results in an effective technique. Unfortunately, since it is not a polynomial procedure, it is possible to construct examples where the amount of computation required using this method is extensive.

10.3   Multi-Item Inventory Models

In many practical situations, the coordination of inventory and ordering policies involves a variety of different products and this complicates the problem considerably. Consider the uncapacitated case once again, and assume there are n products. Each product faces a known demand during the next T periods. In addition, a fixed order cost of K_i is incurred every time product i is ordered.

For each product i, define the following.

- Let y_{it} be the amount of product i ordered in period t, for $t = 1, 2, \ldots, T$.

- Let h_i be the inventory holding cost for product i.

- Let I_{it} be the amount of product i in inventory at the start of period t, for $t = 1, 2, \ldots, T$.

- Let d_{it} be the demand in period t for product i, for $t = 1, 2, \ldots, T$.

Making the same assumptions as in the Wagner-Whitin model, the problem is then:

Problem P : Min $\displaystyle\sum_{t=1}^{T}\sum_{i=1}^{n}\left[K_i\delta(y_{it}) + h_i I_{it}\right]$

s.t.

$$I_{it} = I_{i,t-1} + y_{it} - d_{it}, \quad i = 1, 2, \ldots, n, \ t = 1, 2, \ldots, T \quad (10.6)$$

$$I_{i0} = 0, \quad i = 1, 2, \ldots, n \quad\quad\quad\quad\quad\quad\quad\quad\quad (10.7)$$

$$I_{it}, y_{it} \geq 0, \quad i = 1, 2, \ldots, n, \ t = 1, 2, \ldots, T \quad . \quad\quad (10.8)$$

Here (10.6) are inventory-balance constraints for each product, while (10.7) specify starting inventory for each product.

It is easy to see that P decomposes into m single product problems. Each of these single product problems can be solved using the algorithms for the Wagner-Whitin model.

A more realistic version of this problem is when a *joint set-up cost* K_0 is present. This cost is incurred whenever *any* product is ordered. The problem then becomes

$$\text{Problem } P': \quad Min \sum_{t=1}^{T} \left[K_0\delta(\sum_{i=1}^{n} y_{it}) + \sum_{i=1}^{m} \left(K_i\delta(y_{it}) + h_i I_{it} \right) \right]$$

$$s.t. \text{ (10.6), (10.7) and (10.8).}$$

Unfortunately, this problem is considerably more difficult to solve than the simple Wagner-Whitin model. In fact, Arkin et al. (1989) prove that it is $\mathcal{NP}$-Complete. Several researchers have proposed heuristics for this problem, including Silver (1976), Atkins and Iyogun (1988) and Joneja (1990). We present here the approach of Joneja.

The *cost covering* heuristic of Joneja proceeds period by period in a forward direction. Specifically, at period t, the ordering policy of periods $1, 2, \ldots, t-1$ has been determined and the decision is which items to order, if any, in period t. Let t_i be the last period in which item i was ordered. Let H_{it} denote the total inventory holding cost incurred by item i since period t_i assuming no order for item i is placed in period t. That is,

$$H_{it} = h_i \sum_{j=t_i+1}^{t} (j - t_i)d_{ij}.$$

Intuitively, if we forget for the moment, the joint order cost and $H_{it} > K_i$, then it is worth ordering item i in period t, since it costs more to keep an item in inventory from period t_i (the last time item i was ordered) to t than to order it in period t. The quantity $\max\{H_{it} - K_i, 0\}$ can be seen as the *savings* that are accrued by ordering item i in period t. This approach is basically the Silver-Meal heuristic adapted to the multiple item case. With the joint order cost present, an order should only be placed if the total savings accrued by ordering a set of items in period t exceeds the joint order cost. Therefore, Joneja proposes the following ordering rule.

Rule 1. In period t, order those items i such that $H_{it} \geq K_i$, if $\sum_{i=1}^{n} \max\{H_{it} - K_i, 0\} \geq K_0$.

Joneja shows that this single rule is not quite strong enough to ensure that the schedule of orders is cost efficient. For instance, consider the following example with two products. The holding costs are equal ($h_1 = h_2 = 1$). Pick an integer m and set the demands to

$$d_{1t} = 0, \text{ for } t = 1, 2, \ldots, m-1$$

$$d_{1m} = \frac{K_0 + K_1}{m - 1}$$

$$d_{2t} = 0, \text{ for } t = 1, 2, \ldots, m$$

$$d_{2,m+1} = \frac{K_0 + K_2}{m}.$$

Using Rule 1, item 1 will be ordered at time m, but not item 2. Item 2 will be ordered at time $m + 1$. If both items were ordered at time m, then we pay $h_2 d_{2,m+1} = \frac{K_0 + K_2}{m}$ in extra holding cost but save K_0 in ordering costs. Therefore, for large m, we see that we can be far from optimal.

To counteract this behavior, Joneja proposed the following additional feature. Let t_0 be the time at which the last joint order was placed, and assume item i was not included in this order (since $H_{it_0} < K_i$). It may, in some cases, be advantageous to order item i at time t_0 even though Rule 1 would specify the opposite. Define

$$S_{it} = h_i(t_0 - t_i) \sum_{j=t_0}^{t} d_{ij}.$$

Then S_{it} is the savings in inventory holding cost accrued by ordering item i at time t_0. Since a joint order is already placed in period t_0, the following rule was proposed.

Rule 2. In period t, if the last joint order was in period t_0, item i was not ordered in period t_0 and $S_{it} \geq K_i$, then order item i in period t_0.

Computational experiments with this heuristic, whose complexity is $O(nT)$, show that it produces solutions fairly close to optimal.

10.4   Exercises

Exercise 10.1. Assume order costs are general concave and time-dependent functions of the number of items produced. Also, assume holding costs are general concave and time-dependent functions of the number of items held in inventory. Prove that the Zero-Inventory Ordering Property holds in this general setting as well.

Exercise 10.2. The Silver-Meal Heuristic works as follows. Let $d_1, d_2, \ldots, d_n$ be the demands in the n period planning horizon. Define $C(T)$ to be the per period average holding and set-up cost under the condition that the current order covers demand in the next T periods. Then $C(1) = K$, $C(2) = \frac{1}{2}(K + hd_2)$, etc. In the Silver-Meal Heuristic we calculate these until $C(i) > C(i - 1)$. In this case, we stop and produce in period 1 to meet the demand of the first $i - 1$ periods. We then start over with the ith period.

Construct an example where the Silver-Meal Heuristic provides a nonoptimal solution.

Exercise 10.3. Determine the complexity of Baker et al.'s algorithm.

11
Stochastic Inventory Models

11.1 Introduction

The inventory models considered so far are all deterministic in nature; demand is assumed to be known and either constant over the infinite horizon or varying over a finite horizon. In many logistics systems, however, such assumptions are not appropriate. Typically, demand is a random variable whose distribution may be known.

Stochastic inventory models have attracted considerable attention in the last three decades. The pioneering work of Scarf (1960), Iglehart (1963a and b) and Veinott and Wagner (1965) for a single warehouse, Clark and Scarf (1960) for multi-echelon systems, Eppen and Schrage (1981) and Federgruen and Zipkin (1984a-c) for distribution systems, and Rosling (1989) for assembly systems, all represent milestones in our understanding of complex stochastic logistics systems. More recently, the work of Zheng (1991), Zheng and Federgruen (1991) and Chen and Zheng (1994) reveal new insights and provide more efficient algorithms for these problems. For recent reviews, we refer the reader to Lee and Nahmias (1993), Porteus (1990) and the recent book by Zipkin (1997).

In this chapter we review some of the main results in stochastic inventory models. We start with the analysis of a single warehouse model. To build our intuition, Section 11.2 considers a single period model. In Sections 11.3 and 11.4 we show that the insight obtained in the previous section can be used to analyze a multi-period model. Section 11.5 extends the analysis further to the infinite horizon model. Finally, Section 11.6 describes the development of interesting bounds on the optimal cost for multi-echelon systems.

11.2   Single Period Models

Consider a company that designs, produces and sells winter fashion items such as skijackets, coats, etc. About six months before the winter season, the company must commit itself to specific production quantities for all its products. Since there is no clear indication as to how the market will respond to the new designs, these decisions are typically based on realized sales from the last few years, current economic conditions and professional judgment.

To assist management in selecting production quantities, the marketing department assumes that demand D for each new product is randomly distributed, generated from a product-specific distribution with continuous cdf $F(\cdot)$. Additional information available to the decision makers includes the variable production cost per unit c, the selling price per unit r, and the salvage value per unit v. Clearly, these variables should satisfy $r > c > v$, otherwise the problem can trivially be solved.

Since demand is a random variable, the decision concerning how many units to produce is based on the *expected cost* $z(y)$, which is a function of the amount produced y. This expected cost is

$$z(y) = cy - r \int_D \min(y, D) dF(D) - v \int_{D=0}^{y} (y - D) dF(D) \quad \text{for } y \geq 0.$$

Note that $\int_D \min(y, D) dF(D) = \int_0^y D dF(D) + y \int_y^{\infty} dF(D)$. Adding and subtracting the quantity $r \int_{D=y}^{\infty} D dF(D)$ to $z(y)$, we get

$$z(y) = cy - rE(D) - r \int_{D=y}^{\infty} (y - D) dF(D) - v \int_{D=0}^{y} (y - D) dF(D). \quad (11.1)$$

The objective is, of course, to choose y so as to minimize the expected cost $z(y)$. This is the so-called *newsboy problem*.

Taking the derivative of $z(y)$ with respect to y and using the Leibnitz rule, we get the optimality condition:

$$c - r(1 - \Pr\{D \leq y\}) - v \Pr\{D \leq y\} = 0,$$

which implies that the optimal production quantity S should satisfy

$$\Pr\{D \leq S\} = \frac{r - c}{r - v}.$$

Since by assumption, $r - c < r - v$ and $F(D)$ is continuous, a finite value S, $S > 0$ always exists. In addition, it can easily be verified that the expected cost $z(y)$ is *convex* for $y \in (0, \infty)$, and that the value of $z(y)$ tends to infinity as $y \to \infty$. Hence, the quantity S is a minimizer of $z(y)$.

Observe that, implicitly, three assumptions have been made in the above analysis. First, there is no initial inventory. Second, there is no fixed set-up cost for starting production. Third, the excess demand is lost; that is, if the demand D happens to be greater than the produced quantity y, then the additional revenue $r(D - y)$ is lost.

The tools developed so far allow us to extend the above results to models with initial inventory y_0, and set-up cost K. We now relax the first two assumptions. Observe that the expected cost of producing $(y - y_0)$ units is

$$K - cy_0 + z(y).$$

Hence, S clearly minimizes this expected cost if we decide to produce. Consequently, there are two cases to consider.

1. If $y_0 \geq S$, we should not produce anything.

2. If $y_0 < S$, the best we can do is to raise the inventory to level S. However, this is optimal only if $-cy_0 + z(y_0)$, the cost associated with not producing anything, is larger than or equals $K - cy_0 + z(S)$, the cost associated with producing $S - y_0$. That is, if $y_0 < S$, it is optimal to produce $S - y_0$ only if $z(y_0) \geq K + z(S)$.

Let s be a number such that

$$z(s) = K + z(S).$$

The discussion above implies that the optimal policy has the following structure.

Order $S - y_0$ if the initial inventory level y_0 is at or below s, otherwise do not order.

We refer to such a policy as an (s, S) policy. The quantity S is called the *order-up-to level* while s is referred to as the *reorder point*.

11.3   Finite Horizon Models

We are now ready to consider the finite horizon (multi-period) inventory problem. This problem can be described as follows. At the beginning of each period, for example, each week or every month, the inventory of a certain item at the warehouse is reviewed and the inventory level is noted. Then an order may be placed to raise the inventory level up to a certain level. Replenishment orders arrive instantly. The case with the nonzero leadtime will be discussed at the end of the Section 11.5.

We assume that demands for successive periods are independent and identically distributed. If the demand exceeds the inventory on hand, then the additional demand is backlogged and is filled when additional inventory becomes available. Thus, the backlogged units are viewed as negative inventory. The inventory left over at the end of the final period has a value of c per unit, and all unfilled demand at this time can be backlogged at the same cost c. As we shall see, these assumptions ensure that the expected (gross) revenue in each period is a constant, and therefore we will not include the revenue term in our formulation.

Costs include ordering, holding and shortage costs. Ordering cost consists of a set-up cost, K, charged every time the warehouse places a replenishment order, and a proportional purchase cost c. There is a holding cost of h^+ for each unit of the inventory on hand at the end of a period and a shortage cost of h^- per unit whenever demand exceeds the inventory on hand. To avoid triviality, we assume $h^-, h^+ > 0$ (why?). The objective is to determine an inventory policy that minimizes the expected cost over m periods. In what follows, we show that an (s_k, S_k) policy is optimal, and develop a dynamic programming algorithm to determine the optimal (s_k, S_k) values for $k = 1, 2, \ldots, m$. Of course, an (s_k, S_k) policy is similar to the (s, S) policy described earlier except that the parameters s and S may vary from period to period.

To characterize the optimal policy for the finite horizon model we first develop a dynamic programming formulation of the problem. Here we follow the convention of letting the index k represent the number of remaining periods; for example, $k = 1$ refers to the last period, and $k = m$ refers to the first period. Similarly, y_1 is the inventory level at the start of the final period (before possible ordering) and y_m is the initial inventory at the beginning of the first period.

If the inventory level immediately after ordering is y, then the expected one-period shortage and holding cost for that period is

$$G(y) = h^+ \int_D \max(y - D, 0) dF(D) + h^- \int_D \max(D - y, 0) dF(D), \quad (11.2)$$

which is the so-called one-period *loss function*. Since the maximum of convex functions is convex and since convexity is preserved under integration, we see that $G(y)$ is convex.

Given a policy $Y = (y^1, y^2, \cdots, y^m)$, where y^k are the order-up-to levels (random variables) and may be contingent upon other variables, the sum of the total expected proportional purchasing cost and salvage value P_Σ is given by

$$P_\Sigma = E\left[\sum_{k=1}^m c(y^k - y_k) - c(y^1 - D_1) \right],$$

where D_k is the realized demand in period k. Noting that $y_{k-1} = y^k - D_k$, we have

$$P_\Sigma = cE[y^m - y_m + y^{m-1} - (y^m - D_m) + \cdots + y^1 - (y^2 - D_2) + D_1 - y^1]$$
$$= cmE(D).$$

Thus, P_Σ is independent of the ordering policy, and we can drop off the linear ordering cost component from the formulation. This observation is quite intuitive, since all backlogged demand is filled at the end of the last period while all remaining inventory left at this period is salvaged, both at the same price c. We also remark that whenever possible, we will suppress the subscript k from D_k (because demands are iid) and superscript k from y^k.

To formulate the dynamic program, define the following two expected cost functions. Denote by y_k the inventory level, prior to ordering, at the beginning of period $m - k + 1$. Let $G^k(y_k)$ be the *expected cost* for the remaining k periods if *we do not order* in period $m - k + 1$ and act *optimally in the remaining $k - 1$ periods*. Let $z^k(y_k)$ be the *minimal expected cost* incurred through the remaining k periods if we *act optimally in period $m - k + 1$ and all the remaining $k - 1$ periods*. It follows that

$$G^k(y_k) = G(y_k) + \int_D z^{k-1}(y_k - D)dF(D),$$

and

$$z^k(y_k) = Min_{y \geq y_k} \quad \{K\delta(y - y_k) + G^k(y)\}, \tag{11.3}$$

where $\delta(x)$ is 1 if $x > 0$ and it is 0 otherwise.

Note that if we order up to the level $y > y_k$ in period $m - k + 1$, the cost for the final k periods is $K + G^k(y)$.

It remains to show that an (s_k, S_k) policy is optimal for every $k, k = 1, 2, \ldots, m$. For this purpose, it is sufficient to prove that the function $G^k(y)$ is K-convex, and $G^k(y) \to \infty$ as $|y| \to \infty$, for each period $k, k = 1, 2, \ldots, m$.

Definition 11.3.1 *A function g is K-convex if*

$$K + g(a + x) - g(x) - (a/b)(g(x) - g(x - b)) \geq 0$$

for any $a \geq 0, b \geq 0$ and for all $x \in (-\infty, \infty)$ (Scarf, 1960).

Note that a convex function is 0-convex, and a K_1-convex function is also K_2-convex if $K_2 > K_1$. To understand this definition we examine Figure 11.1. Here one observes that if initial inventory is y, then raising inventory to level S_1 is not optimal. This is true since the total cost at S_1, $g(S_1)$ plus K, is more than $g(y)$. Since the same holds for each of S_i, it follows that S is the (only) optimal order up to level. Note, on the other hand, that if the curve in the figure satisfies $K + g(S_1) < g(y)$, then it would have contradicted the definition of K-convexity. This is seen as follows. In the above definition, let $a + x = S_1$ and $x = y$ and hence,

$$K + g(S_1) - g(y) \geq \frac{S_1 - y}{b}[g(y) - g(y - b)] > 0,$$

for some small $b, b > 0$.

Lemma 11.3.2 *A K-convex function $g(y)$ is bounded for any finite y and continuous on $(-\infty, \infty)$.*

Proof. The finiteness of $g(y)$ for any $|y| < \infty$ follows directly from the definition of K-convexity. Now suppose, to the contrary, that $g(y)$ is not continuous. For some discontinuous point y ($|y| < \infty$), there are two possibilities: $g(y^+) \neq g(y^-)$ and $g(y) \neq g(y^-) = g(y^+)$. In either case, it is possible to choose x, a and b in Definition 11.3.1, such that K-convexity is always violated. For this purpose, choose the parameters such that $a/b \to \infty$, while $g(x) - g(x - b) < -p$ where p is a positive constant. ∎

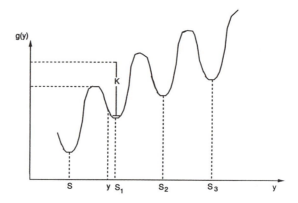

FIGURE 11.1. A K-convex function.

As in the single period problem, analyzed in Section 11.2, to prove that an (s_k, S_k) policy is optimal we must also show the existence of s_k and S_k, and that the typical graph for $G^k(y_k)$ is as illustrated in Figure 11.1, for $k = 1, \dots, m$. The proof is constructive in nature and proceeds in several steps. First, we assume that $G^k(y)$ is K-convex for all k, $k = 1, \dots, m$ and show the existence of an optimal (s_k, S_k) policy; then we show that $G^k(y)$ is indeed K-convex. The next two lemmas establish the optimality of (s_k, S_k) policies under the assumption that $G^k(y)$ is K-convex.

Lemma 11.3.3 $G^k(y) \to \infty$ as $|y| \to \infty$.

Proof. We prove by induction. For $k = 1$, $G^1(y) = G(y) > 0$ for all y and $G(y) \to \infty$ as $|y| \to \infty$. This implies that $z^1(y) > 0$. Now assume that $G^{k-1}(y) > 0$ for all y and is unbounded as $|y| \to \infty$. Then $z^{k-1}(y) > 0$ and $G^k(y) = G(y) + E_D[z^{k-1}(y - D)] > 0$ for all y, and hence $G^k(y) \to \infty$ as $|y| \to \infty$. ∎

Suppose that $G^k(y)$ is K-convex. Unfortunately, even with this assumption, the above two lemmas are still not sufficient to prove the optimality of (s_k, S_k) policies. The difficulty is that we have not ruled out the possibility of multiple (s_k, S_k) policies in period $m - k + 1$.

For this purpose, we need the following result.

Lemma 11.3.4 *Suppose that $G^k(y_k)$ is K-convex; then we have:*

(i) *there exists a number S_k minimizing $G^k(y_k)$;*

(ii) *there exists a number s_k such that $G^k(s_k) = K + G^k(S_k)$ and $s_k \leq S_k$. In case of multiple s_k, we choose the biggest one;*

(iii) *for $y_k \leq s_k$, $G^k(y_k)$ is nonincreasing, and there are no two points y_{k1} and y_{k2} such that $s_k < y_{k1} < y_{k2}$ and $G^k(y_{k1}) - G^k(y_{k2}) > K$.*

Before proving the Lemma, we demonstrate what happens if part (iii) does not hold. Suppose the second part of (iii) fails to hold. In this case, if we are facing inventory level y_{k1}, we will be better off raising the inventory level up to y_{k2}, since $G^k(y_{k2}) + K < G^k(y_{k1})$. Similarly, if the first part of (iii) fails to hold, it may be the case that $G^k(y_k) < G^k(S_k) + K$.

Proof. Parts (i) and (ii) follow easily from the continuity of $G^k(y_k)$ and the infiniteness of $G^k(y_k)$ as $|y| \to \infty$. Note that if there exist multiple numbers s_k, we choose the largest one.

To see that $G^k(y_k)$ is nonincreasing for $y_k \le s_k$, we suppose that, to the contrary, $G^k(y_k)$ has a local maximum at y^0. Without loss of generality, assume $G^k(y^0) \ge G^k(s_k)$. Then there must exist some positive number $\rho > 0$ so that $G^k(y^0) - G^k(y^0 - \rho) \ge 0$. Let $x = y^0$, $a + x = a + y^0 = S_k$ and $x - b = y^0 - \rho$. First assume that $G^k(y^0) > G^k(s_k)$. The K-convexity of $G^k(y_k)$ implies that

$$K + G^k(S_k) - G^k(y^0) - ((S_k - y^0)/\rho)(G^k(y^0) - G^k(y^0 - \rho)) \ge 0,$$

which, together with $K + G^k(S_k) = G^k(s_k)$, contradicts the hypothesis. Now assume that $G^k(y^0) = G^k(s_k)$; again, the K-convexity will not hold unless $G^k(y^0 - \rho) = G^k(s_k)$. This proves the first part of (iii).

We now show that there are no two points y_{k1} and y_{k2} such that $S_k < y_{k1} < y_{k2}$ and $G^k(y_{k1}) - G^k(y_{k2}) > K$. Again, assume that, to the contrary, such points exist. Let $x = y_{k1}$, $x - b = S_k$ and $x + a = y_{k2}$. The K-convexity of $G^k(y_k)$ gives

$$K + G^k(y_{k2}) - G^k(y_{k1}) - ((y_{k2} - y_{k1})/(y_{k1} - S_k))(G^k(y_{k1}) - G^k(S_k)) \ge 0,$$

which again contradicts the hypothesis, since $G^k(y_{k1}) \ge G^k(S_k)$.

Finally, it follows from (ii) that $G^k(y_{k1}) - G^k(y_{k2}) \le K$ for $s_k < y_{k1} \le y_{k2}$. ∎

The above lemma can be interpreted as follows. For $y_k \in (-\infty, s_k)$, $G^k(y_k) \ge G^k(s_k)$ and is nonincreasing; for $y_k \in (s_k, S_k]$, $G^k(y_k) - G^k(S_k) < K$; and finally, for $y_k > S_k$, $G^k(y_k) - G^k(y_k + a) \le K$ for any $a \ge 0$.

The next result follows directly from the above two lemmas.

Corollary 11.3.5 *If $G^k(y)$ satisfies the conditions specified in the above two lemmas, then the optimal inventory policy solving (11.3) is an (s_k, S_k) policy for all k, $k = 1, 2, \ldots, m$.*

Thus, the optimality of (s_k, S_k) policy in period k implies that

$$z^k(y_k) = \begin{cases} K + G^k(S_k) & \text{if } y_k \le s_k, \\ G^k(y_k) & \text{if } y_k > s_k. \end{cases} \tag{11.4}$$

It now remains to show that $G^k(y_k)$ is indeed K-convex.

Lemma 11.3.6 *The function $G^k(y)$ is K-convex for all k, $k = 1, \ldots, m$.*

Proof. We start by stating two properties of K-convex functions, whose proof follows directly from the definition of K-convexity. See, for instance, Dreyfus and Law (1977), Bertsekas (1987) or Exercise 11.6.

1. If $g_1(y)$ and $g_2(y)$ are K-convex and L-convex, respectively, then for $\alpha, \beta \geq 0$, $\alpha g_1(y) + \beta g_2(y)$ is $(\alpha K + \beta L)$-convex.

2. If $g(y)$ is K-convex, then $E_D[g(y - D)]$ is also K-convex.

We prove the lemma in two steps. In the first step we show that if the (s_{k-1}, S_{k-1}) policy is optimal in period $k - 1$ and $G^{k-1}(y)$ is K-convex, then $G^k(y)$ is also K-convex. In the second step, we demonstrate that $G^1(y)$ is K-convex. By Lemmas 11.3.2, 11.3.3 and 11.3.4, these two steps are sufficient to show that $G^k(y)$ is K-convex.

Consider Step 1. The definition of $G^k(y)$,

$$G^k(y) = G(y) + E_D[z^{k-1}(y - D)],$$

together with the two properties stated above implies that it suffices to show that $z^{k-1}(y)$ is K-convex. Our objective is to prove that

$$K + z^{k-1}(x + a) - z^{k-1}(x) - \frac{a}{b}(z^{k-1}(x) - z^{k-1}(x - b)) \geq 0$$

for any $a, b \geq 0$ and for all $x \in (-\infty, \infty)$. For this purpose, and following the treatment in Dreyfus and Law (1977), we differentiate between four cases, depending upon where x, $x + a$ and $x - b$ lie.

Case 1: $x - b > s_{k-1}$. Clearly, $x, x + a > s_{k-1}$. By (11.4), $z^{k-1}(x) = G^{k-1}(x)$ and hence, $z^{k-1}(x)$ is K-convex in this region.
Case 2: $x - b \leq s_{k-1} < x$. From (11.4),

$$K + z^{k-1}(x + a) - z^{k-1}(x) - \frac{a}{b}[z^{k-1}(x) - z^{k-1}(x - b)]$$

$$= K + G^{k-1}(x + a) - G^{k-1}(x) - \frac{a}{b}[G^{k-1}(x) - G^{k-1}(S_{k-1}) - K]$$

$$= K + G^{k-1}(x + a) - G^{k-1}(x) - \frac{a}{b}[G^{k-1}(x) - G^{k-1}(s_{k-1})]$$

$$\doteq W.$$

To see that $z^{k-1}(x)$ is K-convex in this region, we further consider two subcases: (2.1) $G^{k-1}(x) \leq G^{k-1}(s_{k-1})$ and (2.2) $G^{k-1}(x) > G^{k-1}(s_{k-1})$. In (2.1), $W \geq 0$ because of Lemma 11.3.4 (iii) and the K-convexity of $G^{k-1}(x)$. For (2.2), consider

$$K + G^{k-1}(x + a) - G^{k-1}(x) - \frac{a}{x - s_{k-1}}[G^{k-1}(x) - G^{k-1}(s_{k-1})] \doteq W'.$$

Because $G^{k-1}(x)$ is K-convex, $W' \geq 0$. By the assumption $x - b \leq s_{k-1} < x$, we see that $b \geq x - s_{k-1}$. Hence, $0 \leq W' \leq W$ and $z^{k-1}(x)$ is K-convex in this interval.
Case 3: $x \leq s_{k-1} < x + a$. In this case,

$$K + z^{k-1}(x + a) - z^{k-1}(x) - \frac{a}{b}[z^{k-1}(x) - z^{k-1}(x - b)]$$

$$= G^{k-1}(x + a) - G^{k-1}(S_{k-1}) \geq 0,$$

where the last inequality holds since S_{k-1} is a minimizer of $G^{k-1}(y)$.
Case 4: $x + a \le s_{k-1}$. In this case,

$$z^{k-1}(x) = z^{k-1}(x + a) = z^{k-1}(x - b) = K + G^{k-1}(S_{k-1}),$$

and therefore, $z^{k-1}(y)$ is obviously K-convex.

As for Step 2, the proof is straightforward. In the final period,

$$G^1(y_1) = G(y_1), \tag{11.5}$$

where the function $G(\cdot)$ is defined in equation (11.2). Since $G(y_1)$ is convex in y_1, $G^1(y_1)$ is thus K-convex. In addition, $G(y) \to \infty$ as $|y| \to \infty$. Hence, the (s_1, S_1) policy is optimal for the final period. The proof is now completed. $\blacksquare$

We now show how to solve the dynamic programming problem, that is, how to compute the optimal (s_k, S_k) policy for every $k \ge 1$. We start computing the optimal policy for the final period, and then recursively calculate the functions $G^k(y)$ and $z^k(y)$. These functions are used to determine the optimal (s_k, S_k) for $k = 2, \ldots, m$.

We know that the functions $G^1(y)$ and $z^1(y)$ as well as the optimal (s_1, S_1) can be found as described in Section 11.2. Given the functions $G^j(y)$ and $z^j(y)$ and the optimal (s_j, S_j), for $j = 1, 2, \ldots, k-1$, we determine the functions $G^k(y)$ and $z^k(y)$. As in the single period model, let

$$G_o^k(y_k) = K + G^k(S_k).$$

That is, $G_o^k(y_k)$ is the expected cost given that we start in period $m - k + 1$ with on-hand inventory of y_k units, order up to S_k in that period, and act optimally in the remaining $k - 1$ periods.

Clearly, the optimal S_k will be the value of y that minimizes $G^k(y)$. Alternatively, to compute the optimal S_k we find the point at which the function $G_o^k(y_k)$, a line with slope 0, is tangent to $G^k(y_k) + K$.

To determine s_k, we look for y smaller than S_k such that

$$G^k(y) = K + G^k(S_k).$$

We thus conclude that

$$z'^k(y) = \begin{cases} 0 & \text{if } y \le s_k, \\ G'^k(y) & \text{if } y > s_k. \end{cases} \tag{11.6}$$

What can we say about the relationship between the different quantities (s_k, S_k), $k = 1, 2, \ldots, m$? Very little! The only result known was obtained by Iglehart (1963a).

Theorem 11.3.7 *The optimal policy solving (11.3) satisfies* $S_1 \le S_k$, $2 \le k \le m$.

Proof. It is sufficient to show that $G'^k(y) \le 0$ for all $y < S_1$. Suppose that we choose the smallest S_1 that minimizes $G(y)$. The convexity of $G^1(y)(= G(y))$

implies that $G'^1(y) < 0$ for all $y < S_1$, and hence $z'^1(y) \leq 0$ for all $y < S_1$; see equation (11.6). Now assume $z'^k(y) \leq 0$ for all $y < S_1$ and observe that

$$G'^{k+1}(y) = G'(y) + \int_D z'^k(y - D)dF(D) < 0,$$

which completes the proof.   ∎

11.4   Quasiconvex Loss Functions

The above proof on the optimality of (s_k, S_k) policies relies on the fact that the one-period loss function $G(y)$ is convex. In many practical situations this assumption is not appropriate. For instance, consider the previous model, but assume that whenever a shortage occurs, an emergency shipment is requested. Suppose further, that this emergency shipment incurs a fixed cost plus a linear cost proportional to the shortage level. It can be easily shown that the new loss function $G(y)$ is, in general, not convex.

To overcome this difficulty, Veinott (1966) offers a different yet elegant proof for the optimality of (s_k, S_k) policies under the assumption that $-G(y)$ is unimodal or $G(y)$ is quasiconvex. Here we provide a slightly simplified proof suggested by Chen (1996) for the model considered here.

Definition 11.4.1 *A function f is quasiconvex on a convex set X if for any x and $y \in X$ and $0 \leq q \leq 1$,*

$$f(qx + (1 - q)y) \leq \max\{f(x), f(y)\}.$$

It is easily verified that a convex function is also quasiconvex. An alternative definition may be as follows: f is said to be quasiconvex if

$$-f(x) \text{ is unimodal.}$$

Consider the following m-period model:

$$z^k(y_k) = \min_{y \geq y_k}\{K\delta(y - y_k) + G^k(y)\} \tag{11.7}$$

where

$$G^k(y) = G(y) + E_D[z^{k-1}(y - D)], \quad \text{for } k = 1, 2, \ldots, m. \tag{11.8}$$

In the analysis below we use the following assumptions on $G(y)$.

(i) $G(y)$ is continuous and quasiconvex.

(ii) $G(y) > \inf_x G(x) + K$ as $|y| \to \infty$.

Other assumptions on ordering costs and demands are the same as in the previous section.

If (i) and (ii) hold, there is a number y^* that minimizes $G(y)$. In addition, there are two numbers $\underline{s}(\leq y^*)$ and $\overline{S}(\geq y^*)$ such that

$$G(\overline{S}) = G(y^*) + K \tag{11.9}$$
$$G(\underline{s}) = G(y^*) + K. \tag{11.10}$$

It is also worth mentioning that $G(y)$ is decreasing (nonincreasing) in y on $(-\infty, y^*]$ and increasing (nondecreasing) in y on (y^*, ∞).

To prove the optimality of (s_k, S_k) policy for all k, we need the next two lemmas.

Lemma 11.4.2 *For $k = 1, \ldots, m$, and $y \leq y'$,*

$$z^k(y) \leq z^k(y') + K \quad and \tag{11.11}$$
$$G^k(y') - G^k(y) \geq G(y') - G(y) - K. \tag{11.12}$$

Proof. It follows that

$$\begin{aligned}
z^k(y) &= \min\{G^k(y), K + \min_{x \geq y} G^k(x)\} \\
&\leq K + \min_{x \geq y} G^k(x) \\
&\leq K + \min_{x \geq y'} G^k(x) \\
&\leq K + z^k(y').
\end{aligned}$$

We also provide an alternative proof here. The result obviously holds for $y' = y$. Now assume that $y' > y$. Suppose that at the beginning of the period, the inventory level prior to any ordering is y. Consider the following strategy: we first raise the inventory level up to y' and then act optimally as if we started with the inventory level y' (prior to any ordering). Such a strategy incurs cost equal to $K + z^k(y')$. Because this strategy is not necessarily optimal, it follows that

$$z^k(y) \leq K + z^k(y'),$$

which also proves (11.11).

Inequalities in (11.11) implies that

$$\begin{aligned}
G^k(y') - G^k(y) &= G(y') - G(y) + E_D[z^{k-1}(y' - D)] - E_D[z^{k-1}(y - D)] \\
&\geq G(y') - G(y) - K,
\end{aligned}$$

which completes the proof.   ∎

Lemma 11.4.3 *For $k = 1, \ldots, m$, and $y \leq y' \leq y^*$,*

$$G^k(y') - G^k(y) \leq G(y') - G(y) \leq 0 \quad and \tag{11.13}$$
$$z^k(y') \leq z^k(y). \tag{11.14}$$

Proof. The proof is by induction. Note that $G(y)$ is decreasing in y for $y \leq y^*$.

For $k = 1$, $G^1(y') - G^1(y) = G(y') - G(y) \leq 0$, which implies that $\min_{x \geq y'} G^1(x) = \min_{x \geq y} G^1(x)$. Then,

$$
\begin{aligned}
z^1(y') &= \min\{G^1(y'), K + \min_{x \geq y'} G^1(x)\} \\
&\leq \min\{G^1(y), K + \min_{x \geq y'} G^1(x)\} \\
&= \min\{G^1(y), K + \min_{x \geq y} G^1(x)\} = z^1(y).
\end{aligned}
$$

Assume that for $k - 1 \geq 0$, and $y \leq y' \leq y^*$,

$$
\begin{aligned}
G^{k-1}(y') - G^{k-1}(y) &\leq G(y') - G(y) \leq 0 \quad \text{and} \\
z^{k-1}(y') &\leq z^{k-1}(y).
\end{aligned}
$$

Now it follows immediately that

$$
\begin{aligned}
G^k(y') - G^k(y) &= G(y') - G(y) + E_D[z^{k-1}(y' - D)] - E_D[z^{k-1}(y - D)] \\
&= G(y') - G(y) + E_D[z^{k-1}(y' - D) - z^{k-1}(y - D)] \\
&\leq G(y') - G(y) \leq 0, \quad\quad\quad\quad\quad\quad\quad (11.15)
\end{aligned}
$$

and

$$
\begin{aligned}
z^k(y') &= \min\{G^k(y'), K + \min_{x \geq y'} G^k(x)\} \\
&\leq \min\{G^k(y), K + \min_{x \geq y} G^k(x)\} = z^k(y).
\end{aligned}
$$

This completes the proof. ∎

We are now ready to show the optimality result.

Theorem 11.4.4 (Veinott, 1966) *If* (i) *and* (ii) *hold, an* (s_k, S_k) *policy is optimal for the model (11.7). Moreover,* $\underline{s} \leq s_k \leq y^*$ *and* $y^* \leq S_k \leq \overline{S}$.

Proof. The proof proceeds in several steps. We start with the assumption that $G^k(y)$ is continuous in y. This assumption will be confirmed at the end.

(1) S_k is a global minimizer of $G^k(y)$. For this purpose, we first show that $G^k(y)$ is decreasing for $y \leq y^*$, which follows directly from (11.13). Because $G^k(y)$ is continuous, there exists a number S_k that minimizes $G^k(y)$ over $[y^*, \overline{S}]$. Now it is clear that S_k minimizes $G^k(y)$ on $(-\infty, \overline{S})$. By the definition of $\overline{S}$ and Lemma 11.4.2, it follows that for $y > \overline{S}(\geq y^*)$,

$$
\begin{aligned}
G^k(y) - G^k(y^*) &\geq G(y) - G(y^*) - K \\
&\geq G(\overline{S}) - G(y^*) - K = 0,
\end{aligned}
$$

where $G(y) \geq G(\overline{S})$ due to the quasiconvexity of $G(y)$. Hence, S_k is indeed a global minimizer of $G^k(y)$ and $y^* \leq S_k \leq \overline{S}$.

(2) There exists a number s_k such that

$$G^k(S_k) + K = G^k(s_k) \text{ and } \underline{s} \le s_k \le y^*.$$

The definitions of S_k, $\underline{s}$ and y^* imply that

$$G^k(S_k) + K - G^k(\underline{s}) \le G^k(y^*) + K - G^k(\underline{s})$$
$$\le G(y^*) + K - G(\underline{s}) = 0,$$

where the first inequality follows from the definition that S_k is the minimizer of $G^k(y)$ while the second inequality holds due to Lemma 11.4.3. From the definition of y^* and Lemma 11.4.2, we see

$$G^k(S_k) + K - G^k(y^*) \ge G(S_k) - G(y^*) - K + K \ge 0.$$

Together with the continuity assumption of $G^k(y)$ and the fact that $G^k(y)$ is decreasing on $(-\infty, y^*]$, the above two inequalities imply that there exists a number s_k such that

$$G^k(S_k) + K = G^k(s_k) \text{ and } \underline{s} \le s_k \le y^*.$$

(3) For $y^* < y < y'$,

$$[K + G^k(y')] - G^k(y) \ge 0.$$

This follows directly from Lemma 11.4.2 and the fact that $G(y') \ge G(y)$:

$$G^k(y') - G^k(y) \ge G(y') - G(y) - K \ge -K.$$

Note that this observation implies that placing an order does not reduce the expected cost when $y > y^*$.

(4) We conclude, therefore, that an (s_k, S_k) policy is optimal.

(5) It remains to prove that $G^k(y)$ is continuous in y.

Again, we proceed by induction. It is true for $k = 1$ because $G^1(y) = G(y)$ (by assumption (i)). Suppose now that $G^{k-1}(y)$ is continuous for $k > 1$. From (4),

$$z^{k-1}(y) = \begin{cases} K + G^{k-1}(S_k) & \text{if } y \le s_k, \\ G^{k-1}(y) & \text{if } y > s_k. \end{cases}$$

Define $\bar{z}'(y) = \max_x\{|z'^{k-1}(x)| : s_k < x \le y\}$ for $y < \infty$. Obviously, $\bar{z}'(y)$ is the largest slope in the interval $(s_k, y]$. The existence of $\bar{z}'(y)$ is due to the continuity of $z^{k-1}(y)$ and the fact that $z'^{k-1}(y) = 0$ for $y \le s_k$.

For any given $\theta > 0$, there exists a number $\epsilon > 0$ such that

$$\bar{z}'(y) \cdot \epsilon < \theta$$

and

$$|E_D[z^{k-1}(y - D) - z^{k-1}(y + \epsilon - D)]| \le \bar{z}'(y) \cdot \epsilon < \theta.$$

Hence, $E_D[z^{k-1}(y - D)]$ is continuous. ∎

The above proof for the optimality of (s_k, S_k) policies is based on the assumption that demands are independent and identically distributed. If demands are not independent and identically distributed, Lemma 11.4.3 will generally fail to hold for the following reason. In the proof of Lemma 11.4.3, we require that $z^{k-1}(y' - D) - z^{k-1}(y - D) \le 0$ for all D in (11.15), which holds only if $y - D \le y' - D \le y^*$. When demands are not independent and identically distributed, the minimizer of $G(y)$ may vary from period to period, and the requirement that $z^{k-1}(y' - D) - z^{k-1}(y - D) \le 0$ may not be met. In the proof of K-convexity, however, no requirement is imposed upon demands. Thus, while the result in this section is more general than the results of Section 11.3, when demands are independent and identically distributed, it is not a generalization of the first.

11.5   Infinite Horizon Models

In this section we consider a *discrete time* infinite horizon model in which an order may be placed by the warehouse at the beginning of any period. To simplify the analysis, we assume a discrete distribution of the one period demand D. Let $p_j = \Pr\{D = j\}$ for $j = 0, 1, 2, \ldots$. The objective is to minimize the long-run expected cost per period. All other assumptions and notation are identical to those in the previous section.

This problem has attracted considerable attention in the last three decades. The intuition developed in the previous section (for the finite horizon models) suggests and is proved by Iglehart (1963b) and Veinott and Wagner (1965), that an (s, S) policy is optimal for the infinite horizon case. A simple proof is proposed by Zheng (1991). Various algorithms have been suggested by Veinott and Wagner (1965), Bell (1970) and Archibald and Silver (1978) as well as others; see, for instance, Porteus (1990) or Zheng and Federgruen (1991). This section describes a recent, surprisingly simple, algorithm developed by Zheng and Federgruen (1991) for finding the optimal (s, S) policy. We follow their paper, as well as the insight provided in Denardo (1996).

Let $c(s, S)$ be the long-run average cost associated with the (s, S) policy. Given a period and an initial inventory y, recall that the loss function $G(y)$ is the expected holding and shortage cost minus revenue at the end of the period. In what follows the loss function $G(y)$ is assumed to be quasiconvex.

Let $M(j)$ be the expected number of periods that elapse until the next order is placed when starting with $s + j$ units of inventory. That is, $M(j)$ is the expected number of periods until total demand exceeds j units. It is obvious that for all j we have

$$M(j) = \sum_{k=0}^{j} p_k[1 + M(j - k)] + \sum_{k=j+1}^{\infty} p_k \qquad (11.16)$$

$$= \sum_{k=0}^{j} p_k M(j - k) + 1,$$

with $M(0) = 0$.

Let $\mathcal{F}(s, y)$ be the expected total cost in all periods until placing the next order, when we start with y units of inventory.

Observe that since orders are received immediately, each time an order is placed the inventory level increases to S. Hence, replenishment times can be viewed as *regeneration points*, see Ross (1970). The theory of regeneration processes tells us that

$$c(s, S) = \frac{\mathcal{F}(s, S)}{M(S - s)}. \tag{11.17}$$

That is, $c(s, S)$, the long-run average cost, is the ratio of the expected cost between successive regeneration points and the expected time between successive regeneration points.

To calculate $M(S - s)$, one need only solve the recursive equation (11.16). In addition,

$$\mathcal{F}(s, S) = K + H(s, S),$$

where $H(s, S)$ is the expected holding and shortage cost until placing the next order, when starting with S units of inventory. How can we calculate the quantity $H(s, S)$? For this purpose, observe that $M(j) \geq M(j - 1)$ and let

$$m(j) \doteq M(j) - M(j - 1),$$

for $j = 1, 2, 3, \ldots .$ To interpret $m(j)$, observe that for any j, $j < S-s$, the expected time between successive regeneration points consists of two components: the first is $M(j)$ the expected time until demand exceeds j units while the second is the expected time, prior to placing the next order, until demand exceeds $(S - s - j)$ units. Thus, the definition of $M(j)$ implies that $m(j)$ is the expected number of periods, prior to placing the next order, for which the inventory level is exactly $S - j$. Hence,

$$H(s, S) = \sum_{j=0}^{S-s-1} m(j)G(S - j). \tag{11.18}$$

To summarize, given an (s, S) policy we have

$$c(s, S) = \frac{K + H(s, S)}{M(S - s)}.$$

Recall that y^* is the smallest y minimizing the function $G(y)$. That is,

$$y^* = \min\{y | G(y) = \min_{x} G(x)\}.$$

Zheng and Federgruen's algorithm is essentially based on the following results.

Lemma 11.5.1 *There exists an optimal (s, S) policy satisfying $s < y^* \leq S$.*

Proof. Observe that $G(y)$ is a quasiconvex function of y and therefore $G(y)$ is nonincreasing for $y \leq y^*$ and nondecreasing for $y \geq y^*$. Consider now $s \geq y^*$. Equation (11.18) together with the quasiconvexity of $G(y)$ implies that $H(s-1, S-1) \leq H(s, S)$. Hence, $c(s, S) \geq c(s-1, S-1)$. Suppose now that $y^* \geq S$. A similar argument shows that $H(s+1, S+1) \leq H(s, S)$ and hence $c(s, S) \geq c(s+1, S+1)$ which completes the proof.   ∎

The following property is given without proof; the interested reader is referred to Zheng and Federgruen.

Lemma 11.5.2 *For any order-up-to level S, a reorder level $s^0 < y^*$ is optimal if*

$$G(s^0) \geq c(s^0, S) \geq G(s^0 + 1). \tag{11.19}$$

Similarly, for any order-up-to level S, there exists an optimal reorder level s^0 such that $s^0 < y^*$ and (11.19) holds.

An immediate byproduct of the lemma is an algorithm for finding an optimal reorder point s^0 for any given S.

Corollary 11.5.3 *For any value of S, $s^0 = \max\{y < y^* | c(y, S) \leq G(y)\}$ is the optimal reorder level associated with S.*

Proof. Let

$$\alpha = \frac{M(S - s - 1)}{M(S - s)}$$

and observe that (11.17) and (11.18) imply that

$$c(s, S) = \alpha c(s + 1, S) + (1 - \alpha)G(s). \tag{11.20}$$

The definition of s^0 implies that $G(s^0) \geq c(s^0, S)$ and hence, using (11.20), we have $c(s^0, S) \geq c(s^0 + 1, S)$. In addition, the same definition also implies $G(s^0 + 1) < c(s^0 + 1, S)$. Hence, $G(s^0 + 1) < c(s^0, S) \leq G(s^0)$. Thus, by Lemma 11.5.2, s^0 is an optimal reorder point associated with S.   ∎

Lemma 11.5.4 *For two order-up-to levels S^0, $S \geq y^*$, let s^0 and s be the corresponding optimal reorder points, respectively. The (s, S) policy improves on (has smaller cost than) (s^0, S^0) if and only if*

$$c(s^0, S) < c(s^0, S^0).$$

Proof. We need only show that if $c(s, S) < c(s^0, S^0)$, then $c(s^0, S) < c(s^0, S^0)$. By contradiction, assume $c(s^0, S) \geq c(s^0, S^0)$. We prove that this implies $c(s, S) \geq c(s^0, S^0)$ for $y^* > s$. We distinguish between two cases. First we look at $s > s^0$. Define $\beta = M(S - s)/M(S - s^0)$ and observe that $0 < \beta \leq 1$. The definition of $c(s^0, S)$ together with Lemma 11.5.2 implies that

$$c(s^0, S) \leq \beta c(s, S) + (1 - \beta)c(s^0, S).$$

Hence, $c(s^0, S) \leq c(s, S)$ which together with $c(s^0, S) \geq c(s^0, S^0)$ shows that $c(s, S) \geq c(s^0, S^0)$, a contradiction. The proof when $s < s^0$ is identical.   ∎

Finally, we state the following lemma without proof.

Lemma 11.5.5 *Let* (s^*, S^*) *denote an optimal* (s, S) *policy. Then* $c(s^*, S^*) \geq G(S^*)$.

These results suggest the following simple algorithm. Start with $S^0 = y^*$ and find the best reorder point s^0 applying Lemma 11.5.3. Now increase S by increments of 1 each time comparing $c(s^0, S^0)$ to $c(s^0, S)$. If $c(s^0, S) < c(s^0, S^0)$, set $S^0 = S$ and find the corresponding reorder point. Continue until you've identified (s^0, S^0) such that no $S, S > S^0$ has $c(s^0, S) < c(s^0, S^0)$ and $G(S) > c(s^0, S^0)$.

We conclude this section with a discussion of the impact of leadtimes on the analysis. So far we have assumed zero leadtimes; if this fails to hold, and a fixed delivery leadtime has to be incorporated, the problem can be transformed into one with zero leadtime by a fairly simple change in the loss function $G(\cdot)$; see, for instance, Veinott and Wagner (1965), Veinott (1966), Heyman and Sobel (1984) or the third exercise at the end of this chapter. For this purpose, let the *inventory position* at the warehouse be defined as the inventory at that warehouse plus inventory in transit to the warehouse. The loss function $G(y)$ is calculated such that y is the inventory position and D is the total demand during the leadtime plus one period.

11.6 Multi-Echelon Systems

Consider a distribution system with a single warehouse, denoted by the index 0, and n retailers, indexed from 1 to n. Incoming orders from an outside vendor with unlimited stock are received by the warehouse that replenishes the retailers. We refer to the warehouse or the retailers as *facilities*. The transportation leadtime to facility $i = 0, 1, 2, \ldots, n$, is a constant L_i.

As in the previous section, we analyze a discrete time model in which customer demands are independent and identically distributed and are faced only by the retailers. Every time a facility places an order, it incurs a set-up cost K_i, $i = 0, 1, 2, \ldots, n$. The echelon inventory holding cost (see Chapter 9) is h_i^+ at facility i, $i = 0, 1, 2, \ldots, n$. Finally, demand is backlogged at a penalty cost of h_i^-, $i = 1, 2, \ldots, n$ per unit per period. The objective is to find a centralized strategy, that is, a strategy that uses systemwide inventory information, so as to minimize long-run average system cost.

As the reader no doubt understands, the analysis of stochastic distribution models is quite difficult and finding an optimal strategy is close to impossible; consider the difficulty involved in finding an approximate solution for its deterministic, constant demand counterpart; see Chapter 9. As a result, limited literature is available. The rare exceptions are the approximate strategy suggested by Eppen and Schrage (1981) and the lower bounds developed by Federgruen and Zipkin (1984a-c) and Chen and Zheng (1994). We briefly describe these two bounds here.

For this purpose, let the *echelon inventory position* at a facility be defined as the echelon inventory at that facility plus inventory in transit to that facility.

Consider the following approach suggested by Federgruen and Zipkin

(1984a-c). Given an inventory position y_i at retailer i, let the loss function $G_i(y_i)$ be

$$G_i(y_i) = h_i^+ \max\{0, y_i - D\} + (h_i^- + h_0^+) \max\{0, D - y_i\},$$

where D is total demand faced by retailer i during $L_i + 1$ periods (see the end of the previous section for a discussion).

Consider now any inventory policy with echelon inventory of y units at the warehouse and inventory position y_i at retailer i. The expected one period holding and shortage cost in the system is

$$G(y) = h_0^+(y - \mu) + \sum_{i=1}^{n} G_i(y_i),$$

where μ is the expected single period systemwide demand. Since, by definition, $y \geq \sum_{i=1}^{n} y_i$, a lower bound on $G(y)$ is obtained by finding

$$G_0(y) \doteq \min_{y_1,\ldots,y_n} \left\{ h_0^+(y - \mu) + \sum_{i=1}^{n} G_i(y_i) \middle| \sum_{i=1}^{n} y_i \leq y \right\}. \qquad (11.21)$$

Thus, a lower bound on the long-run average system cost C^{FZ} is obtained by solving a single facility inventory problem with loss function G_0 and set-up cost K_0. Notice that this bound does not take into account the retailer-specific set-up costs. This is incorporated in the next lower bound of Chen and Zheng (1994).

To describe their lower bound consider the following *assembly-distribution system* associated with the original distribution system. In the assembly-distribution system each retailer sells a product consisting of two components. A basic component, denoted by a_0 and a retailer-specific component, denoted by a_i. Each retailer receives component a_0 from the warehouse which receives it from the outside supplier. On the other hand, component a_i is supplied directly from the vendor to retailer i. The arrival of a basic component at retailer i is coordinated with the arrival of component a_i. That is, at the time the warehouse delivers basic components to retailer i, the same number of a_i components are shipped to the retailer from the supplier. These two shipments arrive at the same time and the final product is assembled, each containing one basic component and one a_i component.

To ensure that the original distribution system and the assembly-distribution system are, in some sense, equivalent, we allocate cost in the new system as follows. Associated with retailer i is a single facility inventory model with set-up cost K_i, holding cost h_i^+ and shortage cost $h_0^+ + h_i^-$. Delivery leadtime to the facility is L_i and demand is distributed according to demand faced by retailer i. This is, of course, a standard inventory model for which an (s_i, S_i) policy is optimal. Let C_i be the long-run average cost associated with this optimal policy. Given an inventory position y, let $G_i(y)$ be the associated loss function. Finally, let

$$G_i^i(y) = \begin{cases} C_i & \text{if } y \leq s_i \\ G_i(y) & \text{if } y > s_i \end{cases}$$

and $G_i^0(y) = G_i(y) - G_i^i(y)$.

In the assembly-distribution system costs are charged as follows. A set-up cost K_0 is allocated to the basic component and a set-up cost K_i to each component a_i, and an expected holding and penalty cost, that is, loss function, of G_i^0 to the basic component and G_i^i to component a_i. Notice that since shipments are coordinated, there is no difference between long-run average cost in the original system and in the assembly-distribution system.

To find a lower bound on the long-run average cost of the original system, we consider a relaxation of the assembly distribution system in which the basic components can be sold independently of the other components. Thus, C_i, $i = 1, 2, \ldots, n$ is exactly the long-run average cost associated with the distribution of component a_i. Let C_0 be a lower bound on the long-run average cost of the basic component. Consequently, $\sum_{i=0}^{n} C_i$ is a lower bound on the long-run average cost of the original distribution system.

It remains to find C_0. This is obtained following the approach suggested by Federgruen and Zipkin and described above. For this purpose, we replace G_i by G_i^0 in (11.21) and take C^{FZ} as C_0.

11.7 Exercises

Exercise 11.1. In (11.1), we assume that $F(D)$ is continuous. Now suppose that $F(D)$ is not necessarily continuous. Does there exist an S such that $z(y)$ is minimized at $y = S$? If there exists such an S, how can you determine it ?

Exercise 11.2. Prove (11.20).

Exercise 11.3. Consider the single warehouse inventory model analyzed in Section 11.5 with leadtime $l > 0$. Prove that the inventory on hand at the end of period t for some $t > l$ can be written as

$$S_{t-l} - \sum_{i=t-l}^{t} D_i,$$

where S_{t-l} is the order-up-to-level in period $t - l$ and D_i is the demand in period i. Conclude that any nonzero leadtime model can be replaced by a model with zero leadtime for which the loss function $G(y)$ is calculated according to (11.2) with y being the inventory position and D the total demand during the leadtime.

Exercise 11.4. It is now June and your company has to make a decision regarding how many skijackets to produce for the coming Winter season. It costs c dollars to produce one skijacket which can be sold for r dollars. Skijackets not sold during the Winter season are lost. Suppose your marketing department estimates that demand during the season can take one of the values $D_1, D_2, \ldots, D_k$, $k \geq 3$. Since this is a new product, they do not know what probabilities to attach to each possible demand D_i; that is, they do not have estimates of p_i, the probability that demand during the Winter season will be D_i, $i = 1, 2, \ldots, k$. They have, however, a good estimate of average demand μ, and the variance of the demand σ^2. Your objective is to find production quantity y that will protect you against the worst probability distribution possible while maximizing profit. For this purpose you would like to consider the following optimization model.

$$\text{MAXIMIZE }_y \text{ MINIMIZE }_{p_1,\ldots,p_k \in \mathcal{P}} \text{ Average Profit}, \qquad (11.22)$$

where $\mathcal{P}$ is the set of all possible discrete distribution functions with mean μ and variance σ^2.

(a) Write an expression for the average profit as a function of the production quantity y and the unknown probabilities $p_1, p_2, \ldots, p_k$.

(b) Suppose we have already determined the production quantity, y. Write a linear program that identifies the worst possible distribution, that is, the one that minimizes average profit.

(b) Given a value of y characterize the worst possible distribution; that is, identify the number of demand points that have positive probabilities in the probability distribution found in the previous question.

(c) Can you formulate a linear program that finds the optimal production quantity; that is, can you write a linear program that solves equation (11.22)?

Exercise 11.5. Consider the following discrete version of the newsboy problem. Demand for product can take the values $D_1, D_2, \ldots, D_n, n \geq 3$, with probabilities $p_1, p_2, \ldots, p_n$, where $\sum_{i=1}^{n} p_i = 1$. Let r be a known selling price per unit and c be a known cost per unit. Our objective is to find an order quantity y that maximizes expected profit. Prove that the optimal order quantity that maximizes the expected profit must be one of the demand points, $D_1, D_2, \ldots, D_n$.

Exercise 11.6. Prove the following properties.

(a) If $g_1(y)$ and $g_2(y)$ are K-convex and L-convex, respectively, then for $\alpha, \beta \geq 0$, $\alpha g_1(y) + \beta g_2(y)$ is $(\alpha K + \beta L)$-convex.

(b) If $g(y)$ is K-convex, then $E_D[g(y - D)]$ is also K-convex.

Exercise 11.7. Consider the newsboy problem with demand D being a random variable whose density, $f(D)$, is known. Let r be a known selling price per unit and c be a known cost per unit. Assume no initial inventory and no salvage value. The objective is to find an order quantity y that maximizes expected profit.

(*a*) Let a **service level** be defined as the probability that demand is no more than the order quantity, y. Our objective is to find the order quantity, y, that maximizes expected profit subject to the requirement that the service level is **at least** α. What is the optimal order quantity as a function of α, c, r and $f(D)$.

(*b*) Suppose there is no service level requirement; however, there is a capacity constraint, C, on the amount we can order. That is, the order quantity, y, cannot be more than C. What is the optimal order quantity, y, that maximizes expected profit subject to the capacity constraint, C.

(*c*) Suppose there is a service level requirement, α, and a capacity constraint, C. What is the optimal order quantity, y, that maximizes expected profit subject to the constraints that service level is at least α and the capacity constraint, C.

Part IV

HIERARCHICAL MODELS

12
Facility Location Models

12.1 Introduction

One of the most important aspects of logistics is deciding where to locate new facilities such as retailers, warehouses or factories. These strategic decisions are a crucial determinant of whether materials will flow efficiently through the distribution system.

In this chapter we consider several important warehouse location problems: the p-Median Problem, the Single-Source Capacitated Facility Location Problem and a distribution system design problem. In each case, the problem is to locate a set of warehouses in a distribution network. We assume that the cost of locating a warehouse at a particular site includes a *fixed* cost (e.g., building costs, rental costs, etc.) and a *variable* cost for transportation. This variable cost includes the cost of transporting the product to the retailers as well as possibly the cost of moving the product from the plants to the warehouse. In general, the objective is to locate a set of facilities so that total cost is minimized subject to a variety of constraints which might include:

- each warehouse has a capacity which limits the area it can supply.

- each retailer receives shipments from *one and only one* warehouse.

- each retailer must be within a fixed distance of the warehouse that supplies it, so that a reasonable delivery lead time is ensured.

Location analysis has played a central role in the development of the operations research field. In this area lie some of the discipline's most elegant results and theories. We note here the paper of Cornuéjols et al. (1977) and the two excellent books devoted to the subject by Mirchandani and Francis (1990) and Daskin (1995). Location problems encompass a wide range of problems such as the location of emergency services (fire houses or ambulances), the location of hazardous materials, problems in telecommunications network design, etc. just to name a few.

In the next section, we present an exact algorithm for one of the simplest location problems, the p-Median Problem. We then generalize this model and algorithm to incorporate additional factors important to the design of the distribution network, such as warehouse capacities and fixed costs. In Section 12.4, we present a more general model where all levels of the distribution system (plants and retailers) are taken into account when deciding warehouse locations. We also present an efficient algorithm for its solution. All of the algorithms developed in this chapter are based on the Lagrangian relaxation technique described in Chapter 4.3 which has been applied successfully to a wide range of location problems. Finally, in Section 12.5, we describe the structure of the optimal solution to problems in the design of large-scale logistics systems.

12.2   An Algorithm for the p-Median Problem

Consider a set of retailers geographically dispersed in a region. The problem is to choose where in the region to locate a set of p identical warehouses. We assume there are $m \geq p$ sites that have been preselected as possible locations for these warehouses. Once the p warehouses have been located, each of n retailers will get its shipments from the warehouse closest to it. We assume:

- there is no fixed cost for locating at a particular site, and

- there is no capacity constraint on the demand supplied by a warehouse.

Note that the first assumption also encompasses the case where the fixed cost is not site-dependent and therefore the fixed set-up cost for locating p warehouses is independent of where they are located.

Let the set of retailers be N where $N = \{1, 2, \ldots, n\}$, and let the set of potential sites for warehouses be M where $M = \{1, 2, \ldots, m\}$. Let w_i be the demand or flow between retailer i and its warehouse for each $i \in N$. We assume that the cost of transporting the w_i units of product from warehouse j to retailer i is c_{ij}, for each $i \in N$ and $j \in M$.

The problem is to choose p of the m sites where a warehouse will be located in such a way that the total transportation cost is minimized. This is the p-Median Problem.

The continuous version of this problem, where any point is a potential warehouse location, was first treated as early as 1909 by Weber. The discrete version was analyzed by Kuehn and Hamburger (1963) as well as Hakimi (1964), Manne (1964), Balinski (1965) and many others.

We present here a highly effective approach to the problem. Define the following decision variables:

$$Y_j = \begin{cases} 1, & \text{if a warehouse is located at site } j, \\ 0, & \text{otherwise,} \end{cases}$$

for $j \in M$, and

$$X_{ij} = \begin{cases} 1, & \text{if retailer } i \text{ is served by a warehouse at site } j, \\ 0, & \text{otherwise,} \end{cases}$$

for $i \in N$ and $j \in M$. The p-Median Problem is then:

$$\text{Problem } P : \text{Min} \sum_{i=1}^{n} \sum_{j=1}^{m} c_{ij} X_{ij}$$

$$s.t. \sum_{j=1}^{m} X_{ij} = 1, \quad \forall i \in N \tag{12.1}$$

$$\sum_{j=1}^{m} Y_j = p \tag{12.2}$$

$$X_{ij} \leq Y_j, \quad \forall i \in N, \ j \in M \tag{12.3}$$

$$X_{ij}, Y_j \in \{0, 1\}, \quad \forall i \in N, \ j \in M. \tag{12.4}$$

Constraints (12.1) guarantee that each retailer is assigned to a warehouse. Constraint (12.2) ensures that p sites are chosen. Constraints (12.3) guarantee that a retailer selects a site only from among those that are chosen. Constraints (12.4) force the variables to be integer.

This formulation can easily handle several side constraints. If a handling fee is charged for each unit of product going through a warehouse, these costs can be added to the transportation cost along all arcs leaving the warehouse. Also, if a particular limit is placed on the length of any arc between retailer i and warehouse j, this can be incorporated by simply setting the per unit shipping cost (c_{ij}) to $+\infty$. In addition, the model can be easily extended to cases where a set of facilities are already in place and the choice is whether to open new facilities or *expand* the existing facilities.

Let Z^* be an optimal solution to Problem P. One simple and effective technique to solve this problem is the method of Lagrangian relaxation described in Chapter 4.3.

As described in Chapter 4.3, Lagrangian relaxation involves relaxing a set of constraints and introducing them into the objective function with a multiplier vector. This provides a lower bound on the optimal solution to the overall problem. Then, using a subgradient search method, we iteratively update our multiplier vector in an attempt to increase the lower bound. At each step of the subgradient procedure (i.e., for each set of multipliers) we also attempt to construct a feasible solution to the location problem. This step usually consists of a simple and efficient subroutine. After a prespecified number of iterations, or when the solution found is within a fixed error tolerance of the lower bound, the algorithm is terminated.

To solve the p-Median Problem, we choose to relax constraints (12.1). We incorporate these constraints in the objective function with the multiplier vector $\lambda \in I\!R^n$. The resulting problem, call it P_λ, with optimal objective function value Z_λ, is:

$$\text{Min } \sum_{i=1}^{n}\sum_{j=1}^{m} c_{ij}X_{ij} + \sum_{i=1}^{n}\lambda_i\left(\sum_{j=1}^{m}X_{ij} - 1\right)$$

subject to $(12.2) - (12.4)$.

Disregarding constraint (12.2) for now, the problem decomposes by site, that is, each site can be considered separately. Let subproblem P_λ^j, with optimal objective function value Z_λ^j, be the following.

$$\text{Min } \sum_{i=1}^{n}(c_{ij} + \lambda_i)X_{ij}$$

$$s.t. \ X_{ij} \le Y_j, \quad \forall i \in N$$

$$X_{ij} \in \{0, 1\}, \quad \forall i \in N$$

$$Y_j \in \{0, 1\}.$$

Solving Subproblem P_λ^j

Assume λ is fixed. In Problem P_λ^j, site j is either selected $(Y_j = 1)$ or not $(Y_j = 0)$. If site j is not selected, then $X_{ij} = 0$ for all $i \in N$ and therefore $Z_\lambda^j = 0$. If site j is selected, then we set $Y_j = 1$ and assign exactly those retailers i with $c_{ij} + \lambda_i < 0$ to site j. In this case:

$$Z_\lambda^j = \sum_{i=1}^{n}\min\{c_{ij} + \lambda_i, 0\}. \tag{12.5}$$

We see that P_λ^j is solved easily and its optimal objective function value is given by (12.5).

To solve P_λ, we must now reintroduce constraint (12.2). This constraint forces us to choose only p of the m sites. In P_λ, we can incorporate this constraint by choosing the p sites with smallest values Z_λ^j. To do this, let π be a permutation of the numbers $1, 2, \ldots, m$ such that

$$Z_\lambda^{\pi(1)} \le Z_\lambda^{\pi(2)} \le Z_\lambda^{\pi(3)} \le \cdots \le Z_\lambda^{\pi(m)}.$$

Then the optimal solution to P_λ has objective function value:

$$Z_\lambda \doteq \sum_{j=1}^{p}Z_\lambda^{\pi(j)} - \sum_{j=1}^{n}\lambda_j.$$

The value Z_λ is a lower bound on the optimal solution of Problem P for any vector $\lambda \in I\!R^n$. To find the best such lower bound, we consider the Lagrangian dual:

$$\max_\lambda \{Z_\lambda\}.$$

Using the subgradient procedure (described in Chapter 4.3), we can iteratively improve this bound.

Upper Bounds

It is crucial to construct good upper bounds on the optimal solution value as the subgradient procedure advances. Clearly, solutions to P_λ will not necessarily be feasible to Problem P. This is due to the fact that the constraints (12.1) (that each retailer choose *one and only one* warehouse) may not be satisfied. The solution to P_λ may have facilities choosing a number of sites. If, in the solution to P_λ, each retailer chooses only *one* site, then this must be the optimal solution to P and therefore we stop. Otherwise, there are retailers that are assigned to several or no sites. A simple heuristic can be implemented which fixes those retailers that are assigned to only one site, and assigns the remaining retailers to these and other sites by choosing the next site to open in the ordering defined by π. When p sites have been selected, a simple check that each retailer is assigned to its closest site (of those selected) can further improve the solution.

Computational Results

Below we give a table listing results of various computational experiments. The retailer locations were chosen uniformly over the unit square. For simplicity, we made each retailer location a potential site for a warehouse, thus $m = n$. The cost of assigning a retailer to a site was the Euclidean distance between the two locations. The values of w_i were chosen uniformly over the unit interval. We applied the algorithm mentioned above to many problems and recorded the relative error of the best solution found and the computation time required. The algorithm is terminated when the relative error is below 1% or when a prespecified number of iterations is reached. The numbers below "Error" are the relative errors averaged over ten randomly generated problem instances. The numbers below "CPU Time" is the CPU time averaged over the ten problem instances. All computational times are on an IBM Risc 6000 Model 950.

Table 1: Computational results for the p-Median algorithm

n	p	Error	CPU Time
10	3	0.3%	0.2s
20	4	1.7%	2.6s
50	5	1.4%	20.7s
100	7	1.3%	87.7s
200	10	2.4%	715.4s

12.3   An Algorithm for the Single-Source Capacitated Facility Location Problem

Consider the p-Median Problem where we make the following two changes in our assumptions.

- The number of warehouses to locate (p) is not fixed beforehand.

- If a warehouse is located at site j:
  - a fixed cost f_j is incurred, and
  - there is a capacity q_j on the amount of demand it can serve.

The problem is to decide where to locate the warehouses and then how the retailers should be assigned to the open warehouses in such a way that total cost is minimized. We see that the problem is considerably more complicated than the p-Median Problem. We now have capacity constraints on the warehouses and therefore a retailer will not always be assigned to its nearest warehouse. Allowing the optimization to choose the appropriate number of warehouses also adds to the level of difficulty.

This problem is called the single-source Capacitated Facility Location Problem (CFLP), or sometimes the Capacitated Concentrator Location Problem (CCLP). This problem was successfully used in Chapter 6 as a framework for solving the Capacitated Vehicle Routing Problem.

Using the same decision variables as in the p-Median Problem, we formulate the single-source CFLP as the following integer linear program.

$$\text{Min} \quad \sum_{i=1}^{n}\sum_{j=1}^{m} c_{ij} X_{ij} + \sum_{j=1}^{m} f_j Y_j$$

$$s.t. \quad \sum_{j=1}^{m} X_{ij} = 1 \qquad \forall i \in N \qquad (12.6)$$

$$\sum_{i=1}^{n} w_i X_{ij} \leq q_j Y_j \quad \forall j \in M \qquad (12.7)$$

$$X_{ij}, Y_j \in \{0, 1\} \qquad \forall i \in N, \ j \in M. \qquad (12.8)$$

Constraints (12.6) (along with the integrality conditions (12.8)) ensure that each retailer is assigned to exactly one warehouse. Constraints (12.7) ensure that the warehouse's capacity is not exceeded, and also that if a warehouse is not located at site j, no retailer can be assigned to that site.

Let Z^* be the optimal solution value of single-source CFLP. Note we have restricted the assignment variables (X) to be integer. A related problem, where this assumption is relaxed, is simply called the (multiple-source) Capacitated Facility Location Problem. In that version, a retailer's demand can be *split* between any number of warehouses. In the single-source CFLP, it is required that each retailer have only *one* warehouse supplying it. In many logistics applications, this is a realistic assumption since without this restriction optimal solutions might have a retailer receive many deliveries of the same product (each for, conceivably, a very small amount of the product). Clearly, from a managerial, marketing and accounting point of view, restricting deliveries to come from only one warehouse is a more appropriate delivery strategy.

Several algorithms have been proposed to solve the CFLP in the literature; all are based on the Lagrangian relaxation technique. This includes Neebe and Rao (1983), Barcelo and Casanovas (1984), Klincewicz and Luss (1986) and Pirkul (1987). The one we derive here is similar to the algorithm of Pirkul which seems to be the most effective.

We apply the Lagrangian relaxation technique by including constraints (12.6) in the objective function. For any $\lambda \in \mathbb{R}^n$, consider the following problem P_λ.

$$\text{Min} \quad \sum_{i=1}^{n}\sum_{j=1}^{m} c_{ij}X_{ij} + \sum_{j=1}^{m} f_jY_j + \sum_{i=1}^{n} \lambda_i\left(\sum_{j=1}^{m} X_{ij} - 1\right)$$

$$\text{subject to } (12.7) - (12.8).$$

Let Z_λ be its optimal solution and note that

$$Z_\lambda \leq Z^*, \quad \forall \lambda \in \mathbb{R}^n.$$

To solve P_λ, as in the p-Median Problem, we separate the problem by site. For a given $j \in M$, define the following problem P_λ^j, with optimal objective function value Z_λ^j:

$$\text{Min} \quad \sum_{i=1}^{n}(c_{ij} + \lambda_i)X_{ij} + f_jY_j$$

$$s.t. \quad \sum_{i=1}^{n} w_iX_{ij} \leq q_jY_j$$

$$X_{ij} \in \{0, 1\} \qquad \forall i \in N$$

$$Y_j \in \{0, 1\}.$$

Solving P_λ^j

Problem P_λ^j can be solved efficiently. In the optimal solution to P_λ^j, Y_j is either 0 or 1. If $Y_j = 0$, then $X_{ij} = 0$ for all $i \in N$. If $Y_j = 1$, then the problem is no more difficult than a single constraint 0-1 Knapsack Problem, for which efficient algorithms exist; see, for example, Nauss (1976). If the optimal knapsack solution is less than $-f_j$, then the corresponding optimal solution to P_λ^j is found by setting $Y_j = 1$ and X_{ij} according to the knapsack solution, indicating whether retailer i is assigned to site j. If the optimal knapsack solution is more than $-f_j$, then the optimal solution to P_λ^j is found by setting $Y_j = 0$ and $X_{ij} = 0$ for all $i \in N$.

The solution to P_λ is then given by

$$Z_\lambda \doteq \sum_{j=1}^{m} Z_\lambda^j - \sum_{i=1}^{n} \lambda_i.$$

For any vector $\lambda \in I\!R^n$, this is a lower bound on the optimal solution Z^*. In order to find the best such lower bound we use a subgradient procedure.

Note that if the problem has a constraint on the number of warehouses (facilities) that can be opened (chosen), this can be handled in essentially the same way as it was handled in the algorithm for the p-Median Problem.

Upper Bounds

For a given set of multipliers, if the values $\{X\}$ satisfy (12.6), then we have an optimal solution to Problem P, and we stop. Otherwise, we perform a simple subroutine to find a feasible solution to P. The procedure is based on the observation that the knapsack solutions found when solving P_λ give us some information concerning the benefit of setting up a warehouse at a site (relative to the current vector λ). If, for example, the knapsack solution corresponding to a given site is 0, that is, the optimal knapsack is empty, then this is most likely not a "good" site to select at this time. In contrast, if the knapsack solution has a very negative cost, then this is a "good" site. Given the values Z_λ^j for each $j \in M$, let π be a permutation of $1, 2, \ldots, m$ such that

$$Z_\lambda^{\pi(1)} \leq Z_\lambda^{\pi(2)} \leq \cdots \leq Z_\lambda^{\pi(m)}.$$

The procedure we perform allocates retailers to sites in a myopic fashion. Let M be the minimum possible number of warehouses used in the optimal solution to CFLP. This can be found by solving the Bin-Packing Problem defined on the values w_i with bin capacities Q_j; see Section 2.2. Starting with the "best" site, in this case site $\pi(1)$, assign the retailers in its optimal knapsack to this site. Then, following the indexing of the knapsack solutions, take the next "best" site (say site $j \doteq \pi(2)$) and solve a new knapsack problem: one defined with costs $\bar{c}_{ij} \doteq c_{ij} + \lambda_i$ for each retailer i still unassigned. Assign all retailers in this knapsack solution to site j. If this optimal knapsack is empty, then a warehouse is not located at that site, and we go on to the next site. Continue in this manner until M warehouses are located.

The solution may still not be a feasible solution to P since some retailers may not be assigned to a site. In this case, unassigned retailers are assigned to sites that are already chosen where they fit with minimum additional cost. If needed, additional warehouses may be opened following the ordering of π. A local improvement heuristic can be implemented to improve on this solution, using simple interchanges between retailers.

Computational Results

We now report on various computational experiments using this algorithm. The retailer locations were chosen uniformly over the unit square. Again, for simplicity, we made each retailer location a potential site for a warehouse; thus, $m = n$. The fixed cost of a site was chosen uniformly between 0 and 1. The cost of assigning a retailer to a site was the Euclidean distance between the two locations. The values of w_i were chosen uniformly over the interval 0 to $\frac{1}{2}$ with warehouse capacity equal to 1. We applied the algorithm mentioned above to ten problems and recorded the average relative error of the best solution found and the average computation time required. The algorithm is terminated when the relative error is below 1% or when a prespecified number of iterations is reached. The numbers below "Error" are the relative errors averaged over the ten randomly generated problem instances. The numbers below "CPU Time" is the CPU time averaged over the ten problem instances. All computational times are on an IBM Risc 6000 Model 950.

Table 2: Computational results for the
single-source CFLP algorithm

n	Error	CPU Time
10	1.2%	1.2s
20	1.0%	8.1s
50	1.1%	110.0s
100	1.1%	558.3s

12.4   A Distribution System Design Problem

So far the location models we have considered have been concerned with minimizing the costs of transporting products between warehouses and retailers. We now present a more realistic model that considers the cost of transporting the product from manufacturing facilities to the warehouses as well.

Consider the following warehouse location problem. A set of plants and retailers are geographically dispersed in a region. Each retailer experiences demands for a variety of products which are manufactured at the plants. A set of warehouses must be located in the distribution network from a list of potential sites.

The cost of locating a warehouse includes the transportation cost per unit from warehouses to retailers but also the transportation cost from plants to warehouses. In addition, as in the CFLP, there is a site-dependent fixed cost for locating each warehouse.

The data for the problem are the following.

- L = number of plants; we will also let $L = \{1, 2, \ldots, L\}$

- J = number of potential warehouse sites, also let $J = \{1, 2, \ldots, J\}$

- I = number of retailers, also let $I = \{1, 2, \ldots, I\}$

- K = number of products, also let $K = \{1, 2, \ldots, K\}$

- W = number of warehouses to locate

- $c_{\ell jk}$ = cost of shipping one unit of product k from plant ℓ to warehouse site j

- d_{jik} = cost of shipping one unit of product k from warehouse site j to retailer i

- f_j = fixed cost of locating a warehouse at site j

- $v_{\ell k}$ = supply of product k at plant ℓ

- w_{ik} = demand for product k at retailer i

- s_k = volume of one unit of product k

- q_j = capacity (in volume) of a warehouse at site j

We make the additional assumption that a retailer gets delivery for a product from one warehouse only. This does not preclude solutions where a retailer gets shipments from different warehouses, but these shipments must be for different products. On the other hand, we assume that the warehouse can receive shipments from any plant and for any amount of product.

The problem is to determine where to locate the warehouses, how to ship the product from the plants to the warehouses and also how to ship the product from the warehouses to the retailers. This problem is similar to one analyzed by Pirkul and Jayaraman (1996).

We again use a mathematical programming approach. Define the following decision variables:

$$Y_j = \begin{cases} 1, & \text{if a warehouse is located at site } j, \\ 0, & \text{otherwise,} \end{cases}$$

and

$$U_{\ell jk} = \text{amount of product } k \text{ shipped from plant } \ell \text{ to warehouse } j,$$

for each $\ell \in L$, $j \in J$ and $k \in K$. Also define:

$$X_{jik} = \begin{cases} 1, & \text{if retailer } i \text{ receives product } k \text{ from warehouse } j, \\ 0, & \text{otherwise,} \end{cases}$$

for each $j \in J$, $i \in I$ and $k \in K$.

Then the Distribution System Design Problem can be formulated as the following integer program.

$$\text{Min} \quad \sum_{\ell=1}^{L}\sum_{j=1}^{J}\sum_{k=1}^{K} c_{\ell jk} U_{\ell jk} + \sum_{i=1}^{I}\sum_{j=1}^{J}\sum_{k=1}^{K} d_{jik} w_{ik} X_{jik} + \sum_{j=1}^{J} f_j Y_j$$

$$\text{s.t.} \quad \sum_{j=1}^{J} X_{jik} = 1 \qquad \forall i \in I, \ k \in K \qquad (12.9)$$

$$\sum_{i=1}^{I}\sum_{k=1}^{K} s_k w_{ik} X_{jik} \le q_j Y_j \quad \forall j \in J \tag{12.10}$$

$$\sum_{i=1}^{I} w_{ik} X_{jik} = \sum_{\ell=1}^{L} U_{\ell jk} \quad \forall j \in J,\, k \in K \tag{12.11}$$

$$\sum_{j=1}^{J} U_{\ell jk} \le v_{\ell k} \quad \forall \ell \in L,\, k \in K \tag{12.12}$$

$$\sum_{j=1}^{J} Y_j = W \tag{12.13}$$

$$Y_j,\, X_{jik} \in \{0, 1\} \quad \forall i \in I,\, j \in J,\, k \in K \tag{12.14}$$

$$U_{\ell jk} \ge 0 \quad \forall \ell \in L,\, j \in J,\, k \in K. \tag{12.15}$$

The objective function measures the transportation costs between plants and warehouses, between warehouses and retailers and also the fixed cost of locating the warehouses. Constraints (12.9) ensure that each retailer/product pair is assigned to one warehouse. Constraints (12.10) guarantee that the capacity of the warehouses is not exceeded. Constraints (12.11) ensure that there is a conservation of the flow of products at each warehouse; that is, the amount of each product arriving at a warehouse from the plants is equal to the amount being shipped from the warehouse to the retailers. Constraints (12.12) are the supply constraints. Constraints (12.13) ensure that we locate exactly W warehouses.

The model can handle several extensions such as a warehouse handling fee or a limit on the distance of any link used just as in the p-Median Problem. Another interesting extension is when there are a fixed number of possible warehouse types from which to choose. Each type has a specific cost along with a specific capacity. The model can be easily extended to handle this situation (see Exercise 12.1).

As in the previous problems, we will use Lagrangian relaxation. We relax constraints (12.9) (with multipliers λ_{ik}) and constraints (12.11) (with multipliers θ_{jk}). The resulting problem is:

$$\text{Min} \quad \sum_{\ell=1}^{L}\sum_{j=1}^{J}\sum_{k=1}^{K} c_{\ell jk} U_{\ell jk} + \sum_{j=1}^{J}\sum_{i=1}^{I}\sum_{k=1}^{K} d_{jik} w_{ik} X_{jik} + \sum_{j=1}^{J} f_j Y_j$$

$$+ \sum_{j=1}^{J}\sum_{k=1}^{K} \theta_{jk}\left[\sum_{i=1}^{I} w_{ik} X_{jik} - \sum_{\ell=1}^{L} U_{\ell jk}\right] + \sum_{i=1}^{I}\sum_{k=1}^{K} \lambda_{ik}\left[1 - \sum_{j=1}^{J} X_{jik}\right],$$

subject to (12.10), (12.12) − (12.15).

Let $Z_{\lambda,\theta}$ be the optimal solution to this problem. This problem can be decomposed into two separate problems P_1 and P_2. They are the following.

$$\text{Problem } P_1 : Z_1 \doteq \text{Min} \quad \sum_{\ell=1}^{L}\sum_{j=1}^{J}\sum_{k=1}^{K} [c_{\ell jk} - \theta_{jk}] U_{\ell jk}$$

$$s.t. \quad \sum_{j=1}^{J} U_{\ell jk} \leq v_{\ell k}, \forall \ell \in L, \, k \in K \qquad (12.16)$$

$$U_{\ell jk} \geq 0, \quad \forall \ell \in L, j \in J, k \in K.$$

$$\text{Problem } P_2 : Z_2 \doteq \text{Min} \quad \sum_{j=1}^{J}\sum_{i=1}^{I}\sum_{k=1}^{K}[d_{jik}w_{ik} - \lambda_{ik} + \theta_{jk}w_{ik}]X_{jik} + \sum_{j=1}^{J} f_j Y_j$$

$$s.t. \quad \sum_{i=1}^{I}\sum_{k=1}^{K} s_k w_{ik} X_{jik} \leq q_j Y_j, \quad \forall j \in J \qquad (12.17)$$

$$\sum_{j=1}^{J} Y_j = P, \qquad (12.18)$$

$$Y_j, X_{jik} \in \{0, 1\}, \quad \forall i \in I, j \in J, k \in K.$$

Solving P_1

Problem P_1 can be solved separately for each plant/product pair. In fact, the objective functions of each of these subproblems can be improved (without loss in computation time) by adding the constraints:

$$s_k \sum_{\ell=1}^{L} U_{\ell jk} \leq q_j, \quad \forall j \in J, \, k \in K. \qquad (12.19)$$

For each plant/product combination, say plant ℓ and product k, sort the J values $\overline{c}_j \doteq c_{\ell jk} - \theta_{jk}$. Starting with the smallest value of $\overline{c}_j$, say $\overline{c}_{j'}$, if $\overline{c}_{j'} \geq 0$, then the solution is to ship none of this product from this plant. If $c_{\ell j'k} < 0$, then ship as much of this product as possible along arc (ℓ, j') subject to satisfying constraints (12.16) and (12.19). Then if the supply $v_{\ell k}$ has not been completely shipped, do the same for the next cheapest arc, as long as it has negative reduced cost ($\overline{c}$). Continue in this manner until all of the product has been shipped or the reduced costs are no longer negative. Then proceed to the next plant/product combination repeating this procedure. Continue until all the plant/product combinations have been scanned in this fashion.

Solving P_2

Solving Problem P_2 is similar to solving the subproblem in the CFLP. For now we can ignore constraints (12.18). Then we separate the problem by warehouse. In the problem corresponding to warehouse j, either $Y_j = 0$ or $Y_j = 1$. If $Y_j = 0$, then $X_{jik} = 0$ for all $i \in N$ and $k \in K$. If $Y_j = 1$, then we get a Knapsack Problem with NK items, one for each retailer/product pair. Let Z_2^j be the objective function value when Y_j is set to 1 and the resulting knapsack problem is solved. After having solved each of these, let π be a permutation of the numbers $1, 2, \ldots, J$ such that

$$Z_2^{\pi(1)} \le Z_2^{\pi(2)} \le \cdots \le Z_2^{\pi(J)}.$$

The optimal solution to P_2 is to choose the W smallest values:

$$Z_2 \doteq \sum_{j=1}^{W} Z_2^{\pi(j)}.$$

For fixed vectors λ and θ, the lower bound is

$$Z_{\lambda,\theta} \doteq Z_1 + Z_2 + \sum_{i=1}^{I} \sum_{k=1}^{K} \lambda_{ik}.$$

To maximize this bound, that is,

$$\max_{\lambda,\theta}\{Z_{\lambda,\theta}\},$$

we again use the subgradient optimization procedure.

Upper Bounds

At each iteration of the subgradient procedure, we attempt to construct a feasible solution to the problem. Consider Problem P_2. Its solution may have a retailer/product combination assigned to several warehouses. We determine the set of retailer/product combinations that are assigned to one and only one retailer and fix these. Other retailer/product combinations are assigned to warehouses using the following mechanism. For each retailer/product combination we determine the cost of assigning it to a particular warehouse. After determining that this assignment is feasible (from a warehouse capacity point of view), the assignment cost is calculated as the cost of shipping all of the demand for this retailer/product combination through the warehouse plus the cost of shipping the demand from the plants to the warehouse (along one or more arcs from the warehouse to the plants). For each retailer/product combination we determine the penalty associated with assigning the shipment to its second best warehouse instead of its best warehouse. We then assign the retailer/product combination with the highest such penalty and update all arc flows and remaining capacities. We continue in this manner until all retailer/product combinations have been assigned to warehouses.

Computational results for this problem appear at the end of Chapter 15.

12.5   The Structure of the Asymptotic Optimal Solution

In this section we describe a region partitioning scheme to solve large instances of the CFLP.

Assume there are n retailers located at points $\{x_1, x_2, \ldots, x_n\}$. Each retailer also serves as a potential site for a warehouse of fixed capacity q. The fixed cost of locating a warehouse at a site is assumed to be proportional to the distance the site is from a manufacturing facility located at x_0 which is assumed (without loss of generality) to be the origin $(0, 0)$. Retailer i has a demand w_i which is assumed to be less than or equal to q. Without loss of generality, we assume $q = 1$ and therefore $w_i \in [0, 1]$ for each $i \in N$. Let α be the per unit cost of transportation between warehouses and the manufacturing facility, and let β be the per unit cost of transportation between warehouses and retailers.

We assume the retailer locations are independently and identically distributed in a compact region $A \subset \mathbb{R}^2$ according to some distribution μ. Assume the retailer demands are independently and identically distributed according to a probability measure ϕ on $[0, 1]$. The bin-packing constant associated with the distribution ϕ (denoted by γ_ϕ or simply γ) is the asymptotic number of bins used per item in an optimal packing of the retailer demands into unit size bins, when items are drawn randomly from the distribution ϕ (see Section 3.2).

The following theorem shows that if the retailer locations and demand sizes are random (from a general class of distributions), then as the problem size increases, the optimal solution has a very particular structure. This structure can be exploited using a region partitioning scheme as demonstrated below.

Theorem 12.5.1 *Let x_k, $k = 1, 2, \ldots, n$ be a sequence of independent random variables having a distribution μ with compact support in $\mathbb{R}^2$. Let $\|x\|$ be the Euclidean distance between the manufacturing facility and the point $x \in \mathbb{R}^2$, and let*

$$E(d) = \int \|x\| d\mu(x).$$

Let the demands w_k, $k = 1, 2, \ldots, n$ be a sequence of independent random variables having a distribution ϕ with bin-packing constant equal to γ. Then, almost surely,

$$\lim_{n \to \infty} \frac{1}{n} Z_n^* = \alpha \gamma E(d).$$

This analysis demonstrates that simple approaches which consider only the geography and the packing of the demands can be very efficient on large problem instances. Asymptotically, this is in fact the optimal strategy. This analysis also demonstrates that, asymptotically, the cost of transportation between retailers and warehouses becomes a very small fraction (eventually zero) of the total cost.

12.6   Exercises

Exercise 12.1. In the Distribution System Design Problem, explain how the solution methodology changes when there are a fixed number of possible warehouse capacities. For example, at each site, if we decide to install a warehouse, we can install a *small*, *medium* or *large* one.

Exercise 12.2. Prove Theorem 12.5.1.

Exercise 12.3. Show how any instance of the Bin-Packing Problem (see Part I) can be formulated as an instance of the Single-Source CFLP.

Exercise 12.4. Consider Problem P_1 of Section 12.4.
  (*a*) Show that this formulation can be strengthened by adding the constraints:

$$\sum_{\ell=1}^{L} \sum_{k=1}^{K} s_k U_{\ell j k} \le q_j, \quad \forall j \in J.$$

  (*b*) Show that this new formulation can be transformed to a specialized kind of linear program called a transportation problem.
  (*c*) Why might we not want to use this stronger formulation?

Exercise 12.5. (Mirchandani and Francis, 1990) Define the Uncapacitated Facility Location Problem (UFLP) in the following way. Let F_j be the fixed charge of opening a facility at site j, for $j = 1, 2, \ldots, m$.

$$\text{Problem UFLP} \;:\; \text{Min} \; \sum_{i=1}^{n} \sum_{j=1}^{m} c_{ij} X_{ij} + \sum_{j=1}^{m} F_j Y_j$$

$$\text{s.t.} \; \sum_{j=1}^{m} X_{ij} = 1, \quad \forall i \in N$$

$$X_{ij} \le Y_j, \quad \forall i \in N, \; j \in M$$

$$X_{ij}, Y_j \in \{0, 1\}, \quad \forall i \in N, \; j \in M.$$

Show that UFLP is $\mathcal{NP}$-Hard by showing that any instance of the $\mathcal{NP}$-Hard Node Cover Problem can be formulated as an instance of UFLP. The Node Cover Problem is defined as follows: given a graph G and an integer k, does there exist a subset of k nodes of G that cover all the arcs of G? (Node v is said to cover arc e if v is an end-point of e.)

Exercise 12.6. (Mirchandani and Francis, 1990) It appears that the p-Median problem can be solved by solving the resulting problem UFLP (see Exercise 12.5) for different values of $F = F_j, \forall j$, until a value F^* is found where the UFLP opens exactly p facilities. Show that this method does not work by giving an instance of a 2-Median problem for which no value of F provides an optimal solution to UFCLP with two open facilities.

13

Integrated Logistics Models

13.1 Introduction

The vehicle routing models discussed in Part II assume that the frequency, timing and sizes of customer deliveries are predetermined. There are however many distribution problems in which the vehicle schedules and the timing and size of the customer deliveries are (or should be) simultaneously determined. This is clearly the case in *internal* distribution systems in which the depot and the customers represent (part of) consecutive layers in the distribution network of a single company (see, e.g., Chapter 12).

In addition, the need to integrate inventory control and routing decisions arises in many *external* distribution processes in which deliveries need to be made to *external* customers. An example is the gas industry where the gas producers install tanks at their customers' locations and assume the responsibility for maintaining an adequate inventory level by determining the replenishment frequency and delivery sizes of all customers. Suppliers of supermarkets and department stores, to give another example, often acquire shelf space and are given the responsibility for replenishing the stock. They often adopt the complete inventory management function of their retailer customers. By billing a retailer only at the time it makes a sale to a consumer, the capital costs associated with the retailer's inventories are borne by the supplier. The supplier is given the responsibility to replenish the retailer's inventory at its discretion while guaranteeing a given fill rate or being charged for any lost sales or backlogs.

This arrangement alleviates the industrial retailer of its costly inventory investments and the intricacies of inventory planning; the supplier has the advantage of being able to determine when and in what quantities to deliver to its retailer customers. Moreover, when demands are subject to a considerable degree of uncertainty, the system as a whole derives additional benefits from this arrangement because the supplier can meet a given service level with an aggregate safety stock significantly smaller than the sum of the safety stocks required by the individual retailers, a phenomenon known as *risk pooling*.

There are many potential models integrating inventory control and vehicle routing problems. These include:

- Single-period models with stochastic customers demands; see, for instance, Federgruen and Zipkin (1984) who consider the following model. At the beginning of the period, the initial inventory, perhaps supply remaining from the previous period, for each location is reported to the central depot. This information is used to determine the allocation of the available product among the locations. At the same time, the assignment of customers to vehicles and their routes are determined. After the deliveries are made, the demands occur and inventory-carrying and shortage costs are incurred at each location proportional to the end-of-the-period inventory level. Observe that in this model it is possible that some locations will not be visited in a particular period.

- Multi-period models with deterministic (known) customer demands. Dror and Ball (1987) and Chien et al. (1989) suggest decomposing the multi-period problem into a series of single-period problems using a cost adjustment in each single-period model to reflect the effect of decisions made in one time period on later time periods. For further discussion of the multi-period inventory-routing problem the reader is referred to Golden et al. (1984), Assad et al. (1982), Dror et al. (1986), Dror and Ball (1987) and Chandra and Fisher (1990).

- Infinite horizon models where demands are at a customer-specific constant and *deterministic* rate. Here one needs to determine infinite horizon replenishment *policies* for all customers as well as efficient vehicle routes.

The impact of integrated inventory and routing strategies was recently highlighted by Stalk et al. (1992) who review the evolution of the discount retailing industry. They attribute Wal-Mart's success in developing into the largest and highest profit retailer in the world to a relentless focus on *efficient logistical design and planning*. "The key to achieving these goals was to make the way the company replenished inventory the centerpiece of its competitive strategy." Stalk et al. identify a number of major components in this strategic vision, most importantly, a logistics technique referred to as "cross docking." This refers to a distribution strategy in which the stores are supplied by central warehouses which act as coordinators of the supply process, and as transshipment points for incoming orders from outside vendors, but which do not keep stock themselves. In this chapter we analyze models that will to some extent explain the observed effectiveness of the cross docking strategy.

The models below assume that the firm operates its own private fleet of vehicles. Therefore, vehicle and maintenance costs are essentially sunk and the only remaining costs are fuel and labor. The analysis below differs substantially from the situation where the distribution is done through outside distributors such as truck-load carrier, less-than-truckload carrier, couriers, UPS etc. Models of this type will not be analyzed here.

13.2   Single Warehouse Models

The single warehouse distribution planning problem can be modeled as follows: a single warehouse serves retailers geographically dispersed in a given area. Stock for a single item is delivered to the retailers by a fleet of vehicles of limited capacity. Each retailer faces a deterministic, retailer-specific demand rate. The inventory holding costs are accrued at a retailer-specific constant rate. No inventory is kept at the depot. Each time a vehicle is sent out to replenish inventory, it incurs a fixed cost plus a cost proportional to the total distance traveled by the vehicle. The objective is to determine an inventory policy and a routing strategy such that each retailer satisfies its demands and the long-run average transportation and inventory costs are minimized.

In a distribution system of this type, one may have an additional constraint limiting the frequency with which each retailer is visited. Such a constraint may, for example, be due to limited material handling capacity and/or to the set-up time required for unloading deliveries at the retailers.

It is highly improbable that an optimal strategy will be identified in the near future for this model; such attempts have long been abandoned even for far simpler models, for example, the special case where the cost of dispatching a vehicle to a group of retailers only consists of the fixed component and is independent of the distance traveled. Such models, with joint replenishment costs of this type, are often referred to as Joint Replenishment Problems; see Jackson et al. (1985) and Federgruen and Zheng (1992). Most important, the structure of a fully optimal strategy may be so complex that it might fail to be implementable even if it could be determined in a reasonable amount of time. As a consequence, various authors have restricted themselves at the outset to specific classes of strategies and have developed methods to identify optimal or asymptotically optimal rules within the chosen class.

It is noteworthy that all of the proposed classes of policies for these and related problems are subsets of the class of *Zero Inventory Ordering Property* (ZIO) policies (see Chapter 9) under which a retailer is replenished if and only if its inventory is zero. In the absence of constraints on the vehicle capacity and the frequency with which retailers can be served, it is easily verified that an optimal policy must satisfy the ZIO property. However, in the presence of these constraints, ZIO policies may fail to be optimal, as we shall demonstrate shortly.

Even the structure of an optimal ZIO policy may be too complex to permit implementation or identification by a reasonable algorithm; this is why all of the literature on this model has restricted itself to specific subclasses of the ZIO policies. One attractive class is the class of *Fixed Partition* (FP) policies analyzed by Bramel and Simchi-Levi (1995). A FP policy partitions the set of retailers into a number of regions such that each region is served separately and independently from all other regions. Moreover, whenever a retailer in a set is visited by a vehicle, all other retailers in the set are visited as well. Fixed partition policies are easy to implement: they allow for an easy integration of the distribution, marketing and customer service functions.

Other strategies have been considered as well. For instance, Anily and Federgruen (1990), the first to analyze this model, focus on a class of replenishment strategies Ψ with the following properties: a replenishment strategy in Ψ specifies a collection of regions (subset of retailers); if a retailer belongs to several regions, a specific fraction of its sales is assigned to each of these. Each time one of the outlets in a given region gets a delivery, this delivery is made by a vehicle which visits all other outlets in the region as well. Anily and Federgruen show that regions can be formed by a simple regional partitioning scheme similar to those introduced in Section 5.4 and a combined inventory and routing strategy can thus be computed which is asymptotically optimal within the class Ψ.

Subsequent work considers restrictions to other classes of strategies. Gallego and Simchi-Levi (1990) show that Direct Shipping (DS) policies, that is, policies in which each vehicle visits a single retailer, are within 6% of optimality under certain restrictions on the problem parameters. We present these results in Section 13.3.

Herer and Roundy (1990) and Viswanathan and Mathur (1993) show good empirical performance for the so-called power-of-two strategies under which each retailer is replenished at constant intervals which are power-of-two multiples of a common base planning period. For a detailed discussion of power-of-two policies see Chapter 9. Bramel and Simchi-Levi (1995) analyzed the class of Fixed Partition policies. They show good empirical performance for medium-size problems in the absence of frequency constraints.

Observe that all the approaches suggested for the problem use strategies that belong to the class of ZIO policies. The question, of course, is how much is lost when one restricts itself to this class. Following the work of Chan et al. (1996) we perform, in Section 13.4, a probabilistic analysis of the class of ZIO and the class of FP policies.

Finally, in Section 13.5, we discuss multi-echelon systems and present recent results obtained by Chan and Simchi-Levi (1996) on the effectiveness of the cross-docking strategy; a strategy introduced in the previous section.

13.3   Worst-Case Analysis of Direct Shipping Strategies

In view of the worst-case results developed for the Capacitated Vehicle Routing Problem (see Chapters 5 and 6), one wonders whether similar results can be obtained for models integrating inventory control and transportation policies. Here we demonstrate that this is possible for infinite horizon inventory-routing problems where the warehouse does not hold inventory. For this model, Gallego and Simchi-Levi characterize the effectiveness of so-called *direct shipping* strategies.

Consider a model with a set of retailers N. For each retailer $i \in N$, we define

- D_i = demand per unit of time

- d_i = distance from the warehouse

- h_i = holding cost per unit per unit of time

- K_i = set up cost for ordering.

Items are shipped from a central depot to the retailers using vehicles of capacity q. Each time a vehicle is sent out to replenish inventory to a set of retailers S, it incurs a cost proportional to the total distance traveled by the vehicle, that is, a cost proportional to $L^*(S)$, the length of the optimal traveling salesman tour through the warehouse and the retailers in the set S. Without loss of generality, we set the cost per mile equal to one. We seek a combined inventory control and routing strategy that replenishes retailer inventories in time to meet their demands and minimizes the long-run average total inventory holding and transportation cost per unit of time. As in traditional joint replenishment inventory models, it is not clear that one "optimal" policy always exists. That is, it is possible that a series of policies successively has smaller and smaller cost without the existence of a "limiting" policy. Thus, here we let Z^* denote the infimum of the long-run average cost values over all feasible policies.

13.3.1 A Lower Bound

A lower bound on the long-run average cost over all inventory-routing strategies is obtained by combining lower bounds on the long-run average ordering and holding costs and a lower bound on the long-run average transportation cost.

Lemma 13.3.1 *A lower bound B on the long-run average cost over all inventory routing strategies is given by*

$$B = \sum_{i \in N} \left\{ \sqrt{2D_i K_i h_i} + \frac{2d_i D_i}{q} \right\}. \tag{13.1}$$

Proof. Let B denote the lower bound obtained by minimizing separately,

(*a*) the ordering and holding costs, and

(*b*) the total vehicle routing costs required to allow all retailers to meet their demands, and then adding these two values.

The minimum of (a) is given by the average costs of n independent EOQ models (see Chapter 9), that is, by

$$\sum_{i \in N} \sqrt{2 D_i K_i h_i}.$$

To find a lower bound for (b) we use a similar analysis to the proof of Lemma 5.2.1. Consider the distance traveled by vehicles of capacity q serving a set of geographically dispersed retailers (N) located at distances d_i from the depot and facing demands w_i. A lower bound on the total distance traveled is given by

$$\frac{2}{q} \sum_{i \in N} d_i w_i. \tag{13.2}$$

Let us now consider the distance traveled up to time t. The cumulative demand at retailer i up to time t is $D_i t$, and since no shortages or backlogging are allowed, the minimal amount shipped to retailer i up to time t is $D_i t$ for all $i \in N$. Therefore, the minimal distance traveled up to time t is obtained by substituting $D_i t$ for w_i in equation (13.2). Consequently, a lower bound on the distance traveled per unit time is given by $\frac{2}{q} \sum_{i \in N} d_i D_i$. Adding this expression to the lower bound on the long-run inventory ordering and holding cost we obtain equation (13.1).   ∎

13.3.2   The Effectiveness of Direct Shipping

We now analyze the cost of supplying all retailers separately. We call this the class of direct shipping strategies. An important subclass, called fully loaded direct shipping strategies, consists of direct shipping strategies where all shipments are made by fully loaded vehicles. We obtain an upper bound on the optimal cost in this subclass of policies. This bound, together with the lower bound of Lemma 13.3.1, characterizes an upper bound on the worst-case performance of direct shipping.

Let Q_i be the *lot size* for retailer $i \in N$, that is, the amount brought to the retailer at equal intervals of time. The cost per unit of time for retailer $i \in N$ is given by

$$z_i(Q_i) = \frac{K_i D_i}{Q_i} + \frac{h_i Q_i}{2} + 2 d_i \left\lceil \frac{Q_i}{q} \right\rceil \frac{D_i}{Q_i}.$$

Let $Z^{DS} = \sum_{i \in N} z_i(Q_i)$ be the total cost per unit of time for the policy corresponding to the order quantities $\{Q_1, Q_2, \ldots, Q_n\}$. We find an upper bound on Z^{DS} by restricting the choice of lot sizes to fully loaded vehicles, that is, the order quantities are restricted to the set $F \doteq \{mq : m = 1, 2, \ldots\}$.

Clearly, Z^{DS} is separable, so it is enough to find an upper bound on z over F, where z is identical to z_i omitting the index i. Let $f(Q) = \frac{KD}{Q} + \frac{hQ}{2}$ and note that, in F, the functions f and z differ only by the constant $\frac{2dD}{q}$. Thus, Q^f, the minimizer of f over F, is also the minimizer of z over the same set. Finally, let $Q^e \doteq \sqrt{2 K D h}$, $\eta \doteq \max\{\frac{q}{Q^e}, \sqrt{2}\}$ and $\epsilon(\eta) \doteq \frac{1}{2}(\eta + \frac{1}{\eta})$. We have

Lemma 13.3.2 $z(Q^f) \leq \left(f(Q^e) + \frac{2dD}{q} \right) \epsilon(\eta).$

Proof. It is easily verified (see Maxwell and Singh (1983)) that $Q^f = mq$ minimizes f over F if and only if

$$\sqrt{\frac{m-1}{m}} \leq Q^e / Q^f \leq \sqrt{\frac{m+1}{m}}. \tag{13.3}$$

Consider the following two cases. If $Q^e \geq \frac{q}{\sqrt{2}}$, then by (13.3), $\frac{1}{\sqrt{2}} \leq \frac{Q^e}{Q^f} \leq \sqrt{2}$. Since f is convex and $f(Q^e \sqrt{2}) = f(\frac{Q^e}{\sqrt{2}})$ we obtain (with $\eta = \sqrt{2}$)

$$f(Q^f) \leq f(Q^e)\epsilon(\eta). \tag{13.4}$$

If, on the other hand, $Q^e < \frac{q}{\sqrt{2}}$, then $Q^f = q$. Hence,

$$f(Q^f) = f(Q^e)\epsilon(\eta). \tag{13.5}$$

Combining (13.4) and (13.5), $\epsilon(\eta) \geq 1$ and the definition of z we obtain

$$z(Q^f) = f(Q^f) + \frac{2dD}{q} \leq \left[f(Q^e) + \frac{2dD}{q} \right]\epsilon(\eta). \qquad \blacksquare$$

We are now ready to characterize the worst-case performance of direct shipping. For this purpose, let $\eta_i \doteq \max\{\frac{q}{Q_i^e}, \sqrt{2}\}$, $\eta \doteq \max_{i \in N}\{\eta_i\}$ and $Z^{FDS} \doteq \sum_{i \in N} z(Q_i^f)$. It is easy to see that the lower bound B obtained in Lemma 13.3.1 together with the upper bound of Lemma 13.3.2 yields:

Theorem 13.3.3 *For any instance,* $\frac{Z^{FDS}}{B} \leq \epsilon(\eta)$.

This implies that the worst-case ratio of the cost of direct shipping to a lower bound on the optimal cost is no more than 1.061 whenever the economic lot sizes exceed 71% of the vehicle capacity, that is, whenever $Q_i^e \geq \frac{q}{\sqrt{2}}$ for all $i \in N$. The worst-case ratio increases as the economic lot sizes decrease. For instance, if the minimum lot size is 50% (respectively, 33%) of the vehicle capacity, then the worst-case ratio is 1.25 (respectively, 1.68).

13.4   Asymptotic Analysis of ZIO Policies

In this section our objective is to characterize the asymptotic effectiveness of the class of ZIO and the class of FP policies described in Section 13.2. For this purpose we analyze the following model.

Consider a distribution system with a set $N = \{1, 2, \ldots, n\}$ of geographically dispersed retailers. A central warehouse with an unlimited supply of a given product serves the retailers using vehicles of limited capacity q. Retailer i, located at a distance d_i from the warehouse, faces a deterministic demand rate D_i per unit of time and incurs a linear holding cost at a constant rate h per unit of product stored there per unit of time. Demand at each retailer must be met over an infinite horizon without shortages or backlogging. The frequency with which a given retailer can be visited is bounded from above by f; that is, the time that elapses between two consecutive deliveries to a retailer should be at least $\frac{1}{f}$. As mentioned earlier, this upper bound on the delivery frequency to each retailer may be due to the set-up time required for unloading at the retailers or may be due to other material handling constraints.

Each time a vehicle is sent out to replenish inventory to a set of retailers S, it incurs a fixed cost c plus a cost proportional to the total distance traveled by the vehicle, that is, a cost proportional to $L^*(S)$, the length of the optimal traveling salesman tour through the warehouse and the retailers in the set S. Without loss of generality, we set the cost per mile equal to one. We seek a combined inventory control and routing strategy that replenishes retailer inventories in time to meet their demands and minimizes the long-run average total inventory holding and transportation cost per unit of time.

Let Z_{zi}^* denote the infimum of the long-run average cost over all Zero-Inventory Ordering policies. The following example shows that Z^*, the infimum of the long-run average costs over all possible policies, can be strictly smaller than Z_{zi}^* even in an asymptotic sense, that is, we can construct a sequence of problem instances in which as $n \to \infty$ we have $\lim_{n\to\infty} \frac{Z^*}{n} < \lim_{n\to\infty} \frac{Z_{zi}^*}{n}$.

An Example

Consider a problem in which there are $3n$ retailers, each one with demand rate $D = 2$, located at the same point a distance $d = 1$ from the warehouse. Let $f = 1$ and $q = 3$. The fixed cost of sending out a vehicle c equals 1 and the holding cost rate h is 1.

Lemma 13.4.1 *There exists a feasible policy with long-run average cost $Z_{zi}^* - \frac{n}{2}$.*

Proof. Consider policies that satisfy the Zero-Inventory Ordering property. Let w be the size of a single delivery to a retailer in a policy of this type. The frequency constraint implies that $w \geq \frac{D}{f} = 2$ and hence each delivery to a retailer must be made by a separate vehicle. Since $\frac{2(2d_i+c)D}{h} = 12 > 9 = q^2$, the optimal ZIO policy delivers a full truck load (3 units) to each retailer every 1.5 units of time. The long-run average transportation cost of this policy is $(3n)\frac{2d+c}{1.5} = 6n$ while the long-run average holding cost is $3n(1.5) = 4.5n$.

Consider now a different policy which fails to satisfy the Zero-Inventory Ordering property. Under this policy, each retailer receives a delivery every unit of time. The frequency constraint is clearly satisfied. Without loss of generality, assume the system starts with zero-inventory at each retailer. Partition the retailers into groups of three retailers each. For each such group of three retailers, let the delivery sizes be $(2,2,3)$ at time 0, $(2,3,1)$ at time $2t - 1$ and $(2,1,3)$ at time $2t$ for each $t = 1, 2, \ldots$. Hence, for each $t = 1, 2, \ldots$, only two fully loaded vehicles are needed to visit each group of three retailers. It is easy to see that the long-run average transportation cost of this policy is $(2d + c)2n = 6n$ while the long-run average holding cost is $n[1 + 1.5 + 1.5] = 4n$. ∎

13.4.1   A Lower Bound on the Cost of Any Policy

We start by constructing a lower bound on the cost of any feasible policy.

Lemma 13.4.2

$$B = \sum_{i=1}^{n} \left[\frac{D_i(2d_i + c)}{q} + \frac{hD_i}{2f} \right]$$

is a lower bound on the long-run average cost over all feasible policies over the infinite horizon.

Proof. Let $I_i \geq 0$ be the initial inventory level at retailer i for every i. Consider an arbitrary policy $\mathcal{P}$ over an infinite horizon. Let $C(\mathcal{P}, t)$ be the average cost per unit of time incurred by this policy over the interval $[0, t)$. It suffices to show that $C(\mathcal{P}, t) \geq (\frac{1}{t+\frac{1}{f}})B - \frac{c'}{t}$ for some constant c' for all $t > \max_i \frac{I_i}{D_i}$.

Assume the retailers are ordered so that $d_1 \geq d_2 \geq \ldots \geq d_n$. Let M be the number of vehicles sent out from the warehouse during the interval $[0, t)$, S_j the set of retailers visited by vehicle $j = 1, 2, \ldots, M$, and w_i^j the number of units of product received by retailer i from vehicle j during $[0, t)$. Let Q_j be the amount of product delivered by the jth vehicle during the interval $[0, t)$; that is, $Q_j = \sum_{i=1}^{n} w_i^j$.

We first construct a lower bound on the total transportation cost incurred by policy $\mathcal{P}$. Consider the jth vehicle and a retailer $i \in S_j$. Clearly, $L^*(S_j) + c \geq 2d_i + c$ and hence,

$$Q_j[L^*(S_j) + c] = \sum_{i \in S_j} w_i^j[L^*(S_j) + c] \geq \sum_{i \in S_j} w_i^j(2d_i + c).$$

Since $Q_j \leq q$,

$$L^*(S_j) + c \geq \sum_{i \in S_j} \frac{w_i^j}{q}(2d_i + c).$$

Hence, the total transportation cost is no smaller than

$$\sum_{j=1}^{M}[L^*(S_j) + c] \geq \sum_{j=1}^{M} \sum_{i \in S_j} \frac{w_i^j}{q}(2d_i + c)$$

$$= \sum_{i=1}^{n} \sum_{j | i \in S_j} \frac{w_i^j}{q}(2d_i + c)$$

$$\geq \sum_{i=1}^{n} \frac{D_i t - I_i}{q}(2d_i + c).$$

Consider now the holding cost for each retailer i. Let r_i be the number of deliveries received by retailer i over the interval $[0, t)$. Due to the frequency constraint, $r_i \leq (t + \frac{1}{f})f$. Hence, the holding cost incurred by retailer i is no smaller than when the total delivery quantity to retailer i in $[0, t)$ is the minimum required, that is, $D_i t - I_i$, and the quantity is delivered at r_i equidistant epochs when inventories fall to zero; see Chapter 9. In this case the average inventory level equals $\frac{D_i t - I_i}{2r_i}$. The total holding cost incurred by retailer i in $[0, t)$ is thus bounded from below by

$$ht \frac{D_i t - I_i}{2r_i} \geq \frac{h D_i t}{2} \frac{t}{(t + \frac{1}{f})f} - \frac{ht I_i}{2(t + \frac{1}{f})f}.$$

Let $c' = \sum_{j=1}^{M} \frac{I_i}{q}(2d_i + c)$. Combining the lower bounds on the transportation and the holding costs, we have

$$C(\mathcal{P}, t) \geq \frac{t}{t + \frac{1}{f}} \sum_{i=1}^{n} \left[\frac{D_i(2d_i + c)}{q} + \frac{h D_i}{2f} \right] - \frac{c'}{t} - \frac{h \sum_i I_i}{2f} \frac{1}{t + \frac{1}{f}}$$

$$= \left(\frac{t}{t + \frac{1}{f}} \right) B - \frac{c'}{t} - \frac{h \sum_i I_i}{2f} \frac{1}{t + \frac{1}{f}}. \qquad \blacksquare$$

13.4.2   An Efficient Fixed Partition Policy

We construct a FP policy which is close to optimal in a specific sense described below. In particular, we show that the cost of this FP policy is, asymptotically, related to the asymptotic optimal solution of a related Bin-Packing Problem.

Given the retailers' demand rates, $D_1, D_2, \ldots, D_n$, consider the Bin-Packing Problem defined by items of size equal to these demand rates and bins of capacity $\bar{b}$, where $\bar{b} \doteq qf$. Without loss of generality we assume $\bar{b}$ is an integer. Feasibility implies that for every retailer $i \in N$, its demand rate D_i must satisfy $D_i \leq \bar{b}$. Assume the retailer demand rates D_i, $i = 1, 2, \ldots, n$ are independent and identically distributed according to a probability measure Φ defined on $[1, \bar{b}]$ with expected value $E(D)$. Let b^* be the number of bins used in the optimal solution to this Bin-Packing Problem. Then it follows from the analysis in Section 3.2 that there exists a constant γ such that $\lim_{n \to \infty} \frac{b^*}{n} = \gamma$ almost surely. If $\gamma = \frac{E(D)}{\bar{b}}$, the distribution is said to allow *perfect packing*. In that case, the constant $\alpha \doteq \gamma \frac{\bar{b}}{E(D)}$ equals one. If the distribution does not allow perfect packing, that is, $\gamma > \frac{E(D)}{\bar{b}}$, then the constant α is in $(1, 2]$.

The next theorem uses the constant α to characterize the difference between the long-run average cost of the FP policy and the long-run average cost of the best possible policy for any distribution Φ of the retailer demand rates.

Theorem 13.4.3 *Let the set of n retailer locations be a sequence of independent random variables having a distribution μ with compact support $A \subset \mathbb{R}^2$. Let the retailer demand rates be a sequence of independent random variables having a* *distribution* Φ. *Let* Z^*, Z^*_{zi} *and* Z^*_{fp} *denote the infimum of the total costs among* <u>all</u> *possible strategies,* <u>all</u> *zero-inventory strategies and* <u>all</u> *FP policies, respectively. Then with probability one,*

$$\lim_{n \to \infty} \frac{Z^*_{zi}}{Z^*} \leq \lim_{n \to \infty} \frac{Z^*_{fp}}{Z^*} \leq \sqrt{\alpha}.$$

Observe that when the distribution Φ allows perfect packing $\alpha = 1$ and therefore, in that case, and when the number of retailers tends to infinity, Z^*_{fp} has the same cost as the cost of the best Zero-Inventory Ordering policy which is also the cost of the best policy.

To prove the theorem, we construct a FP policy using the following two-step procedure. In the first step, we partition the region A where the retailers are distributed into subregions. The retailers in each subregion are then partitioned into subsets of retailers by solving the Bin-Packing Problem defined by the retailer demand rates and bins of size $\bar{b}$. Each such set is then served in an efficient way.

The Region Partitioning Scheme

Similarly to what we have done in Chapter 6, let $G(u)$ be an infinite grid of squares with edges parallel to the coordinate axes and side length $\frac{u}{\sqrt{2}}$. Let $\{A_1, A_2, \ldots, A_m\}$ denote the intersections of the squares with the compact region A.

Let $N(j)$ be the set of retailers in subregion A_j with $n(j) = |N(j)|$, $j = 1, 2, \ldots, m$. Given subregion A_j, let $\underline{d}_j$ be the distance from the warehouse to its closest point in A_j, $j = 1, 2, \ldots, m$.

To construct the fixed partition policy, we group all the retailers in subregion A_j, $j = 1, 2 \ldots, m$ into sets by solving the Bin-Packing Problem defined by the demand rates of the retailers in $N(j)$ and bins of capacity $\bar{b}$. Each such set S of retailers is served together using a reorder interval that depends on $D(S) \doteq \sum_{i \in S} D_i$ and the subregion where the retailers are located. If S is a set of retailers in subregion A_j, then the reorder interval is

$$t_S = \begin{cases} \frac{1}{f}, & \text{if } \sqrt{2D(S)(2\underline{d}_j + c)/h} \leq D(S)/f, \\ \sqrt{\frac{2(2\underline{d}_j + c)}{D(S)h}}, & \text{if } D(S)/f < \sqrt{2D(S)(2\underline{d}_j + c)/h} \leq q, \\ \frac{q}{D(S)} & \text{otherwise.} \end{cases}$$

That is, the reorder interval is chosen so that $q_S = D(S)t_S$ is the value of w achieving the following.

$$\min_{D(S)/f \leq w \leq q} \left\{ \frac{D(S)(2\underline{d}_j + c)}{w} + \frac{hw}{2} \right\}.$$

Consequently, these reorder intervals satisfy the capacity as well as the frequency constraints.

For any set of retailers $S \subseteq N(j)$, we use the following routing strategy. The vehicle travels from the warehouse to its closest point in A_j, visits the retailers in

S in any order, and then returns to the warehouse. It is clear that the total distance traveled is no more than $2\underline{d}_j + (|S| + 1)u$.

Analysis of the Upper Bound

For each subregion A_j, let $b^*(j)$ be the optimal solution to the Bin-Packing Problem defined by the demand rates of the retailers in $N(j)$, $j = 1, 2, \ldots, m$. Let $S_\ell(j)$, $\ell = 1, 2, \ldots, b^*(j)$ be the set of retailers assigned to the ℓth bin in this optimal solution.

We first need the following technical lemma presented without proof (the interested reader can consult Chan et al. (1996) for details).

Lemma 13.4.4 *(a) The function*

$$F(b, d) = \min_{b/f \le w \le q} \left[\frac{b(2d + c)}{w} + \frac{hw}{2} \right]$$

is concave in b for all $b \in [1, \bar{b}]$.

(b) $F(b, d) \le F(\bar{b}, d)\sqrt{\frac{b}{\bar{b}}}$ for all $b \in [1, \bar{b}]$.

We now derive an upper bound on the cost of the above-defined FP policy and hence on Z^*_{fp}, the infimum of the cost among all FP policies. This bound depends on the number of routes $b^*(N(j))$ into which the customers of A_j are partitioned, for $j = 1, 2, \ldots, m$. For each subregion $j = 1, 2, \ldots, m$, we express the number of routes generated in the subregion *relative* to the minimum possible number of routes, that is, the number of routes required if the demand rates $\{D_i : i \in N(j)\}$ could be perfectly packed into bins of size $\bar{b}$; in other words, we express the number of routes employed by the FP policy in terms of

$$\beta_j = \frac{b^*(N(j))\bar{b}}{\sum_{i \in N(j)} D_i} \ge 1,$$

where in the notation we have omitted the dependence of β_j on n.

Theorem 13.4.5

$$Z^*_{fp} \le \sum_{j=1}^{m} \sqrt{\beta_j} \sum_{i \in N(j)} D_i \frac{F(\bar{b}, d_i)}{\bar{b}} + 2nuf.$$

Proof. We bound Z^*_{fp} by the cost of the particular FP policy described above. Under this policy, the reorder interval for every subset of retailers $S_\ell(j)$, $\ell = 1, 2 \ldots, b^*(N(j))$, is $t_{S_\ell(j)} \ge \frac{1}{f}$. Hence, Z^*_{fp} is bounded by

$$Z^*_{fp} \leq \sum_{j=1}^{m} \sum_{\ell=1}^{b^*(N(j))} \left\{ \frac{2\underline{d}_j + c + u(|S_\ell(j)| + 1)}{t_{S_\ell(j)}} + \frac{hD(S_\ell(j))t_{S_\ell(j)}}{2} \right\}$$

$$\leq \sum_{j=1}^{m} \sum_{\ell=1}^{b^*(N(j))} \left\{ \frac{2\underline{d}_j + c}{t_{S_\ell(j)}} + \frac{hD(S_\ell(j))t_{S_\ell(j)}}{2} \right\} + 2nuf$$

$$= \sum_{j=1}^{m} \sum_{\ell=1}^{b^*(N(j))} \min_{D(S_\ell(j))/f \leq w \leq q} \left\{ \frac{D(S_\ell(j))(2\underline{d}_j + c)}{w} + \frac{hw}{2} \right\} + 2nuf.$$

$$= \sum_{j=1}^{m} \sum_{\ell=1}^{b^*(N(j))} F(D(S_\ell(j)), \underline{d}_j) + 2nuf.$$

By Lemma 13.4.4(a), $F(b, \underline{d}_j)$ is a concave function of b for every $j = 1, 2, \ldots, m$ and therefore for every j,

$$\sum_{\ell=1}^{b^*(N(j))} F(D(S_\ell(j)), \underline{d}_j) \leq b^*(N(j)) F\left(\frac{D(N(j))}{b^*(N(j))}, \underline{d}_j \right) = b^*(N(j)) F\left(\frac{\bar{b}}{\beta_j}, \underline{d}_j \right).$$

Then

$$Z^*_{fp} \leq \sum_{j=1}^{m} b^*(N(j)) \left(\frac{\bar{b}}{\beta_j} \right) \frac{F(\frac{\bar{b}}{\beta_j}, \underline{d}_j)}{\bar{b}/\beta_j} + 2nuf$$

$$= \sum_{j=1}^{m} D(N(j)) \frac{F(\frac{\bar{b}}{\beta_j}, \underline{d}_j)}{\bar{b}/\beta_j} + 2nuf.$$

Hence, by Lemma 13.4.4(b), we have

$$Z^*_{fp} \leq \sum_{j=1}^{m} \sqrt{\beta_j} D(N(j)) \frac{F(\bar{b}, \underline{d}_j)}{\bar{b}} + 2nuf$$

$$\leq \sum_{j=1}^{m} \sqrt{\beta_j} \sum_{i \in N(j)} D_i \frac{F(\bar{b}, d_i)}{\bar{b}} + 2nuf.$$

The last inequality follows since F is nondecreasing in its second argument. ∎
We can now finish the proof of Theorem 13.4.3.

Proof. Lemma 13.4.2 tells us that

$$B = \sum_{i=1}^{n} \left[D_i \frac{2d_i + c}{q} + \frac{h}{2f} \right]$$

$$= \sum_{i=1}^{n} D_i \left[\frac{2d_i + c}{\sqrt{\frac{\bar{b}}{f}q}} + \frac{h}{2\bar{b}} \sqrt{\frac{\bar{b}}{f}q} \right]$$

$$\geq \sum_{i=1}^{n} D_i \min_{\bar{b}/f \leq w \leq q} \left[\frac{2d_i + c}{w} + \frac{hw}{2\bar{b}} \right].$$

Hence,

$$B \geq \sum_{i=1}^{n} \frac{D_i F(\bar{b}, d_i)}{\bar{b}}$$

and since

$$\lim_{n \to \infty} \beta_j = \alpha$$

for each $j = 1, 2, \ldots, m$ we get that almost surely

$$\lim_{n \to \infty} \frac{Z_{fp}^*}{n} \leq \sqrt{\alpha} \lim_{n \to \infty} \frac{B}{n} + 2uf.$$

Finally, since u was arbitrary, we obtain that almost surely

$$\lim_{n \to \infty} \frac{Z_{fp}^*}{n} \leq \sqrt{\alpha} \lim_{n \to \infty} \frac{B}{n} \leq \sqrt{\alpha} \lim_{n \to \infty} \frac{Z^*}{n}. \qquad \blacksquare$$

13.5   Asymptotic Analysis of Cross-Docking Strategies

We are now ready to analyze a more general distribution system consisting of a single outside vendor, a number of warehouses and a large number of retailers. For this purpose, consider a distribution system with a set N of retailers, $N = \{1, 2, \ldots, n\}$, geographically dispersed in a given area A and a set M of warehouses, $M = \{1, 2, \ldots, m\}$. An outside vendor with an unlimited supply of a product serves the warehouses using "big" vehicles of capacity Q; each warehouse serves the retailers using "small" vehicles of capacity q. The terms "small" and "big" do not necessarily reflect the actual sizes of the vehicles; we use them just to distinguish between vehicles that deliver items to the warehouses and vehicles that deliver items to the retailers. We assume that each small vehicle is assigned to a unique warehouse.

Warehouse j, located at a distance d_j from the outside vendor, incurs a linear holding cost at a constant rate H per unit of product per unit of time. Retailer i, located a distance d_{ij} from warehouse $j = 1, \ldots, m$, faces a deterministic demand rate of D_i units of product per unit of time and incurs a linear holding cost at a constant rate h per unit of product per unit of time.

Demand at each retailer must be met over an infinite horizon without shortages or backlogging. The frequency with which a given retailer can be visited is bounded from above by f, that is, the time that elapses between two successive deliveries to a retailer should be at least $\frac{1}{f}$.

Each time a big vehicle is sent out to replenish inventory at the warehouses, it incurs a fixed cost C plus a cost proportional to the total distance traveled by it. Similarly, each time a small vehicle is sent out to replenish inventory at the retailers, it incurs a fixed cost c plus a cost proportional to the total distance it travels. In what follows the variable transportation cost for either a big or small vehicle is scaled so that it is equal to the total distance it travels. We seek a dispatching and routing strategy that delivers items from the outside vendor to the warehouses and from there to the retailers such that its long-run average cost is as small as possible. Long-run average cost is defined as total inventory holding cost per unit of time at the warehouses and the retailers plus transportation cost per unit of time from the outside vendor to the warehouses and from the warehouses to the retailers.

Let Z^* denote the infimum of the long-run average cost over all feasible policies. Similarly, let Z_{zi}^* denote the infimum of the long-run average cost over all Zero-Inventory Ordering policies. Define $\overline{b} \doteq qf$, b^*, Φ, γ and α as in Section 13.4.2.

Our main results are summarized in the following theorems.

Theorem 13.5.1 *Let the set of retailer locations be a sequence of independent random variables having a distribution μ with compact support $A \subset \mathbb{R}^2$. Let the retailer demand rates be a sequence of independent random variables having a distribution Φ. If Φ allows perfect packing, then there exists a Zero-Inventory Ordering policy which is asymptotically optimal with respect to all possible policies and satisfies the following properties.*

(a) *There is direct shipping from the outside vendor to the warehouses. That is, each big vehicle visits only a single warehouse in each trip.*

(b) *No inventory is held at the warehouses. That is, the warehouses serve as coordinators of the time and sizes of deliveries rather than storing points.*

(c) *Each retailer is served by exactly one warehouse.*

Observe that these properties imply a distribution strategy that is *very similar* to the "cross-docking" strategy identified by Stalk et al. in their analysis of Wal-Mart (see Section 13.1). In particular, the result may explain why a distribution system in which the warehouses serve only as a coordinator of the timing and size of deliveries but hold no inventory is so effective in practice.

The above results are explained as follows. Since the total number of retailers tends to infinity while the number of warehouses is fixed, independent of n, the number of retailers served by a single warehouse goes to infinity as well. Hence, each warehouse is faced with large demands, enough to fill up the entire capacity of a big truck. This explains part (a) of the theorem. To explain part (b), observe that once a big truck arrives at the warehouse, the warehouse can group enough retailers and immediately deliver the items that arrived so that no inventory is held at the warehouse. Finally, part (c) is justified by the fact that the distribution Φ allows perfect packing and thus, with high probability, the small trucks assigned to a single warehouse depart the warehouse fully loaded. This implies that there is no incentive to assign a retailer to more than one warehouse; it does not substantially improve the utilization of either the small trucks or the big trucks. Thus, in an asymptotically optimal strategy, a retailer should be served by its most efficient warehouse.

The proof of Theorem 13.5.1 is based on constructing a Fixed Partition Zero Inventory Ordering policy that satisfies all the properties established in the theorem.

The policy is similar to the one described in the previous section in terms of the distribution of products from the warehouses to the retailers. The cost of this policy Z_{fp}^* converges to the cost of a lower bound on the long-run average cost of all possible policies, when the distribution Φ allows perfect packing. The interested reader may refer to Chan and Simchi-Levi for details.

In the next theorem we characterize the difference between the long-run average cost of the best FP policy and the long-run average cost of the best possible strategy for any distribution Φ, even those that do not allow perfect packing. We remark that this theorem is essentially an extension of similar results presented in Section 13.4 for the single warehouse multi-retailer inventory-routing problem.

Theorem 13.5.2 *Under the assumptions of Theorem 13.5.1, and for any distribution Φ of the retailer demand rates we have*

$$\lim_{n \to \infty} \frac{Z_{zi}^*}{Z^*} \leq \lim_{n \to \infty} \frac{Z_{fp}^*}{Z^*} \leq \sqrt{\alpha} \leq \sqrt{2} \qquad (a.s.).$$

Observe that when the distribution Φ allows perfect packing, $\alpha = 1$. Therefore, in this case, when the number of retailers tends to infinity, Z_{fp}^* has the same asymptotic cost as the cost of the best Zero-Inventory Ordering policy which is also the asymptotic cost of the best policy.

13.6   An Algorithm for Multi-Echelon Distribution Systems

The previous results suggest a new algorithm for general multi-echelon distribution problems. Here we outline the general steps of the algorithm that generates a Fixed Partition Zero-Inventory Ordering policy.

Multi-Echelon Distribution Algorithm

Step 1: Assign each retailer to one warehouse.

Step 2: For each set of retailers assigned to the same warehouse
        Step 2.1: Partition the retailers into clusters.
        Step 2.2: Combine the clusters into groups and determine the reorder interval of each group.

Thus, in this multi-echelon distribution strategy each retailer is assigned to a unique warehouse and it receives deliveries only from that warehouse. Retailers assigned to the same warehouse are then partitioned into clusters such that all retailers in each cluster are served together by a single small vehicle. Each small vehicle serves a cluster of retailers assigned to a warehouse by following an optimal traveling salesman tour through the warehouse and all the retailers in the cluster. Clusters of retailers are combined into sets such that all retailers in the same set have the same reorder interval.

The deliveries are then coordinated by the warehouses as follows. Each warehouse j serving retailers in clusters belonging to a set S, with reorder interval t_S, arranges the deliveries so that small vehicles serving clusters in S leave warehouse j at the same time. The warehouse coordinates the deliveries such that the minimum number of big vehicles needed to carry the total load of the small vehicles (that are used to serve the retailers in S) arrive directly from the outside vendor just in time to transfer their loads to the small vehicles before these vehicles leave. With the total load of the big vehicles exactly equal to that of the small vehicles, warehouse j does not carry any inventory.

The interested reader may refer to Chan and Simchi-Levi for more details on the algorithm and its effectiveness from both practical and theoretical points of view.

13.7 Exercises

Exercise 13.1. Consider the following distribution problem. We are given a set of manufacturing facilities M, a set of warehouses W and a set of customers S. Each warehouse and each customer has a limit on the amount that can be stored at the facility. Each customer has forecasted demands for a single product for the next T periods and transportation cost between the facilities is a linear function of the amount delivered. Transportation cost per item may change from one period to the next. Inventory holding cost is charged on items carried at a facility from one period to the next. How would you design a delivery schedule that does not allow for shortages?

Part V

LOGISTICS ALGORITHMS

IN PRACTICE

14
A Case Study: School Bus Routing

14.1 Introduction

We now turn our attention to a case study in transportation logistics. We highlight particular issues that arise when implementing an optimization algorithm in a real-life routing situation. The case concerns the routing and scheduling of school buses in the five boroughs of New York City.

Many of the vehicle routing problems we have discussed so far (see Part II) have been simplified versions of the usually more complex problems that appear in practice. Typically, a vehicle routing problem will have many constraints on the types of routes that can be constructed including multiple vehicle types, time and distance constraints, complex restrictions on what items can be in a vehicle together, etc. The problems that appear in the context of school bus routing and scheduling could be characterized as the most difficult types of vehicle routing problems since they have aspects of all these constraints. This is the problem we will consider here.

School bus routing and scheduling is an area where, in general, computerized algorithms can have a large impact. User-friendly software that call routing and scheduling algorithms at the click of a button and that result in workable solutions can greatly affect the day-to-day operations of a dispatching unit. With increasingly affordable high-speed computing power in desktop computers and the possibility of displaying geographic information on-screen, it is not surprising that many communities are using expert systems to perform the daunting task of routing and scheduling their school buses. In most cases, this has led to improved solutions in fractions of the time that was previously required.

Unfortunately, providing workable solutions for such an application as this is not as simple as just "clicking" the right button. Anyone who has been involved in a real-life optimization application knows that much discussion is involved in determining what the problem is and how we are to "solve" it. In this chapter we concern ourselves with some of the details that make it possible to put modeling assumptions and algorithms into action.

14.2   The Setting

The New York City school system is composed of 1,069 schools and approximately one million students. Most of these students either walk to school or are given public transportation passes. About 125,000 students ride school buses that are leased by the Board of Education. The majority, or about 83,000, of these are classified as General Education students. These students walk to their neighborhood bus stop in the morning and wait for a bus to take them to school. In the afternoon, a bus takes them from their school and drops them off back at their bus stop. The rest of these students with particular needs, classified as Special Education, are picked up and dropped off directly at their homes.

This is one distinction that makes the transportation policies governing Special Ed students fundamentally different from those of General Ed students. Another fundamental difference is that, in many cases, Special Ed students enroll in schools with specific services and therefore may be bused over long distances. General Ed students usually go to schools only a few miles from their homes and almost exclusively to schools within the same borough. In addition, Special Ed students, such as wheelchair-bound students, are transported in specially designed vehicles with much smaller carrying capacities.

For General Ed student transportation, currently the Board of Education leases approximately 1,150 buses a year. Many companies bid for the contract to transport the students and currently the companies winning contracts design the routes. Independent of the company, the leasing cost to the Board is approximately $80,000 annually for each bus (and driver). The total yearly budget for General Education student transportation alone is therefore close to $100 million.

The routing of Special Education students is done differently. Using colored pins and large maps placed on walls, a team of inspectors/routers at the Board of Education Office of Pupil Transportation mark the students' homes and schools. Then, using their knowledge of the geography and street conditions acquired through their many years of work, they literally string pins together to form routes. Although the inspectors clearly do this well, this is very time consuming. For example, a group of five people took approximately three months to manually generate routes just for the Borough of Manhattan.

Several years ago, the New York City Board of Education appropriated funds to develop a computerized system, called CATS (Computer-Assisted Transportation System). This system is supposed to help in the design of routes for both the General and Special Ed students. The project consists of three phases.

Phase I: Replicate the pinning and stringing approach on a computer. The purpose of this phase is to emulate on the computer screen what was previously done with maps, pins and string. First, a database is needed to keep track of all relevant student and school information. The student data consist of address, bus stop and school. For each school, the data consist of an address, as well as starting and ending times for all sessions. This makes data easily retrievable and updatable, and provides some of the basic information that is needed for routing and scheduling. In addition to the database, a method of generating maps on the computer is needed as well; this is the geographic information system (GIS). These systems, widely available only in the last few years, truly offer a new dimension to many decision-support systems. With this software, color-coded objects designating students or schools can easily be displayed on a computer screen. This enables the user to visualize the relative locations of important points. In addition, the user can "click and drag" with a mouse and get information about the area outlined. This information can include U.S. Census data such as number of households, median age, income, etc. More importantly, in this application, by designating two points, the GIS can calculate exact locations (latitude and longitude coordinates) and also the distance between the two points along the street network. By "stringing" together a series of points, the software can give the total distance traveled. When this phase is completed, inspectors currently designing Special Ed routes will be able to "click" on bus stops with a mouse and "string" them together on the computer screen. This is the method called "blocking and stringing."

Phase II: Extend the functionality developed in Phase I to the General Education stop-to-school service. The goal is to create a system whereby one could construct routes for the General Ed population on the computer screen. For example, by choosing a set of schools with a mouse, the pertinent bus stops (those with students going to the set of schools) are highlighted. The inspector can then string together the stops and schools to form a route directly on the computer screen, or again let the computer determine a good route through the stops. The immediate *visualization* of a possible solution (routes) along with relevant statistics (bus load, total travel time, total students picked up) makes it much easier to check feasibility of the routes. This alone considerably simplifies the task of building efficient routes.

Phase III: Create an optimization module. The aim here is to build software that uses the student and school data and the GIS to generate efficient bus routes and schedules meeting existing transportation policies. The software should include subroutines that check feasibility of suggested routes or design routes for any subset of the population, be it a school, a district, a borough or the entire city. This is the phase in which we are the most interested.

We present here a range of issues related to the development of this optimization module (Phase III) and to the problem of routing buses through the New York City streets. We focus on routing the General Ed students; the routing of Special Ed is currently being done at the Office of Pupil Transportation using the "blocking and stringing" approach.

In Section 14.3, we give a short summary of some of the important papers that have appeared in the literature in the area of school bus routing and scheduling and related vehicle routing problems. In Section 14.4, we present details of the school bus routing and scheduling problem in Manhattan. In Section 14.5, we give a brief overview of methodologies we used to estimate distances, travel times and the pickup and dropoff times.

In designing a computerized system for this problem it is important to consider the following questions. First, is it possible to design an algorithm that will generate quality solutions in a reasonable amount of computing time? Second, are routes constructed by the computerized system truly *driveable*? Third, what is the best way to make these computerized algorithms of use to the people designing the routes? To answer the first two questions, we designed a school bus routing and scheduling algorithm and ran it on the Manhattan data. The algorithm is presented in Section 14.6. To answer the third question, in Section 14.8 we discuss some of the ways in which a computerized system for school bus routing can be made more interactive. In Section 14.9, we present results on the Manhattan data.

14.3   Literature Review

In the operations research literature, we find quite a few references to the problem as well as many different solution techniques. A standard way the school bus routing and scheduling problem has been analyzed is to decompose it into two problems: a route generation problem where simple routes are designed (usually with only one school), and a route scheduling problem where these routes are linked to form longer routes (routes that visit more than one school).

As early as 1969, Newton and Thomas looked at a bus routing problem for a single school. Using some of the first local improvement procedures for vehicle routing problems, they designed a tour through all the bus stops and then partitioned it into smaller feasible routes that each could be covered by a bus.

In 1972, Angel et al. considered a clustering approach to generating routes. First, bus stops are grouped by their proximity using a clustering algorithm. Then an attempt is made to find minimum length routes through these clusters in such a way that the constraints are satisfied. Finally, some clusters are merged if this is feasible. The algorithm was applied to an instance consisting of approximately 1,500 students and 5 schools in Indiana.

In 1972, Bennett and Gazis considered the problem of generating routes. They modified the Savings Algorithm of Clarke and Wright (1964) (see Section 6.2). They also experimented with different objective functions such as minimizing total student-miles. The problem considered had 256 bus stops and approximately 30 routes in Toms River, New Jersey.

In 1979, Bodin and Berman used a 3-opt procedure to generate an initial traveling salesman tour which is then partitioned into feasible routes. This algorithm uses two additional components: a lookahead feature and a bus stop splitter. The lookahead feature allows the initial order to be changed slightly. The bus stop splitter allows a bus stop to be split into smaller bus stops. Two problems were studied. One dealt with a school district in a densely populated suburban area with 13,000 students requiring bus transportation each day and 25 schools. A second district, also in a suburban area, had 4,200 students transported.

In 1984, Swersey and Ballard addressed only the problem of scheduling a set of routes that had already been designed. Given a set of routes that delivered all students from their bus stops to their schools, the authors devised a method to find the minimum number of buses that could "cover" these routes. This scheduling problem can be formulated as a difficult integer program. The authors used some simple cutting planes to solve it heuristically. The size of the problem considered was approximately 30-38 buses and 100 routes.

Finally, in 1986, Desrosiers et al. studied a bus routing problem in Montréal, Canada. Using several techniques, depending on whether the stops were in rural or urban areas, they generated a set of routes. To schedule them, they formulated the problem as an integer program and solved it using a column generation approach. The problem solved had 60 schools and 20,000 students.

14.4   The Problem in New York City

The School Bus Routing and Scheduling Problem can take many forms depending on how generally it is formulated. In its most general form, the problem consists of a set of students distributed in a region who have to be brought to and from their schools every school day. The problem consists of determining bus stop locations, assigning students to bus stops, and finally routing and scheduling the buses so as to minimize total operating cost while following all transportation guidelines. The difficulty, of course, is that each of these subproblems are dependent and therefore should be looked at simultaneously. That is, any determination of bus stop locations, and who gets assigned to each, clearly has an impact on the routes and schedules of the buses. Hence, an integrated approach is required to avoid suboptimality. However, due to the complexity and the size of the problem this has historically never been attempted. In addition, often it is not necessarily possible to reoptimize all aspects of the problem, such as bus stop locations or assignments.

To understand why this problem is so complex, consider for instance the bus stop location problem on its own. There are numerous constraints and requirements: no more than a certain number of students can be assigned to the same bus stop; bus stops cannot be within a certain distance of each other; each student must be within a short walk of the bus stop and must not cross a major thoroughfare, etc.

In our case, the Board of Education decided that the bus stops that are currently being used will remain in use. Thus, the position of the bus stops as well as which students are assigned to each was assumed fixed. These stops satisfy all the requirements mentioned above. Our routing and scheduling problem thus starts with a set of bus stops, each with a particular number of students assigned to it destined for a particular school. Each school has starting and ending times for each session. In addition to bus stop and school data, it is assumed that distance and travel time between any two points in the area are readily available. This issue will be discussed in more detail in Section 14.5.

We formally define a *route* as follows. A route is a sequence of stops and possibly several schools that can be feasibly driven by one bus. For example, routes for the morning problem always start with a pickup at a stop and end with dropoff at a school. In contrast, an afternoon route always starts with a pickup at a school and ends with a dropoff at a stop.

The goal is to design a set of minimum cost routes satisfying all existing transportation guidelines. The major cost component to the Board of Education is the cost of leasing each bus and driver, and hence the objective is essentially to minimize the number of buses needed to feasibly transport the students. Clearly, safety is the first consideration, and it is the view of the Board of Education that bus routes that meet all transportation guidelines provide a high level of safety. The rest is up to the drivers.

Route feasibility is the most complex aspect of the problem. There are numerous side constraints. First, the bus can hold only a limited number of students at one time (*capacity constraint*). Second, each student must not be on the bus for more than a specific amount of time and/or distance (*time* or *distance constraint*). This is motivated by the simple observation that the less time spent on the bus the safer and more desirable it is for the students. And finally, there are restrictions on the time a bus can arrive at a school in the morning, and on the time a bus can leave the school in the afternoon (*time window constraints*). In many school bus routing and scheduling problems, transportation policies specify that students from different schools not be put on the same bus at the same time; that is, no *mixed loads* are allowed. Clearly, allowing mixed loads provides increased flexibility and therefore can lead to savings in cost. In New York City, for the most part, mixed loads are allowed. We list here the primary constraints. There are several other constraints which we talk about in Section 14.7.

We will deal exclusively here with the problem of delivering the students to their school in the *morning*. Researchers have noted that this problem is usually more critical than the *afternoon* problem for two reasons. First, in the afternoon the time windows are usually less constraining. For example, in Manhattan (in the morning), school starting times fall between 7:30am and 9:00am. That gives roughly a one and a half hour time window to pickup all students and take them to their schools. In the afternoon, schools end at times over a wider range: anywhere between 1:00pm and 4:15pm. Second, traffic congestion is usually higher in the morning hours than in the afternoon hours when the students are being bused. Therefore, it is very likely more buses will be needed in the morning than in the afternoon. Indeed, our computational experiments reported in Section 14.9 verify that this is true in Manhattan. Note that the solution found in the morning *cannot* be simply replicated in the afternoon, that is, having each bus travel the same route as in the morning but in the opposite direction. This is true since the sequencing of school ending times in the afternoon is different from the sequencing of school starting times and therefore schools visited in one order in the morning cannot always be visited in the same or opposite order in the afternoon.

For the morning problem in Manhattan, the specific problem parameters are given below. During the 1992-93 academic year, 4,619 students were transported by school buses from 838 bus stops to 73 schools. The constraints were as follows.

- *Vehicle capacity constraint*. At most 66 students can be on the bus at one time.

- *Distance constraint*. Each student cannot be on the bus for more than 5 miles.

- *Time window constraints*: Buses must arrive at a school no earlier than 25 minutes before and no later than 5 minutes before the start of school.

- The earliest pickup must not be before 7:00 a.m.

- Mixed loads are allowed.

The 5-mile distance constraint is not applied uniformly to all students; students in District 6 (upper Manhattan) are often transported out of their district due to overcrowding. Therefore, since this involves longer trips, sometimes traversing most of the island, the 5-mile constraint is not applied to these students. Approximately 36% of the students in our application were in this group.

The Manhattan school bus routing problem presents many challenges. First of all, the number of bus stops and schools is much larger than those encountered in most vehicle routing applications. Second, there are many difficulties involved in calculating accurate distances and travel times in New York City. We now consider these two points.

14.5   Distance and Time Estimation

To accurately estimate distances one needs a precise geographic representation of the area. This is achieved using a geographic information system (GIS) which is based on data files built from satellite photographs. These files store geographic objects, such as streets, highways, parks and rivers that can be presented on a computer screen. An important feature is the ability to calculate exact latitudes and longitudes of any point. Given a street address, the process of *geocoding* returns the coordinates of the address with very high accuracy. Given these coordinates, it is then easy to calculate "as the crow flies" or "Euclidean" distances. Some GISs also have the capability of calculating exact road network distances, that is, the distance between two points on the actual street network, sometimes even taking into account one-way streets.

The Office of Pupil Transportation at the Board of Education uses a GIS called MapInfo for Windows. The MapInfo version used by the City does not have a street network representation of New York City. However, such a network has been developed by a subcontractor and therefore accurate shortest distances between any two points along the street network are readily available. The current version also takes into account one-way streets. Although incorporating one-way street information may seem like a trivial task, it turned out to be very difficult. We believe most current geographic information systems are highly inaccurate with regard to one-way streets and are probably unusable without substantial error checking. The New York City Department of Transportation does not keep the information in an easily retrievable format. We had to resort to checking the *one-way street sign* database at the NYC DOT to reconstruct accurate information about one-way streets. Needless to say, the data collection and error checking was extremely time consuming.

Estimating accurate travel times in New York City is probably the trickiest part of the problem. As described above, a GIS with a street network representation simplifies the calculation of street distances. In addition, in the GIS each data structure corresponding to a street segment has space to store the average travel speed and/or travel time along the segment. These estimates would make it possible to calculate travel times along any path. The difficulty lies, of course, in determining these travel speeds.

Most existing vehicle routing implementations that we are aware of use a fixed travel speed throughout the area of interest. Travel times are then determined by simply dividing the distance traveled by this universal speed. This method is most likely not satisfactory for New York City. Anyone who has driven in New York City knows the multitude of different street types and congestion levels that can produce a wide variety of different travel speeds. We decided to try to get some idea of the average speed in different parts of New York City.

In addition to performing various timing experiments, we obtained several reports from the New York City Department of Transportation. These include "Midtown Auto Speeds–Spring 1992" and "Midtown Auto Speeds–Fall 1992." These reports provide data on Midtown Manhattan average travel speeds as well as some data on the variance of these speeds. (Midtown Manhattan is defined as the rectangular area between First and Eighth Avenues and 30th and 60th Streets.) The data seem to suggest that speeds vary from an average of 6 miles per hour up to about 14 miles per hour, depending on street type, direction and time of day.

Our approach was to choose an estimate of speed that would be specific to each district; thus, a district in the Bronx would not have the same speed estimate as one in Midtown Manhattan. These range from about 7 miles per hour to 12 miles per hour. An important observation made when collecting data was that when a bus experienced below average travel times along the beginning of the route, the bus driver will slow down or spend more time at the stops to get back on schedule. In addition, since the students have a scheduled pickup time, the bus cannot, as a rule, leave early. It must wait until a specific time before leaving the bus stop. If the bus experiences above average travel times (below average speeds), then the bus driver can speed up (slightly) and make sure to leave when all students are on the bus. Consequently, the travel time is not as random as one might think.

To make sure that school buses meet the time window constraints, information about travel time along the streets of New York City is not sufficient. The time to pick up students from their bus stops and to drop off students at their schools must also be taken into account. By riding the buses, we collected data on the time it takes to pick up or drop off students at stops or at schools. A linear regression was performed on the data providing the following model for the pickup time:

$$PTime = 19.0 + 2.6N,$$

where $PTime$ = pickup time (in seconds), and N = number of students picked up at the bus stop. This regression was performed on 30 data points. The R^2 was 77.7% and the p-value of the independent variable was very small (< 0.001). The regression performed on the dropoff times resulted in the equation:

$$DTime = 29.0 + 1.9N,$$

where $DTime$ = dropoff time (in seconds), and N = number of students dropped off at the school. This regression was performed on 30 data points. Here the R^2 was 41.9% and the p-value of the independent variable was 0.01%. In our implementation, we used these equations to determine approximate pickup and dropoff times.

Overall, the approximations and calculations made in testing the optimization module were designed with the goal of ensuring that a route constructed by the algorithm would be a driveable one. The next question is how to generate a good feasible solution to the school bus routing and scheduling problem.

14.6   The Routing Algorithm

There are many existing algorithms for school bus routing and scheduling. Numerous communities throughout the world have implemented computerized algorithms to perform these tasks. Overall, the success seems to be universally recognized. Almost all papers published in the literature mention cost savings of around 5–10%. We recognize that it may be useless to even contemplate the meaning of these savings numbers since the savings may not only come from reduction in cost but also from increased control of the bus routes. The magnitude of the "savings" is also highly dependent on what methods were in use before the computerized system was put into place.

Transferability seems to be the critical factor. It is difficult to compare algorithms for this problem directly from the literature. Each problem has its own version of the constraints and even objectives. It is not always simple or even possible to take an existing algorithm in use in one community and simply apply it to another. Each problem has its peculiarities and may also have very different constraints. For instance, in an implementation in Montréal, the people designing the routes have the freedom to change existing school starting and ending times at their convenience. Clearly this added flexibility can simplify the problem to some extent, and can lead to additional savings in cost. In New York City this was not possible.

Finally, this is all within the framework of an optimization problem, which we have seen is extremely difficult to solve. There is an absence of any strong lower bounds on the minimum number of buses required.

In determining what type of algorithm to apply to this large vehicle routing problem, we considered several important aspects of the problem and also the setting in which the algorithm would be used.

Efficiency This is an extremely large problem, so the solution method must be efficient in computation time and in space requirement. Assuming optimization might be done by district, some districts have as many as 1,500 bus stops. Even though complete optimization of the solution might only be done once a year, the time involved in testing and experimenting with the problem parameters is reduced considerably if the algorithm is time and space efficient.

Transparency The algorithm would most likely need to be constructive in nature thereby providing a dispatcher with the ability of viewing the algorithm progression in real-time. This makes it possible to detect "problem routes" and correct errors without having to wait until the termination of the algorithm. That is, the approach should build routes in a sequential fashion and not, for example, work for hours and finally, in the last moments provide a solution.

Flexibility The heuristic should be flexible enough to handle, not only the constraints currently in place, but additional constraints that might be imposed in the future.

Interactivity From our discussions with the inspectors it is clear that the algorithm implemented must have an interactive component that would allow an experienced inspector to help construct routes using his or her prior knowledge. That is, the algorithm must be able to work in two different modes. First, it must be able to act like a black box, where data are input and a solution is output. Second, it must also serve as an interactive tool, where a starting solution can be presented along with a set of unrouted stops and the algorithm finds the best way to *add on* to this starting solution.

Multiple Solutions The algorithm should be capable of producing a series of solutions, not simply one solution. This last point is important since each solution would have to be checked by an inspector, and it is possible that the inspector will rule out some solutions.

Finally, the urban nature of our application, in contrast to many of the problems seen in the literature, should also be taken into account. As many researchers have noted (see Bodin and Berman, 1979, and Chapleau et al., 1983), the vehicle capacity constraint tends to be the most binding constraint when routing in an urban area. This is due to the general rule that the bus will tend to "fill up" before the time constraints become an issue. Therefore, it seems as though algorithms developed for the Capacitated Vehicle Routing Problem (CVRP) (see Chapter 6) should be a good starting point. The difficulty is that the CVRP generally has a different objective function: minimize the total distance traveled, not the number of vehicles used. Fortunately (see Chapter 6 or Bramel et al., 1991), if the number of pickup points is very large and distances follow a general norm, when the distance is minimized, a byproduct of the solution is that the minimum number of vehicles will be used. Observe that distances in New York City come from the street network, not from a norm; however, since the blocks are short and somewhat uniform in size, the street network distance is fairly close to a norm distance, and similar results most likely hold.

For these reasons, our starting point for the algorithm for the school bus routing and scheduling problem was the Location Based Heuristic (LBH) (see Section 6.7) developed for the CVRP. This algorithm has the important property that it is *asymptotically optimal* for the CVRP (see Section 6.7); that is, the relative error between the value of the solution generated by the algorithm and the optimal solution value tends to zero as the number of pickup points increases.

Due to the size and complexity of the problem, we made several changes to the LBH. The algorithm is *serial* in nature as it constructs one route at a time and not in parallel. To describe the algorithm, let the bus stops be indexed $1, 2, \ldots, n$. Let a route run by a single bus be denoted R_i. Let a full solution to the school bus routing and scheduling problem be written as a set of routes $\{R_1, R_2, \ldots, R_M\}$, where M is the number of buses used. For each bus stop j, let $school[j]$ be the index of the school to which the students at stop j are destined. Let U be the set of indices of all unvisited pickup points.

The following algorithm creates one solution to the school bus routing and scheduling problem. More solutions can be generated by starting the algorithm with different random seeds.

Randomized LBH:

Let $U = \{1, 2, \ldots, n\}$ and $m = 0$.
while $(U \neq \emptyset)$ *do*
{
Pick a seed stop from U using a selection criterion. Call it j.
Let $U \leftarrow U \setminus \{j\}$.
Let the current route be $R_m = \{j \rightarrow school[j]\}$.
repeat
{
For each $i \in U$, calculate $c_i = routelength(i, R_m)$.
Let $c_k = \min_{i \in U}\{c_i\}$.
If $c_k < +\infty$ then
{
Let $R_m \leftarrow buildroute(k, R_m)$.
Let $U \leftarrow U \setminus \{k\}$.

```
        }
      } until c_k = +∞.
    m ← m + 1.
    }
  }
M ← m.
```
The heuristic solution is $\{R_1, R_2, \ldots, R_M\}$.

The selection of the seed stops can be done in one of several different ways. One approach is to simply select these stops at random from the set of unvisited stops. Another approach is to select stops with large loads or stops that have tight delivery windows (i.e., the distance and time constraints force these stops to be delivered almost directly from the stop to the school with very few stops in between). Other criteria were used according to which constraints were binding at particular stops.

The function *routelength*(i, R) determines the approximate cost of inserting stop i into route R. Route R consists of a path through several stops and schools. While preserving the order of the stops and schools in route R, we determine the best insertion point for stop i. We check each consecutive pair of points (either stops or schools) along route R and check whether stop i can be inserted between these two. If *school*$[i]$ is not in route R, then we must not only find the best insertion point for stop i, but also the best insertion point for *school*$[i]$. It is possible that no insertion point(s) can be found that results in a feasible route. Checking whether a stop can be inserted requires checking all the constraints. If no feasible insertion point exists, then the value of *routelength*(i, R) is made $+\infty$. This indicates that it is not possible (while preserving the order of R) to insert stop i into route R. If an insertion is found that results in a feasible route, then the value of *routelength*(i, R) is made to be exactly the additional distance traveled.

To illustrate the difficulty of this step, consider simply the capacity constraint. In the case of the CVRP, all loads are dropped off at the same point (the final stop); therefore, the maximum load that is carried by the vehicle is when it picks up its last load. Therefore, it is easy to check whether a stop can be added to a route since we need only check that the maximum load is less than the vehicle capacity. This maximum load is always at the last stop, so the calculation is easy. By contrast, performing a similar calculation in the school bus routing and scheduling problem is much more complicated since there is more than one dropoff point. Checking feasibility when adding a stop to a route requires knowing *when* the student is getting on and off the bus, since this will affect whether there is room for a student at future points on the bus route. Therefore, checking whether the capacity constraint is violated in the school bus routing problem is much more complicated than in the CVRP.

The function *buildroute*(k, R) creates the route that results from the insertion of stop k into route R. Again, stop k is simply inserted between the two consecutive points (stops or schools) that result in the shortest total route. This route is guaranteed to be feasible since $c_k < +\infty$.

The algorithm satisfies the requirements that we described above. It runs efficiently for problems of large size and builds routes sequentially. It is very flexible in the sense that constraints of almost any type can be included (e.g., disallowing mixed loads for some schools). Of course each additional constraint causes the algorithm to take a little longer to find a solution. In terms of its interactivity (see the next section for details), the algorithm can be used in an interactive mode if this is desired. In this mode, a partial routing solution can be used as a starting point and unrouted stops can be added efficiently. The inspector can also have a major impact on the routes generated by the algorithm via the selection of the seed points (see Section 14.8 below for a further discussion on this point). Since the algorithm can be easily randomized (by randomizing the seed stop selection procedure), starting the algorithm with different random numbers makes it generate different solutions. Finally, the most important advantage of this heuristic is that it does not decompose the problem into subproblems, but solves the routing and scheduling components simultaneously.

14.7   Additional Constraints and Features

In the course of the implementation of our algorithm, several additional "soft" constraints came to our attention. These are subtle rules that inspectors used when constructing feasible routes, which were only determined once a set of routes were shown to the inspectors.

Limit on the number of buses to a particular school This is best explained with an example. Consider the situation where a school, say school A, has a late starting time relative to other schools, say 9:30am, where all other schools start at 9am, and assume only a dozen of the students from school A require bus service. Previously, if a solution required 20 buses to serve all schools, routers would take one of these and have it alone serve school A. That is, some time between 9am and 9:30am one bus would pick up the dozen students and deliver them to school A. Since 20 buses are used in the solution, this solution is equivalent to, for example, having 6 of the 20 buses each deliver 2 students to school A between 9am and 9:30am. This, from a cost point of view, is just as good a solution. However, school A may only be able to handle one or two buses at a time due to limited driveway space. We therefore needed to add a constraint on the number of buses that could deliver students to each school. This constraint only became active for a few schools.

Multi-level relational distance constraints When delivering packages to warehouses or to customers, a distance constraint is usually set on the complete route thus limited to the driver's working day. When delivering students to schools, the distance constraint is really *student specific*. That is, each student's trip is limited, not just the driver's. In the school bus routing and scheduling problem, the distance constraint also illustrates the difficulty of modeling, through simple constraints, a real-life problem. To illustrate this, consider the 5-mile distance constraint discussed earlier. We found that this simple constraint was actually unsatisfactory for this problem. For example, if a student was only 1 mile from school, then it was not considered desirable to have him or her end up traveling 5 miles on the bus. This student (and maybe more vociferously his or her parents) would not consider this an equitable solution. We therefore decided to implement what we call a relational distance constraint. That is, for a multiplier α, say $\alpha = 2$, a student could not travel on the bus for more than α times the distance the student's bus stop was from school. The question was then to what do we set α. We determined that the best rule was to divide the region around a particular school into concentric rings. For example, if the first ring was 3 miles in radius, then a stop that was $d \leq 3$ miles from the school would have a distance constraint (on the bus) of $\alpha_1 d$ miles. Ring i was assigned a multiplier α_i and this was repeated for each ring. Although it took some time to determine appropriate multipliers, eventually this is the type of distance constraint that was implemented.

Waiting time constraint Another constraint that did not come to our attention until we presented our routes to the inspectors was the waiting time constraint. Again, this is something that is specific to the routing of people as opposed to packages. Consider a simple problem with two schools, school A starting at 8am and school B starting at 9am. At 7:30 a bus picks up both students for schools A and B and then arrives at school A in the time window (say at 7:45) and drops off only those students that are going to school A. Since school B starts at 9am, the bus waits for half an hour at school A until proceeding to pick up some more students for school B and then arriving at school B at 8:45 and dropping off all the students. A route of this type, where students wait on the bus for half an hour, was definitely not deemed acceptable. Therefore, we needed to add a constraint on the amount of time a bus (with students on it) can wait idle. Five minutes was the number that was eventually used.

Route balancing It is desirable that the routes in a solution be of similar duration and total distance. It does not seems fair if one driver serves morning routes from 7am to 7:30am while another works from 7am to 9:30am. The balancing of the workloads is partially achieved by implementation of a *route-balance()* subroutine that is called once, at the end of the algorithm. This subroutine essentially moves stops and schools from heavily loaded routes to less heavily loaded routes while maintaining feasibility of the solution. This seemed to work very well.

Single route optimization Once a solution is determined, we may (and should) optimize the sequencing of the stops and schools on each route individually. That is, given a set of stops and schools that can be feasibly served by one bus, in terms of service level, what is the "best" route to actually drive? An objective that guarantees a high service level is to minimize the total number of student-miles traveled (see e.g., Bennett and Gazis (1972)). For each route created, we call a procedure called *route-opt( )* which minimizes the total number of student-miles while maintaining feasibility of the route.

14.8   The Interactive Mode

As we mentioned earlier, the complete rescheduling of all buses might only be done once a year (in August). However, throughout the course of the school year there are quite a few small changes that must be made to the solution. These changes could be caused by, for example:

- A school, which previously did not request bus service, requests service in mid-year.

- A student changes address or school.

- A school's session time changes.

One option might be simply to reoptimize all routes that are affected by the changes. This might cause major disruptions in a large number of routes. These disruptions may translate to disruptions in the parents' morning schedules which might over-load the Office of Pupil Transportation telephone switchboard. In essence, it is desirable to implement the changes while making the fewest disruptions to other students' schedules.

This was the impetus for the development of the algorithm's *interactive mode*. Here it is possible to start the algorithm with a number of routes already created and to simply add stops to or delete stops from these routes. Let's consider what happens when a stop is added to an existing set of routes. The user has the ability to select from one of three options:

- *Complete reoptimization.* This corresponds to starting the reoptimization from scratch, that is, throwing away all previously created routes. Optimization then starts with all new stops added to the list of stops.

- *Single route reoptimization.* This corresponds to selecting a route and check-ing whether a particular stop can be added to it. This is done through a simple *route-check( )* subroutine. In this case, the route may be completely resequenced.

- *No reoptimization.* In this case, the stop is simply inserted between two stops on existing routes without any reoptimization.

Deleting a stop is somewhat easier to do, the user simply clicks the mouse on the stop in question and deletes it from the current solution. The fact that this may actually render the remaining route infeasible is a good illustration of the complexity of the bus routing and scheduling problem. This is due to the waiting time constraint mentioned in the previous section. In either case, the user can specify whether a reoptimization of the route is desired.

These optimization tools proved quite useful as they provided simple ways to test what-if scenarios; tests that previously would have taken weeks if not months.

14.9   Data, Implementation and Results

To assess the effectiveness of our algorithm, we attempted to solve the problem using the Manhattan data given to us by the Office of Pupil Transportation, that is, to use our algorithm to generate a solution and to check it for actual drivability.

We solved both the morning and the afternoon problem. We first calculated the shortest distance matrix between all 911 points of interest (838 stops and 73 schools) along the street network. We used a speed of 8 miles per hour for the entire borough. This was the lowest average speed in Midtown Manhattan along a street or avenue between 7am and 10am (the time interval that the bus would be traveling in the morning) reported by the Department of Transportation. We feel that this average speed is quite conservative and a bus can on average travel more quickly. One reason for this is that the measurement was made in Midtown Manhattan, a location with very high congestion throughout the day. The algorithm was run on a PC (486DX2/50 megahertz) under Windows over a period of several hours. To generate its first feasible solution, the algorithm takes about 40 minutes. We repeated the algorithm 40 times keeping track of the best solution. The algorithm has a detailed schedule and directions for each bus.

In order to determine the sensitivity of the results to some of the assumptions we have made, we ran the algorithm with several settings for the average travel speed. We used 8 mph, 10 mph and 12 mph. Note again these speeds are conservative, as we have also taken into account the time to stop and pick up or drop off students. The following table lists the number of buses used in the best solutions found for each of these settings and for the morning and afternoon problems.

Table 1: General education routing

Universal	Number of Buses Used	
Speed	Morning	Afternoon
8 mph	74	67
10 mph	64	60
12 mph	59	56

As a comparison, these solutions use substantially fewer buses than are currently in use. We do not expect that the number of buses used will be as low as indicated by our preliminary results, due to the fact that the routes have not been checked by the inspectors. However, it is reasonable to assume that they will serve as a starting solution which can be modified by the inspectors.

15

A Decision Support System for Network Configuration

15.1   Introduction

In this chapter we present some of the issues involved in the development of a decision support system for logistics network configuration. These are issues that are often not dealt with in traditional operations research analyses. However, they are essential in transforming raw data and problem characteristics to modeling assumptions and input data for the models.

Network configuration may involve issues relating to plant, warehouse and re-tailer location. As explained in Chapter 1, these are strategic decisions since they have a lasting effect on the firm. In the discussion below, we concentrate on a decision support system for the following key strategic decisions: (1) determining the appropriate number of warehouses, (2) determining the location of each warehouse, (3) determining the size of each warehouse, (4) allocating space for products in each warehouse and (5) determining which products customers will receive from each warehouse. We therefore assume that plant and retailer locations will not be changed. The objective is to design or reconfigure the logistics network so as to minimize annual system-wide costs including production and purchasing costs, inventory holding costs, facility costs (storage, handling and fixed costs) and transportation costs, subject to a variety of *service level* requirements.

In this setting, the tradeoffs are clear. Increasing the number of warehouses typically yields:

- an improvement in service by reducing travel time to customers,

- an increase in inventory costs due to increased safety stocks required to protect the warehouse against uncertainties in customer demands,

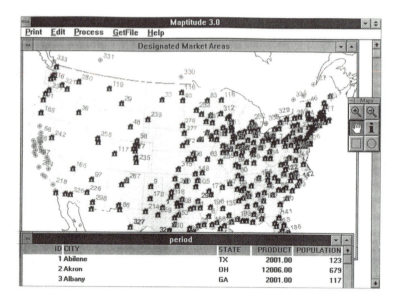

FIGURE 15.1. The DSS screen representing data prior to optimization.

- an increase in overhead and set-up costs,

- a reduction in outbound transportation costs; transportation costs from the warehouses to the customers,

- an increase in inbound transportation costs; transportation costs from the suppliers and/or manufacturers to the warehouses.

In essence, the firm must balance the costs of opening new warehouses with the advantages of being "close" to the customer. In this way, decisions in warehouse location are crucial determinants of whether the supply chain is an efficient channel for the distribution of the products.

We describe below some of the issues related to data collection and the calculation of costs required for the optimization models. In addition, we discuss how these are performed in the context of a decision support system (DSS) for distribution network design. Some of the information provided is based on logistics textbooks such as Ballou (1992), Johnson and Wood (1986) and Robeson and Copacino (1994). Most of it, however, is based on our experience with the development of a DSS, called LogicTools, that includes a geographic information system (see Chapter 14), various database features and optimization tools. The latter is comprised mainly of an algorithm similar in nature (although incorporating many more features) to the one described in Section 12.4. Figure 15.1 and Figure 15.2 present two typical screens that the user would see at different stages of the optimization. One represents the network prior to optimization and the second represents the optimized network.

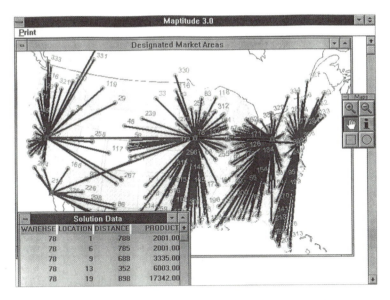

FIGURE 15.2. The DSS screen representing the optimized logistics network.

15.2   Data Collection

A typical network configuration problem involves large amounts of data. This includes information on:

1. Location of customers, retailers, existing warehouses and distribution centers, manufacturing facilities and suppliers.

2. All products, including volumes, special transport modes (e.g., refrigerated).

3. Annual demand for each product by customer location.

4. Transportation rates by mode.

5. Warehousing costs including labor, inventory carrying charges and fixed operating costs.

6. Shipment sizes and frequencies for customer delivery.

7. Order processing costs.

8. Customer service requirements and goals.

Data Aggregation

Of course, a quick look at the above list suggests that the amount of data involved in any optimization model for this problem is overwhelming. For instance, in a typical soft drink distribution system there are between 10,000 to 120,000 accounts (customers). Similarly, in a retail logistics network, such as Wal-Mart or J. C. Penney, the number of different products that flow through the network is in the thousands or even hundreds of thousands.

For that reason, a typical first step is data aggregation. This is done using the following criteria:

- Customers located in close proximity to each other are aggregated using a grid network or other clustering technique. All customers within a single cell or a single cluster are replaced by a single customer located at the centroid of the cell or cluster. We refer to a cell or a cluster as a customer zone. A technique that is commonly used and which we have found to be effective is to aggregate customers according to the five-digit zip code.

- Items are aggregated into a reasonable number of product groups, based on

    1. *Distribution pattern*. All products picked up at the same source and destined to the same customers are aggregated.

    2. *Product type*. In many cases, different products might simply be variations in product models or style or might differ only in the type of packaging. These products are typically aggregated.

An important consideration, of course, is the impact on the model's effectiveness due to replacing the original detailed data with the aggregated data. We address this issue in two ways. First, even if the technology exists to solve the logistics network design problem with the original data, it still may be useful to aggregate data. This is true, since our ability to forecast customer demand at the account and product levels is usually poor. Because of the reduction in variance achieved through aggregation (see Exercise 15.1) forecast demand is significantly more accurate at the aggregated level. Second, various researchers report that aggregating data into about 150–200 points usually results in no more than about 1% error in the estimation of total transportation costs; see Ballou (1992) and House and Jamie (1981).

In practice, the following guidelines are used when aggregating the data.

- Aggregate demand points to between 150–200 zones.

- Make sure each zone has about an equal amount of total demand. This implies that the zones may be of different sizes.

- Place the aggregated points at the center of gravity of the zone.

- Aggregate the products into 20–50 product groups.

Transportation Rates

The next step in constructing the distribution network design model is estimating transportation costs. An important characteristic of most transportation rates including truck, rail and others, is that the rates are almost linear with distance and volume. We distinguish here between transportation costs associated with an *internal* and an *external* fleet.

Estimating transportation costs for company-owned trucks is typically quite simple. It involves annual costs per truck, annual mileage per truck, annual amount delivered and the truck's effective capacity. All this information can be used to easily calculate cost per mile per SKU (Stock Keeping Unit).

Incorporating in the model transportation rates for an external fleet is more complex. These rates typically belong to one of three basic types of freight rates: *class, exception* and *commodity*. The *class* rates are standard rates that can be found for almost all products or commodities shipped. They are found with the help of a *classification tariff* which gives each shipment a *rating* or a *class*. For instance, the railroad classification includes 31 classes ranging from 400 to 13 which are obtained from the widely used *Uniform Freight Classification*. The National Motor Freight Classification, on the other hand, includes only 23 classes ranging from 500 to 35. In all cases, the higher the rating or class, the greater the relative charge for transporting the commodity. There are many factors involved in determining a product's specific class. These include product density, ease or difficulty of handling and transporting, and liability for damage.

Once the rating is established it is necessary to identify the *rate basis number*. This number is the approximate distance between the load's origin and destination. With the commodity rating or class and the rate basis number, the specific rate per hundred pounds can be obtained from a freight rate table.

The two other freight rates, namely, *exception* and *commodity*, are specialized rates used to provide either less expensive rates (exception), or commodity-specific rates (commodity). For an excellent discussion, see Johnson and Wood (1986) and Patton (1994). Most carriers provide an easy-to-use database with all their transportation rates; these databases are typically incorporated as part of the decision support system.

Mileage Estimation

As in the previous case study (Chapter 14), we can estimate distances using either street network or straight line distances. Specifically, suppose we want to estimate the distance between two points a and b. Since the decision-support system uses a GIS, geo-coding makes it possible to obtain lon_a and lat_a, the longitude and latitude of point a (similarly for point b). Then the straight line distance in miles from a to b, D_{ab} is calculated as follows

$$D_{ab} = 69\sqrt{(lon_a - lon_b)^2 + (lat_a - lat_b)^2}.$$

The value 69 is approximately the number of miles per degree (for the latitudes of the continental United States), since longitude and latitude are given in degrees. This equation is accurate for short distances only; it does not take into account the curvature of the Earth. To measure fairly long distances and correct for the Earth's curvature, we use the approximation (see Lindsey, 1996) suggested by the U.S. Geological Survey:

$$D_{ab} = 2(69)\sin^{-1}\sqrt{\sin\left(\frac{lat_a - lat_b}{2}\right)^2 + \cos(lat_a) \times \cos(lat_b) \times \sin\left(\frac{lon_a - lon_b}{2}\right)^2}.$$

Note the $\sin^{-1}$ should return degrees in order for D_{ab} to be in miles. These equations result in very accurate distance calculations; however, in both cases the equations underestimate the actual road distance. Therefore, to correct for this we multiply D_{ab} by a *circuitry* factor ρ. Typically, $\rho = 1.3$.

Warehouse Costs

Warehousing and distribution center costs include three main components:

- *Fixed costs.* These capture all cost components that are not proportional to the amount of material that flows through the warehouse.

- *Handling costs.* These include labor and utility costs.

- *Storage costs.* These are proportional to inventory level.

The first two cost components are fairly easy to estimate; the third is not so simple. The problem is that inventory, or storage costs, are proportional to *average* inventory levels (see Chapter 9), and not to the *annual flow* of material through the warehouse. To see this difference, suppose that during the entire year 1,000 units of product are required by a particular customer. These 1,000 units are not required to flow through the warehouse *at the same time*. Thus, when constructing the data for the DSS we need to convert these annual flows into actual inventory amounts over time. To overcome this difficulty, we call upon a concept often used by practitioners: the *inventory turnover ratio*. This is defined as follows.

$$\text{Inventory Turnover Ratio} = \frac{\text{annual sales}}{\text{average inventory level}}.$$

In our case, the inventory turnover ratio is the ratio of the total annual flow through the warehouse to the average inventory level. Thus, if the ratio is λ, then the average inventory level is total annual flow divided by λ. Finally, multiplying the average inventory level by the inventory holding cost gives the annual storage costs.

Warehouse Capacities

Another important input to the distribution network design model are the actual warehouse capacities. The question, of course, is how to estimate the actual space required, given a specific annual flow of material through the warehouse. We use the inventory turnover ratio again. As before, annual flow through a warehouse divided by the inventory turnover ratio allows us to calculate the average inventory level. Assuming a regular shipment and delivery schedule, such as that given by Figure 9.1, it follows that the required storage space is approximately *twice* that amount. Of course, in practice, every pallet stored in the warehouse requires an empty space to allow for a convenient approach to the pallet. Thus, considering this space as well as space for aisles, picking, sorting and processing facilities and AGVs, we typically multiply the required storage space by a factor ($>$ 1). This factor depends on the specific application and allows us to more accurately assess the amount of space available in the warehouse. A typical factor used in practice is 3. This factor would be used in the following way. Consider a situation where the annual flow through the warehouse is 1,000 units and the inventory turnover ratio is 10.0. This implies that average inventory per day is about 100 units and hence if each unit takes 10 square feet of floor space, the required space for the products is 2,000 square feet. The total space, therefore, required for the warehouse is about 6,000 square feet.

Potential Warehouse Locations

Another major part of the development of the model is identifying potential locations for new warehouses. Typically, these locations must satisfy a variety of conditions:

- geographical and infrastructure conditions,

- natural resources and labor availability,

- local industry and tax regulations,

- public interest.

As a result, there are only a limited number of locations that would meet all the requirements. These are the potential location sites for the new facilities.

Service Level Requirements

There are various ways to define service levels. For example, we might specify an upper bound on the distance between every customer and the warehouse serving it. This is due to the requirement that a warehouse will be able to serve its customers within a reasonable time. A related service level requirement recognizes that for some customers, maybe those in rural or isolated areas, it is harder to satisfy the same service level as most other customers. For this purpose, we define the service level as the proportion of customers whose distance to their assigned warehouse is no more than a given distance. For instance, we may require that 95% of the customers are within 200 miles of the warehouses serving them.

Future Demand

As observed in Chapter 1, decisions at the strategic level, which include distribution network design, have a long-lasting effect on the firm. In particular, decisions regarding the number, locations and sizes of warehouses have an impact on the firm for at least the next three to five years. This implies that changes in customer demands over the next few years should be taken into account when designing the network. Our approach here is to use a *scenario*-based approach incorporating net present value calculations. For example, one generates various possible scenarios representing a variety of possible states for demand over the planning horizon. These scenarios can then be directly incorporated into the model to determine the best distribution strategy.

15.3   The Baseline Feature

The previous section documents the difficulties in collecting, tabulating and cleaning the data for a network configuration DSS. Once this is done, how do we ensure that the data accurately reflect the network design problem? For this purpose we use what we call a *baseline feature*. This tool is an integral feature of the decision support system. It serves two main functions. It allows the user to:

(*a*) reconstruct the current existing network, and

(*b*) perform a set of "what-if" scenarios.

The importance of (*a*) cannot be overstated. The baseline feature presents the user with the current state of operation. It lists all costs, including warehousing, inventory, production and transportation costs generated under the current network configuration. These data can then be compared to the company's accounting information. In our experience, it usually identifies errors in the data, problematic assumptions, modeling flaws, etc. For instance, in one implementation, the transportation costs calculated by the baseline feature were consistently underestimating the costs suggested by the accounting data. After a careful review of the distribution practices, we concluded that the effective truck capacity was only about 30% of the truck's physical capacity. That is, trucks were being sent out with very little payload. Thus, the baseline feature not only helped calibrate some of the parameters used in the model but also suggested potential improvements in the utilization of the existing network.

The second feature also plays an important role in making the user "believe in" the system. The baseline feature allows the user to make local changes in the network configuration and estimate their impact on costs and service levels. Specifically, this step involves positing a variety of "what if" questions. This includes estimating the impact on system performance of closing an existing warehouse. Or, to give another example, it allows the user to change the flow of material through the existing network and see the changes in the costs.

It is our belief that a *baseline feature* as suggested above is a useful tool because it makes the connection for the user, between the current operation, which the user can see in the baseline feature, and possible improvements, after optimization. In our experience, this is a critical factor in determining how well the DSS will be received.

15.4   Flexibility and Robustness

One of the key requirements of any decision support system is flexibility. In the context of distribution network design, we define flexibility as the ability of the system to incorporate a large set of preexisting network characteristics. Indeed, in our experience, many users want their system to be able to make decisions of increasing flexibility. At one end of this spectrum is complete reoptimization of the existing network. This means each warehouse can be either opened or closed and all transportation flows can be redirected. At the other end of the spectrum we find users that may want the optimization to incorporate the following features.

1. *Customer-specific service level requirements.*

2. *Existing warehouses.* In most cases, there are warehouses already existing and the lease has not yet expired. Therefore, the model should not permit the closing of the warehouse.

3. *Expansion of existing warehouses.* Existing warehouses may be expandable.

4. *Specific flow patterns.* In a variety of situations, specific flow patterns (from, say a particular warehouse to a set of customers) may not need to be changed.

5. *Warehouse-to-warehouse flow.* In some cases, material may flow from a warehouse to a warehouse.

The decision support system must have the capability of dealing with all these issues with little or no reduction in its *effectiveness*. The latter requirement is directly related to the so-called *robustness* of the system. This stipulates that the relative quality of the solution generated by the system, that is, cost and service level, should be independent of the specific environment, the variability of the data or the particular setting.

Another important requirement is that the system running time be reasonable. Of course, as discussed in Chapter 1, the term *reasonable* depends on the particular problem at hand.

In the next table, we report running times, in seconds, on an IBM PC 166MHz machine for a variety of problem sizes. The results are given as a function of various parameters. In all cases, the number of potential locations for warehouses is 32, the number of suppliers is 9 and the numbers of products is also 9. In each case, we require that the distance between a customer and a warehouse serving it will be no more than 100 miles. The optimization was terminated when the relative difference between the cost of the solution generated and the optimal cost was within a specified gap. Thus, the column "Running Time 5%" provides the running times when the gap is 5%, while "Running Time 1%" provides the running times when the gap is 1%. Finally, these six test problems represent real-world data that we have received from a producer and distributor of soft drinks in the Northeastern part of the United States.

Table 1: Running times

Number of Customers*	Number of Warehouses	Running Time 5%	Running Time 1%
144	6	64s	106s
144	5	95s	209s
144	4	99s	227s
73	6	31s	60s
73	5	19s	54s
73	4	20s	37s

* after aggregation.

15.5 Exercises

Exercise 15.1. Consider n independent and identically distributed random variables, $X_1, X_2, \ldots, X_n$. Let $S_n = \frac{1}{n} \sum_{i=1}^{n} X_i$. Find the variance of the random variable S_n as a function of the variance of X_i.

References

Aggarwal, A. and J. K. Park (1990), Improved Algorithms for Economic Lot-Size Problems. Working Paper, Laboratory for Computer Science, MIT, Cambridge, MA.

Aho, A. V., J. E. Hopcroft and J. D. Ullman (1974), *The Design and Analysis of Computer Algorithms*, Addison-Wesley, Reading, MA.

Altinkemer, K. and B. Gavish (1987), Heuristics for Unequal Weight Delivery Problems with a Fixed Error Guarantee. *Oper. Res. Lett.* **6**, pp. 149–158.

Altinkemer, K. and B. Gavish (1990), Heuristics for Delivery Problems with Constant Error Guarantees. *Transportation Sci.* **24**, pp. 294–297.

Angel, R. D., W. L. Caudle, R. Noonan and A. Whinston (1972), Computer-Assisted School Bus Scheduling. *Management Sci. B* **18**, pp. 279–288.

Anily, S. (1991), Multi-Item Replenishment and Storage Problems (MIRSP): Heuristics and Bounds. *Oper. Res.* **39**, pp. 233–239.

Anily, S. and A. Federgruen (1990), One Warehouse Multiple Retailer Systems with Vehicle Routing Costs. *Management Sci.* **36**, pp. 92–114.

Anily, S., J. Bramel and D. Simchi-Levi (1994), Worst-Case Analysis of Heuristics for the Bin-Packing Problem with General Cost Structures. *Oper. Res.* **42**, pp. 287–298.

Archibald, B. and E. Silver (1978), (s, S) Policies Under Continuous Review and Discrete Compound Poisson Demand. *Management Sci.* **24**, pp. 899-908.

Arkin, E., D. Joneja and R. Roundy (1989), Computational Complexity of Uncapacitated Multi-Echelon Production Planning Problems. *Oper. Res. Lett.* **8**, pp. 61–66.

Assad, A., B. Golden, R. Dahl and M. Dror (1982), Design of an Inventory/ Routing System for a Large Propane Distribution Firm. C. Gooding, ed., *Proc. 1982 Southeast TIMS Conference*, Myrtle Beach, pp. 315–320.

Atkins, D. R. and P. Iyogun (1988), A Heuristic with Lower Bound Performance Guarantee for the Multi-Product Dynamic Lot-Size Problem. *IIE Transactions* **20**, pp. 369–373.

Azuma, K. (1967), Weighted Sums of Certain Dependent Random Variables. *Tohoku Math. J.* **19**, pp. 357–367.

Baker, B. S. (1985), A New Proof for the First-Fit Decreasing Bin Packing Algorithm. *J. Algorithms* **6**, pp. 49-70.

Baker, K. R., P. Dixon, M. J. Magazine and E. A. Silver (1978), An Algorithm for the Dynamic Lot-Size Problem with Time-Varying Production Capacity Constraints. *Management Sci.* **24**, pp. 1710–1720.

Balinski, M. L. (1965), Integer Programming: Methods, Uses, Computation. *Management Sci.* **12**, pp. 253–313.

Balinski, M. L. and R. E. Quandt (1964), On an Integer Program for a Delivery Problem. *Oper. Res.* **12**, pp. 300-304.

Ball, M. O., T. L. Magnanti, C. L. Monma and G. L. Nemhauser (eds.) (1995), Network Routing, *Handbooks in Operations Research and Management Science* North-Holland, North-Holland, Amsterdam.

Ballou, R. H. (1992), *Business Logistics Management*. Prentice-Hall, Englewood Cliffs, NJ, 3rd edition.

Barcelo, J. and J. Casanovas (1984), A Heuristic Lagrangian Algorithm for the Capacitated Plant Location Problem. *Eur. J. Oper. Res.* **15**, pp. 212–226.

Beardwood, J., J. L. Halton and J. M. Hammersley (1959), The Shortest Path Through Many Points. *Proc. Cambridge Phil. Soc.* **55**, pp. 299–327.

Beasley, J. (1983), Route First–Cluster Second Methods for Vehicle Routing. *Omega* **11**, pp. 403–408.

Bell, C. (1970), Improved Algorithms for Inventory and Replacement Stock Problems. *SIAM J. Appl. Math.* **18**, pp. 558-566.

Bennett, B. and D. Gazis (1972), School Bus Routing by Computer. *Transportation Res.* **6**, pp. 317–326.

Bertsekas, D. P. (1987), *Dynamic Programming*. Prentice-Hall, Englewood Cliffs, NJ.

Bertsimas, D. and D. Simchi-Levi (1996), The New Generation of Vehicle Routing Research: Robust Algorithms Addressing Uncertainty. *Oper. Res.* **44**, pp. 286-304.

Bienstock, D. and D. Simchi-Levi (1993), A Note on the Prize Collecting Traveling Salesman Problem. Working Paper, Columbia University.

Bienstock, D., J. Bramel and D. Simchi-Levi (1993), A Probabilistic Analysis of Tour Partitioning Heuristics for the Capacitated Vehicle Routing Problem with Unsplit Demands. *Math. Oper. Res.* **18**, pp. 786–802.

Bienstock, D., M. Goemans, D. Simchi-Levi and D. Williamson (1993), A Note on the Prize Collecting Traveling Salesman Problem. *Math. Programming*, **59**, pp. 413–420.

Bodin, L. and L. Berman (1979), Routing and Scheduling of School Buses by Computer. *Transportation Sci.* **13**, pp. 113–129.

Braca, J., J. Bramel, B. Posner and D. Simchi-Levi (1994), A Computerized Approach to the New York City School Bus Routing Problem. To appear in *IIE Transactions*.

Bramel, J. and D. Simchi-Levi (1994), On the Effectiveness of Set Partitioning Formulations for the Vehicle Routing Problem. To appear in *Oper. Res.*.

Bramel, J. and D. Simchi-Levi (1995), A Location Based Heuristic for General Routing Problems. *Oper. Res.* **43**, pp. 649–660.

Bramel, J. and D. Simchi-Levi (1996), Probabilistic Analysis and Practical Algorithms for the Vehicle Routing Problem with Time Windows. *Oper. Res.* **44**, pp. 501–509.

Bramel, J., E. G. Coffman Jr., P. Shor and D. Simchi-Levi (1991), Probabilistic Analysis of Algorithms for the Capacitated Vehicle Routing Problem with Unsplit Demands. *Oper. Res.* **40**, pp. 1095–1106.

Chan, L. M. A. and D. Simchi-Levi (1996), Probabilistic Analysis and Practical Algorithms for Multi-Echelon Distribution Models. Submitted to *Management Sci.*.

Chan, L. M. A., A. Federgruen and D. Simchi-Levi (1996), Probabilistic Analysis and Practical Algorithms for Inventory Routing Models. To appear in *Oper. Res.*.

Chan, L. M. A., D. Simchi-Levi and J. Bramel (1995), Worst-Case Analyses, Linear Programming and the Bin-Packing Problem. To appear in *Math. Programming*.

Chandra, P. and M. L. Fisher (1990), Coordination of Production and Distribution Planning. Working Paper, 90-11-06, The Wharton School, University of Pennsylvania.

Chandra, B., H. Karloff and C. Tovey (1995), New Results on the Old k-Opt Algorithm for the TSP. Working Paper, University of Chicago.

Chapleau, L., J. A. Ferland and J.-M. Rousseau (1983), Clustering for Routing in Dense Area. *Eur. J. Oper. Res.* **20**, pp. 48–57.

Chen, F. and Y. S. Zheng (1994), Lower Bounds for Multi-Echelon Stochastic Inventory Systems. *Management Sci.* **40**, pp. 1426–1443.

Chen, Y. F. (1996), On the Optimality of (s, S) Policies for Quasiconvex Loss Functions. Working Paper, Northwestern University.

Chien, T. W., A. Balakrishnan and R. T. Wong (1989), An Integrated Inventory Allocation and Vehicle Routing Problem. *Transportation Sci.* **23**, pp. 67–76.

Christofides, N. (1976), Worst-Case Analysis of a New Heuristic for the Traveling Salesman Problem. Report 388, Graduate School of Industrial Administration, Carnegie-Mellon University, Pittsburgh, PA.

Christofides, N. (1985), Vehicle Routing. In *The Traveling Salesman Problem: A Guided Tour of Combinatorial Optimization*, Lawler, E. L., J. K. Lenstra, A. H. G. Rinnooy Kan and D. B. Shmoys (eds.), John Wiley & Sons Ltd., New York, pp. 431–448.

Christofides, N., A. Mingozzi and P. Toth (1978), The Vehicle Routing Problem.

In *Combinatorial Optimization*, Christofides, N., A. Mingozzi, P. Toth and C. Sandi (eds.), John Wiley & Sons Ltd., New York, pp. 318–338.

Christofides, N., A. Mingozzi and P. Toth (1981), Exact Algorithms for the Vehicle Routing Problem Based on Spanning Tree and Shortest Path Relaxations. *Math. Programming* **20**, pp. 255–282.

Churchman, C. W., R. L. Ackoff and E. L. Arnoff (1957), *Introduction to Operations Research*. John Wiley & Sons Ltd., New York.

Clark, A. J. and H. E. Scarf (1960), Optimal Policies for a Multi-Echelon Inventory Problem. *Management Sci.* **6**, pp. 475–490.

Clarke, G. and J. W. Wright (1964), Scheduling of Vehicles from a Central Depot to a Number of Delivery Points. *Oper. Res.* **12**, pp. 568–581.

Coffman, E. G. Jr. and G. S. Lueker (1991), *Probabilistic Analysis of Packing and Partitioning Algorithms*, John Wiley & Sons Ltd., New York.

Cornuéjols, G. and F. Harche (1993), Polyhedral Study of the Capacitated Vehicle Routing Problem. *Math. Programming* **60**, pp. 21–52.

Cornuéjols, G., M. L. Fisher and G. L. Nemhauser (1977), Location of Bank Accounts to Optimize Float: An Analytical Study of Exact and Approximate Algorithms. *Management Sci.* **23**, pp. 789–810.

Council on Logistics Management, mission statement, Council on Logistics Management Web Site, www.clm1.org/mission.html.

Cullen, F., J. Jarvis and D. Ratliff (1981), Set Partitioning Based Heuristics for Interactive Routing. *Networks* **11**, pp. 125–144.

Daskin, M. S. (1995), *Network and Discrete Location: Models Algorithms and Applications*. John Wiley & Sons Ltd., New York.

Dematteis, J. J. (1968), An Economic Lot Sizing Technique: The Part-Period Algorithm. *IBM Syst. J.* **7**, pp. 30–38.

Denardo, E. V. (1996), Dynamic Programming. In *Mathematical Programming for Industrial Engineers*, Avriel, M. and B. Golany (eds.), Marcel Dekker, Inc., Englewood Cliffs, NJ, pp. 307–384.

Deng, Q. and D. Simchi-Levi (1992), Valid Inequalities, Facets and Computational Results for the Capacitated Concentrator Location Problem. Columbia University, Working paper.

Desrochers, M., J. Desrosiers and M. Solomon (1992), A New Optimization Algorithm for the Vehicle Routing Problem with Time Windows. *Oper. Res.* **40**, pp. 342–354.

Desrosiers, J., J. A. Ferland, J.–M. Rousseau, G. Lapalme and L. Chapleau (1986), TRANSCOL: A Multi-Period School Bus Routing and Scheduling System. *TIMS Stud. Management Sci.* **22**, pp. 47–71.

Dobson, G. (1987), The Economic Lot Scheduling Problem: A Resolution of Feasibility Using Time Varying Lot Sizes. *Oper. Res.* **35**, pp. 764–771.

Dreyfus, S. E. and A. M. Law (1977), *The Art and Theory of Dynamic Programming*. Academic Press, Inc., New York.

Dror, M. and M. Ball (1987) Inventory/Routing: Reduction from an Annual to a Short-Period Problem. *Naval Research Logistics* **34**, pp. 891–905.

Dror, M., M. Ball and B. Golden (1986), A Computational Comparison of Algorithms for the Inventory Routing Problem. *Ann. Oper. Res.* **4**, pp. 3–23.

Edmonds, J. (1965), Maximum Matching and a Polyhedron with 0,1-Vertices. *J. Res. Nat. Bur. Standards* **69B**, pp. 125–130.

Edmonds, J. (1971), Matroids and the Greedy Algorithm. *Math. Programming* **1**, pp. 127-136.

Eppen, G. and L. Schrage (1981), Centralized Ordering Policies in a Multiwarehouse System with Lead Times and Random Demand. In *Multi-Level Production/Inventory Control Systems: Theory and Practice*, Schwarz, L. (Ed.), North-Holland Publishing Company, Amsterdam.

Erlenkotter, D. (1990), Ford Whitman Harris and the Economic Order Quantity Model. *Oper. Res.* **38**, pp. 937–946.

Federgruen, A. and G. van Ryzin (1992), Probabilistic Analysis of a Generalized Bin Packing Problem with Applications to Vehicle Routing and Scheduling Problems. To appear in *Oper. Res.*.

Federgruen, A. and D. Simchi-Levi (1995), Analytical Analysis of Vehicle Routing and Inventory Routing problems. In *Handbooks in Operations Research and Management Science*, the volume on *Network Routing*, Ball, M. O., T. L. Magnanti, C. L. Monma and G. L. Nemhauser (eds.), North-Holland, Amsterdam, pp. 297–373.

Federgruen, A. and M. Tzur (1991), A Simple Forward Algorithm to Solve General Dynamic Lot Sizing Models with n periods in $O(n \log n)$ or $O(n)$ time. *Management Sci.* **37**, pp. 909–925.

Federgruen, A. and Y. S. Zheng (1992) The Joint Replenishement Problem with General Joint Cost Structures. *Oper. Res.* **40**, pp. 384–403.

Federgruen, A. and P. Zipkin (1984), A Combined Vehicle Routing and Inventory Allocation Problem. *Oper. Res.* **32**, pp. 1019–1032.

Federgruen, A. and P. Zipkin (1984a), Approximation of Dynamic, Multi-Location Production and Inventory Problems. *Management Sci.* **30**, pp. 69–84.

Federgruen, A. and P. Zipkin (1984b), Computational Issues in the Infinite Horizon, Multi-Echelon Inventory Model. *Oper. Res.* **32**, pp. 818–836.

Federgruen, A. and P. Zipkin (1984c), Allocation Policies and Cost Approximation for Multi-Location Inventory Systems. *Naval Research Logistics Quart.* **31**, pp. 97–131.

Few, L. (1955), The Shortest Path and the Shortest Road through n Points. *Mathematika* **2**, pp. 141-144.

Fisher, M. L. (1980), Worst-Case Analysis of Algorithms. *Management Sci.* **26**, pp. 1–17.

Fisher, M. L. (1981), The Lagrangian Relaxation Method for Solving Integer Programming Problems. *Management Sci.* **27**, pp. 1–18.

Fisher, M. L. (1994), Optimal Solution of Vehicle Routing Problems Using Minimum K-Trees. *Oper. Res.* **42**, pp. 626–642.

Fisher M. L. (1995), Vehicle Routing. In *Handbooks in Operations Research and Management Science*, the volume on Network Routing, Ball, M. O., T. L.

Magnanti, C. L. Monma and G. L. Nemhauser (eds.), North-Holland, Amsterdam, pp. 1–33.

Fisher, M. L. and R. Jaikumar (1981), A Generalized Assignment Heuristic for Vehicle Routing. *Networks* **11**, pp. 109–124.

Florian, M. and M. Klein (1971), Deterministic Production Planning with Concave Costs and Capacity Constraints. *Management Sci.* **18**, pp. 12–20.

Florian, M., J. K. Lenstra and A. H. G. Rinnooy Kan (1980), Deterministic Production Planning: Algorithms and Complexity. *Management Sci.* **26**, pp. 669–679.

Gallego, G. and D. Simchi-Levi (1990), On the Effectiveness of Direct Shipping Strategy for the One Warehouse Multi-Retailer R-Systems. *Management Sci.* **36**, pp. 240–243.

Gallego, G., M. Queyranne and D. Simchi-Levi (1996), Single Resource Multi-Item Inventory System. *Oper. Res.* **44**, pp. 580–595.

Garey, M. R. and D. S. Johnson (1979), *Computers and Intractability.* W. H. Freeman and Company, New York.

Garey, M. R., R. L. Graham, D. S. Johnson and A. C. Yao (1976), Resource Constrained Scheduling as Generalized Bin Packing. *J. Combinatorial Theory Ser. A* **21**, pp. 257–298.

Gaskel, T. J. (1967), Bases for Vehicle Fleet Scheduling. *Oper. Res. Quart.* **18**, pp. 281–295.

Gillett, B. E. and L. R. Miller (1974), A Heuristic Algorithm for the Vehicle Dispatch Problem. *Oper. Res.* **22**, pp. 340–349.

Goemans M. X. and D. J. Bertsimas (1993), Survivable Networks, Linear Programming Relaxations and the Parsimonious Property. *Math. Programming* **60**, pp. 145–166.

Golden, B. L. and W. R. Stewart (1985), Empirical Analysis of Heuristics. In *The Traveling Salesman Problem: A Guided Tour of Combinatorial Optimization*, Lawler, E. L., J. K. Lenstra, A. H. G. Rinnooy Kan and D. B. Shmoys (eds.), John Wiley & Sons Ltd., New York, pp. 207–249.

Golden, B. L., A. Assad and R. Dahl (1984), Analysis of a Large Scale Vehicle Routing Problem with Inventory Component. *Large Scale System* **7**, pp. 181–190.

Goyal, S. K. (1978), A Note on "Multi-Product Inventory Situation with One Restriction." *J. Opl. Res. Soc.* **29**, pp. 269–271.

Graves, S. C. and L. B. Schwarz (1977), Single Cycle Continuous Review Policies for Arborescent Production/Inventory Systems. *Management Sci.* **23**, pp. 529–540.

Graves, S. C., A. H. G. Rinnooy Kan and P. H. Zipkin (eds.) (1993), Logistics of Production and Inventory. In *Handbooks in Operations Research and Management Science*, North-Holland, Amsterdam.

Hadley, G. and T. M. Whitin (1963), *Analysis of Inventory Systems.* Prentice-Hall, Englewood Cliffs, NJ.

Haimovich, M. and A. H. G. Rinnooy Kan (1985), Bounds and Heuristics for Capacitated Routing Problems. *Math. Oper. Res.* **10**, pp. 527–542.

Haimovich, M., A. H. G. Rinnooy Kan and L. Stougie (1988), Analysis of Heuristics for Vehicle Routing Problems. In *Vehicle Routing: Methods and Studies,* Golden, B. L. and A. A. Assad (eds.), Elsevier Science Publishers, B.V., pp. 47–61.

Hakimi, S. L. (1964), Optimum Locations of Switching Centers and the Absolute Centers and Medians of a Graph. *Oper. Res.* **12**, pp. 450–459.

Hall, N. G. (1988), A Multi-Item EOQ Model with Inventory Cycle Balancing. *Naval Research Logistics* **35**, pp. 319–325.

Hariga, M. (1988), The Warehouse Scheduling Problem. Ph. D. Thesis, School of Operations Research and Industrial Engineering, Cornell University.

Harris, F. (1915), *Operations and Costs*. Factory Management Series, A. W. Shaw Co., Chicago, IL, pp. 48–52.

Hartley, R. and L. C. Thomas (1982), The Deterministic, Two-Product, Inventory System with Capacity Constraint. *J. Opl. Res. Soc.* **33**, pp. 1013–1020.

Hax, A. C. and D. Candea (1984), *Production and Inventory Management*. Prentice-Hall, Englewood Cliffs, NJ.

Held, M. and R. M. Karp (1962), A Dynamic Programming Approach to Sequencing Problems. *SIAM J. Appl. Math.* **10**, pp. 196–210.

Held, M. and R. M. Karp (1970), The Traveling Salesman Problem and Minimum Spanning Trees. *Oper. Res.* **18**, pp. 1138–1162.

Held, M. and R. M. Karp (1971), The Traveling Salesman Problem and Minimum Spanning Trees: Part II. *Math. Programming* **1**, pp. 6–25.

Herer, Y. and R. Roundy (1990), Heuristics for a One Warehouse Multi-Retailer Distribution Problem with Performance Bounds. Technical Report No. 916, Cornell University, Ithaca, NY.

Heyman, D. P. and M. J. Sobel (1984), *Stochastic Models in Operations Research*. Vol I, McGraw-Hill, New York.

Hodgson, T. J. and T. J. Howe (1982), Production Lot Sizing with Material-Handling Cost Considerations. *IIE Trans.* **14**, pp. 44–51.

Hoffman, K. L. and M. Padberg (1993), Solving Airline Crew Scheduling Problems by Branch-and-Cut. *Management Sci.* **39**, pp. 657–682.

Holt, C. C. (1958), Decision Rules for Allocating Inventory to Lots and Cost Foundations for Making Aggregate Inventory Decisions. *J. Ind. Engn.* **9**, pp. 14–22.

Homer, E. D. (1966), Space-Limited Aggregate Inventories with Phased Deliveries. *J. Ind. Engn.* **17**, pp. 327–333.

House, R. G. and K. D. Jamie (1981), Measuring the Impact of Alternative Market Classification Systems in Distribution Planning. *J. Business Logistics* **2**, pp. 1–31.

Iglehart, D. (1963a), Optimality of (s, S) Policies in the Infinite Horizon Dynamic Inventory Problem. *Management Sci.* **9**, pp. 259–267.

Iglehart, D. (1963b), Dynamic Programming and Stationary Analysis in Inventory Problems. In *Multi-Stage Inventory Models and Techniques*, Scarf H., D. Guilford and M. Shelly (eds.). Stanford University Press, Stanford CA, pp. 1–31.

Jackson, P. L., W. L. Maxwell and J. A. Muckstadt (1985), The Joint Replenishement Problem with Powers of Two Restrictions. *AIIE Trans.* **17**, pp. 25–32.

Jaillet, P. (1985), Probabilistic Traveling Salesman Problem. Ph.D. Dissertation. Operations Research Center, Massachusetts Institute of Technology, Cambridge, MA.

Johnson, D. S. and C. H. Papadimitriou (1985), Performance Guarantees for Heuristics. In *The Traveling Salesman Problem: A Guided Tour of Combinatorial Optimization*, Lawler, E. L., J. K. Lenstra, A. H. G. Rinnooy Kan and D. B. Shmoys (eds.), John Wiley & Sons Ltd., New York, pp. 145–180.

Johnson, D. S., A. Demers, J. D. Ullman, M. R. Garey and R. L. Graham (1974), Worst-Case Performance Bounds for Simple One-Dimensional Packing Algorithms. *SIAM J. Comput.*, **3**, pp. 299–325.

Johnson, J. C. and D. F. Wood (1986), *Contemporary Physical Distribution and Logistics*. Macmillan, New York, 3rd edition.

Joneja, D. (1990), The Joint Replenishment Problem: New Heuristics and Worst-Case Performance Bounds. *Oper. Res.* **38**, pp. 711–723.

Jones, P. C. and R. R. Inman (1989), When is the Economic Lot Scheduling Problem Easy? *IIE Trans.* **21**, pp. 11–20.

Karlin, S. and H. M. Taylor (1975), *A First Course in Stochastic Processes* Academic Press, Inc., San Diego, CA.

Karmarkar, N. (1982), Probabilistic Analysis of Some Bin-Packing Algorithms. *Proc. 23rd Ann. Symp. Foundat. Comput. Sci.*, pp. 107–111.

Karp, R. M. (1977), Probabilistic Analysis of Partitioning Algorithms for the Traveling Salesman Problem. *Math. Oper. Res.* **2**, pp. 209–224.

Karp, R. M. and J. M. Steele (1985), Probabilistic Analysis of Heuristics. In *The Traveling Salesman Problem: A Guided Tour of Combinatorial Optimization*, Lawler, E. L., J. K. Lenstra, A. H. G. Rinnooy Kan and D. B. Shmoys (eds.), John Wiley & Sons Ltd., New York, pp. 181–205.

Karp, R. M., M. Luby and A. Marchetti-Spaccamela (1984), A probabilistic analysis of multidimensional bin packing problems. *Proc. Sixteenth Annual ACM Symposium on Theory of Computing*, pp. 289–298.

Kingman, J. F. C. (1976), Subadditive Processes. *Lecture Notes in Math. 539*, Springer-Verlag, Berlin, pp. 168–222.

Klincewicz, J. G. and H. Luss (1986), A Lagrangian Relaxation Heuristic for Capacitated Facility Location with Single-Source Constraints. *J. Opl. Res. Soc.* **37**, pp. 495–500.

Kuehn, A. A. and M. J. Hamburger (1963), A Heuristic Program for Location Warehouses. *Management Sci.* **9**, pp. 643–666.

Lawler, E. L. (1976), *Combinatorial Optimization: Networks and Matroids*. Holt, Rinehart and Winston, New York.

Lawler, E. L., J. K. Lenstra, A. H. G. Rinnooy Kan and D. B. Shmoys (1993), Sequencing and Scheduling: Algorithms and Complexity. In *Handbooks in Operations Research and Management Science*, the volume on Logistics of Production and Inventory, Graves, S. C., A. H. G. Rinnooy Kan and P. H. Zipkin (eds.), North-Holland, Amsterdam, pp. 445–522.

Lawler, E. L., J. K. Lenstra, A. H. G. Rinnooy Kan and D. B. Shmoys (eds.) (1985), *The Traveling Salesman Problem: A Guided Tour of Combinatorial Optimization.* John Wiley & Sons Ltd., New York.

Lee, H. L. and S. Nahmias (1993), Single Product, Single Location Models. In *Handbooks in Operations Research and Management Science*, the volume on Logistics of Production and Inventory, Graves, S. C., A. H. G. Rinnooy Kan and P. H. Zipkin (eds.), North-Holland, Amsterdam, pp. 3–55.

Li, C. L. and D. Simchi-Levi (1990), Worst-Case Analysis of Heuristics for the Multi-Depot Capacitated Vehicle Routing Problems. *ORSA J. Comput.* **2**, pp. 64–73.

Lindsey (1996), A communication to the AGIS-L list server.

Lovasz, L. (1979), *Combinatorial Problems and Exercises.* North-Holland, Amsterdam.

Love, S. F. (1973), Bounded Production and Inventory Models with Piecewise Concave Costs. *Management Sci.* **20**, pp. 313–318.

Manne, A. S. (1964), Plant Location Under Economies of Scale–Decentralization and Computation. *Management Sci.* **11**, pp. 213–235.

Maxwell, W. L. and H. Singh (1983), The Effect of Restricting Cycle Times in the Economic Lot Scheduling Problem. *IIE Trans.* **15**, pp. 235–241.

Mirchandani, P. B. and R. L. Francis (1990), *Discrete Location Theory.* John Wiley & Sons Ltd., New York.

Muckstadt, J. M. and R. O. Roundy (1993), Analysis of Multistage Production Systems. In *Handbooks in Operations Research and Management Science*, the volume on Logistics of Production and Inventory, Graves, S. C., A. H. G. Rinnooy Kan and P. H. Zipkin (eds.), North-Holland, Amsterdam, pp. 59–131.

Nauss, R. M. (1976), An Efficient Algorithm for the 0-1 Knapsack Problem. *Management Sci.* **23**, pp. 27–31.

Neebe, A. W. and M. R. Rao (1983), An Algorithm for the Fixed-Charged Assigning Users to Sources Problem. *J. Opl. Res. Soc.* **34**, pp. 1107–1113.

Newton, R. M. and W. H. Thomas (1969), Design of School Bus Routes by Computer. *Socio-Economic Planning Sci.* **3**, pp. 75–85.

Page, E. and R. J. Paul (1976), Multi-Product Inventory Situations with One Restriction. *J. Opl. Res. Soc.* **27**, pp. 815–834.

Papadimitriou, C. H. and K. Stieglitz (1982), *Combinatorial Optimization: Algorithms and Complexity.* Prentice-Hall, Englewood Cliffs, NJ.

Park, K. S. and D. K. Yun (1985), Optimal Scheduling of Periodic Activities. *Oper. Res.* **33**, pp. 690–695.

Patton, E. P. (1994), Carrier Rates and Tariffs. In *The Distribution Management Handbook*, Tompkins, J. A., and D. Harmelink (eds.), McGraw-Hill, NY, Chapter 12.

Pinedo, M. (1995), *Scheduling: Theory, Algorithms and Systems.* Prentice-Hall, Englewood Cliffs, NJ.

Pirkul, H. (1987), Efficient Algorithms for the Capacitated Concentrator Location Problem. *Comput. Oper. Res.* **14**, pp. 197–208.

Pirkul, H. and V. Jayaraman (1996), Production, Transportation and Distribution Planning in a Multi-Commodity Tri-Echelon System. *Transportation Sci.* **30**, pp. 291–302.

Polyak, B. T. (1967), A General Method for Solving Extremum Problems (in Russian). *Doklady Akademmi Nauk SSSR* **174** , pp. 33–36.

Porteus, E. L. (1985), Investing in Reduced Setups in the EOQ Model. *Management Science* **31**, pp. 998-1010. Porteus, E. L. (1990), Stochastic Inventory Theory. In *Handbooks in Operations Research and Management Science*, the volume on Stochastic Models, Heyman, D. P., and M. J. Sobel (eds.), North-Holland, Amsterdam, pp. 605–652.

Psaraftis, H. N. (1984), On the Practical Importance of Asymptotic Optimality in Certain Heuristic Algorithms. *Networks* **14**, pp. 587–596.

Rhee, W. T. (1988), Optimal Bin Packing with Items of Random Sizes. *Math. Oper. Res.* **13**, pp. 140–151.

Rhee, W. T. (1991), An Asymptotic Analysis of Capacitated Vehicle Routing. Working Paper, The Ohio State University, Columbus, OH.

Rhee, W. T. and M. Talagrand (1987), Martingale Inequalities and NP-Complete Problems. *Math. Oper. Res.* **12**, pp. 177–181.

Robeson, J. F. and W. C. Copacino (eds.) (1994), *The Logistics Handbook.* Free Press, New York.

Rosenblatt, M. and U. Rothblum (1990), On the Single Resource Capacity Problem for Multi-Item Inventory Systems. *Oper. Res.* **38**, pp. 686–693.

Rosenkrantz, D. J., R. E. Stearns and P. M. Lewis II (1977), An Analysis of Several Heuristics for the Traveling Salesman Problem. *SIAM J. Comput.* **6**, pp. 563–581.

Rosling, K. (1989), Optimal Inventory Policies for Assembly Systems Under Random Demand. *Oper. Res.* **37**, pp. 565–579.

Ross, S. (1970), *Applied Probability Models with Optimization Applications.* Holden-Day, San Francisco.

Roundy, R. (1985), 98%-Effective Integer-Ratio Lot-Sizing for One-Warehouse Multi-Retailer Systems. *Management Sci.* **31**, pp. 1416–1430.

Russell, R. A. (1977), An Effective Heuristic for the M-Tour Traveling Salesman Problem with Some Side Constraints. *Oper. Res.* **25**, 521-524.

Sahni, S. and T. Gonzalez (1976), P-Complete Approximation Algorithms. *J. Assoc. Comput. Mach.* **23**, pp. 555-565.

Scarf, H. E. (1960), The Optimalities of (s, S) Policies in the Dynamic Inventory Problem. In *Mathematical Methods in the Social Sciences,* Arrow, K., S. Karlin and P. Suppes (eds.), Stanford University Press, Stanford, CA, pp. 196–202.

Shmoys, D. and D. Williamson (1990), Analyzing the Held-Karp TSP Bound: A Monotonicity Property with Application. *Inf. Process. Lett.* **35**, pp. 281–285.

Silver, E. A. (1976), A Simple Method of Determining Order Quantities in Joint Replenishments Under Deterministic Demand. *Management Sci.* **22**, pp. 1351–1361.

Silver, E. A. and H. C. Meal (1973), A Heuristic for Selecting Lot Size Quantities for the Case of a Deterministic Time-Varying Demand Rate and Discrete Opportunities for Replenishment. *Prod. Invent. Management* **14**, pp. 64–74.

Silver E. A. and R. Peterson (1985), *Decision Systems for Inventory Management and Production Planning.* John Wiley & Sons Ltd., New York.

Simchi-Levi, D. (1994), New Worst Case Results for the Bin-Packing Problem. *Naval Research Logistics* **41**, pp. 579-585.

Simchi-Levi, D. and J. Bramel (1990), On the Optimal Solution Value of the Capacitated Vehicle Routing Problem with Unsplit Demands. Working Paper, Department of IE&OR, Columbia University, New York.

Simchi-Levi, D., P. Kaminsky and E. Simchi-Levi (1997), *Managing the Supply Chain: A Structured Approach.* Irwin, Burr Ridge, IL.

Solomon, M. M. (1986), On the Worst-Case Performance of Some Heuristics for the Vehicle Routing and Scheduling Problem with Time Window Constraints. *Networks* **16**, pp. 161–174.

Solomon, M. M. and J. Desrosiers (1988), Time Window Constrained Routing and Scheduling Problems: A Survey. *Transportation Sci.* **22**, pp. 1–13.

Stalk, G., P. Evans, and L. E. Shulman (1992), Competing on Capabilities: The New Rule of Corporate Strategy. *Harvard Bus. Rev.* **70**, No. 2, pp. 57–69.

Steele, J. M. (1981), Subadditive Euclidean Functionals and Nonlinear Growth Geometric Probability. *The Annals of Probability* **9**, pp. 365–375.

Steele, J. M. (1990), Lecture Notes on "Probabilistic Analysis of Algorithms."

Stout, W. F. (1974), *Almost Sure Convergence.* Academic Press, Inc., NY.

Swersey, A. J. and W. Ballard (1984), Scheduling School Buses. *Management Sci.* **30**, pp. 844–853.

Thomas, L. C. and R. Hartley (1983), An Algorithm for Limited Capacity Inventory Problem with Staggering. *J. Opl. Res. Soc.* **34**, pp. 81–85.

Veinott, A. (1966), On the Optimality of (s, S) Inventory Policies: New Condition and a New Proof. *J. SIAM Appl. Math.* **14**, pp. 1067–1083.

Veinott, A. and H. Wagner (1965), Computing Optimal (s, S) Inventory Policies. *Management Sci.* **11**, pp. 525–552.

Viswanathan S. and K. Mathur (1993), Integrating Routing and Inventory Decisions in One Warehouse Multi-Retailer Multi-Product Distribution Systems. Working paper.

Wagelmans, A., S. Van Hoesel and A. Kolen (1992), Economic Lot Sizing: An $O(n \log n)$ Algorithm That Runs in Linear Time in the Wagner-Whitin Case. *Oper. Res.* **40**, Suppl. No. 1, pp. S145–S156.

Wagner, H. M. and T. M. Whitin (1958), Dynamic Version of the Economic Lot Size Model. *Management Sci.* **5**, pp. 89–96.

Weber, A. (1909), *Theory of the Location of Industries.* (Friedrich, C. J., ed. and transl.) Chicago University Press, Chicago, IL.

Wolsey, L. (1980), Heuristic Analysis, Linear Programming and Branch and Bound. *Math. Prog. Study* **13**, pp. 121–134.

Yellow, P. (1970), A Computational Modification to the Savings Method of Vehicle Scheduling. *Oper. Res. Quart.* **21**, pp. 281–283.

Zangwill, W. I. (1966), A Deterministic Multi-Period Production Scheduling Model with Backlogging. *Management Sci.* **13**, No. 1, pp. 105–199.

Zavi, A. (1976), *Introduction to Operations Research, Part II: Dynamic Programming and Inventory Theory* (in Hebrew). Dekel, Tel-Aviv, Israel.

Zheng, Y. S. (1991), A Simple Proof for the Optimality of (s, S) Policies for Infinite Horizon Inventory Problems. *J. Appl. Prob.* **28** pp. 802–810.

Zheng, Y. S. and A. Federgruen (1991), Finding Optimal (s, S) Policies is About as Simple as Evaluating a Single Policy. *Oper. Res.* **39**, pp. 654–665.

Zipkin, P. H. (1997), *Foundations of Inventory Management.* Irwin, Burr Ridge, IL.

Zoller, K. (1977), Deterministic Multi-Item Inventory Systems with Limited Capacity. *Management Sci.* **24**, pp. 451–455.

Index